Yale Publications in Religion, 18

The icon of Rāmānuja in the temple of his birthplace, Srīperumbūdūr, traditionally believed to have been fashioned and consecrated during his lifetime. (This photograph is used with the permission of its owner, Tiru K. K. A. Ramanujachari, whose brother, Tiru K. K. A. Venkatachari, arranged for its use in this book.)

The Theology of Rāmānuja

An Essay in Interreligious Understanding

John Braisted Carman

New Haven and London, Yale University Press, 1974

Library of Congress catalog card number: 73-77146
International standard book number: 0-300-01521-6 (cloth).

Designed by John O. C. McCrillis
and set in IBM Baskerville type.
Printed in the United States of America by
The Murray Printing Co., Forge Village, Massachusetts.

Published in Great Britain, Europe, and Africa by
Yale University Press, Ltd., London.
Distributed in Latin America by Kaiman & Polon, Inc., New York City; in Australasia and Southeast Asia by John Wiley & Sons Australasia Pty. Ltd., Sydney; in India by UBS Publishers' Distributors Pvt., Ltd., Delhi; in Japan by John Weatherhill, Inc., Tokyo.

To Ineke

Contents

Preface

This book is a revision of my dissertation, "The Ideas of Divine Supremacy and Accessibility in the Theology of Rāmānuja," which was submitted to the Yale University Graduate School in September 1962 in partial fulfillment of the requirements of the Doctor of Philosophy.

The principal expansion concerns the treatment of Rāmānuja's biography in chapter 2 and the relation of Rāmānuja to subsequent Śrī Vaiṣṇava tradition in chapter 17. The last chapter has been rewritten twice, but it remains no more than an effort to raise certain theological questions that seem to me to arise from this study. To attempt to answer those questions responsibly would call for another book.

There is clearly a need for further scholarly work on the Śrī Vaiṣṇava tradition before and after Rāmānuja. It is my hope that in the next generation a number of us will be able to increase collaboration between traditional Śrī Vaiṣṇava scholars and scholars trained in various modern academic disciplines. It seems to me of special interest at this juncture to study the Tamil hymns of the Āḻvārs and their utilization by the Śrī Vaiṣṇava community in corporate worship, private meditation, and theological reflection.

In general I have followed the standard international system for transliterating Sanskrit words in roman script used, for example, by Franklin Edgerton in his text of the *Bhagavadgītā* in roman script. However, I have not indicated the guttural *n* with *ṅ*, since this sound is usually pronounced as a guttural *n* in English when it occurs before *g* or *k* (e.g., in *sing* or *sink*). I have written Krishna rather than Kṛṣṇa because this has now become a common English term. Sanskrit words recurring in quotations from modern authors writing in western languages are generally spelled as found in the work cited, unless this deviates so much from the standard transliteration as to be confusing. In the case of the names of Indian authors and editors, their own choice of English spelling is followed, but when such a name appears on the Sanskrit title page of a work, it is spelled according to international scholarly usage.

Tamil terms are transliterated following the same rules, rather than those of many contemporary Tamil scholars, who use the same letter in roman script to designate a particular Tamil consonant regardless of its actual sound. In so doing I am following the spirit of the premodern Śrī Vaiṣṇava practice of writing in Telugu script (supplemented by two Tamil letters) in order to transcribe both Tamil and Sanskrit with phonetic accuracy. I have used *ḷ*, not to denote the rare Sanskrit vocalic *l*, but to indicate the frequent Dravidian retroflex *l*, and I have used *ḻ*, rather than *l* or *zh*, to indicate the Tamil guttural *l*.

In the translation of Sanskrit passages I have utilized all the translations available to me. I was fortunate during the writing of the dissertation to have the guidance of Dr. N. S. Anantha Rangachar, then a professor in the Government Sanskrit College in Bangalore and currently District Educational Officer in Bangalore City. I must especially acknowledge his assistance in passages cited from Rāmānuja's *Vedārthasaṃgraha.* More recently I have been greatly assisted by Pandit K. K. A. Venkatachari of Madras City with Sanskrit passages, and I am entirely dependent on him in the translation of Tamil passages.

In the case of Rāmānuja's writings, I have frequently altered existing translations to secure a more standard use of English equivalents, and in some cases I have made more substantial changes. In cases where a text with translation was available, I have referred to that (sometimes by paragraph rather than by page in order to refer simultaneously to Sanskrit and English). For the texts of the *Śrībhāṣya* (except the lengthy 1.1.1.), the *Bhagavadgītābhāṣya,* and the *Nityagrantha,* I have used Annangarācārya's edition of Rāmānuja's collected works, and my references in the case of those works are to this Sanskrit edition.

I should like to thank specifically some of the many people who have been of assistance during this study. In the first place my thanks are due to Professor Norvin Hein of Yale Divinity School, who guided my early studies of Hinduism and the dissertation behind this book and has continued to give me wise counsel on the preparation of this work for publication. The first chapter will make clear the extent of my indebtedness to Professor K. A. H. Hidding, with whom I studied history and phenomenology of religion at the University of Leiden. I am grateful to the late Dr. P. D. Devanandan for inviting me to become a Research Fellow of the Christian Institute for the Study of Religion and Society in Bangalore and for introducing me to a number of distinguished Hindu scholars. I should like especially to acknowledge the generous hospitality and continuing counsel of the late Professor M. Yamunacharya of Mysore City, who helped me to decide upon the specific focus of this study. He introduced me to Dr. N. S. Anantha Rangachar without whose help at every stage the original dissertation could not have been completed. In the subsequent revision I have been greatly aided by Pandit K. K. A. Venkatachari, not only in the interpretation of texts but also in the understanding of many facets of traditional and contemporary life of Tengalai Śrī Vaiṣṇavas. My work has been aided by the translations of Professor S. S. Raghavachar of Mysore University, Professor J. A. B. van Buitenen of the University of Chicago, and Professor M. R. Rajagopala Ayyangar of Chromepet. I have been fortunate in being able to discuss issues related to the study with all of them. I have received illuminating comments on the interpretation of Rāmānuja's thought from a number of scholars in South India: Pandit Agnihothram Ramanuja Thathachariar of Kumbakonam, Professor K. Seshadri of Trivandrum, Professors K. C. Varadachari and D. T. Tatacharya of Tirupati, and Professor V. Ramanujachari of Madras. I have had illuminating discussions on points of Śrī Vaiṣṇava history with Professor B. V. Ramanujam of Annamalai University and Professor N. Subrahmanian of the University of Madras. Valuable help was given me in the earlier work by two colleagues engaged in studies of Rāmānuja and his school, Professors Robert Lester and James H. K. Norton. More recently I have been greatly aided by Professors D. Dennis Hudson and H. Daniel Smith and by my student, Mr. Walter G. Neevel, Jr., now completing a dissertation on Rāmānuja's predecessor Yāmuna. In the final stages of typing of the dissertation, I was rescued by the editorial assistance of Professor Eugene Irschick. In reviewing this manuscript I have been similarly greatly helped by Dr. Cheever M. Brown. I am grateful to all those institutions that have assisted me through their libraries and their teachers and through giving me the opportunity to present aspects of this study under their auspices. The American Baptist Foreign Mission Society gave me permission to write the dissertation during my term of service with them (1957-63). I am particularly grateful for the support of Dr. Marlin D. Farnum, then secretary for South India. My return to India for three years under the auspices of the Center for the Study of World Religions at Harvard University was made possible by its director and my colleague there, Professor Wilfred Cantwell Smith. I want to thank him for his encouragement of my writing and for assuming many extra burdens during my absence.

I appreciate the cooperation of Mrs. Merle Speigel of the Yale University Press, and I am especially grateful for the painstaking and patient assistance in the final editing given me by Mrs. Barbara Palmer.

Our three children have grown up with the writing of this book and have encouraged me with it. I am dedicating the book to my wife as a sign of affection and appreciation, not only for help at various stages but also for her encouraging presence through the years.

Belmont, Massachusetts J.B.C.
June 1973

1 A Phenomenological and Historical Approach to Rāmānuja's Theology

A Western Christian's Study of a Hindu Theology

This is a study of the doctrine of God (Īśvaratattva) of one of the most important medieval Hindu theologians, Rāmānuja. I approach this study as a Western Protestant Christian. This means negatively that I do not belong to the Hindu community in general or to Rāmānuja's own sect, the Śrī Vaiṣṇava Saṃpradāya. It means positively that I belong to a branch of the Christian church that has exhibited a generally negative attitude toward Hindu religion but has occasionally evinced some friendly interest in the teachings of Rāmānuja and his school because of some apparent similarities between Śrī Vaiṣṇavism and Christianity, most obviously with respect to the doctrines of Divine incarnation and Divine grace. As a Western Christian I share in a Western academic tradition which has, especially during the last two centuries, explored Indian culture with the various scholarly tools and cultural predilections of the West.

This Western exploration of Indian culture has been closely connected with the Western colonial domination of India, only recently concluded, which has left among its legacies a system of Western education. For Hindus who have been educated in that system, as well as for Westerners, it no longer seems novel or strange that a Western student should seek to understand a Hindu thinker. However, the entire effort of intercultural and interreligious understanding is something relatively new in human history.

The study of a religious leader's thought is first of all the task of those who follow in his own tradition, but the study of the positions of opposing thinkers has a long history in India, as in the West. What is novel in the recent Western scholarly interest in India is that much of it has been concerned neither to follow nor to oppose but to understand. This understanding has been of various kinds—literary, historical, or sociological—but it has usually claimed to be objective, to be concerned with the accurate determination of historical facts and not with the supposed supramundane realities that are of paramount importance for the religious person or group being studied.

It is only very recently that the specific *problem* of intercultural understanding has begun to concern those engaged in this task. The prejudices of Christian theological interpreters of Hinduism have been much more evident to "objective" Western scholars than the obstacles in the way of their own understanding. If the historically minded Western scholar has recognized the gulf between his understanding of the facts of Hindu history and society and the self-understanding of contemporary Hindus, he has been inclined to ascribe it to the distortion of history caused by tradition or to the rewriting of history by modern Hindu reformers. Western orientalists, however, have recently become much more aware of the limitations of their own approach and have attempted to utilize more extensively both traditional Hindu materials and the works of modern Indian scholars who have tried to combine traditional Indian and modern Western approaches to historiography and literary criticism.[1]

Western Christian interpreters have been aware for a longer time of the problem of relating their theological convictions to their "objective" survey of the "facts," but they have paid less attention to the difficulty of their *not* belonging to the particular Hindu group they are studying than to the problem of their belonging to the Christian church. There have, of course, been Western interpreters who have proceeded on the basis of a thoroughgoing identification with a particular school of Indian philosophy or at least with the general spirit of Indian philosophy and religion. These interpreters have usually been very critical or even contemptuous of both Christian scholars and uncommitted orientalists. I feel that they have generally been lacking in self-criticism; they have failed to see the problems for understanding posed by their own admiration of Indian spirituality or by a conversion to some particular form of it. Hindu scholars have been generally tolerant and often appreciative of the efforts of Western orientalists, and they have frequently been exceedingly generous in assisting Western students in their writing and research projects, even when they knew that the conclusions these Western students would reach would seem to them at least one-sided and perhaps quite unacceptable.

Relatively little detailed study of Rāmānuja and the Śrī Vaiṣṇava tradition has been undertaken by Western scholars. Orientalists have generally been interested in earlier periods of Indian literary and cultural history, and most Western students with interests in the medieval philosophical schools have devoted their time to Śankara and the Advaita school of the Vedānta. Indeed, the emphasis of these scholars and of Indian scholars writing in English has given the semischolarly public in Western countries the impression that

Śankara's philosophy is the *only* significant type of orthodox Hindu thought. Insofar as Rāmānuja is known at all in these circles, it is as the representative of a subphilosophical piety. Christian students of Hinduism have often had a general interest in Rāmānuja and his school, but few have undertaken extensive research.

In recent years, however, there has been a marked increase in scholarly studies of Rāmānuja by Western and Hindu scholars, both Śrī Vaiṣṇavas and others. A few Indian Christian scholars have also engaged in the study of aspects of the Śrī Vaiṣṇava tradition.[2]

My approach shares certain features with some of these other studies, and my indebtedness to many of them will be evident in the following pages. Yet there is sufficient distinctiveness in my conception of the task of a Western Christian student of Rāmānuja's theology to warrant spending this first chapter elaborating that conception and discussing certain problems that it may raise.

When I was writing the doctoral dissertation that underlies this book, I felt that I was addressing an audience primarily of fellow Christians, especially in the West, both in the methodological introduction and in the book as a whole. Since the dissertation was finished, however, I have shared some of its contents with a variety of audiences in both India and the United States. I have found that the term *phenomenology of religion* has now come into vogue in the United States, though it is so variously used as to make a particular definition imperative. In India, on the other hand, while the term *phenomenological* is still strange, the approach I have been trying to follow in this study has been received with sufficient sympathy by Śrī Vaiṣṇavas as well as other Hindus that it now seems important to explain to them, too, what I am attempting to do. My increasing interest in trying to relate the phenomenological and historical approaches to the study of religion seems to me to find echoes in much recent thinking of my colleagues in such study in the universities of the United States and Canada.

An Understanding of Phenomenology of Religion Based on Kristensen and van der Leeuw

I approach this subject as a Western Christian trying to understand a Hindu thinker as sympathetically as is possible for one who stands quite outside the Śrī Vaiṣṇava tradition in particular and Hinduism in general. In doing so, I am trying to follow the principles and the example of the historians of religion in the Netherlands who have developed what they call the phenomenology of religion.[3]

Professor W. Brede Kristensen has summarized the task of the historian or phenomenologist of religion as follows:

> The requirement is, negatively expressed: self-denial, letting the believer himself speak without mixing our praise or blame into what he tells us; positively expressed, having an attitude of sympathetic and loving understanding toward the alien faith, which "sympathy" alone can lead toward comprehension and proper evaluation.[4]

Thus, the first side of this requirement is that the one who seeks to understand another religion must make a continued and disciplined effort to refrain from evaluating the truth or value of the things he observes in other religions on the basis of his own religious norms or his own cultural prejudices.

This does not mean that such a student may not make any such judgments at any time in his life. In the course of witnessing to the truth of the Divine revelation as it is understood in his own religion, it may well be necessary for him to come to some definite conclusions in his evaluation of another religion, whether or not he voices these judgments directly in his contact with adherents of that religion. If he himself or a recent ancestor has been converted from one religion to another, he inevitably assesses the value of different elements of the old religion for his life in the new religious community. In all such judgments, however, he is within the sphere of theology, not of phenomenology of religion. When he is not thinking as a phenomenologist, he may also make a variety of other judgments about the truth or value of another religion that are based, not on the revealed truth that he accepts in his own religion, but on some philosophical or scientific truth, or perhaps on the grounds of some deep-seated cultural assumption. The phenomenologist of religion, therefore, does not deny himself the freedom to evaluate other religions throughout his life as a person or as a scholar, but he does try his best to discipline himself to refrain from judgment while he is about the task of understanding another religion from the standpoint of its own believers. The term that Professor G. van der Leeuw borrowed from the philosophical phenomenologists to describe this attitude is *epoché,* restraint or refraining from judgment.[5]

The second part of the task is, according to Kristensen, only the positive expression of the same requirement that in the first part is negatively expressed. The German word that both Kristensen and van der Leeuw either use directly or have in mind is *einfühlen,* which is usually translated into English as "empathy." This Kristensen further explains as the attempt to relive in one's own experience that which is "alien" or "strange" (Dutch *vreemd*) or the "imaginative reexperiencing of a situation strange to us." In following this second rule, or the positive side of the single basic rule, one must draw on one's entire religious background, not in order to evaluate, but in order to understand. One has to use, at least to some extent, his own religious concepts and categories in order to grasp the meaning of something in another religion. The phenomenologist within the sphere of phenomenology of religion cannot decide whether there is any ontological significance in the use of familiar religious ideas in order to grasp concepts that at first appear and perhaps are in reality utterly alien, though that is a legitimate and relevant question for the theologian or philosopher. The phenomenologist simply presses into service those concepts or mental images that may help him in his difficult task of understanding other religions as they are understood by their own serious believers.[6]

That the phenomenologist must draw on his own religious experience to understand the thoughts, feelings, and behavior of someone in another religion underlines the fundamental fact that he is studying that religion as an outsider and his best efforts can only bring him to an approximate understanding of the other religion. As Kristensen says, he can never experience another religion as a power in life. If he should really do so, he would become an adherent of that religion, and his study as a phenomenologist would come to an end.[7]

Kristensen's two rules, or two aspects of the same basic requirement, do not constitute a simple method that can easily be followed. Rather, they are a challenge to a total involvement of one's personality in the scholarly task of understanding the religion of others, an involvement that may include one's emotions but that also calls for a constant discipline of both mind and heart. It is difficult for anyone to judge how successfully he has met these requirements in his studies, and it frequently happens that a person with some artistic sensitivity and with a loving concern for others, who has never heard of phenomenology of religion, proves to be a better phenomenologist than a scientific student of religion who has evolved an elaborate methodology. Yet it is precisely when we do not possess the genius and the artistic touch of such scholars as Kristensen and van der Leeuw that we need continually to remind ourselves of these basic requirements of self-restraint and self-giving in the study of another religion.

Van der Leeuw conceives phenomenology of religion as a study of similar phenomena in all religions, producing an understanding of the fundamental types or categories common to all religions. His teacher Kristensen, on the other hand, limits himself almost entirely to the ancient religions of the peoples living around the eastern Mediterranean and in western Asia. Kristensen does not make as sharp a distinction as does van der Leeuw between history and phenomenology, for he believes that a proper historical study of even a single phenomenon in one particular religion ought to be animated by the same desire to understand the faith of the believer that is the phenomenologist's concern. Indeed the phenomenologist's comparative study of similar features of different religions is not an end in itself but a useful means of understanding the particular religion of some particular believer. The particular or historical study and the comparative study are interrelated, for even to understand one particular phenomenon one must draw on his own understanding of the meaning of similar religious phenomena that he has already studied or has personally encountered. Nevertheless, there is a clear difference between the two types of study, and if the number of religions one is comparing becomes too large or the difference between them is too great, one can no longer work toward Kristensen's goal of understanding the religion of the believer. There is a limit to the number of religions that an outside observer can know well enough to enter into the inner feelings and attitudes of their adherents; and for most students of other religions that limit is much narrower than it was for Kristensen, who had mastered a number of ancient languages and had carefully studied the religious literature in those languages.

In this study I am trying to practice the phenomenological method more nearly in the sense in which Kristensen defines and uses it. Actually, this study is not "systematic" or comparative in the strict sense, since it is concerned with a single mind in a single religious tradition. It is therefore "historical" as well as "phenomenological." It is concerned with determining certain historical events—in the first place, determining what the historical Rāmānuja actually wrote. This involves making certain judgments on historical facts that are avoided in a purely phenomenological inquiry concerned only with determining patterns of meaning. I shall return later in the chapter to a consideration of some of the problems this involves.

In the course of this effort to understand Rāmānuja's conception of God, it is necessary for a Western Christian to utilize concepts drawn from Christian religious traditions and, to a lesser extent, from the entire background of Western culture. Within this particular study, however, I shall try to refrain from any judgments concerning the value or truth of Rāmānuja's ideas about God. This does not mean that these questions are without interest. They are doubtless the reason why a Christian student is often drawn to make a close study of Rāmānuja or of some aspect of the religious tradition with which he is associated rather than to study one of a host of other subjects in the history of religion. The interest in questions of truth and value helps to determine the subject for phenomenological study, and the result of such study—that is, the clearer understanding of the subject—is indispensable for any serious assessment of this religious material by philosophy of religion or Christian theology. In phenomenology of religion, however, the questions of truth and value are put aside, because they tend to distract the phenomenologist from the immediate and specific object of his study: the understanding of the pattern of belief and practice in the life of the believers of some other religion.

THE SERIOUS BELIEVER AND THE RELIGIOUS PATTERN

Professor Hendrik Kraemer has described the difference in his approach from that of Kristensen, his revered teacher and friend, as follows.

> As I see it, the weakness in his strength is that, with his exclusive stress on the full right of the diverse religious intuitions, he is involuntarily driven towards a blurring of the majestic problem of Truth, which lies behind the undeniable reality of experience and value. . . . His brilliant phenomenological approach leaves the mind with an indelible impression of the seriousness and relevance of Religion, but it offers no way to uncover and tackle such a disturbing problem as that of the perennial ambiguity of Religion. Such a problem can only be really and adequately tackled by a theological approach, which

> is nevertheless fully aware of the indispensable preparatory training given by phenomenology.[8]

One important meaning of "the perennial ambiguity of Religion" is that most people do not take their religion seriously. The ambiguity lies in the fact that every religion, and every element within a religion, inherently claims absolute significance. Yet that claim is not taken seriously by most of those who hold that belief or participate in that practice; they use their religion for their own ends. All the major religions have their own theological explanation of this fact, which may be called "religious worldliness." As Rāmānuja (following Yāmuna) understands the *Bhagavadgītā,* this distinction between different kinds of people, all of them supposedly religious, is one of that sacred poem's central themes. Rāmānuja expands on the *Gītā*'s statement that the highest type of devotee, who worships God only for His sake and not for his own benefit, is very rare indeed.[9]

It is this worldly practice of religion that furnishes the most obvious material for those psychologists and sociologists who try to reduce all religious thoughts and practices to something that is not religious. Even if we reject such efforts to explain religion away, it is possible that in any particular case such a psychological or sociological explanation may contain a great deal of truth, for religious worldliness has subtle forms that can appear as the most devout forms of piety, a fact which the devotional and theological writings of many religions have themselves recognized.

Phenomenology of religion, as Kristensen defines it and to a remarkable extent practices it, assumes that the believer takes his religion seriously and that it is of absolute and quite incomparable significance for him. It is into the minds of these serious believers that the phenomenologist tries to penetrate with all the powers of imagination and sympathy at his disposal.[10] But if the average religious man is really not so utterly serious and dedicated to the goals of his religion, what relevance or validity, then, remains in the description offered by the phenomenologist of religion?

Apart from the deeper theological problem to which Kraemer refers, this obvious side of "the perennial ambiguity of Religion" indicates a serious limitation of phenomenology of religion, but it does not negate the validity of its approach within its limited field. The phenomenologist of religion, therefore, ought not to object if other types of study of religion also claim to "understand" that religion or those who profess it. To his mind, these other so-called understandings may appear to be only theological or metaphysical interpretations of the religious phenomena, or psychological or sociological attempts to explain the religion away, but these interpretations or explanations are also to some extent an understanding of the total situation of a man practicing his religion. Nevertheless, there is a special kind of understanding that may be obtained from a patient and sympathetic effort to understand the mind of one who seriously believes and practices a particular religion. Because of his own religious and cultural background, every phenomenologist will have a somewhat different understanding of the mind of the believer. Nonetheless, to some extent (sometimes to a very great extent) that mind is made intelligible to us through such phenomenological understanding.[11]

Phenomenology of religion has a valid sphere of operation precisely because any religion, even the most primitive, is distinct from the use that men make of it. No religion measures its own validity by how fully its adherents believe in its doctrines or practice its sacred rites, for its very claim to absolute value and truth implies a relation or avenue of approach to the ultimate power or powers underlying existence, a relation that, in principle, is independent of man's personal involvement in it. To say that our goal is to understand the mind of the serious believer really means that understanding his mind is the best means we have toward an understanding of what for him is the ultimate reality, to which he believes that his ritual actions as well as his beliefs are divinely inspired responses.

It is probable that the religious life of even a serious devotee is influenced by what are actually nonreligious factors, yet the phenomenologist has no choice but simply to ignore all such factors and proceed on the assumption that the person (or group) in question really acts or thinks according to the religious norms that he claims to uphold. This means that phenomenology of religion, like all other human sciences, is an abstraction from the total reality of the situation that it tries to study and understand. This is the phenomenologist's limitation, but this does not mean that he gains no real knowledge of what he is studying, for he is abstracting something that is really there, namely, the pattern of that religion as it is expressed in the life of one who takes it with utmost seriousness. Although it may interest him as a theologian or as a psychologist, it makes no difference to him as a phenomenologist that alongside this serious believer there are ninety-nine people who use some or even all the elements of this religion for a variety of nonreligious purposes.

In this respect, the phenomenologist's interest is similar to that of the grammarian, who tries to discover the characteristic structure determining the use of a particular language and is not deterred from his goal by the fact that most people do not speak the language with complete grammatical correctness. The phenomenologist runs the same risk as the grammarian of imposing a pattern on the language that is not really there, or at least does not exactly fit, because it is really the pattern of the grammarian's own language or of some language that he takes to be norm of all language. (Latin served as such a not altogether appropriate norm in describing the grammars of western European languages, and the South Indian languages have had grammars composed on the patterns of Sanskrit grammar.) Yet both the phenomenologist of religion and the grammarian rightly assume that there is a pattern to be discovered and that its discovery is possible, not by taking some average of the believers of that religion or of the speakers of that language, but by concentrating on those in whom that pattern really lives. Every individual, of course, remains an individual and not simply the exemplification of some ideal pattern. Nevertheless, it is the religious pattern such a person exemplifies that is the phenomenologist's chief concern.

Some Implications of a Phenomenological Stance

In this study I have used the word *God,* spelled with a capital *G.* If this were a study in Christian theology, such capitalization would imply a crucial theological judgment, that the One whom Rāmānuja considers as the Supreme Being is identical with the God in whom Christians believe, the Divine Trinity. If, on the other hand, in such a theological study Brahman or Īśvara were consistently to be translated with "the deity," it would imply the opposite theological judgment: that the Lord about whom Rāmānuja is talking is not the same Lord as the One Christians worship. However, this is not a theological study, and it does not require such a theological decision—indeed, it requires precisely that I refrain from making it. The positive requirement of imaginative and sympathetic understanding causes me to use the English term *God* in order to convey to myself, and to other Christians, the meaning that is present in Rāmānuja's mind when he uses any one of several different Sanskrit designations for the Supreme Deity.

Now, there are gods to whom Rāmānuja refers whom it would be misleading to call God, since for Rāmānuja and his community they are no more than exalted creatures. There are, moreover, notions of ultimate reality held by other Hindu schools that a phenomenologist of Christian background might well hesitate to refer to with the English word *God* (capital *G*) simply because the meaning of these conceptions is so different from that which Christians have in mind when they think of God. In these cases, there are English words that serve better to convey the meaning of the Sanskrit original for the people who hold these views—such terms as *ultimate reality, absolute principle,* and *primal power.* These terms also have their place in the effort to make Rāmānuja's theology understandable to Western Christians, but there seems to me no doubt that the English term that brings Christians the closest to what Rāmānuja had in mind is the single word *God.*

I shall be focusing on two sides of Rāmānuja's conception of God, which I designate with the terms *supremacy* and *accessibility,* translations of the Sanskrit words *paratva* and *saulabhya,* respectively. The English words are only approximate equivalents, but I have used them for two reasons. First, it is my aim to help Western Christians understand the beliefs of a particular Hindu theologian, and it is therefore desirable, if this can be done without undue distortion, to express that Hindu theologian's concepts in terms that have some meaning for Western Christians, that is to say, some emotional associations as well as a certain intellectual content. Even if the Sanskrit terms *paratva* and *saulabhya* were carefully paraphrased and explained, they could hardly have any emotional associations for those who are not familiar with their use in Sanskrit, especially in hymns and other devotional works. There are, to be sure, some Sanskrit terms in Rāmānuja's vocabulary that are so difficult to translate that it is better, after some explanation, to continue to employ them in the middle of an English sentence. The use of such untranslated terms should be kept to a minimum, however, not merely to avoid the appearance of pedantry and to spare the ingenuity of those who do not know Sanskrit but primarily to reduce the obstacles on the difficult path of phenomenological understanding.

The second reason for the use of English equivalents of paratva and saulabhya instead of the original Sanskrit words is that these terms are not used by Rāmānuja in the general sense that is my primary concern in this study. They are rather the terms used by some of the leading commentators on Rāmānuja's writings as the names for two contrasting categories of Divine attributes. It is therefore not the Sanskrit terms themselves that form the subject matter of this study but the two aspects of Rāmānuja's conception of God to which they point. This content is expressed with fair approximation by the English words *supremacy* and *accessibility*.

Why not take the further step of using the familiar concepts of transcendence and immanence as an aid to understanding Rāmānuja's conception of God? This has been done by some previous modern interpreters of Rāmānuja, but for reasons I shall indicate in the last two chapters, I have come to believe that the polarity of transcendence and immanence is more useful in understanding other schools and sects of Hinduism than it is in understanding Rāmānuja.

It seems to me doubtful, moreover, whether the polarity of Divine transcendence and immanence is an accurate abstraction from the theologies of Western religious systems, whether Jewish, Christian, or Muslim. These terms have indeed been widely used in Western philosophy of religion and in some schools of Christian theology, but I am doubtful whether they fit the experience of followers of any of the Western religions. This is partly because many of these believers object to such a bifurcation of their religious experience, even for the purpose of discussion or abstract thought. More fundamentally, however, it is because the God whom they experience reveals Himself in such a way that His immanence and transcendence are always combined, or, put differently, because the Divine reality they experience does not correspond to the philosophical definitions of either immanence or transcendence. For Christian faith, the great marvel (regarded by some as a paradox) is not the general immanence in His creation of the transcendent Creator but the specific event of God's incarnation in a particular man, Jesus of Nazareth. How could One so high stoop so low to save us? This has been both the worshiper's reverent praise and the theologian's puzzled question. The Śrī Vaiṣṇava doctrines of creation and incarnation are quite different from the Christian ones, and the concepts of transcendence and immanence have different meanings in the two religions, yet Śrī Vaiṣṇavism like Christianity is a religion based on faith in Divine revelation, incarnation, and redemption, and the same significant polarity occurs in the experience and understanding of the Divine nature: that between the Divine supremacy (paratva) and the Divine accessibility (saulabhya).

I make use of the polarity of supremacy and accessibility, in the first place, because I believe that it is really present in Rāmānuja's thought, as has been pointed out by his followers. In the second place, however, I believe that this polarity is so close to one present in the Christian understanding of God's incarnation that I can use it to help Christians understand this conception of God in a religion quite different from their own.

The fact that the interpretive concepts that I employ have been used by Rāmānuja's followers to understand his theology does not in itself prove that these concepts are appropriate for understanding his thought, since there are certain points where later Śrī Vaiṣṇava tradition seems to have diverged from Rāmānuja. It is Rāmānuja's own thought, not that of his followers, that is the subject of this book. The later comments are of interest only as they elucidate Rāmānuja's own conception of God. It will be a major task of this study to prove that this is in fact the case.

The significance of the terms *paratva* and *saulabhya* in the Śrī Vaiṣṇava conception of God seems to have declined in the generations after Sudarśana Sūri and Vedānta Deśika. It is not found in the later manual of Śrīnivāsadāsa's *Yatīndramatadīpikā.* Professor M. Yamunacharya suggested to me that it is the emphasis on saulabhya that gives the distinctive stamp to Rāmānuja's thought. Further study led me to conclude that it is not saulabhya by itself but the way in which it is held in combination with paratva that gives Rāmānuja's thought its distinctive unity and its fundamental importance for the later Śrī Vaiṣṇava tradition.

Some Complications of History

In deciding to focus this study on the thought of a single religious leader, one is forced to deal with certain difficult historical questions, as well as with patterns of religious meaning. One can avoid most of these questions if he makes a study of a particular religious tradition as a whole. Orthodox Śrī Vaiṣṇavas assume complete agreement between all the *ācāryas* in the orthodox line, which means in effect that one's own teachers, of the northern or southern school as the case may be, are the source of the correct interpretation of

Rāmānuja. Many students of Rāmānuja outside the Śrī Vaiṣṇava community have adopted much of this procedure, for example, the late Professor Surendranath Dasgupta in his *History of Indian Philosophy.*[12] Now, there are good reasons why any outside student must read Rāmānuja in the light of the subsequent tradition; it would be foolish to ignore the help of the later commentaries, especially those of Sudarśana Sūri, and a knowledge of the later definitions of certain key terms that Rāmānuja used but did not himself define is indispensable.[13] But the question remains whether a distinction should be made in principle. Krishna Dhatta Bharadwaj states that such a distinction is essential but then proceeds to quote from the much later Śrī Vaiṣṇava manual, the *Yatīndramatadīpikā,* not only to elucidate what Rāmānuja said but to fill in the system at the points where Rāmānuja said little or nothing.[14] This filling in is certainly the legitimate function of subsequent tradition, and it need not be any distortion of the original conception; but it is nevertheless an addition to it and therefore distinct from it.

If the phenomenologist of religion wishes to consider the Śrī Vaiṣṇava tradition as an undivided whole, he has the problem of reconciling the different emphases of the two schools that crystallized about two hundred years after Rāmānuja's death. Whether one takes the tradition as a whole or one of the two branches, what he actually has to understand is the tradition of the recent past, that which contemporary Śrī Vaiṣṇavas, as represented by the teachers they themselves most respect, consider the correct view of the tradition. If one were to undertake such a study of the contemporary Śrī Vaiṣṇava community, he would seek to understand its view of the unchanging character of tradition.

If, on the other hand, one takes the thought of a single Śrī Vaiṣṇava ācārya as the object of his study, one can gratefully accept the help of later tradition in understanding the earlier teacher without accepting its claim to substantial identity with the views of that teacher. That claim would in any case need to be scrutinized. In this particular case, one would have to decide which of the later schools faithfully incorporates Rāmānuja's views. To do this one would first have to determine what Rāmānuja's views themselves are; this is precisely the aim of the present study, but I shall limit myself to one aspect of Rāmānuja's thought, his doctrine of God.

The frequent Western alternative to the traditionalist view is to concentrate entirely on a certain written work or works of the person who is to be studied, paying as little attention as possible to the traditional commentaries on those works and being very skeptical indeed of any oral traditions concerning the author being studied. This attitude of the Western literary critic, including the "higher critics" of the Bible, goes back to a protest against the domination of commentaries and oral tradition in the medieval church, a protest voiced by the Renaissance and Reformation, giving rise to a demand for the plain text, whether of Aristotle or Paul, preferably in the original Greek. The protest was certainly justified in terms of the values of modern European culture, and Western literary criticism of the last four centuries has been an impressive cultural achievement, not least the work of the Western orientalists during the last two hundred years. Nevertheless, I believe that the Western student of a Hindu religious leader like Rāmānuja needs to be self-critical about the possible one-sidedness of the Western literary approach, especially if he is concerned not only with determining the meaning of a text but also with the total pattern of meaning expressed by a particular historical figure.

The work by which Rāmānuja is best known in India outside of his own school is his great commentary on the *Vedānta Sūtras,* called the *Śrībhāṣya.* He is said to have been given the title "Bhāṣyakāra" (commentator) by the goddess Sarasvatī in Kashmir, and this has remained a favorite title for him among his own followers, especially those of the more Sanskrit-oriented northern school (Vaḍagalai).[15] It is therefore understandable for the outside student to treat Rāmānuja primarily as the author of this commentary and to evaluate any other evidence available concerning Rāmānuja's thought on the basis of this touchstone, the *Śrībhāṣya.* There do not seem to me, however, to be sound historical grounds for such a procedure. The earliest extant commentary on the *Śrībhāṣya,* written almost two centuries later, is by the same author (Sudarśana Sūri) who wrote commentaries on other works of Rāmānuja, and there are references to much earlier commentaries (now lost) on the recently disputed work, the *Gadyatraya.*[16] There is, moreover, a serious question as to how much an Indian commentary reveals about the individual views of a particular commentator. This might seem to be less the case with the commentaries on the *Vedānta Sūtras,* since that work consists only of a string of brief and often enigmatic statements which have been diversely interpreted. The commentators on the *Vedānta Sūtras,* however, also relied on a number of previous commentaries that have since been lost, and even those with personal views as different as Śankara and Rāmānuja tended to follow the earlier commentators as far as they possibly could.[17] It is difficult to know, for example, whether Rāmānuja's comment in the *Śrībhāṣya* defending the killing of animals in the Vedic sacrifice indicates his stand in a current controversy or the repetition of arguments first made several centuries earlier. It would certainly be hazardous to conclude from this comment that he was not a vegetarian. The only major work of Rāmānuja that is not in the form of a commentary is the *Vedārthasaṃgraha,* which, though brief, treats a large number of important topics. But no one has yet suggested that this work is either the sole touchstone or the final authority in interpreting Rāmānuja's thought.

An alternative procedure, still following the literary critical approach, would be to make a separate analysis of each writing attributed to Rāmānuja, after which one could compare the teachings contained in each, decide which works were genuine, and form a composite picture of the teachings contained in the genuine works. Such a procedure is certainly possible (I did something of this kind in the early stages of this study), but we should not expect that the composite of the doctrines contained in various writings would bring us to a full understanding of the theology of this historical religious leader. There is simply no reason to expect that a complete picture of Rāmānuja's thought would emerge from an analysis of any single writing or even from all the writings. There are also a number of Tamil sayings attributed to Rāmānuja, and there is a rich biographical tradition. Both the sayings and the stories, however, were passed on orally for a hundred years or more before they were written down and are therefore precisely the kind of material that the Western critic finds most suspect. I shall consider all the evidence from various sources concerning Rāmānuja's teachings as a number of clues to that elusive whole of the teacher's position. The Sanskrit writings, insofar as they are genuine, are the most dependable clues we have, and they will be so treated in this study.

The question of the historical usefulness of the traditional biographies of the Śrī Vaiṣṇava saints and teachers is one that deserves far more attention than it has so far received.[18] I believe that they contain a great deal of material of historical value, especially in illuminating the social context of Rāmānuja's life and the religio-social significance of his work as the leader of the Śrī Vaiṣṇava community in the late eleventh and early twelfth centuries A.D. Stories that indicate some imperfection in Rāmānuja seem to me especially likely to contain genuine memories, since they would be least likely to be invented. There is considerable other material that is probably not historically accurate but is valuable for the evidence it furnishes concerning Rāmānuja's impact on his disciples and/or concerning typical modes of pious thought and behavior within the Śri Vaiṣṇava community, some of them of a kind that we catch but a glimpse of in the Sanskrit writings of the school.

In the following chapter, I shall present the most probable facts (and/or community beliefs) about the life of Rāmānuja, and a few references to the biographies will be made in subsequent chapters at points where I believe they shed some light on the views of Rāmānuja as expressed in his Sanskrit writings. The historian needs to be extremely cautious about accepting the actual words attributed to Rāmānuja in the oral tradition, for they frequently so much reflect later doctrinal concerns that they tell us nothing about Rāmānuja's own thought. However, I shall indicate a few instances where words attributed to Rāmānuja in the oral tradition seem to me both genuine and important, especially where the view of Rāmānuja is contrasted with that of his predecessor Yāmuna and is manifestly different from that taken by subsequent Śrī Vaiṣṇavas.[19]

When a point of Śrī Vaiṣṇava doctrine is absent from Rāmānuja's Sanskrit writings, one faces the question of whether to "fill in" this "silence" from the tradition of sayings or from the explanatory written comments by Rāmānuja's later followers. The particular problems will be discussed as they arise in the following chapters. Some of the use I make of the later commentators is indirect; I use English translations and consult secondary works that themselves depend heavily on the commentaries, especially those of Sudarśana Sūri and Vedānta Deśika.

It is surprising that Rāmānuja never defines most of the string of Divine attributes that he so frequently lists before the Divine name, especially those terms that express virtues of the finite spirit raised to the plane of the Supreme Spirit.[20] He does give careful definitions of such terms as *śarīrī* (embodied soul), which are of crucial metaphysical importance, and he defines the five "defining attributes" of Brahman. There is no alternative to consulting the later commentators in order to determine the meaning that the various Divine attributes held for Rāmānuja, but it cannot be simply assumed that the commentators have correctly interpreted their teacher's mind. I shall begin, therefore, with those aspects of the concept of the Deity about which Rāmānuja is most explicit. These are the various terms designating God's relation to the cosmos in the respects of creation, rule, and so forth, and the Divine attributes prominently mentioned in the Upaniṣads. Beginning in this way will provide certain definitions in Rāmānuja's own thought that can be compared with the later definitions of his followers.

Rāmānuja did not define many of the Divine attributes because there was no controversy surrounding them to make such definition necessary. The Karma Mīmāṃsā (as well as a number of heterodox systems) denied the existence of a Supreme Person in toto; they were not interested in arguing over particular attributes. Śankara and his followers admitted all the "anthropomorphic" Divine qualities at the level of the lower wisdom and in the context of devotion to the Saguṇa Brahman. When this view was transcended, all these qualities vanished at once along with the personal Lord (Īśvara) Himself. Here again, therefore, there was no purpose in debate over the meaning of particular qualities. When Rāmānuja wanted to give some particular shade of meaning to a term that might be understood differently, he did define it.[21]

The problem is further complicated by the fact that for Rāmānuja's successors some of the terms have both general (exoteric) and special Śrī Vaiṣṇava (esoteric) meanings and sometimes even multiple esoteric meanings. It seems to me likely but not certain that Rāmānuja also accepted this scheme of multiple meanings. The correspondence between the few terms that Rāmānuja does define and the later definitions, as well as the apparent lack of controversy about most of these terms, leads me to conclude that the later definitions reflect the traditional view shared by Rāmānuja. There are some exceptions, and these relate to a characteristic shift away from Rāmānuja's position on some points (these will be discussed in chapter 17).

THE QUESTION OF THE AUTHENTICITY OF THE SHORTER WRITINGS ASCRIBED TO RĀMĀNUJA

One of the most difficult and most inescapable historical questions intruding into the phenomenologist's realm of meanings is that of determining the genuineness of the works ascribed to the religious leader who is the object of study. No one has questioned the authenticity of the three major works of Rāmānuja: the *Vedārthasaṃgraha,* the *Śrībhāṣya,* and the *Bhagavadgītābhāṣya.* Some modern scholars have questioned the genuineness of the other six works. The *Vedāntadīpa* and the *Vedāntasāra* have been questioned because of the assumed implausibility that a teacher who had not written commentaries on individual Upaniṣads would write three distinct commentaries on the *Vedānta Sūtras;* the three Gadyas (prose hymns) and the *Nityagrantha* (manual of daily worship) because of the assumed incompatibility between the doctrines and terminology they contain and the doctrines in Rāmānuja's admittedly genuine works.

Determining the authenticity of authorship is an old and thorny problem in many fields of literary criticism. Competent scholars may consider such a question and arrive at diametrically opposite conclusions. The underlying attitude that influences the way in which a particular scholar deals with this problem is revealed by the answer he gives to the question: on whom does the burden of proof lie? Since there is no universal answer to that question on scientific grounds, this is an inquiry into which one's "unscientific" prejudice easily enters.

In this study I am trying to enter as sympathetically and imaginatively as possible into a tradition that is foreign to my own religious background and experience. I am therefore attempting to be "prejudiced" in favor of the tradition. It is best to state this at the outset, especially since my conclusion seems to confirm that initial predisposition toward the tradition. The object of this study is the thought of Rāmānuja himself, not that of his followers, and if I should be forced to conclude that certain writings are contrary to the spirit of Rāmānuja's thought, they obviously could not be used to penetrate more deeply into the basic conceptions of that thought.

There is also a major objective difficulty in solving the problem of authorship: that of determining the unity in the thought of the same individual writing at different times and on different subjects, as distinguished from the similarity in thought between a teacher and his students. Such determination is often difficult, but it is possible, provided that we know the thought of both the teacher in question and his followers well enough to establish the distinctive personal characteristics of each individual's thought, characteristics persisting throughout the lifetime of that individual, notwithstanding marked changes in his views. In many other cases of disputed authorship—for example, the books of the Bible—we simply do not have the writings of the disputed authors' followers. Fortunately, many of the writings of Rāmānuja's followers have been preserved. It would therefore seem possible to institute such close comparison and thus to arrive at a definite conclusion concerning the disputed works attributed to Rāmānuja. However, this material in Sanskrit and in Tamil is extensive and has not yet been critically analyzed. My study of these writings is still quite incomplete. My conclusions, therefore, are necessarily tentative. Even after a close study of the post-Rāmānuja tradition, the strict proof of the logical demonstration cannot be expected and certainly not the believing certainty of a faithful member of that tradition.

One indication of the relative reliability of the Śrī Vaiṣṇava ascriptions of authorship is a comparison with the ascription of authorship in the school of Śankara. According to Belvalkar, there are "some 400 works generally attributed to the great name of Śankarācārya" consisting of commentaries, hymns, and religio-philosophic tracts. Of them Belvalkar regards eleven commentaries "as most probably coming, in the main, from Śankarācārya himself" with another five debatable. Only eight of the more than two hundred *stotras* (hymns of praise) can be regarded as "very probably . . . genuine" with another three "plausible." There is a similar proportion of genuine to spurious works among the *prakaraṇagranthas* (tracts): five out of almost one hundred and ten. There is thus a total of twenty-four works "which we can almost confidently call Śankara's own."[22] There is a similar uncertainty about the traditional biographies of Śankara.

> Even such fragmentary and highly exaggerated biographical details about the *Ācārya* as happen to be preserved by the zeal of partisans and the animus of opponents are seen to be inconsistent and contradictory. The differences between the partisans begin even from the *Ācārya*'s nativeplace and parentage.[23]

The tradition concerning Rāmānuja contains no such proliferation of writings attributed to him, nor are there sharply contradictory accounts of his life by the partisans of different maths or sects. This is all the more remarkable when one bears in mind that the split between Vaḍagalais and Tengalais was more serious, both in doctrinal significance and in practical effect, than the rivalry between the different maths founded or claimed to be founded by Śankara. There are many passages in the biographies that quite probably reflect later points of view, and there are considerable differences in detail between the different biographies, but there is not a wholesale manufacture of either oral traditions or spurious writings in the interest of securing the great teacher's support in the doctrinal disputes of later generations. In striking contrast to the tradition of Śankara, there has always been complete agreement between the two schools in ascribing only nine writings to Rāmānuja, four of which are very short. The tradition has preserved the names of the outstanding scholars of each generation after Rāmānuja (and to a more limited extent of those before, back to Nāthamuni) and of their writings—even when the writings themselves are no longer extant.

What accounts for this characteristic of the Śrī Vaiṣṇava tradition? It is tempting to suppose that the emphasis of Viśiṣṭādvaita on a plurality of distinct persons might have had something to do with it. A more certain factor is the desire to honor all the ācāryas in the tradition, beginning with one's own teacher, going back to his teacher, and so on. This would not encourage the ascribing of all works to the greatest teacher of the tradition. There is the related fact that Rāmānuja does not so entirely dominate his tradition as Śankara does the school of Kevalādvaita. Rāmānuja is the authoritative commentator on the *Vedānta Sūtras*, and he is regarded as the mediator of salvation, especially by the Tengalais, since by his own faith and act of surrender he has secured the redemption of all his followers. As a teacher, however, he continues to be regarded as simply one in a long line. Since the hymns of the Āḻvārs were so important for Śrī Vaiṣṇavas, it would have been quite natural if a commentary on these hymns had been attributed to Rāmānuja. The biographies state that Rāmānuja named a disciple's child after Nammāḻvār and that this disciple later wrote a Tamil commentary called the "Six Thousand." Since Rāmānuja is said to have lectured on the Tamil *Prabandham,* Śrī Vaiṣṇavas presume that the contents of that commentary are faithful to Rāmānuja's own teaching, but neither this nor any other writing in Tamil is ascribed to Rāmānuja himself.[24]

Most of the previous modern studies of Rāmānuja have not been concerned with this problem of the authenticity of certain disputed works. In the case of many Vaiṣṇava authors this has been quite understandable, since they have simply accepted the traditional list. Since no challenge of this traditional ascription had come to their notice, they have not felt it necessary to deal with the subject at all. A number of other scholars have apparently had grave reservations about the authenticity of some of these works, but they have either solved the problem by simply ignoring the disputed works or dealt inadequately with the question of their authenticity. For example, Sukhtankar, who in 1908 wrote the first modern thesis on Rāmānuja for a Western university (Vienna), stated that he had not seen the *Vedāntasāra* but had concluded on the basis of a statement of the Reverend J. J. Johnson, who did examine it, that it was not genuine.[25] A number of earlier studies of Rāmānuja in this century ignored certain works because they were not available to the author.

The entire body of Rāmānuja's writings should be considered before deciding on the exact nature of his views on any particular subject. If certain works have been clearly demonstrated to be secondary, they can, of course, be excluded from this corpus. However, if works are in a disputed category and it is not possible at present to reach a definite decision about their authenticity, it would be as wrong to ignore them completely as it would be to accept their evidence without recognizing its possibly secondary character. My own tentative conclusion is that all the nine works that the tradition ascribes to Rāmānuja are genuine. However, since I still lack sufficient evidence for decisive historical demonstration, the six minor works, especially the three Gadyas and the *Nityagrantha,* must be considered as still "in dispute." Material from these works, therefore, will be used as supplementary rather than primary evidence.

LIMITS OF PHENOMENOLOGICAL UNDERSTANDING

This study of Rāmānuja will seem incomplete, not only because it is limited to the doctrine of God but also because the phenomenological approach imposes certain limitations or boundaries on this inquiry in order to concentrate more effectively on the grasping of the religious conceptions in the mind of Rāmānuja. I have indicated above that I have felt it necessary at times to overstep one of these boundaries and enter the realm of historical facts. This study is thus concerned with Rāmānuja as a historical person, a significant leader in the development of Śrī Vaiṣṇavism, but on the whole the concern with historical facts is peripheral to the question of their religious meaning.

Questions concerning the social and psychological motivations of

Rāmānuja and his community have not been considered. I have tried to investigate Rāmānuja's social context, but I have not tried to answer the question of *why*, in terms of his social environment or his psychological constitution, he did what he did or wrote what he wrote. The answers of any modern inquirer outside of the Śrī Vaiṣṇava community to such questions would be very different from the "ideological" explanations that Rāmānuja himself might have given, and these modern answers do not, I believe, help us to a more profound grasp of Rāmānuja's own self-understanding.

I have discussed briefly above the reasons for excluding what for most students of Rāmānuja has been the most obvious and certainly the most significant area of concern: the metaphysical reality apprehended in Rāmānuja's religious faith and experience. It may be well to repeat here that the phenomenological approach to religious studies does not deny the importance of ultimate questions, but it deliberately holds them at bay in the interest of better illuminating a less important but still significant area in the foreground, the area of human religious experience. There are students of religion whose interest is limited to a study and comparison of different types of religious experience, and there have been "objective" historians who have been interested in Rāmānuja as a South Indian religious leader without having any significant interest in what were for Rāmānuja himself the all-important questions. Like many of those attempting a phenomenological approach to religious studies, however, I am deeply interested in the philosophical and religious questions that Rāmānuja was seeking to answer. Yet precisely in the interest of more adequate theological reflection, it seems to me highly desirable to postpone consideration of ultimate questions until one has gained a better understanding of Rāmānuja's thought at the more superficial level of human religious experience. In the last chapter, however, I shall raise two questions of importance for Christian theologians and possibly for other religious thinkers as well. These are questions that can be asked, but not answered, within this study.

2 Rāmānuja's Life

Early Leaders of the Śrī Vaiṣṇava Community

Rāmānuja is regarded by Hindus as the leading exponent of one of the theistic interpretations of the dominant Hindu philosophy, the Vedānta. He belonged to the sect of Viṣṇu devotees centered in the Tamil-speaking area of South India. This sect is known as the Śrī Vaiṣṇava Saṃpradāya: the religious community that worships Viṣṇu (also called Nārāyaṇa) as the Supreme Lord, in conjunction with His Consort Śrī (also called Lakṣmī). About two centuries after Rāmānuja, the sect split in two, but both branches regard Rāmānuja as the third great teacher (ācārya) of the distinct Śrī Vaiṣṇava tradition and as in some respects the most important teacher of all.

The first of the great teachers, Nāthamuni, is said to have taken the first steps toward the correct expression of Vaiṣṇava philosophy and theology (namely, through an interpretation of *nyāya* or logic and an interpretation of the Sanskrit scriptures). The names of his two Sanskrit writings are remembered, but neither has survived.[1] A few sentences from a logical treatise are quoted four centuries later by the Śrī Vaiṣṇava teacher Venkaṭanātha (Vedānta Deśika).[2] Nāthamuni is also remembered as the one who gathered together the hymns of the Tamil Vaiṣṇava saints, known as Āḻvārs, into a collection of four thousand verses and arranged for these "Tamil Vedas" to be sung along with the verses from the Sanskrit Veda in the worship of the most important temple of Viṣṇu in South India at Śrīrangam. Finally, he is remembered as the last great master of the ancient Indian tradition of Yoga: the achievement of salvation or release from the cycle of bodily existences through a difficult process of mental and physical disciplines.

Nāthamuni has thus been regarded by his disciples who followed as the end of one great Hindu tradition—the effort to achieve salvation through one's own human powers—and the founder of a new community that brought firmly together the Sanskrit tradition going back to the Vedas and the equally ancient tradition of Tamil hymns to Viṣṇu. Nāthamuni was a Brahmin from a family with a tradition of Sanskrit scholarship. It may well have been one of the Brahmin families that had migrated from North India a few centuries before under the inducement of land from the Hindu dynasty of the Pallavas. The traditional biography of the ācāryas begins with the account of a pilgrimage that Nāthamuni and his entire family, including his father and his son, made to a number of sacred places of Viṣṇu in North India where the family decided to settle on the banks of the Yamuna River at a spot where the Supreme Lord Viṣṇu had lived on earth during his incarnation as Krishna. However, Mannanār, the form of Lord Viṣṇu present in Nāthamuni's village temple in South India, appeared to him in a dream and ordered him to come home to Vīranārāyaṇapuram. When Nāthamuni returned home, he was commended by Mannanār (through the medium of His priests or arcakas), assured of a house and a living, and given a position of some responsibility at Mannanār's temple. Later in his life Nāthamuni may have had some influence at the much larger Vaiṣṇava temple at Śrīrangam, an island in the Kāveri River across from the modern city of Tiruchirapalli; indeed, according to the temple record, he was given the title of Śrīkāryam (temple manager).[3]

The Āḻvārs came from a number of different castes; some were Brahmins, some Śūdras, and one was an outcaste. The small Vaiṣṇava community that treasured their memory and sang their hymns was also made up of different castes, and most of the Brahmins among them did not have the Sanskrit learning and prestige of Nāthamuni's family, who were therefore welcomed in the community and given positions of leadership, especially in carrying on and strengthening the tradition of scholarship.[4]

Nāthamuni was succeeded, in turn, by two of his disciples, who are said to have regarded themselves as waiting for the next great ācārya—Nāthamuni's grandson, Yāmuna or Āḷavandār, who had to be won away from a position of secular wealth and persuaded to accept the trust of the family "treasure": the Lord Viṣṇu and His Consort Śrī incarnate in the famous images of the Śrīrangam temple. Yāmuna gave up all his family possessions to become an ascetic (sannyāsī) and take instruction from his grandfather's disciples. He missed the chance to learn the secret of Nāthamuni's powerful yoga when the disciple to whom Nāthamuni had entrusted the secret died just after Yāmuna had missed an appointment with him.[5] It is significant that what made Yāmuna forget his appointment was his preoccupation with a visit to another famous Viṣṇu temple, that of Ananta Padmanābha in Trivandrum. Henceforth worship of the Deity in the image form would increasingly displace private spiritual disciplines of self-effort as the center of Śrī Vaiṣṇava piety, and scholarship would be concerned with the theory and the practice of the worship of the Divine Person.

Most of Yāmuna's writings have been preserved, though the most important doctrinal work, the *Siddhitraya,* appears to be rather seriously incomplete. The main outline and many of the details of later Śrī Vaiṣṇava thought emerge clearly in his works. His extant writings are in Sanskrit, and it is clear that he was attempting to go further with Nāthamuni's program of establishing the Vedic orthodoxy and logical cogency of a tradition making important use in its devotional life of sectarian works in Sanskrit (the *Pāñcarātra Āgamas*) as well as of the Tamil hymns to Lord Viṣṇu. Yāmuna is also said to have lectured on the meaning of the Tamil hymns (called collectively the "Four Thousand" or *Divya Prabandham*). Some of his comments or particular verses are quoted in the later written commentaries. His Sanskrit writings do not appeal to the Tamil hymns as a scriptural authority in the same way in which they claim to be based on the Sanskrit Vedas, but the influence of the Tamil hymns is clear in Yāmuna's two Sanskrit hymns, the four verses in praise of Śrī and the much longer and very significant hymn of confession, petition, and praise, the "Jewel of Hymns" (*Stotraratna*). The same type of devotion to Viṣṇu is evident in his brief verse summary of the *Bhagavadgītā,* called the *Gītārthasaṃgraha.*

Yāmuna is said to have gathered around him a group of devoted disciples, some of whom later attached themselves as respected lay devotees and teachers to other important Viṣṇu temples in South India. The number of his disciples remembered by name by the tradition is only twenty, and Yāmuna did not find among them the scholar who could carry on his work.

RĀMĀNUJA'S YOUTH

At this point the scene of the traditional biographies shifts to the northeastern part of the Tamil country, near the modern city of Madras. One of Yāmuna's most able disciples was Periya Tirumalai Nambi (the Sanskrit equivalent is Śrī Śaila Pūrṇa). Sometime before, he had left Śrīrangam and attached himself to the famous temple of Śrī Venkaṭeśvara in the Tirumalai hills near Tirupati, now in Telugu-speaking country but in ancient time considered the northern boundary of the Tamil country. This scholar-devotee had two sisters, named after the two favorite consorts of Viṣṇu, Śrī and Bhūmī, living in villages near Madras, both married into Brahmin families with traditions of Vedic scholarship. The elder sister, Bhūmī, was married to Āsūri Keśava Perumāḻ of Śrī Perumbūdūr, a town twenty-six miles from Madras City. In due course a son was born to them, whom the saintly uncle Śrī Śaila Pūrṇa was given the privilege of naming: he was called Lakṣmaṇa (the brother of Rāma) or Iḷaiyāḻvān in Tamil; he was later to be known by another form of the same name, Rāmānuja. Eight years later Bhūmī's younger sister Śrī had a son, who was called Govinda.

The traditional dates for Rāmānuja correspond to A.D. 1017-1137, following the dates of 823 to 923 for Nāthamuni and 916 to 1036 for Yāmuna.[6] Apart from a certain suspicious neatness about the life span of 120 years (twice the normal span of 60 years), there are certain features in the biographies and references to contemporary history that suggest that the date of Rāmānuja's death might well be 20 years later and his date of birth between 20 and 60 years later. Since Yāmuna is represented as suffering from ill health, his exceptionally long life span seems somewhat improbable; he may have been born considerably later, or he may not in fact have lived during Rāmānuja's lifetime. If Rāmānuja lived for only 80 years, his dates might have been A.D. 1077 to 1157.[7] This uncertainty of a generation or two is less significant than the fact that all three Śrī Vaiṣṇava teachers lived in the period when most of the Tamil country—and at times much of the rest of South India and Ceylon —was united in the Coḻa kingdom, whose various capitals in the Kāveri delta were within fifty miles of Śrīrangam. In spite of numerous wars with neighboring kingdoms, the Coḻa kingdom encouraged economic prosperity and cultural developments through its efficient central administration, its stimulation to effective local government in the villages, and its benefactions to temples and religious establishments of different sects and religions. The Coḻa kings were generally Śaivite, but they protected and enriched both Śaivite and Vaiṣṇava temples, and sometimes Jain and Buddhist establishments as well. It is perhaps particularly significant that Tanjore and Śrīrangam, instead of being on the changing boundary between the Pallavas to the north and the Pandyas to the south, were now in the middle of the kingdom and also that the ancient Pallava capital of Kāñcīpuram, with its tradition of Sanskrit scholarship under more recent Brahmin immigrants from North India, should be part of the same kingdom with the ancient centers of Tamil culture in Tanjore, Madurai, and the Tāmbraparṇī valley north of Cape Comorin.[8]

Rāmānuja's family belonged to the Vaḍama subcaste of Brahmins, a group upholding traditions of Vedic scholarship. Many of this group today are Smārta Brahmins, neither sectarian Vaiṣṇavas nor sectarian Śaivites but honoring five chief Hindu deities: Viṣṇu, Śiva, Śiva's consort Pārvatī, Śiva's son Gaṇeśa, and Sūrya, the sun-god. Each family or individual is free to choose one of these five deities and direct most of his worship to that god. At the present time all Smārta Brahmins in South India are in principle followers of the Advaita philosophy of Śankara, according to which the true Brahman lies beyond the conception of any personal Lord. The majority of them are devotees of Śiva, but they are not sectarian Śaivites; they are not initiated into a special sectarian community. To this day, a significant minority of Tamil Smārta Brahmins are devotees of Viṣṇu. It seems likely that this group of Smārta Brahmins with Vaiṣṇava leanings was relatively even larger before Rāmānuja, for he himself and many of his early "converts" to exclusive loyalty to Lord Viṣṇu and His devotees seemed to have belonged to the group of Vaiṣṇava Smārtas.[9] The family name and the close relationships to Periya Tirumalai Nambi would certainly indicate Vaiṣṇava leanings, but the biographies do not claim that Rāmānuja was initiated into the Śrī Vaiṣṇava sect as a boy, and they report his study with his father of Sanskrit Scriptures but not of the Tamil hymns. Moreover, soon after his marriage, Rāmānuja moved away from his family home and joined the student disciples of Yādava Prakāśa, represented in the traditional biographies as an Advaitin but probably the teacher of a particular variant of the Bhedābheda philosophy (the view that there is both difference and nondifference between God and the universe), which is perhaps the earliest form of Vedānta and one that was associated in the mind of an earlier Bhedābheda teacher, Bhāskara, with a very strict Vedic orthodoxy. Rāmānuja's decision (or his father's decision for him) to study with Yādava Prakāśa probably means that Yādava was considered the most able teacher of the Vedānta in the vicinity, an abler student of the Upaniṣads than any Śrī Vaiṣṇava devotee with whom Rāmānuja might have studied. Nevertheless, it seems unlikely that Rāmānuja's family would have allowed him to study with Yādava Prakāśa if they had been Śrī Vaiṣṇavas in the fully sectarian sense. Rāmānuja is represented in the biographies as a

Vedāntin with strong Vaiṣṇava leanings. He had no conversion experience. His Vaiṣṇava leanings were gradually strengthened, first, by his reaction against his teacher's interpretations of Upaniṣadic texts, second, by his personal attachment to a non-Brahmin disciple of Yāmuna's named Tirukacci Nambi (Kāñcīpūrṇa), and third, by his acceptance of, initiation into, and then leadership of the small Śrī Vaiṣṇava community centered among Yāmuna's disciples at Śrīrangam.

The biographies focus on the incidents of disagreement between the teacher and his unusual student, and they also recount Rāmānuja's foiling a murder plot organized by Yādava Prakāśa and most of his other disciples. (Rāmānuja was warned by his cousin and fellow student Govinda while on the way to Banaras, and his escape through the jungle and return to Kāñcīpuram was miraculously assisted by Lord Viṣṇu and His consort Śrī in their special forms as the deities of the great Vaiṣṇava temple in Kāñcīpuram.)[10] The biographies report that after Yādava Prakāśa's return, Rāmānuja rejoined the circle of his disciples and that sometime thereafter Yāmuna made a special trip to Kāñcī to see Rāmānuja. However, seeing him in the company of Yādava Prakāśa, Yāmuna did not go to him but looked at him from a distance with a benevolent glance and prayed to Lord Varada (the name of Viṣṇu at this temple means "the granter of wishes") that Rāmānuja might become the *darśana pravartaka* (propagator of doctrine) of the Śrī Vaiṣṇavas.[11] The beginning of the answer to this prayer was the final disagreement and break between Rāmānuja and Yādava Prakāśa, after which Rāmānuja returned home and sought his mother's advice. (His father had apparently died before this.) His mother advised him to go to the non-Brahmin disciple of Yāmuna, Tirukacci Nambi, a fervent lay devotee in Lord Varada's temple, and seek his advice. Tirukacci Nambi told him to carry a pot of water every morning from a certain well to the temple and offer it for the morning service of Lord Varada.[12] (Such service was one of the characteristic forms of lay worship to the temple image form of the Deity permitted those who were not the temple priests.)

Yāmuna was already in his last illness and had committed his disciples to the care of his senior disciple, Tiruvarangattu Perumāḷ Araiyar, the cantor of the Tamil hymns of the Āḻvārs, when he received word that Rāmānuja had broken with Yādava Prakāśa and was performing the service of a lay devotee in Lord Viṣṇu's temple.

He dispatched one of his younger disciples, named Periya Nambi (Mahā Pūrṇa) to fetch Rāmānuja to Śrīrangam posthaste. This Periya Nambi did, but before they returned Yāmuna died, and when Rāmānuja and Periya Nambi reached Śrīrangam, they saw a crowd gathered at the spot near the river bank where Yāmuna was to be buried. Rāmānuja was terribly disappointed, but after he had composed himself somewhat he pressed on and came to look at the corpse of the great teacher he had hoped to meet and to serve. Rāmānuja noticed that three fingers of Yāmuna's hand were closed and asked whether there was anyone present who had listened to Yāmuna's discourses and had heard him express any wishes. The disciples replied, "We don't know anything except that he used often to express his gratitude toward Vyāsa and Parāśara, his great affection for Nammālvār, and his ambition to write a commentary on the *Vyāsa Sūtras* according to Viśiṣṭādvaita." When Rāmānuja promised to try, with Divine aid, to fulfill these wishes, the three fingers straightened out. Those who were watching acclaimed Rāmānuja as Yāmuna's successor and their new teacher. Rāmānuja, however, was still filled with grief and disappointment. Vexed with Lord Ranga (the image incarnation of Lord Viṣṇu at Śrīrangam) for failing to grant him the favor of even a brief meeting with Yāmuna, he bade good-bye respectfully to Periya Nambi, and without going to the temple to worship Lord Ranga, started back to Kāñcīpuram.[13]

Both this account and the more elaborate stories in the later biographies present certain difficulties to a historian concerned with chronology and with historical probabilities, but it is clear in all the accounts that while Rāmānuja considered himself the disciple and the successor of Yāmuna, the link between them was spiritual rather than physical and temporal; they shared a community of purpose. The influence of Yāmuna was mediated through a number of Yāmuna's disciples.

On his return to Kāñcī, Rāmānuja again sought out Yāmuna's non-Brahmin disciple Tirukacci Nambi as his spiritual guide and soon asked this devoted Vaiṣṇava to become his formal ācārya, the teacher who initiates one into the Śrī Vaiṣṇava community. Tirukacci Nambi refused on the grounds that if he were to become Rāmānuja's ācārya, Rāmānuja would have certain social obligations to him inconsistent with Tirukacci Nambi's lower position in the caste system. Rāmānuja thought that he could at least obtain the sacramental grace of Tirukacci Nambi by eating the remains of his meal (a practice considered degrading except to show obeisance to and gain the sacramental favor of one's spiritual superior) and therefore invited him to dinner. However, Tirukacci Nambi deliberately came early while Rāmānuja was away and asked to be fed immediately so that he could begin his duties at the temple. After he had eaten and left, Rāmānuja's wife picked up with a stick the leaf from which he had eaten and threw it away, purified the room, and took another bath. When Rāmānuja returned home and discovered what had happened, he was furious with his wife and disappointed that his attempt to forge a sacramental bond with Tirukacci Nambi had failed. Tirukacci Nambi then brought Rāmānuja cryptic answers from Lord Varada to six questions in the young scholar's mind. The sixth question asked whom he should take as his ācārya, and the answer was Periya Nambi.[14] Rāmānuja set out for Śrīrangam but had only gone a day's journey when he met Periya Nambi in Madurāntkam. The latter had been commissioned by the rest of Yāmuna's disciples to prepare Rāmānuja for his work as Yāmuna's successor and then to bring him to Śrīrangam.

Rāmānuja was delighted at this unexpected meeting and insisted on being initiated at once: under a Vakuḷa tree in the courtyard of the little temple there. Periya Nambi branded Rāmānuja on the shoulders with the weapons of Viṣṇu, the conch and the wheel (śankha, cakra), marked the vertical Vaiṣṇava lines (tiruman or nāmam) on his body, whispered the sacred mantra, the so-called Dvayam, into his right ear, and then said to him aloud,

> Of old, Śrī Rāmacandra, being prevented by his promise to his father from reigning in person in Ayōdhya, left with Bhārata his sandals as his representative, and proceeded to the forest. Similarly my master, being prevented from initiating you himself, has placed his sacred feet on my head and deputed to me the responsibility. So, it is *he* from whom you have received your initiation and not from *me*.[15]

For six months, Periya Nambi and his wife lived in Rāmānuja's home while the instruction in Śrī Vaiṣṇava doctrine was proceeding. The course came to an abrupt end when the two wives quarreled about the relative purity of their respective water pots. According to one of the later biographies, some drops of water fell from the vessel of Periya Nambi's wife into the vessel of Rāmānuja's wife, whereupon the latter declared that her water pot was polluted and went on to taunt the wife of her husband's teacher about her poverty and lower caste status. (Periya Nambi was one of the so-called forelock Brahmins who wore the sacred tuft of hair further forward on their heads and were considered socially inferior by the Vaḍama Brahmins around Kāñcī.) Periya Nambi is said to have seen the quarrel, rebuked his wife, and left immediately with her for Śrīrangam. When Rāmānuja returned home he was shocked to hear of his ācārya's precipitous departure and was so furious with his wife that he sent her back to her parents and soon thereafter became an ascetic (sannyāsī).[16]

It is important to note that it was not considered necessary for a Śrī Vaiṣṇava to become an ascetic in order to lead a devout life. It is true that Yāmuna and Rāmānuja both became ascetics after several years of marriage, but Nāthamuni never took the vows of sannyāsa, and only a few of Yāmuna's and Rāmānuja's disciples were ascetics. Moreover, even those Śrī Vaiṣṇava ascetics who renounced family life and became sannyāsīs were less cut off from the religious norms of householders than were Smārta and Śaiva ascetics. Śrī Vaiṣṇava ascetics who belonged to one of the three higher or "twice-born" castes continue to wear the sacred thread, and there are certain daily religious duties of householders that they continue to perform. Rāmānuja's theology is an effort to combine into one harmonious life social duties, religious rites, and the higher realms of meditation and devotion. This effort contrasts sharply not only with the theory of Śankara's Advaita but also with the practice of a much more complete world renunciation by Advaitin and Śaiva ascetics. The positive connection between this world and the higher or highest realm, which is to be found in Rāmānuja's theology, has its counterpart in the daily ordering of life by members of the Śrī Vaiṣṇava community. That ordering assumes the validity of the *varnāśramadharma,* the ethic of castes and stages of life, but the community of the Lord's devotees, with its own hierarchy of spiritual excellence, is supposed, in principle if not always in practice, to take precedence over the hierarchies of caste and also of *āśrama* (the respect shown to any ascetic). Rāmānuja's wife had the usual Brahmin attitude toward those of all lower castes and even toward other Brahmins of subcastes considered inferior to one's own, and this attitude is typically expressed as a fear of ritual pollution. For Rāmānuja the superior spiritual rank of Yāmuna's own disciples (which extended in social terms to Periya Nambi's family) was such as to obligate him to the utmost in hospitality and to make him desire precisely that physical or "sacramental" contact that his wife found so polluting.

RĀMĀNUJA AS LEADER OF THE COMMUNITY

Afer Rāmānuja became an ascetic he established his own small math (monastic house) near the temple precincts in Kāñcī. His first disciples were his elder sister's son, Mudali Āṇḍān (Daśarathi) and a scholarly and wealthy Brahmin named Kūraṭṭāḻvān (Kūreśa or Śrī Vatsānka), who either before or after this gave away all his wealth and lived with his wife in great simplicity. (According to the somewhat later Vaḍagalai account, another nephew, Naḍadūr-āḻvān, the son of Rāmānuja's other sister, was also one of the first group of disciples.) Rāmānuja formally initiated his disciples into the Śrī Vaiṣṇava community and started to instruct them in the two branches of Vedic study, the Pūrva and Uttara Mīmāṃsā, namely, the study of Vedic ritual and the study of the philosophy of the Upaniṣads.[17] His next disciple was his former teacher Yādava Prakāśa, whose conversion to Śrī Vaiṣṇavism is said to have been influenced by his mother, a devotee of Lord Varada. Rāmānuja gave him the new name of Govinda Jīyar and asked him to write a book of rules for Śrī Vaiṣṇava ascetics, a work that is still extant (*Yatidharma-samuccaya*).[18]

When the disciples of Yāmuna in Śrīrangam heard that Rāmānuja had become an ascetic and started his own math, they had the temple authorities send a message in the name of the temple deity Lord Ranga to the temple deity in Kāñcīpuram, Lord Varada (both deities considered image incarnations of Viṣṇu-Nārāyaṇa), requesting permission for Rāmānuja to leave the service of Lord Varada and join the service of Lord Ranga at His temple. The first request was refused by Lord Varada (speaking, as on the other occasions, through his priests), but the senior disciple of Yāmuna, Tiruvarangattu Perumāḷ Araiyar, succeeded in a second attempt by so charming Lord Varada through his singing and dancing, while reciting five verses of the Āḻvārs in Lord Varada's praise, that Lord Varada unthinkingly promised him any boon he requested.[19]

When Rāmānuja reached the sacred island of Śrīrangam, he was met by Periya Nambi (Mahā Pūrṇa) and the other disciples of Yāmuna and also by a procession from the temple headed by the image of

Viṣvaksena, the commander of Lord Viṣṇu's army. Rāmānuja was led back through the vast temple precincts to the central shrine where he sang a famous Āḻvār hymn (the "Tirupallāṇḍu") and two verses of Yāmuna's Sanskrit hymn, the "Stotraratna." Then Lord Ranga addressed him as follows: "We have given the wealth of both our realms (this world and the eternal world, *ubhaya-vibhūti-aiśvarya*) for you and your people. After examining everything, manage all the works of our house." Whereupon Rāmānuja turned to Periya Nambi and quoted a verse from Nammāḻvār's *Tiruvāymoḻi* (10.6.10): "If you are connected with great people, you can attain even a good that is both great and difficult" (I owe this honor to you as my ācārya). To this Periya Nambi replied with another line from the *Tiruvāymoḻi* (5.21): "'You will see that Kali [this evil age] is going to be destroyed.' This prophecy is now fulfilled. Take up what the Lord has commanded."[20]

Immediately all the people gathered in the great hall called the Garuḍa Mantapam. Rāmānuja first examined the treasury. Then he inspected the supplies of rice, sandal paste, flower garlands, and lights, looked into the duties of the higher and lower servants of the temple, attended to repairs of the ramparts, and examined the maintenance of the flower gardens. He took Akaḷanga Nattāḻvān (according to the temple record, the non-Brahmin headman of a nearby village) as his disciple and made him the supervisor (business manager) of the daily and periodic rites in the temple.[21]

One might assume from the biographies that the supervision of the temple entrusted to Rāmānuja was of the same kind as that exercised by Yāmuna. The Śrīrangam temple record, the *Kōil Oḻugu,* makes clear, however, that whatever the temple authorities may have originally intended, Rāmānuja proceeded little by little to a thoroughgoing reorganization of the temple administration. This may well have been in the interests of honesty and of sectarian orthodoxy, but it resulted in the displacement of several temple functionaries, the curtailment of the powers of others, and the provision of positions for a number of Rāmānuja's disciples (some of them his relatives), coming from a different group of Brahmins living in the region around Kāñcīpuram. Both the biographies and the temple records mention the attempt of the temple priests (arcakas) to poison Rāmānuja. (According to the temple record, Rāmānuja retired for two years to Tiruveḷḷarai until the repentant temple servants sent Yāmuna's senior disciple, the cantor T. P. Araiyar, to persuade Rāmānuja to come back.[22]

The *Kōil Olugu* gives another story not found in the biographies, however, which illumines the conflict behind the transfer of power. Even after Rāmānuja had been welcomed and given certain powers, the keys to the temple remained in the hands of the hereditary "high priest," Periya Kōil Nambi, and this high priest opposed Rāmānuja's plan to change from a fivefold to a tenfold division of the temple servants (parijanas). Rāmānuja thought of removing him (the oral tradition of the high priest's family claims Rāmānuja thought of poisoning him), but Lord Ranga appeared to Rāmānuja in a dream and pointed out that "for a long time past Periya Kōil Nambi has entrusted himself to Our care. You can do as you please." When Rāmānuja woke up he called his disciple Kūraṭṭāḻvān and reported his dream. "The existence of my enemy . . . seems to be agreeable to the Lord. Let us go to Perumāḷ Kōil (Kāñcīpuram)." Kūraṭṭāḻvān is said to have persuaded his master that the Lord would help to make the high priest his disciple. "If so, you bring him round," said Rāmānuja. The *Kōil Olugu* simply reports that Kūraṭṭāḻvān succeeded in persuading the learned high priest to seek Rāmānuja as his guru and gives after that a story of Kūraṭṭāḻvān's participating in the funeral ceremonies for Periya Kōil Nambi's mother, at the conclusion of which Periya Kōil Nambi gives to Kūraṭṭāḻvān, as the official guest at the eleventh-day feast, "the hereditary office of the high priest and the right to read the purāṇas in the temple . . . and also the document registering these gifts." Kūraṭṭāḻvān immediately turned over these gifts to Rāmānuja.[23]

The oral tradition handed down by the descendants of Periya Kōil Nambi gives a rather different version of the events, one that suggests that Kūraṭṭāḻvān tricked their ancestor out of his inherited status as "high priest." According to this version, Kūraṭṭāḻvān ingratiated himself with the mother of Periya Kōil Nambi, by first singing and later explaining the hymns of the Āḻvārs to her. (Her son is said to have been a Vedic scholar but not well versed in the Tamil hymns.) It was on this account that Kūraṭṭāḻvān received an invitation to be one of the Brahmin guests at the eleventh-day feast. When asked the customary question after the meal of whether he was satisfied, Kūraṭṭāḻvān remained silent. When asked again he replied that all he still wanted were the keys to the temple. The demands of hospitality forced Periya Kōil Nambi to agree. He turned over not only his keys but his house to Kūraṭṭāḻvān and left immediately for his country home where he completed the remaining rites for his mother. When Rāmānuja and Kūraṭṭāḻvān tried to enter the temple the next morning, the priests stopped them. They were allowed to proceed only when Periya Kōil Nambi came back and confirmed that he had indeed turned over all his perquisites to Rāmānuja's lieutenant.[24]

However Rāmānuja may have acquired Periya Kōil Nambi's acquiescence, he was sufficiently pleased to give him a new name, Amudanār (the Tamil form of the Sanskrit word *amrita,* the nectar of immortality), because of his skill in speech, and also a new function, the chanting of one thousand of the four thousand stanzas of the Tamil hymns, the *Divya Prabandham.* This same Amudanār is considered to be the author of a hundred-stanza Tamil poem of praise to Rāmānuja, which may well be the only genuine contemporary work specifically about Rāmānuja. Unfortunately for the historian, this poem gives almost no biographical information about Rāmānuja. It mentions only one of his disciples by name, but that one is, significantly, Kūraṭṭāḻvān.[25] According to tradition, the original version contained much more about Rāmānuja's qualities and deeds, but Rāmānuja disapproved of these verses because they made too little reference to the Āḻvārs. Whatever the explanation, this ode gives very little information of the kind that would have been helpful in lending Rāmānuja's support to positions taken by either of the later schools. This seems to me considerably to increase the possibility of its genuineness. (The first commentary on this work seems to have been by the Tengalai leader, Manavāḷamāmunigaḷ, about three hundred years later, but Vedānta Deśika refers to the ode two generations before that.)[26] It is remarkable, though certainly not inconceivable, that Rāmānuja should have been so highly praised by the man whose authority in the temple he had so seriously diminished.

Perhaps the most important general conclusion to be drawn from the somewhat conflicting traditions is that Rāmānuja did manage to introduce new rules and new temple officers without permanently alienating the representatives of the previous regime. This meant not only a new cooperation between different Brahmin subcastes but also a cooperation between Brahmins and non-Brahmins in the temple administration. The *Kōil Oḻugu* notes two cases when Rāmānuja considered replacing or was asked to replace a non-Brahmin with a Brahmin in the temple administration. In both cases Rāmānuja decided to retain a non-Brahmin in the position.[27] This was not a new policy for the temple, since those particular positions (temple accountant and the person who offered the coconut to the Deity) at the Śrīrangam temple had been traditionally filled by non-Brahmins. This policy was, however, more liberal than the attitude obtaining in the more Sanskrit-oriented group of Brahmins to which Rāmānuja and his first disciples belonged. It is this *relative* liberalism with respect to caste differences within the Srī Vaiṣṇava community that is emphasized in a number of stories about Rāmānuja's relations with non-Brahmin Śrī Vaiṣṇavas. This emphasis may have been increased by the later Tengalai biographers; it certainly was minimized by the alterations and omissions in the still later Vaḍagalai versions of the biography.

Like Nāthamuni and Yāmuna before him, Rāmānuja was the ācārya, the authoritative teacher of the Śrī Vaiṣṇava community. He was also the Śrīkāryam or general manager of the Śrīrangam temple. He seems to have separated these two functions before the end of his life. Before his first long tour away from Śrīrangam, he appointed his nephew Mudali Āṇḍān (Daśarathi) as his deputy in managing temple affairs. After Rāmānuja's death, Āṇḍān became the Śrīkāryam and passed the position on to his own grandson; it remained in the Kaṇḍāḍai family for almost two hundred years until the second Muslim sack of Śrīrangam in 1324.[28] The two later schools differ as to who it was that Rāmānuja appointed to succeed him as ācārya, but in neither case do Mudali Āṇḍān and his descendants figure in the succession of ācāryas.

Rāmānuja came from a Brahmin family that had the duty of studying and teaching the Vedas and also had the right to function as priests in certain Vedic sacrifices. As the chief ācārya of the Śrī Vaiṣṇava community, he also had important priestly duties with respect to all his disciples. He was not, however, a temple priest or arcaka (one who offers worship to the *arca* or image form of the Deity). The arcakas or *pūjārīs* at Śrīrangam and other Vaiṣṇava temples in South India come from a distinct endogamous group of Brahmins who are considered somewhat socially inferior by the more "Vedic" Brahmins. Yet in the actual temple worship so important for Śrī Vaiṣṇavas, the arcakas play the central role; they perform the major acts of worship, which are designed as a continual ministry to the personal needs (bodily as well as mental) of the embodied Lord and His Consorts. It is the arcakas, moreover, who speak on behalf of the Deity enshrined in the temple. This is made clear by the frequent statement that the Lord spoke *arcaka-*

mukhena (by means of his priests). All other worshipers in the temple, including all other Brahmins, are in the position of laymen, though these laymen are allowed to perform certain indirect services toward meeting the bodily needs of the Lord, as Rāmānuja did when he carried a pot of water every day to the temple at Kāñcīpuram. Here again, it was Rāmānuja's task to effect a new degree of cooperation between the Vedic-oriented Brahmin scholars and the temple-oriented Śrī Vaiṣṇava, both Brahmin and non-Brahmin. In the personal religious life of the Śrī Vaiṣṇava, the Vedic and Āgamic types of worship come most closely together in his household worship, for every Śrī Vaiṣṇava is competent to perform worship to his own household image of the Deity. (In Rāmānuja's case, this was a small replica of the form of Lord Viṣṇu in the temple in Kāñcīpuram, known as Peruḷāḷar or Varadarāja.)

While Rāmānuja was thus not a temple priest (arcaka), he exercised many priestly functions. When he assumed the position of ācārya at Śrīrangam, Lord Ranga "by means of His priests" is said to have given Rāmānuja the title of Uḍayavar, a Tamil term meaning "possessor" or "owner." He was entrusted with the management of the Lord's eternal realm as well as with His earthly wealth. Thus Rāmānuja was considered to be not only the steward of the temple but the guardian of the state of eternal bliss of which the temple was an earthly symbol. This was his highest priestly function in the eyes of his followers: mediating salvation to those who depended on him. To those who accepted Rāmānuja as their ācārya, he did indeed fulfill the prophecy of Nammāḻvār by bringing to an end the Kali Yuga. Though outwardly the old evil age continued, his followers believed that he was ushering in the new age, which was only a return to the golden age of righteousness. (There is a reference to Rāmānuja's destroying Kali in Amudanār's *Irāmānuja Nūtranḍādi.*)[29]

Because Rāmānuja had not been instructed and initiated into the esoteric lore of the sect by Yāmuna himself, he had to receive Yāmuna's teaching indirectly from five of Yāmuna's disciples. In his case, moreover, his entire education up to that point had been in the Sanskrit Scriptures, so that he had to be thoroughly instructed in the Tamil hymns going back to Nāthamuni.

The first of the five disciples was Periya Nambi (Mahā Pūrṇa), who formally initiated Rāmānuja into the Śrī Vaiṣṇava Saṃpradāya (sectarian community) and taught him for six months at Rāmānuja's home before the quarrel between their wives abruptly terminated the lessons. In that time they are said to have covered the first two thousand of the four thousand stanzas of the Tamil hymns. The second disciple of Yāmuna to instruct Rāmānuja was Tirukoṭṭiyūr Nambi (Goṣṭhi Pūrṇa), to whom we shall turn below. The third was Tirumālai Āṇḍān (Mālādhara), who taught Rāmānuja Yāmuna's commentary on the four great works of Nammāḻvār, especially the *Tiruvāymoḻi*, and found Rāmānuja an argumentative pupil, who sometimes insisted that he knew Yāmuna's mind better than did his direct disciple. The fourth disciple-teacher was Yāmuna's senior disciple, the cantor Tiruvarangattu Perumāḷ Araiyar, who after keeping Rāmānuja waiting for some time revealed to him the secret of *guru-prapatti,* total reliance on the grace of one's guru, who is to be regarded as God Himself. Finally, Rāmānuja was instructed by his own uncle, Periya Tirumalai Nambi (Śrī Śaila Pūrṇa), who had been a disciple of Yāmuna's before he went to Tirupati. When Rāmānuja visited Tirupati, his uncle spent a year teaching him the meaning of the *Rāmāyaṇa.*

The story of Rāmānuja's instruction from Tirukoṭṭiyūr Nambi (Goṣṭhī Pūrṇa) is one of the favorite parts of the biography and one very often referred to in modern times in order to demonstrate Rāmānuja's liberal spirit. Rāmānuja went eighteen times from Śrīrangam to the home of this disciple of Yāmuna in Tirukoṭṭiyūr. Each time Rāmānuja was sent off without being given the secret doctrine. Finally one of Nambi's disciples interceded. After adjuring Rāmānuja and his two inseparable disciples (Kūraṭṭāḻvān and Mudali Āṇḍān) to secrecy, Tirukoṭṭiyūr Nambi revealed the secret meaning of the eight-syllabled mantra, "Oṃ Namo Nārāyaṇāya." The very next day, however, Rāmānuja went up to the second-floor balcony of the temple tower in Tirukoṭṭiyūr and revealed the secret doctrine to a number of Śrī Vaiṣṇavas congregated in front of the main shrine below. (At the present time, this story is often told as though Rāmānuja had climbed to the *gopuram,* which is the tower over the gate of the temple, and had shouted the secret for all the townspeople to hear. In most temples the gopuram is indeed the only tower that one is permitted to climb. It would be disrespectful to climb up to the top of the *vimāna,* the tower above the central shrine, because one would then be higher than the Deity installed in the image below. In this particular temple, however, there is an image of the Deity on each of the three stories of the vimāna. The image at the top level shows the Deity in standing position, the image on the middle level in sitting position, and the one at ground level in recumbent position. Worshipers are permitted at all three levels. The earliest account makes clear that "Rāmānuja revealed the meaning of the supreme secret to a number of Śrī Vaiṣṇavas." Presumably they had all been duly initiated, but they may not have all been Brahmins. In any case, Tirukoṭṭiyūr Nambi had made Rāmānuja promise not to reveal the secret to anyone else.)

When Nambi heard what had happened, he was amazed and summoned Rāmānuja for an explanation. The ensuing conversation is reported as follows:

Nambi. I heard that you revealed this to a number of Śrī Vaiṣṇavas.

Uḍayavar [*Rāmānuja*]. That is true. Taking your feet (committing myself to your mercy), I revealed it.

Nambi. Do you know the result of disobeying my command, when I told you not to tell anyone?

Uḍayavar. Going against the commandment of the ācārya will result in hell [naraka].

Nambi. Even knowing this, why have you told it?

Uḍayavar. I alone shall go to hell. Keeping your feet in mind I have revealed it. Thus because of their connection with you these souls will be saved.

Nambi then reflected, "I am unable to attain this fullness." Very much pleased with Rāmānuja's thought for the welfare of others, he called him to draw near and embraced him, calling him "Emberumānār" (Our Lord), and said, "What a great person you are. Up to this time this darśana was called *paramavaidika-darśanam.* From now on call it *Emberumānār darśanam.*"[30]

The memory of the original event has been affected by a hundred years of recounting a favorite story, in which thc secretiveness of Tirukoṭṭiyūr Nambi is vividly contrasted with Rāmānuja's openhearted generosity: his desire to share the saving truth with others, not with all but certainly with all those who met the qualifications for such instruction. With each of Yāmuna's disciples, Rāmānuja began as an obedient disciple but then proceeded to demonstrate his own special gifts and finally his unique authority. One interesting feature of Rāmānuja's relation with these five mediators of

Yāmuna's teaching is that each of the five is said to have committed one or more sons to Rāmānuja's care, henceforth to be his disciples.

It does not seem to me inconceivable that the incident at the Tirukoṭṭiyūr temple could have taken place, revolutionary as Rāmānuja's action would have been. Whatever happened, the story clearly captures a concern of Rāmānuja's that was to fill the rest of his life: to spread this darśana, which until now had been the carefully guarded property of a small group of devotees, to spread it both to the communities of devotees at other Vaiṣṇava temples and to the all-Indian scholarly community of students of the Sanskrit Scriptures.

THE MATURE TEACHER OF THEISTIC VEDĀNTA

The next period of Rāmānuja's life consisted of disputations with scholars of other philosophical schools and of teaching disciples, both in Śrīrangam and in various other temple centers, especially in South India. He also went on at least one long tour throughout India.

Rāmānuja's first major debate after becoming the Śrī Vaiṣṇava leader is said to have been with a famous Advaitin ascetic named Yajñamūrti, who came back to South India from Banaras after having defeated scholars of all other schools in debate and having written a number of books. He had heard about this new scholar in Śrīrangam, and he challenged him to a debate, offering, if he should lose, to carry Rāmānuja's sandals, take his name, and enter his sect. Rāmānuja agreed to the debate but would not promise so much: "If we are defeated, we shall abandon books and say, 'Defeated'." For sixteen days of the eighteen-day debate neither gained an advantage, but on the seventeenth day Rāmānuja could make no headway against Yajñamūrti's logic and went home very discouraged. He then prayed for help to his household image, Lord Varada, who answered his prayer by appearing that night to him in a dream and telling him to use all the arguments of Yāmuna against the doctrine of the illusoriness of the world (the māyāvāda). The next morning Yajñamūrti was so impressed with Rāmānuja's confident manner that he confessed defeat before the debate began. Rāmānuja insisted, nonetheless, in reciting the arguments of Yāmuna. After that he welcomed his defeated adversary cordially, initiating him into the Śrī Vaiṣṇava community, and gave him a form of his own title: "Emberumānār by the grace of Perumāḷ" (Viṣṇu, in this case in the form of Lord Varada). He helped his new namesake to establish his own small math, turning over three of his disciples to him.[31] Yajñamūrti is said later to have abandoned his separate monastic establishment because he was embarrassed that visitors to Śrīrangam should be confused by finding two Emberumānār maths.[32] He is said to be the author of two still extant Tamil didactic poems summarizing Śri Vaiṣṇava doctrine "in easily understandable style . . . to save even women and simple people." (These works, called *Jñānasāram* and *Prameyasāram,* do not mention Rāmānuja, and the description of Śrī Vaiṣṇava doctrine is in such general terms as to make it difficult to determine what relation to Rāmānuja the author may have had.)[33]

What are we to think of this story? It seems somewhat improbable in its present form; surely Rāmānuja would have used the arguments of Yāmuna long before the last day. The most intriguing question to me, however, is why Rāmānuja's followers would have remembered and retold this story in a form that seems to reflect so little credit on Rāmānuja's skill as a debater. It is true that the emphasis in the biographical tradition is not on the fine points of metaphysics; there seems at times to be a certain antiintellectualist bias, and certainly there is an emphasis on all occasions of Divine intervention. Nevertheless, this story contrasts strikingly with the story of the youthful Yāmuna confounding the proud court pandit, Ākki Āḻvān, and agrees in its emphasis with the story of the conversion of Rāmānuja's former teacher, Yādava Prakāśa, who may have been shaken but certainly was not convinced by Rāmānuja's objections to his teacher's interpretations of Upaniṣadic texts. He may have been more impressed by Rāmānuja's ability to cast out a demon from the king's daughter when he was unable to do so, but he was finally won over by his pious Vaiṣṇava mother's pleading and by the appearance of Lord Varada in a dream explaining how, as an old man, he could still perform the necessary penance prior to becoming a Śrī Vaiṣṇava.[34]

It is quite probable that the tradition correctly remembers that Rāmānuja as a young man was unable to convince many of his opponents by logical and metaphysical arguments. What the tradition emphasizes is Rāmānuja's utter sincerity and religious zeal, which gave him unusual intellectual courage, the willingness to stand up for what he believed in, even against his elders. This positive emphasis seems to me likewise to rest on an accurate memory of the historical Rāmānuja.

Rāmānuja's tour of India with his disciples probably took him a period of several years. He undoubtedly made other shorter trips to important temple centers in South India. It was and is quite common for a Hindu to go on pilgrimage to a number of the most sacred places in different parts of the country, but Rāmānuja's tour served other purposes as well. It enabled him to meet Vedāntins in other parts of India, both to debate with those of opposing schools and to secure more information about the ancient tradition of theistic interpretation of the Vedānta, which he was attempting to propound. The most significant story in this connection is of Rāmānuja's visit to Kashmir, where he was able to read Bodhāyana's commentary on the *Vedānta Sūtras.* (According to one account he was forced to return the copy to the temple of Sarasvatī after only one night, but fortunately his talented disciple Kūraṭṭāḻvān had memorized the entire manuscript at a single reading.)[35]

Rāmānuja was also concerned to purify the worship at all Vaiṣṇava temples, especially at the great temple centers drawing pilgrims from a wide area. Specifically, he wanted to eliminate the admixture of non-Vaiṣṇava rites. It is not clear to what extent he tried to replace the somewhat less sectarian Vaikhānasa rites with the Pañcarātra rites. Both these types of Vaiṣṇava ritual, using Sanskrit ritual formulas (mantras), were meant not to replace but to supplement Vedic rites; to be used for temple worship which is not provided for in the Vedas, in which worship is offered to the Deity incarnated in an image in which He condescends to dwell in order to make Himself more available to His worshipers.

In his efforts at temple reform, Rāmānuja achieved some success, especially in South India; but he also had experiences of complete failure. He had no success at all at the temple of Ananta Padmanābha in Trivandrum (now in the capital of the state of Kerala, on the southwest coast of India) or at the famous temple of Jagannātha in Purī (in Orissa, on the central east coast of India). Identical stories are told about these two failures of his temple reform. The God incarnate in the temple image sided with his priests and transported Rāmānuja several miles away![36] Some of Rāmānuja's successes were due in part to his arguments, but the defeat of the Śaiva claim to the image of Venkaṭeśvara in the great temple of Tirumalai (on the hill above Tirupati, in southeastern Andhra Pradesh) was accomplished, not by debate, but by a direct indication given by the Lord in the temple: His picking up and wearing the Vaiṣṇava emblems, while leaving the Śaiva emblems unused on the floor.[37]

It is fairly certain that Rāmānuja spent a considerable period during the latter part of his life in the Hoysala kingdom, now the southern part of Mysore State on the central South Indian plateau called the Deccan. According to the biographies, Rāmānuja fled from Śrīrangam to the Hoysala kingdom when the Co̱la king Kulottunga demanded that he come to the Co̱la capital and sign a declaration, "There is no god higher than Śiva." Kūraṭṭāḻvān, dressed to look like Rāmānuja in the saffron-colored robes of an ascetic, and Periya Nambi went to the Co̱la capital in Rāmānuja's stead, where Kūraṭṭāḻvān made a pun on the word "Śiva" when asked to sign the declaration. The king ordered both men's eyes put out. Periya Nambi, then a very old man, died soon after, while Kūraṭṭāḻvān went into retirement at the ancient Vaiṣṇava shrine of Tirumāliruñjolai, near Madurai. Rāmānuja escaped through the hill country to Mysore, where he is said to have converted the Hoysala king Biṭṭideva from Jainism to Śrī Vaiṣṇavism and renamed him Viṣṇuvārdhana. Viṣṇuvārdhana assisted Rāmānuja to found a new Vaiṣṇava temple in Melkote and assisted in establishing five other Vaiṣṇava temples in the kingdom, to which were given the lands previously belonging to a large number of Jain temples.[38] According to some of the biographies, Rāmānuja defeated a thousand Jain ascetics in debate by miraculous means, whereupon the Jain monks committed suicide rather than give up their religion.[39]

The fanatical Śaivite king finally died (according to some accounts he died of a carbuncle in the neck, caused by Rāmānuja's black magic[40]) and Rāmānuja was then able to return to Śrīrangam, where he spent his remaining years in peace, surrounded by a large company of disciples, and died finally at the extreme old age of 120.[41]

THE PROBLEM OF ESTABLISHING DATES

The traditional biographies give a number of dates for this period of Rāmānuja's life, and there is some evidence from temple inscriptions in Mysore State to support the likelihood of Rāmānuja's having been aided by the Hoysala king Viṣṇuvārdhana. Unfortunately, however, it is very difficult to put all the dates given in the traditional biographies (some of them conflicting), inscriptional evidence from Mysore, and our knowledge of the Co̱la kings of the period, together into one coherent pattern.

For some time most students of Śrī Vaiṣṇava history have accepted the chronology proposed by T. A. Gopinatha Rao in 1917. He accepted the traditional dates for Rāmānuja's life given in the later biographies, corresponding to A.D. 1017 to 1137, identified the persecuting Coḻa king with Kulottunga I (who died in 1117), and placed the period of exile from A.D. 1079 to A.D. 1126.[42] This chronology, however, raises several problems, for the tradition maintains that Rāmānuja's exile was only twelve years, and Kulottunga I is not known to have been a fanatical Śaivite. For this reason, various other proposals have been advanced, identifying the persecuting king with some other Coḻa monarch. The most convincing alternative I have seen is that advanced by the Madras government epigraphist, T. N. Subramanian, in a brief article called "A Note on the Date of Rāmānuja."[43] He relies on information contained in three Tamil verses, presumably from an earlier work, contained in the rather late Tamil biography, the *Rāmānujārya Divya Caritai.* This information is (1) that Rāmānuja's largest commentary on the *Vedānta Sūtras,* the *Śrībhāṣya,* was completed in 1077 Śaka (A.D. 1155-56); (2) that Rāmānuja left Śrīrangam in 1059 Śaka (A.D. 1137-38) and returned after a period of eleven years; and (3) that Kūraṭṭāḻvān was refused admission to Śrīrangam (after his blinding) and stayed for eleven years in Tirumāliruñjolai before rejoining his ācārya Rāmānuja. He identifies the persecuting Coḻa king with Kulottunga II (A.D. 1133-50), who is known to have been an active Śaivite who destroyed the shrine to Viṣṇu within the Śaivite temple in Cidambaram and threw the image into the sea.

Subramanian's article does not take up the other dates in Rāmānuja's life or attempt to explain the presence of Rāmānuja and his disciples in Mysore before A.D. 1137. It seems to me quite likely, however, that the later biographers could have telescoped two different visits of Rāmānuja to Mysore, on the first of which he received the favor of the king (Viṣṇuvārdhana was king from A.D. 1110 to 1152) and built the temple at Melkote. It could well have been because he was sure of a friendly welcome that he fled to Mysore in A.D. 1137. Most of the kings of that era were not religious fanatics. Their personal religious preference did not prevent them from supporting religious institutions of Śaivas, Vaiṣṇavas, and often also of Buddhists and Jains. Since Viṣṇuvārdhana seems to have had this Vaiṣṇava name from the beginning of his reign, it is not clear whether his favor to Rāmānuja can be considered a "conversion," nor do we have a record of his withdrawal of support to the Jain monks from a neutral source; but it is clear that Jains declined in influence in this region from about this time and that the Śrī Vaiṣṇavas were henceforth firmly established.

The first piece of information given above, that the *Śrībhāṣya* was not finished until A.D. 1155, ties in with another isolated fragment that the *Śrībhāṣya* was only two-thirds finished when Rāmānuja left Śrīrangam. It is possible that Rāmānuja had not been able to take along the manuscripts he needed when he fled so suddenly to Mysore, but it is also possible that he needed the encyclopedic memory and the literary talents of his amanuensis, Kūraṭṭāḻvān, whom Rāmānuja is said to have told to write down nothing unless he agreed with it.[44] In any case it is clear that Kūraṭṭāḻvān was more than an ordinary disciple; he was an active collaborator in all of Rāmānuja's most cherished projects. He was something of a poet; several Sanskrit hymns survive which there is no reason to doubt he wrote, as well as a cryptic acrostic poem accompanied by a prose commentary, called the *Yamakaratnākaram.* He is also said to have written a commentary on Rāmānuja's three prose hymns, the *Gadyatraya,* but this is no longer extant (see below, chap. 17, n. 25). Kūraṭṭāḻvān is said to have had a saintly and learned wife, who stayed with him when he gave up his wealthy home and property and joined Rāmānuja.[45] The biographies relate the miraculous circumstances surrounding the birth of their twin sons, Parāśara Bhaṭṭar and Śrī Rāma Piḷḷai (Veda Vyāsa Bhaṭṭar), the subsequent "adoption" of these children by Lord Ranga, and the difficulties in finding a bride for Parāśara Bhaṭṭar. Kūraṭṭāḻvān could not find a suitably spiritual (namely, Śrī Vaiṣṇava) girl from among his own relatives, and Rāmānuja had trouble convincing both sides to arrange a match between Parāśara Bhaṭṭar and a girl from Periya Nambi's family, since the latter was of a different Brahmin subcaste (Bṛhaccaraṇas).[46]

THE SUCCESSION AFTER RĀMĀNUJA

According to the Tengalai accounts, Rāmānuja appointed Parāśara Bhaṭṭar his successor as ācārya.[47] In addition to several Sanskrit hymns, Bhaṭṭar wrote a Sanskrit commentary on the ancient Vaiṣṇava work, the "Thousand Names of Viṣṇu," and a manual of daily worship.[48] The Vaḍagalai biographies, on the other hand, state that Rāmānuja appointed his uncle Tirumalai Nambi's son, Tirukkuruhai Pirān Piḷḷān (Kurukeśa), as his successor in the authoritative exposition of both the Sanskrit and the Tamil Scriptures.[49] The first of the written commentaries on the Tamil hymns, written in heavily Sanskritized Tamil, is said to have been written by Piḷḷān on the basis of Rāmānuja's own lectures on the hymns. There seems to me to be earlier evidence for the succession of Parāśara Bhaṭṭar, but since it was part of the genius of Rāmānuja to set his disciples to different tasks, depending upon their talents and also upon his view of the needs of the community, it seems quite possible that he may have commissioned Piḷḷān to write a commentary on the hymns of the Āḻvārs, something he had not done himself and something which marked a new and significant departure from the custom of oral commentaries passed on by oral tradition. The writing of Piḷḷān's "Six Thousand" was an important step in the process of disclosing the "secrets of salvation" to the entire Śrī Vaiṣṇava community and, in these latter days, to the world at large. (There is no comparable tradition of *written* commentaries on the roughly contemporary hymns of the Tamil Śaivite saints.) It is in any case curious that the one considered by the southern school to be Rāmānuja's first successor should have written only in Sanskrit, whereas the one considered by the more Sanskrit-oriented northern school to be Rāmānuja's successor should have written in Tamil. Indeed Piḷḷān initiated the tradition of Sanskritized Tamil commentary on the Tamil hymns, a tradition that was to become a hallmark of the southern school.

I shall discuss in later chapters the light shed by the biographical traditions on Rāmānuja's personality and even on specific teachings. Doubtless the specific words attributed to Rāmānuja after a century or more of oral transmission are often so highly colored by later views of what Rāmānuja *ought* to have said that they tell us little of what he actually taught, but we should not be too skeptical about the relatively accurate transmission of utterances in the oral tradition, especially when they do not conform precisely to later doctrinal developments.

The account in this chapter, however, is concerned not with the oral tradition of Rāmānuja but with the historical person at the source of that tradition. Rāmānuja was not the originator of the traditions he articulated or the founder of the distinctive Śrī Vaiṣṇava community, but he had much to do with articulating those traditions in their distinctive Śrī Vaiṣṇava synthesis in a way that made them known all over India and with greatly enlarging the Śri Vaiṣṇava community, spreading it from a few Vaiṣṇava temples to every part of South India. Rāmānuja came from the Vedic-oriented section of the South Indian Brahmins, and he persuaded many of his kinsmen and others of a similar background to join the Śrī Vaiṣṇava community. In the long run the most striking social effect of this Vaḍama Brahmin influx may have been to increase the Brahmin control of this community, but this is really only one side of the coin. The other side, which was the one closer to Rāmānuja's own intention, was to introduce the educated leadership of all Hindu society to the double tradition of Sanskritic and Tamil Vaiṣṇava theism: the Ubhaya Vedānta.

3 The Sanskrit Writings Attributed to Rāmānuja

The Recorded Teachings of Rāmānuja

Many outside the Śrī Vaiṣṇava community, in India as well as in the West, know Rāmānuja only as the author of a theistic commentary on the *Vedānta Sūtras* called the *Śrībhāṣya*. Indeed, many have read no further than Rāmānuja's long comment on the very first sūtra, a comment that is itself a wide-ranging essay, so comprehensive that some have taken it as a summary of all of Rāmānuja's philosophy. Among a smaller circle of outside students, Rāmānuja is also known as the author of a commentary on the *Bhagavadgītā*. A still smaller number have known that Rāmānuja wrote a small work with an impressive title, "The Summary of the Meaning of the Vedas" (*Vedārthasaṃgraha*).

Within the Śrī Vaiṣṇava community, on the other hand, there is complete agreement between the two schools that Rāmānuja wrote nine works, all in Sanskrit. In addition to the three works just noted, there are two briefer commentaries on the *Vedānta Sūtras,* three Gadyas (prose hymns), and a manual of daily worship (the *Nityagrantha*).

The list of Rāmānuja's works is given in a verse of the *Divya Sūri Carita,* a poetic history of the Śrī Vaiṣṇava saints and teachers that seems to have its original ending before the death of Rāmānuja and purports to be by one of Rāmānuja's immediate disciples, one Garuḍa Vāhana Paṇḍita. There is, however, a strong possibility that this work is a kind of poetic drama actually written more than two hundred years later, possibly by a descendant of the earlier Garuḍa Vāhana Paṇḍita bearing the same name (which is really a family title).[1] The first clearly authentic reference to the writings of Rāmānuja is almost two centuries later in the work of his great commentator, Sudarśana Sūri, the last great teacher before the final split between the northern and southern schools. In any case, the traditions of both Vaḍagalais and Tengalais have always ascribed just these nine works, and no others, to Rāmānuja.

Did Rāmānuja, then, write nothing in Tamil? According to the biographical traditions of both schools, Rāmānuja lectured in Tamil, commenting on the hymns of the Āḻvārs especially in *Tiruvāymoḻi.* The first written commentary on the hymns is said to have been written by one of his own disciples at his behest. It is written in a heavily Sanskritized Tamil called Maṇipravāḷam, and many of its phrases are characteristic of Rāmānuja.[2] In the later and larger commentaries, especially the so-called "Thirty-Six Thousand," the diverse comments of earlier teachers are given on many of the verses in the hymns. The view represented as Rāmānuja's is frequently the position taken in the earlier "Six Thousand." The comments of Rāmānuja are thus scattered throughout the commentaries.[3] There is a small work that partially duplicates this source, the *Vārttamālai,* in which the conversations of a number of the earlier ācāryas are gathered together.[4] There is no written work in Tamil, however, that has been attributed to Rāmānuja, whether classical Tamil or the later Sanskritized Tamil.

A few references will be made to Rāmānuja's oral remarks, as reported in the Tamil tradition, but in the present state of our knowledge of this tradition, they can only be used as materials confirming teachings in his written works, though we should bear in mind the *possibility* that Rāmānuja did communicate to his disciples "secret" or "esoteric" teachings that are not included in his written works. In any case, the writings in Sanskrit, the bulk of which consists of commentary on the *Vedānta Sūtras* and the *Bhagavadgītā,* can hardly be regarded as containing the sum total of his teaching. Nevertheless, it is the portion of his teaching that we have before us in the form in which he wrote it, or dictated it to Kūraṭṭāḻvān.

Rāmānuja's authorship of his shorter works has been challenged. Some of the methodological problems involved in the authentication of authorship were noted in chapter 1. Since the question of the authenticity of the three Gadyas and the *Nityagrantha* is so closely tied to historical questions and to the interpretation of Rāmānuja's teaching as a whole, it will be deferred until a later chapter. The purpose of the present chapter is to describe briefly the nature of all the Sanskrit writings attributed to Rāmānuja.

THE VEDĀRTHASAṂGRAHA

The *Vedārthasaṃgraha* is probably the earliest of Rāmānuja's works. He refers to it several times in the *Śrībhāṣya.* In the auspicious verse introducing his commentary on the *Vedārthasaṃgraha,* Sudarśana Sūri says that Rāmānuja expounded it before the Lord of Śrīśaila, namely, Venkaṭeśvara or Śrīnivāsa, the Deity of the great temple in the Tirumalai hills above Tirupati.[5] Such a specific dedication of a particular theological work to a particular temple Deity occurred fairly frequently. It is possible that precisely because of the less sectarian character of Tirumalai, Rāmānuja chose it as the setting for the first public exposition of his position (in contrast to his private instruction of disciples), addressed to scholars of rival schools. With respect to its significance as a devotional offering to Lord Śrīnivāsa, Professor S. S. Raghavachar says:

> Thus from the standpoint of pious tradition, it embodies both philosophical knowledge and an act of worship. This . . . is a fine illustration of the central affirmation of the work, an affirmation with which it starts and also concludes, that knowledge developing into bhakti is the ultimate value, the consummation of all spiritual endeavour and philosophical exploration.[6]

If Sudarśana Sūri's information is correct, it still does not determine when in Rāmānuja's life this work was first written and delivered as a series of public lectures, but the most likely time would seem to be on his first long visit to Tirupati, after he had been instructed by Yāmuna's four disciples in and near Śrīrangam and had reorganized the Śrīrangam temple administration.

Vedārthasaṃgraha means "summary of the meaning of the Vedas," namely, for the theology of the Upaniṣads. This is a work of medium length commenting on various topics that Rāmānuja feels must be rightly understood in order to grasp the true meaning of the Upaniṣads. After an introduction in which he summarizes his position and those of his opponents, Rāmānuja proceeds to refute the rival positions on the basis of one of their favorite texts, the *Sadvidyā* (the knowledge derived from the meditation on being) in *Chāndogya Upaniṣad* 6.2, containing the famous statement of identity between the soul (ātmā) and Brahman: *tat-tvam-asi* (that Thou art). He expounds two basic metaphysical relations: the unchanging Brahman is the material and the efficient cause of the changing universe, and He ensouls it as its inner Self (Śarīrī). On this basis he explains how all scriptural texts can be shown to have the same meaning, both those stating identity between Brahman and the cosmos and those stating difference. Then he argues that when the Scriptures are rightly understood, they prove that Viṣṇu (Nārāyaṇa) is the Supreme Deity and such rival claimants as Brahmā and Śiva are merely the first among creatures. Then Rāmānuja takes up an attack from a different quarter, the theory of the Prābhākara school of the Karma Mīmāṃsā—the study of the parts of the Veda dealing with religious acts. He refutes the Prābhākara's view that words have meaning only with reference to their commanding some action and also the general Karma Mīmāṃsā doctrine that actions produce their future effect (karma) through an impersonal cosmic force that they generate (apūrva). He concludes that words refer to something that is, not to action that ought to be done, and ultimately and most significantly to Brahman, who is the ground of all finite reality, and that all acts achieve their result by pleasing or displeasing the Supreme Person, who rewards or punishes the doer. The last three sections are concerned with proving that God has a transcendent bodily form, that the Vedas are transhuman in origin, and that bhakti is a special kind of knowledge of God and at the same time a state of service—or even servitude—to Him.

The *Vedārthasaṃgraha* is the only one of the longer works of Rāmānuja that is not a commentary, so it is of special interest, since the author would seem to have been entirely free to determine both its form and its content. However, its difference from the other works is less marked than might thus appear, because the first part is a commentary on a central Upaniṣadic text, in the course of which many other texts are also considered. The other sections are likewise, though to a somewhat lesser extent, commentaries on the crucial texts that must provide the solution to the particular questions taken up. Rāmānuja is also not so "free" as he might appear in the choice of topics; there is not only a long tradition of Vedāntic interpretation behind him but also the particular situation of the tradition in his own day: the particular objections that opposing schools were raising against what he considered the orthodox doctrine. Rāmānuja limits himself to proving the particular point at issue or refuting the particular objection. In the process a certain system emerges—the system of the Śrī Vaiṣṇava tradition, which he is further clarifying and defending—but there is a marked contrast between even this most "systematic" work of Rāmānuja and the logical-metaphysical schemes in the doctrinal manuals of his followers.

THE ŚRĪBHĀṢYA

The *Śrībhāṣya* is the longest work of Rāmānuja and the one on which his fame rests both within and beyond his own community. It is a commentary on the *Vedānta Sūtras,* which itself is a summary of the doctrines of the Upaniṣads in the form of brief and somewhat cryptic statements called sūtras, which were often used for such authoritative works, especially in the formative period of the different philosophies several centuries before Rāmānuja. Because of their brevity they could easily be memorized. Since there was a tradition of elucidation of these brief statements going back possibly to the author of the sūtras himself, they were not as cryptic as they might appear. In the other philosophical schools, such as the Vaiśeṣika, there was little dispute about the meaning of such brief sūtras summarizing the teaching of those schools. But in the case of the Vedānta, the commentators had to interpret the *Vedānta Sūtras* to accord with their own understanding of the Upaniṣads. Even before Śankara, there was some difference between the commentaries (no longer extant) regarding the respective emphasis on the unity of Brahman and the soul and the distinction between them, but Śankara's Bhāṣya brought about a new situation in the Vedānta, because he broke so radically with the previous tradition of interpretation. The four later Vaiṣṇava commentators, Rāmānuja, Nimbārka, Vallabha, and Madhva, all insisted on the heterodox character of Śankara's interpretation and sometimes (especially Madhva) charged him with being a crypto-Buddhist. There is no doubt that Śankara, like his predecessor Gauḍapāda, made use of the weapons of the later Buddhist logic in order to challenge the dominant intellectual position of Buddhism. It is more difficult, however, to determine how much of the content of Buddhist metaphysics, either of the doctrine of the void (śūnyatā) or of the alternative doctrine that reality has only the status of being the object of a cosmic consciousness (vijñāna), entered his own system. However much Buddhist influence there may have been, there is strong critical evidence to support the view of Rāmānuja and the other Vaiṣṇava commentators that Śankara's school was distorting the intended meaning of the *Vedānta Sūtras*.

Here, to be sure, we are primarily concerned, not with the objective fact, but with Rāmānuja's own view of the matter. However, there is a widespread impression in the Western world, fostered by the Advaitins and their Western admirers, that Śankara is *the* commentator on the Upaniṣads and on the *Vedānta Sūtras*. Therefore, it may be well to note that two modern critical studies endorse Rāmānuja's contention that Śankara's interpretation obscures and distorts the meaning of the *Vedānta Sūtras*.[7] This is not to say that Rāmānuja's views coincide exactly with those of the author of the Sūtras. From the standpoint of historical scholarship, such precise correspondence is almost axiomatically excluded, since it ignores the laws of historical change and development. On the other hand, orthodox Śrī Vaiṣṇavas would equally axiomatically affirm a complete identity of doctrine between the Upaniṣads and the *Vedānta Sūtras* and between the latter and Rāmānuja's commentary. Rāmānuja believed that the *Vedānta Sūtras* did correctly summarize the Upaniṣads, and he intended to bring his own thought into conformity with the thought of the Sūtras. Thibaut and Ghate both concluded that Rāmānuja more nearly succeeded in bringing out the intention of the Sūtras than did Śankara, effectively refuting the view that Rāmānuja was a merely sectarian commentator.

In his comment on the *Vedānta Sūtras,* Rāmānuja follows not only what he takes to be the meaning of each particular sūtra but the meaning of the Sūtras as a whole. The subject matter of the Vedānta has been traditionally divided into three parts: *tattva* (ontology), the nature of Brahman and of other entities; *hita,* the means to attain Brahman; and *puruṣārtha,* the nature of man's supreme goal. The author of the Sūtras first tries to establish that Brahman is both the material and the efficient cause of the universe, and then he maintains this view against a large number of objections, most of them based on texts that seem to support some other entity's being the universal cause. The first two pādas of the second adhyāya take up refutations of the rival systems one by one, and the third and fourth pādas are concerned with the details of the process of origination or creation. Rāmānuja says at the beginning of the third adhyāya that up to this poing the Sūtras have set forth the essential nature of Brahman.[8] The third adhyāya is concerned with the means of meditation, the various meditational and devotional disciplines (vidyās), and the fourth adhyāya with the result of meditation: the goal of release from transient, matter-bound existence, the enjoyment of the soul's inherent powers, and the bliss of eternal communion with the Lord.[9]

The unusual thing about the *Śrībhāṣya* is the disproportionate length of the comment on the first sūtra, the greater part of which is called the *Mahāsiddhānta.* This has sometimes been taken as a summary of Rāmānuja's entire system and even oftener as an independent treatise which has only the superficial appearance of a commentary on the first sūtra. Until Dr. A. Hohenberger's recent German translation of the *Vedāntadīpa,*[10] the only translations of Rāmānuja's writings into German and French were of this commentary on the first sūtra. The titles themselves, "Rāmānuja's Siddhānta" (which

Rudolf Otto defines as "the first definitive statement of a doctrine concluding a dialogue with opposing views") and "Rāmānuja's Ethical and Metaphysical Doctrine" (Olivier Lacombe), contribute to this misleading impression. Otto says: "In Rāmānuja's hands . . . this insignificant-looking opening text swells to an entire work in itself, which becomes the magnificent entrance-hall of his book, or more accurately, its most essential and significant part."[11] Lacombe comments similarly: "This fragment detached from Rāmānuja's great commentary on the Brahma Sūtras, which strictly speaking is the commentary on the first sūtra, nevertheless forms in a way a complete treatise, conceived as such by the author."[12]

It is true that the lengthy commentary on the first sūtra refers at least briefly to most of Rāmānuja's doctrines and that one can learn a great deal about his concept of God even by reading this one section. It is correct to say that Rāmānuja intended this as an introduction to his entire commentary, but it is not true that this introduction can stand by itself without that which follows, and it is quite misleading to give Western readers the impression that Rāmānuja may adequately be grasped by reading only *Śrībhāṣya* 1.1.1.

The title *Mahāsiddhānta* was applied by Rāmānuja's followers, not to the entire commentary on the first sūtra, but to the second of the three "Conclusions," each answering one of the corresponding three objections raised by opposing positions (pūrvapakṣa). It is thus preceded by the *Laghusiddhānta* (small conclusion) and followed by the brief *Adhikaraṇasiddhānta* (conclusion of the section). The text of the first sūtra is *atha-ataḥ-brahma-jijñāsā,* which means: Then (atha) therefore (ataḥ) the study (jijñāsā—literally, "desire to know") of Brahman. According to Rangacharya and Varadaraja Aiyangar, the *then* is dealt with in the *Laghusiddhānta* and the *therefore* in the *Mahāsiddhānta.*[13] We might add that *Laghusiddhānta* determines the significance of the *then* by also explaining the concept *jñāna* which is the root of the desiderative *jijñāsā.* The *Laghusiddhānta* establishes that a study of the nature of ritual duties—namely, not merely performing them but also studying their significance—should precede the study of Brahman. It reaches this conclusion after first demonstrating the following points: (1) mere knowledge of the words of Scripture and intellectual realization of the truth are not sufficient to eradicate the ignorance caused by accumulated karma; (2) the knowledge that does have the power to cause the destruction of karma and hence of ignorance is a kind of knowledge that is identical with meditation and devotion; and (3) sacrifices and other religious works are means to originate such devotional knowledge of Brahman. "Knowledge, which is the means of reaching Brahman, thus requires the works prescribed for the different stages of life, and hence the systematic inquiry into works—from which we ascertain the nature of the works required and also the transitoriness and limitation of mere works—forms a necessary antecedent to the systematic inquiry into Brahman."[14]

It is the determination of the term *ataḥ* (therefore) that occupies the bulk of this section, because Rāmānuja believes it necessary decisively to refute Śankara's view of why this study of Brahman should be undertaken at all. Rāmānuja concludes the statement of the Advaitin position as follows: "The purpose of studying the Vedānta texts is to destroy ignorance which is at the root of the illusion that there are the distinctions of knowing subjects, objects of knowledge, and acts of knowledge and thus to obtain a firm knowledge of the oneness of Brahman whose nature is sheer intelligence, free, pure, and eternal."[15]

Rāmānuja agrees with Śankara that the fruits of religious acts are limited and perishable and that only the knowledge of Brahman can bring eternal bliss, but he entirely disagrees as to the nature of that knowledge and the nature of the ignorance that must be destroyed in order to obtain the saving knowledge of Brahman. Whereas for Śankara ignorance (avidyā) is inexplicable, for Rāmānuja its cause is known: the power of karma to blind men to their true nature and relation to God. This is a real power that cannot be overcome simply by cogitation. The power of karma cannot be destroyed by doing more religious acts, which would produce more karma. However, the performance of one's social and religious duties as *duties* (without desiring their merit) is a necessary condition for the development of the kind of knowledge (synonymous with devotion) that does lead to the destruction of karma and hence of ignorance. The necessity of previous study of Vedic ritual is thus reaffirmed, for without an insight into the nature of works we would not know either that "mere works produce only limited and impermanent results" or that "works not aiming at an immediate result but meant to please the Highest Person bring about knowledge of the character of devout meditation, and thereby the unlimited and permanent result of the intuition of Brahman as the Self of all."[16]

The Vedāntadīpa and the Vedāntasāra

It is at first sight curious that among the nine works attributed to Rāmānuja there should be three commentaries on the *Vedānta Sūtras.* In addition to the famous *Śrībhāṣya,* there is a shorter commentary, the *Vedāntadīpa,* and a still briefer commentary, the *Vedāntasāra.* This seems so curious to Professor J. A. B. van Buitenen that he is inclined to doubt that Rāmānuja himself wrote the shorter commentaries.

> The *Vedāntadīpa* seems to be more authentic and its existence has indeed some justification in the length and difficulty of the *Śrībhāṣya.* Yet . . . I find it hard to believe that Rāmānuja, who, after a traditional life of six score, left but few works in comparison with Śankara, would have preferred the clerical and thankless task of abridging his own *chef d'oeuvre* to the more congenial composition of, for example, commentaries on the Upaniṣads.[17]

I do not find it so difficult to believe that Rāmānuja would have preferred writing the *Vedāntadīpa* to writing a commentary on Upaniṣads. Rāmānuja's failure to write separate commentaries on individual Upaniṣads was not because of lack of time. Both the *Vedārthasaṃgraha* and the *Śrībhāṣya* make it clear that Rāmānuja viewed the Upaniṣads, not as a number of discrete works, but as a large collection of authoritative texts, texts that must be reconciled through the correct interpretation. The *Vedānta Sūtras* provide this synthetic interpretation; they are the key to the meaning of all the Upaniṣads. It is therefore reasonable to assume that almost every course of lectures that Rāmānuja gave on the Upaniṣads would have the Sūtras as its basis. Since the *Vedāntadīpa* refers to the *Śrībhāṣya,* it was evidently written later and cannot, therefore, be an earlier and more rudimentary form of the latter, but it seems entirely possible that Rāmānuja might have given a briefer and simpler course of lectures on the Sūtras, either for his less advanced students, for the sake of easier memorization, or in a lecture series during one of his visits to other temples (as Sudarśana Sūri said was the case with the *Vedārthasaṃgraha*).[18]

The *Vedāntadīpa* is not simply an abbreviation of the *Śrībhāṣya,* though it follows it very closely. It has some distinctive features; it is the only one of the three commentaries to have an introduction before the comment on the first sūtra. In this introduction the doctrines of Viśiṣṭādvaita are summarized. It does not follow the *Śrībhāṣya* in having a disproportionately long comment on the first sūtra. With the exception of some illustrations and a few details, the teaching of the *Vedāntadīpa* is the same as that of the *Śrībhāṣya* in each *adhikaraṇa* (a group of sūtras considered by the commentator to form a single unity on a particular subject), but the same comment does not always appear with reference to the same sūtra.

Van Buitenen is also skeptical of the authenticity of the *Vedāntasāra,* and still more so of the comment by Sudarśana Sūri that it was Rāmānuja's first work.

> To me it is inconceivable that Rāmānuja would have put forward his system of Viśiṣṭādvaita for the first time to a highly critical audience of contemporary Vedāntins by merely indicating its barest outlines as is done in the Vedāntasāra. . . . In the most detailed explanation to be found in the booklet, that of Brs. 1,1,2 . . . the bare essentials of Viśiṣṭādvaita are enumerated without the slightest attempt at convincing presentation and plausible argumentation. . . . I think it extremely improbable that Rāmānuja presented his system to the thinkers of his age in such a poor form. If the text was at all composed during Rāmānuja's lifetime, it will at most have been authorized epitome by one of his pupils.[19]

With the exception of a few terms, van Buitenen does not challenge the terminology or the ideas of the *Vedāntasāra.* What he finds impossible to believe is that Rāmānuja could have argued so unconvincingly, considering what we know of his persuasive powers from his indisputably genuine works.

We do not have sufficient evidence to settle the question of whether the *Vedāntasāra,* if genuine, was written prior to the *Vedārthasaṃgraha* but we cannot dismiss the possibility as summarily as van Buitenen does. The *Vedāntasāra* does not pretend to set forth detailed arguments; it states precisely the correct meaning of each sūtra, and the evidence it appends consists of a list of scriptural texts--not of logical arguments. It was used by Rāmānuja's followers as a convenient means of memorizing the gist of Rāmānuja's interpretation. It may have been composed by Rāmānuja himself for precisely this purpose, which would explain the lack of arguments capable of convincing followers of other schools. This in itself does not give any indication of when the *Vedāntasāra* was written, since Rāmānuja was probably teaching students right from the time he moved to Śrīrangam. Indeed, according to the biographies, he started teaching his first disciples while still in Kāñcīpuram.

There are two other points, however, that make it more credible that the *Vedāntasāra* was Rāmānuja's first work. The longest comment in the *Vedāntasāra* is not on the first sūtra, as in the *Śrībhāṣya,* or in an introduction preceding the commentary, as in the *Vedāntadīpa,* but on the second sūtra, *janmādi-asya-yatah* (from whom is the origin, etc., of this [universe]). In many ways this is the most important single sūtra in the Sūtras, because the idea that God is the material cause of the universe and the efficient cause of its periodic origination, continuing existence, and eventual dissolution is basic to the whole theology of the Vedānta. Hence the structure of the *Vedāntasāra* is more in line with the form of the traditional Vedāntic teaching and less original in its conception than the *Śrībhāṣya.*

The second point is brought out in the very passage from the comment on the second sūtra that van Buitenen quotes to show the vagueness of the *Vedāntasāra*'s argumentation. All the schools of Vedānta agree that there is a continuing difference between the three categories of being (God, souls, and matter) even in the state of the dissolution of the manifest universe where the difference is too subtle to be manifest (vyavahāra-anarha-sūkṣma-bhedaḥ), but the other two schools explain this by ascribing imperfection to Brahman, either by connecting Him with inexplicable ignorance, *avidyā* (the Advaitins) or by maintaining that He can be limited and His nature distorted by adjuncts, *upādhis* (the Bhedābhedavādins).[20] This same point is made at the beginning of both the *Vedāntadīpa* and the *Vedārthasaṃgraha.*[21] It is true that it would not have convinced followers of these rival schools, at least not without much further explanation. Nevertheless, it is a key to Rāmānuja's objection to these other schools; their interpretations are an affront to the majesty and supreme perfection of God. There is no emphasis more characteristic of Rāmānuja than that on God's perfection.

If the *Vedāntasāra* was Rāmānuja's first work, its lack of persuasiveness would be in accord with the stories in the biographies that suggest he began his exposition of Śrī Vaiṣṇava theology with more zeal than persuasive power. Considering the nature of the brief commentary itself, however, it seems likely that, whenever the *Vedāntasāra* was written, it was intended, not to convince members of opposing schools, but to instruct Śrī Vaiṣṇava disciples, perhaps especially those in the early stages of their study.

Neither on literary nor on psychological grounds do I see good reason for denying Rāmānuja's authorship of the *Vedāntadīpa* and the *Vedāntasāra*. It would make no difference for this particular study if they should later prove to have been written by some disciple of Rāmānuja, whether on his instruction or independently, since the ideas they contain can be found in the *Śrībhāṣya* and the *Vedārthasaṃgraha*.

THE BHAGAVADGĪTĀBHĀṢYA

Second in length among Rāmānuja's works is his *Bhagavadgītābhāṣya* which appears to have been written later than the *Śrībhāṣya* though many of the comments on particular verses were already fixed and are incorporated in the *Śrībhāṣya.*[22] It is in some ways more like an ordinary commentary than the *Śrībhāṣya* in that the stanzas of the *Gītā* are considerably less cryptic than the stanzas of the Sūtras, so that it is often possible for Rāmānuja to give only a slightly amplified paraphrase. But here again, Rāmānuja is trying to follow not only the text but also the orthodox tradition of interpretation. For Rāmānuja this was epitomized in the brief *Gītārthasaṃgraha* of his predecessor Yāmuna. Van Buitenen has shown how clearly Rāmānuja follows Yāmuna's interpretation of the meaning of each chapter of the *Gītā* as a whole.

> Yāmuna's GAS. [*Gītārthasaṃgraha*] is a very concise summary of the G. [*Gītā*] in 32 ślokas. . . . We do not exaggerate when we say that practically all the salient features of the GBh. [*Bhagavadgītābhāṣya*] are contained in Y.'s [Yāmuna's] scheme. Rāmānuja himself leaves no doubt as to his indebtedness to Yāmuna: he not only dedicated his commentary to Yāmuna with the significant remark that he owes everything to his illustrious predecessor, but he also quotes some of the ślokas of the GAS. and, most important of all, makes a point of using Yāmuna's own words, as often as the occasion arises. . . . R. [Rāmānuja] borrows from Y. [Yāmuna] the tripartition of the eighteen lectures in 3 ṣaṭkas. . . . R. [Rāmānuja] follows in his abstracts of the lectures the summary of the GAS. often to the point of literalness. . . . To Rāmānuja's free use of Yāmuna's terminology corresponds a not less striking fidelity to the main points of the

GAS. Both Y. [Yāmuna] and R. [Rāmānuja] regard jñāna- and karmayoga—whatever their exact relation—only as preparatory stages: they result in the "contemplation of the ātman," but not in the attainment of God himself. God can only be attained through bhakti, to which the former disciplines of jñāna and karman are the indispensable means; and both agree that this doctrine is the essence of the Gītā. . . . Many of Rāmānuja's ideas seem to derive directly from the Gītārthasaṃgraha; for instance, that acts—which are always ritual acts—are propitiations of God: that the contemplation of the ātman is ancillary to the attainment of God through bhakti: and that there are three groups of bhaktas, the aiśvaryārthins, the kaivalyārthins and the jñānins, but that only the last attain God.[23]

The doctrines enunciated in the *Gītābhāṣya* are essentially the same as those of the *Vedārthasaṃgraha* and the *Śrībhāṣya,* but there is a somewhat different mood. On this point van Buitenen comments: "Rāmānuja's views on bhakti, as they appear in the *Gītābhāṣya,* are essentially those of the *Śrībhāṣya;* but in his commentary on the Gītā he loves to dwell upon the devotional and emotional aspects of the continuous representation of God."[24] There is a corresponding shift of emphasis with respect to his doctrine of God in the *Gītābhāṣya:* the aspects of God's nature that are important in redeeming the devotee and bringing him into communion with God receive the most attention in the devotee's praise.

The "text" for this particular study is furnished in Rāmānuja's introduction to this commentary on the *Gītā.* It may well be that the balanced emphasis on two distinct sides of the Divine nature, supremacy and accessibility, is more evident in the *Bhagavadgītābhāṣya* than in any of Rāmānuja's other works. This work is less well known outside the Śrī Vaiṣṇava community than is the *Śrībhāṣya,* and it is less significant in terms of distinctive Śrī Vaiṣṇava cultic practice than the much briefer *Śaraṇāgatigadya.* Nevertheless, as the authoritative commentary on a favorite scripture, it has been important for all the subsequent generations of Śrī Vaiṣṇavas, the more so since the basic ethical and devotional stance (though not detailed rules) of the worshipers of Viṣṇu is taught in the sacred poem itself and is greatly elaborated in this commentary.

This is probably the last major work of Rāmānuja, and it may well reflect the situation of his last years, when doctrinal controversy could be subordinated to the daily remembrance of God. It is an important link between the purely philosophical works, the commentaries on the *Vedānta Sūtras,* and the purely sectarian works to which I next turn. Whether or not those later works were written by Rāmānuja himself, they are related in their emphasis to some of the themes of the commentary on the *Gītā.* This work is thus important for its evidence of Rāmānuja's mature reflection, for its testimony to his synthetic genius as the teacher of Ubhaya Vedānta, and for its hints that its author was himself one of the jñānīs described therein, a man wholly devoted to and dependent upon his Lord.

THE GADYATRAYA AND THE NITYAGRANTHA

The works of Rāmānuja least known to those outside of the Śrī Vaiṣṇava community are four short works, three Gadyas (prose hymns), and a manual of daily worship. The first of these Gadyas, however, has a position of great importance in the cultic life of Śrī Vaiṣṇavas. Called the *Śaraṇāgatigadya,* it is taken as a model of the complete surrender to the mercy of God (śaraṇāgati or prapatti) that in the generations after Rāmānuja became the accepted approach to God for every Śrī Vaiṣṇava. Since the precise nature of the ritual act of surrender became one of the major points of dispute between the northern and southern schools (Vaḍagalai and Tengalai), the three Gadyas and the commentaries on them became not only a devotional exercise but a new field of doctrinal controversy.

The *Śaraṇāgatigadya* is in the form of a dialogue between Rāmānuja on the one hand and the Consort Śrī and the Lord Nārāyaṇa on the other. The author first surrenders himself to the mercy of the Goddess Śrī (Lakṣmī) and prays for Her blessing on his act of surrender to the Lord, which then follows after a brief favorable response from the Goddess. In his prayer to the Lord, Rāmānuja prays for the forgiveness of his many sins, the state of a jñānī or superior devotee described in the *Gītā,* and the gift of "the higher devotion, the higher wisdom, and the highest devotion" (parabhakti, parajñāna, paramabhakti). The last part of the Gadya is the Lord's extended reply, granting Rāmānuja all that he has asked for. The tradition takes this Gadya, not as a literary composition, but as the record of an actual conversation in the Śrīrangam temple between Rāmānuja and the Divine Pair.

The second Gadya is called the *Śrīrangagadya.* It is much shorter and consists of a prayer of surrender uttered at the feet of Lord Ranganātha, requesting that the author be accepted as an eternal servant (*nityakinkara*) of the Lord. The third Gadya is called the *Vaikuṇṭhagadya.* The larger part of this is a detailed description of Vaikuṇṭha, the eternal abode of Lord Viṣṇu, on which one should regularly meditate after he has performed the act of prapatti. The meditation is therefore not a means of *achieving* salvation but a spiritual discipline *after* one has declared himself completely reliant on the Lord's grace to accomplish his salvation. It is the only one of the three Gadyas to have an auspicious verse (mangalaśloka). This verse is in praise of Yāmuna, and the verse itself is modeled on the first three verses of Yāmuna's *Stotraratna.*

The *Nityagrantha* is a manual for daily worship, primarily intended for the individual in his home or monastery (in other words, not for worship in the temple). It makes references to the Gadyas and evidently presupposes their doctrines, but it contains relatively little doctrinal material itself. It is considered to be and has been used as a manual of worship for the *prapanna,* the one who surrendered himself to the Lord without successfully pursuing, or perhaps even attempting, the difficult types of devotional meditation (bhakti-upāsana) that are taught in the Upaniṣads.

The *Nityagrantha* gives detailed instructions for the whole course of the regular (nitya) morning worship, which is directed either to an actual image of the Deity in one's family room for worship or in a monastery chapel or to a mental image upon which one concentrates while worshiping. There is no description of the image itself; nor is there a discussion of its theological significance.

The *Gadyatraya* and the *Nityagrantha* have always been accepted by both Śrī Vaiṣṇava schools as genuine works of Rāmānuja. Recently, however, the respected Vaḍagalai pandit, Agnihothram Rāmānuja Thatachariar of Kumbakonam, has challenged their authenticity with a number of arguments claiming to demonstrate their incompatibility with the genuine works of Rāmānuja in basic theological doctrine and terminology. Professor Robert Lester accepted Pandit Agnihothram's position and has since published his own arguments against their authenticity. He has also shown that if these works are not genuine the later elaborations of the doctrine of prapatti by the two Śrī Vaiṣṇava schools have little connection with Rāmānuja's "genuine" thought and in some respects are sharply opposed to it.

I have not been convinced by Pandit Agnihothram's arguments, but I do not think that the genuineness of these works can be "proved" until much more study has been done of all the Śrī Vaiṣṇava writings that have survived from the century after Rāmānuja. Since many of the arguments turn on the relation of Rāmānuja's thought in his major Sanskrit writings to later Śrī Vaiṣṇava doctrines, it seems to me that such a discussion belongs to the final part of this book after the exposition of Rāmānuja's doctrines of God. Materials from the three Gadyas and the *Nityagrantha* will therefore not be used as primary evidence in establishing Rāmānuja's position. These works will be referred to in the same way as some of the stories in the biographies: to confirm or shed possible additional light on a point that is evident from Rāmānuja's admittedly genuine works.

4 Rāmānuja's Definitions and Descriptions of the Divine Nature

The Significance of Rāmānuja's Mangalaślokas

Most of Rāmānuja's writings begin with an invocation or dedicatory verse called a mangalaśloka. This is meant not only to begin the work auspiciously (mangala) and to express proper reverence to one's Lord or one's guru but also to summarize the content of the work, or at least its main intention.[1] Four of Rāmānuja's writings begin with a mangalaśloka addressed to the Deity and three with one in praise of Yāmuna (including the *Vedārthasaṃgraha,* which has both). The *Śrībhāṣya* has a second śloka in praise of Vyāsa, the author of the *Vedānta Sūtras.*

The *Śaraṇāgatigadya* and *Śrīrangagadya* have no mangalaślokas, but their first paragraphs serve a somewhat similar purpose, since they are addressed in one case to Śrī and in the other to Nārāyaṇa. The *Nityagrantha* also has no mangalaśloka, but it is a work of quite a different kind, being not a doctrinal treatise but a manual of instructions for daily worship. The long introduction of the *Gītābhāṣya* that follows the dedication to Yāmuna could also be considered as serving the function of additional dedicatory verses to Viṣṇu-Nārāyaṇa.

Of the four mangalaślokas that concern us here, two are from works whose authenticity has been disputed: the *Vedāntadīpa* and the *Vedāntasāra.* They may properly be included here, for even if they were not written by Rāmānuja himself, they aptly epitomize his doctrine of God. The same is true of the few quotations from these two works later in this chapter.

These four dedicatory verses addressed to or concerning the Deity are as follows:

> Obeisance to Viṣṇu, who is the treasury of auspicious qualities, which are infinite and untainted by any impurity, who is the Śeṣī of all entities without exception, both spiritual and material, and who reclines on the primordial serpent Śeṣa.[2]

> May my understanding attain the nature of devotion to the Supreme, the abode of Śrī [Lakṣmī], the Brahman who is luminously revealed in the Crown of Scripture [the Upaniṣads], whose sport [līlā] consists in such acts as the origination, maintenance and destruction of all the worlds, who has dedicated

Himself entirely [eka-dīkṣā] to protecting and saving [rakṣā] the hosts of various kinds of creatures who bow before Him.[3]

May my mind be firmly devoted [sakta] to service [paricaraṇa] at the lotus feet of the Primeval Person [Ādi-puruṣa], who is the Consort of Śrī [Śriyaḥ-kāntaḥ], who is infinite, who has a body [vapus] which is the sole substratum of the hosts of excellent qualities, who is the destroyer of all evil, who dwells in the highest heaven, and who is beyond the range [abhūmi] of speech or mind, yet within the range [bhūmi] of the vision of His devotees [natajana].[4]

Obeisance to Viṣṇu united with Śrī, who is an ocean of bliss untainted by any impurity, who is the Self of all, having all entities, both spiritual and material, as His body.[5]

The elements of the concept of God contained in these verses are shown in the following table.

Vedārthasaṃgraha	*Śrībhāṣya*	*Vedāntadīpa*	*Vedāntasāra*
1. treasury of kalyāṇa guṇas (auspicious qualities)		abode of hosts of excellent qualities	the ocean of bliss (ānanda)
2. ananta (infinite)		ananta (infinite)	
3. nirmala (without impurity)		destroyer of all evil	nirmala (without impurity)
4. the Śeṣī of all spiritual and material entities			who is the self of all, having as His body all spiritual and material entities
5. who reclines on Śeṣa		dwelling in the highest heaven	
6. Viṣṇu	Supreme Brahman	the Primeval Person	Viṣṇu
7.	Śrīnivāsa (the abode of Śrī)	Śriyaḥ kāntaḥ (the Consort of Śrī)	Śrīmat (united with Śrī)
8.	whose sport consists in originating, maintaining, and destroying all the worlds		
9.	luminously revealed in the Upaniṣads		

Vedārthasaṃgraha	*Śrībhāṣya*	*Vedāntadīpa*	*Vedāntasāra*
10.	who had dedicated Himself entirely to protecting (saving, *rakṣā*) the hosts of various kinds of creatures who bow before Him	who is beyond the range of speech or mind but within the range of of the vision of His devotees	

Combining these elements gives us the following picture: The Supreme Brahman, the Primeval Person, is Viṣṇu, the Consort of Śrī. He possesses all auspicious qualities and is entirely free of all impurities; indeed He is positively opposed to all evil. He is related to the cosmos of souls and matter as its inner Self (Śarīrī) and as its Owner and Maker (Śeṣī). In sport (līlā) He periodically produces, sustains, and reabsorbs the entire universe. He is also the Lord of His own supreme realm beyond this cosmos where He is faithfully served by His ministers such as the serpent Ādiśeṣa, and He dwells there in utter tranquillity. Though His nature is inconceivable and inexpressible, He reveals Himself in Scripture and grants a vision of Himself to His devotees, whose temporal protection and eternal salvation (rakṣaṇa) is His sole aim. We shall see these same characteristics recurring in Rāmānuja's descriptions of the Divine nature in the body of his writings.

DEFINITIONS AND SUMMARIES OF THE CONCEPT OF GOD

At the very beginning of the *Śrībhāṣya* is a brief definition of Brahman:

> By the word "Brahman" is denoted the Supreme Person [Puruṣottama], who is by inherent nature [svabhāvataḥ] free from all imperfections [doṣa] and possesses hosts of auspicious qualities [kalyāṇaguṇa] which are countless and of matchless excellence [anavadhikātiśaya]. In all contexts the term "Brahman" is applied to whatever possesses the quality of greatness [bṛhattva], but its primary and most significant meaning is that Being whose greatness is of matchless excellence, both in His essential nature and in His other qualities. It is only the Lord of all [Sarveśvara] who is such a Being. Therefore the word "Brahman" is primarily used only to signify Him.[6]

At the beginning of the commentary on the second sūtra, "that from which" or "from whom" (yataḥ) is defined as:

> that Supreme Person who is the Lord of all; whose essential nature is opposed to everything defiling [nikhila-pratyanīka], whose will is ever accomplished [satya-saṃkalpa]; who possesses an infinite number of auspicious qualities, first among which are knowledge and bliss; who is omniscient, omnipotent, and supremely merciful, from whom the creation, continued existence and dissolution of the world proceed–He is Brahman. That is the meaning of this Sūtra.[7]

Likewise the definition given at the end of *Śrībhāṣya* 1.1.3 relates to the subject matter of that sūtra: the nature of that Being about whom we know only through Scripture.

> the Supreme Person, who is the Lord of all, being the Supreme Brahman. The Scriptures declare Him to be distinct in character [visajātīya] from all entities [vastu] cognized by all the other means of knowledge [pramāṇa], to be an ocean of immeasurably generous qualities of matchless excellence, such as omniscience and the power to realize His every will, and to have an essential nature opposed to everything defiling.[8]

The definition at the beginning of the *Vedāntadīpa* stresses the distinction of the Supreme Self from the individual finite self.

> and the Supreme Self [Paramātmā] is utterly distinct in character [atyanta-visajātīya] from the finite self [jīvātmā]... because He is opposed to everything defiling and is solely comprised of auspicious qualities, pervades both souls and matter in all their states, and is their supporter [dhāraka], controller [niyantā] and owner (śeṣī).[9]

Near the end of the *Bhagavadgītābhāṣya* are two passages that that come close to being formal definitions. The first is part of the definition of *āstikyam* (unshakable belief in the Vedas) in 18.42. The second, in 18.73, gives the content of *smṛti-jñāna* (which here means reflection on the Divine nature, culminating in an intuitive vision of the Lord).

> That which is expressed with the term "Supreme Brahman" is the Lord [Bhagavān], the Supreme Person [Puruṣottama]

> and Vāsudeva [Krishna]. He is removed beyond any trace [literally "scent"] of evil. He possesses a host of auspicious qualities such as knowledge and power, which are natural to Him and of matchless excellence. He is the one who is to be known through all the Vedas and Upaniṣads. He is the sole cause of the entire universe and is its support. He causes all things to function. All duties enjoined by the Vedas constitute the worship of Him. Being worshiped through these various duties He grants, according to the petition, the fruit of the nature of dharma, artha, kāma and mokṣa.[10]

> The Supreme Person [Parama Puruṣa], who is meant by the term "Supreme Brahman," has as His sport the origination, maintenance, and dissolution of the entire universe. He is opposed to all evil whatsoever, and His essential nature [svarūpa], consists solely of what is auspicious [kalyāṇa]. He is a great ocean containing a host of all auspicious qualities, the first six of which are knowledge [jñāna], untiring strength [bala], sovereignty [aiśvarya], immutability [vīrya], creative power [śakti], and splendor [tejas], qualities which are natural to Him [svābhāvika] and of matchless excellence.[11]

Somewhat like these "definitions" are the statements occurring in the introductions and summations that Rāmānuja occasionally inserts in his writings. One of them is the résumé of the conclusions of the first three pādas at the beginning of the fourth pāda of the first adhyāya in the *Śrībhāṣya.*

> So far the Sūtras have given instruction about Brahman, the study of whom is a means to attain man's highest goal: final release. He is the cause of the origination, etc., of the universe; He is distinct in character from all nonintelligent things such as Pradhāna [material nature] and from all intelligent beings whether in a state of bondage or release; He is free from even the shadow of anything defiling; He is omniscient and omnipotent, and His will is ever accomplished; His nature [ātmaka] is comprised of all auspicious qualities; He is the inner Self of all, and He possesses unrestricted Lordship.[12]

At the beginning of the *Vedārthasaṃgraha* is a definition of the individual finite self (jīvātman) and the Supreme Person (Puruṣottama). The latter is defined thus:

> The essential nature [svarūpa] of the Inner Controller is as follows: He is the sole cause of the origination, continued existence, and dissolution of the universe consisting of such varieties of intelligent beings and material things, and is the sole cause of the cessation of saṃsāra. His essential nature is distinct from all entities other than Himself by virtue of His opposition to all evil and His being wholly infinite perfection [kalyānatā]. He has a host of such auspicious qualities [kalyāṇaguṇas], which are countless and of matchless excellence. He is known throughout the Upaniṣads by different terms such as "the Self of all," "the Supreme Brahman," "the Supreme Light," "the Supreme Reality," "the Supreme Self" and "Being." He is the Lord (Bhagavān), Nārāyaṇa, the Supreme Person [Puruṣottama].[13]

In the midst of the debate with the Advaitin that occupies the first part of the *Vedārthasaṃgraha,* Rāmānuja sums up his position as follows:

> The Supreme Brahman is by His inherent nature [svabhāva] such that His essential nature [svarūpa] is opposed to impurity and consists solely of infinite knowledge and bliss. He is an ocean of generous qualities that are immeasurable, of matchless excellence, and natural [svābhāvika] to Him. Brahman has a great realm of His glory [mahāvibhūti], which is infinite and untouched by the changes of origination, subsistence, and dissolution brought about by time, whose essential nature comprises countless units from a second to an epoch. He has as instruments of His sport [līlā] an infinite number of intelligent beings, both those bound in saṃsāra and those released from it, all of whom are parts of Himself. Likewise, He possesses all material things, which are subject to infinite, wonderful, and varied changes and which form the objects of enjoyment for intelligent beings. Since He is the Inner Controller of His whole creation, He has all things as His body and His modes.[14]

Certain brief descriptions of God's nature appear in the introductions to some of the chapters of the *Gītābhāṣya.*

> the Supreme Person who is the Supreme Brahman . . . the goal of those who seek salvation [mokṣa] . . . removed from any trace of such imperfections as ignorance [avidyā] and possess-

ing a host of auspicious qualities, which are countless and of matchless excellence.[15]

Nārāyaṇa united with Śrī, who is the supreme goal, the Supreme Brahman, perfect, the sole cause of the entire universe, omniscient, all pervading, whose will is ever accomplished and who possesses the great realm of His Glory [mahāvibhūti].[16]

the Supreme Brahman, Vāsudeva, who is the owner and master [śeṣī] of all spiritual and material entities as well as their cause and support, is the ultimate and most significant meaning of all words [sarva-śabda-vācyatvam] by virtue of having everything as His body and as His modes. He is the controller [niyantā] of all, the One who is higher than anything else [parataratvam] by virtue of His host of auspicious qualities.[17]

OTHER DESCRIPTIONS OF THE NATURE OF GOD

There are many other descriptions of the Divine nature that occur in connection with a particular discussion. This is to some extent true even of some of the passages already noted, but it is even more true of most of Rāmānuja's descriptions of the Divine nature. They serve either to underline the conclusions or to lend support to one of the arguments. At times, however, these descriptions quite overshadow the point of the argument. After the theological affirmation already quoted from the *Vedārthasaṃgraha* and a much longer list of supporting texts which follow it, Rāmānuja humorously admits this by having the hypothetical opponent in the argument reply, "But what is the use of this verbose declamation [āḍambara]? The objection is still not refuted!"[18]

One important context is the resolution of the apparent differences between the scriptural texts that declare a difference (bheda) between God and the cosmos, on the one hand, and those that maintain nondifference (abheda) or nonduality (advaita) on the other. Rāmānuja seeks to prove that his interpretation is the only one that makes sense of both kinds of texts, as well as of a third "mediating" type of text. The outstanding instance of such a passage is in the *Vedārthasaṃgraha.*

The scriptural texts that deal with the immutability of Brahman have their most significant meaning [mukhyārtha] by the very denial of modification in His essential nature [svarūpa]. Those

> stating that He is attributeless are also well established since they pertain to the negation of the defiling qualities of material nature. These that deny plurality are well ensured by the affirmation that all entities, both spiritual and material, are the modes of Brahman by virtue of constituting His body, and that Brahman having everything as His modes exists as the sole reality, because He is the Self of all. The passages speaking of Brahman as different from all modes, as Master [Pati], as Lord [Īśvara], as the abode of all auspicious qualities, as the One whose desires are eternally realized and whose will is ever accomplished, etc., are justly retained by accepting just that. Statements that He is sheer knowledge and bliss are maintained because they express the defining property of the essential nature [svarūpa-nirūpaka-dharma] of the Supreme Brahman, who is different from all, the support of all, the cause of the origination, subsistence, and dissolution of all, faultless, immutable, the Self of all. This defining property is sheer knowledge in the form of bliss opposed to any impurity. Therefore His essential nature, being self-illuminating, is also completely knowledge or consciousness [jñānam-eva]. The declarations of unity are well founded, since by virtue of the body-soul relationship, the identification of the two realities in coordinate predication [sāmānādhikaraṇya] is seen to be the most significant meaning of these texts.[19]

Rāmānuja also describes the Divine nature in the course of discussing a number of other subjects. These include Brahman's distinction from finite selves and from matter, Brahman's possession of a bodily form, Brahman's incarnations (avatāras), and Brahman's rewarding His worshipers. Some of these descriptions will be noted when these subjects are discussed in the following chapters.

In addition, there are a number of passages in the context of meditation, devotion, or commitment in which there is a noticeable shift in emphasis to stress God's gracious and loving nature and His desire to bring His devotees to a state of eternal communion with Him.

One such passage is in Rāmānuja's comment in the *Śrībhāṣya* on the very last sūtra. Having reached the conclusion in 4.4.20 that even the nature of the finite self depends on the Supreme Person and thus also the permanency of the exalted qualities that the soul enjoys after its release from saṃsāra, he has to dispose of a final doubt.

> But if the blissful state of the released soul altogether depends on the Lord, it may happen that by virtue of His being independent, He may will the released soul to return into Saṃsāra. Of this doubt the next Sūtra disposes.
>
> 22. "Nonreturn, according to Scripture."
>
> Just as it is known from Scripture that there is a Supreme Person, whose name is the Supreme Brahman, whose nature is entirely auspicious and opposed to everything defiling, who is the cause of the origination etc., of the universe, who is omniscient, whose will is ever accomplished, who is an ocean full of forgiving love for those who take refuge in Him, who is supremely merciful, who is raised far above the possibility of anyone being equal or superior to Him—even so is it known from Scripture that this Supreme Lord, when pleased by the faithful worship of His devotees . . . frees them from the influence of Ignorance which has the form of karma . . . allows them to obtain that bliss of matchless excellence which has the form of a direct intuition of His own true nature, and certainly does not turn them back [to saṃsāra].[20]

There are also several passages in the *Gītābhāṣya* where Brahman is described as the object of the devotee's meditation and love, or as the one to whom the worshiper has surrendered himself.

> The earnestness in worshiping Me comes from the inordinate desire that impels him to find Me, for the intensity of yearning love that he has for Me is such that he is unable to tolerate a moment's separation from Me,—Me, whose sport [līlā] it is to cause the origination, continued existence, and dissolution of the entire universe filled with a marvelous and infinite variety of objects of enjoyment [material things], enjoyers [finite selves], and instruments of enjoyment [the sense organs]. I am a treasure store of a host of countless auspicious qualities, which are untouched by any evil whatsoever and which are of matchless excellence, the first six of which are knowledge [jñāna], untiring strength [bala], sovereignty [aiśvarya], immutability [vīrya], creative power [śakti], and splendor [tejas].

My celestial form [divyarūpa] is a treasury of infinite qualities, which are in a form entirely agreeable and appropriate to Myself, qualities that are celestial, wondrous, everlasting, flawless, supremely excellent, such as radiance, beauty, fragrance, delicacy, charm, and youthfulness. In my essential and inherent nature [svarūpa-svabhāva] I am beyond the grasp of speech or thought; a boundless ocean of compassion, gracious condescension, forgiving love, and generosity; the refuge for all whatsoever without making any distinction; the remover of the suffering of those who bow down before Me; a sea filled with forgiving love for those who take refuge in Me; the object of the sight of all humanity, incarnated in the family of Vasudeva without losing My own inherent nature [sva-svabhāva]; illuminating the entire universe with My matchless splendor and delighting it with My beauty.[21]

As constantly as a continuous flow of oil, focus your mind on Me. I am the Lord of all lords; I possess all auspicious qualities and am opposed to everything defiling.

Focus your mind on Me. I am all-knowing; My will is ever accomplished; I am the sole cause of the entire universe, the Supreme Brahman, the Supreme Person.

Focus your mind on Me. My eye is long and immaculate like the petal of the white lotus; I have the magnificence of a dark rain cloud and such splendor as the brilliance of a thousand simultaneously rising suns.

Focus your mind on Me. I am an ocean filled with the immortal nectar of loveliness.

Focus your mind on Me. My four arms are broad and stout; My garment is a brilliant yellow, and I am adorned with immaculate diadems, fish-shaped earrings, pearl necklaces, golden bracelets, arm rings, and much more.

Focus your mind on Me. I am an unbounded ocean of mercy, gracious condescension, beauty, sweetness, profundity, generosity, and forgiving love; I am the refuge for all whomsoever without distinction.

Focus your mind on Me. I am the Master of all.[22]

> I am the origin of all the marvelous variety of beings in the universe, both spiritual and material, and everything derives its impulses to action from Me. The wise, knowing Me in My inherent and unrestricted lordship and My association with the hosts of auspicious qualities such as gracious condescension, beauty, and forgiving love, remember these qualities when they worship me.[23]

> . . . those devotees are those who worship Thee fully as the Supreme Lord (Bhagavān), believing that Thou alone art the supreme goal, the possessor of all the glorious realms (vibhūti), and the sea of infinite qualities of matchless excellence, such as beauty, gracious condescension, and the power of ever accomplishing Thy will.[24]

> If you do not immediately succeed in achieving a state of steady concentration of your mind on Me, then try to attain Me by the discipline of practice. This consists in remembering Me with a supremely excellent love [prema]. I am inherently the antithesis of everything defiling and am a sea of infinite qualities of matchless excellence such as beauty, gracious condescension, benevolence, forgiving love, mercy, sweetness, profundity, generosity, courage, immutability [or valor (vīrya)], conquering might, omniscience, the possession of eternally realized objects of My desire, the power of ever accomplishing My will, being the Lord of all and the cause of every single thing.[25]

In much the same strain as the devotional statements just cited in the third person or first person (when the Lord's words in the *Gītā* are amplified) are descriptions in the midst of praise or petition, where the Lord is directly addressed as Thou. Here are three of the important passages of this type from the eleventh chapter of the *Gītābhāṣya,* which deals with Arjuna's vision of Lord Krishna's world-including and world-devouring form. In each case the passage is an explanation of the words in the particular verse of the *Gītā* itself.

> O Supreme Lord [Parameśvara], thus didst Thou describe Thyself. O Supreme Person [Puruṣottama], now I wish directly to experience Thee, actually to see Thy form that is of a different nature from everything else. Thou art an ocean of forgiving love

> for those who resort to Thee; Thou art the Lord; Thou art unique; Thou hast the powers of ruling, protecting, creating, destroying, and supporting all things; Thou art the embodiment of auspicious qualities, and Thou art the most Supreme [paratara].[26]

After Arjuna has seen the awesome cosmic form of Lord Krishna, he prays as follows:

> O Thou of immeasurable might [vīrya] and conquering prowess [parākrama], Thou attainest all things because Thou art their Self, the Self of all kinds of spiritual and material beings which thus constitute Thy body, Thy mode. Hence Thou art the substance of which all else is but mode and every name denotes Thyself.[27]

> Since Thou art the Father of all, the Teacher [Guru] most worthy of worship, Thou who art exalted above all by virtue of Thy compassion and other qualities, bowing and prostrating my body, I beg grace of Thee, Adorable Lord. As a father when humbly entreated is merciful to a son who has done wrong, or a friend forgives a friend, so do Thou, the supremely compassionate, who art the lover, be pleased to bear with me, Thy beloved.[28]

5 Paratva and Saulabhya as Interpretive Concepts

The Introduction to the Gītābhāṣya

Rāmānuja introduces his commentary on the *Bhagavadgītā* with the following passage.

> Śrī's Consort, who is entirely auspicious and utterly opposed to everything defiling, and whose essential nature is wholly knowledge and bliss;
>
> Who is an ocean of auspicious attributes of matchless excellence inherent in His nature, the first six of which are knowledge, untiring strength, sovereignty, immutability, creative power, and splendor;
>
> Whose celestial form is a treasure store of infinite qualities such as radiance, beauty, fragrance, delicacy, charm, and youthfulness, which are completely pleasing to Him and befitting Him, and which are inconceivable, wondrous, everlasting, flawless, and supremely excellent;
>
> Who possesses a magnificent variety of immeasurable celestial ornaments, which are utterly amazing and are never sullied, and who is equipped with countless weapons befitting Him, of inconceivable power, never damaged, and incomparable;
>
> Who is the beloved of Śrī, who Herself possesses countless auspicious attributes of matchless excellence, such as Her essential nature, beautiful form, qualities, glorious realms, sovereignty, and gracious conduct, all of which are eternal and incomparable and are appropriate and pleasing to Him;
>
> Who has innumerable angels at His feet ever praising Him, with infinite qualities of immutable and incomparable knowledge, conduct, sovereignty, etc., whose essence, existence, and various activities are according to His will, and whose sole delight is to be completely subservient to Him;
>
> Whose essential nature and inherent attributes [svarūpa-svabhāva] cannot be grasped by speech or thought;
>
> Who resides in the supreme heaven of immeasurable extent, which is eternal and imperishable, which is filled with a magnificent diversity of objects, instruments, and places of enjoyment, and which is agreeable to Him;
>
> Whose sport [līlā] it is to originate, develop, and dissolve the

entire universe, completely filled with an infinite and magnificent diversity of enjoying subjects and objects of enjoyment;

Who is the Supreme Brahman;

This Nārāyaṇa, the Supreme Person [Puruṣottama], when He created the entire universe of everything from the god Brahmā to motionless stones, remains with His same essential nature [svena-rūpeṇa] and is inaccessible even by such means as the meditation and worship of men or of gods like Brahmā.

But being a shoreless ocean of compassion, gracious condescension, forgiving love [or motherly affection (vātsalya)] and generosity, while still not losing His own inherent nature and attributes [sva-svabhāvam-ajahad-eva], He has assumed His own bodily form [svam-eva-rūpam], which on each occasion has the same generic structure as one of the various classes of creatures, and in these various shapes He has descended again and again to the various worlds where they dwell, where having been worshiped by these different kinds of creatures, He has granted them whatever they prayed for, whether meritorious action, wealth, physical pleasure, or deliverance, according to their own desire.

Although the immediate occasion of His descents is to relieve the earth's burden of evildoers, their deeper intention is to provide a refuge for those who resort to Him, even for such creatures as we, by becoming a visible object to all mankind and accomplishing such Divine feats as captivate the hearts and eyes of all creatures high and low.

Thus he has slain great demons and demonic kings . . . and He has quenched the thirst of all with the immortal nectar of His glances and His words of matchless mercy, friendliness, and tender affection.

He made Akrūra, Mālākāra, and others the most ardent devotees by revealing the multitudes of His unsurpassed virtues such as beauty and gracious condescension.

Finally, using the occasion of having to persuade Arjuna to fight, He has revealed bhaktiyoga [the discipline of devotion], which is promoted by the disciplines of *jñāna* [knowledge] and *karma* [performance of ritual duties], which in the Vedānta [Upaniṣads] is declared to be the means of attaining the supreme goal of human life, *mokṣa* [deliverance from saṃsāra], and of which He Himself is the object.

> Thus, when the Kauravas and Pāṇḍavas began their war with one another, He who is the Supreme Lord [Bhagavān], the Supreme Person [Puruṣottama], the Lord of all lords, who had taken upon Himself a mortal form for helping the universe, and had been overwhelmed by forgiving love for His dependents, placed Arjuna in the war-chariot and Himself undertook the duty of a charioteer so as to be witnessed by all the people.[1]

Rāmānuja has given many other descriptions of the Divine nature, several of which were included in the previous chapter; some of them are more detailed in certain aspects and include qualities omitted here. Nowhere else, however, is there a passage that describes the various aspects of the Deity so clearly or distinguishes between them so distinctly. This passage may therefore well be regarded as the central "text" in this study of Rāmānuja's doctrine of God.

The first thing to be noticed is that the introduction falls clearly into two parts. The first ends with a statement of God's *inaccessibility* to men or even to gods like Brahmā (the lower deity, first among creatures, who fashions the universe under the Lord's direction), even when they attempt to use such effective means as meditation or worship. The second begins with the declaration that this Supreme Person has *made Himself accessible* to His worshipers by descending into the phenomenal realm in a form similar to theirs.

Secondly, we see that the *kalyāṇaguṇas* (the auspicious qualities or attributes), which in the other descriptive statements come together, are here split into two, one group at the beginning of the first part and one at the beginning of the second. The first group consists of the *ṣaḍguṇas,* the "six attributes" of Bhagavān: knowledge (jñāna), untiring strength (bala), sovereignty (aiśvarya), immutability (vīrya), creative power (śakti), and splendor (tejas). The second group consists of compassion or mercy (kāruṇya), gracious condescension (sauśīlya), forgiving and protecting love (vātsalya), and generosity (audārya). Later in the second part, compassion (here dayā instead of kāruṇya) and gracious condescension are repeated, and two related qualities are mentioned: *sauhārda,* concern for His creatures' welfare, and *anurāga,* tender (literally, passionate) affection. The one quality that is repeated from the first part is *saundarya,* beauty of bodily form, for this characterizes the Lord both in His transcendent realm and in His incarnations. These two groups correspond exactly to a later distinction drawn by some of Rāmānuja's successors: on the one hand, essential lordship (īśitṛtva)[2] or supremacy (paratva); and on the other hand, saulabhya, being easily approachable by His worshipers, because He has first descended and drawn near to them.

The two halves of the introduction also describe these two aspects of the Divine nature in more dramatic and dynamic terms. On the one hand, there is the supreme Brahman, Nārāyaṇa, ever united with His Divine Consort Śrī, who dwells in His supreme heaven in His own transcendent form of incomparable beauty, adorned with magnificent ornaments and equipped with inconceivably powerful weapons, and is constantly served by His ministering angels. This Supreme Person causes the origination, continuance, and dissolution of the cosmos out of the sheer urge to self-expression, without necessity and without a determined end; and yet all of this creation of a constantly changing universe does not change Him in His own essential nature.

The second half of the introduction is dominated, not by lists of abstract qualities, but by verbs indicating His actions. Without losing His own inherent nature, He has repeatedly descended (avatīrya, avatīrya) in forms similar to the class of creatures among whom He dwells so that they can see Him and adore Him. When worshiped, He grants them what they pray for, both worldly goods and the supreme good of release from the transient world and communion with Himself. His mighty feats of valor have the immediate purpose of ridding the world of evildoers, but their more significant intent is to captivate men's hearts and, by thus persuasively "compelling" their surrender and awakening their response of devotion, to accomplish their salvation. His final act that is here recounted is His teaching of the way to salvation, the discipline of devotion (bhaktiyoga), to Arjuna, having taken the task of charioteer in the war-chariot and having persuaded the reluctant Arjuna to enter the chariot. Here again the immediate purpose of the teaching is to persuade Arjuna to share in God's work of upholding righteousness and ridding the world of the unrighteous, but the chariot in the midst of the battlefield is transformed by the winsome presence and the gracious words of Lord Krishna into a stage on which He can be witnessed by all the people (literally, all worlds).

The later Śrī Vaiṣṇava teacher Vedānta Deśika commented that there are four terms at the end of the introduction that sum up the entire nature of the Lord (Īśvara), the first two pointing to His supremacy (paratva) and the last two to His accessibility (saulabhya).[3]

The first term is *Puruṣottama* (the Highest Person), Rāmānuja's favorite metaphysical name for God and the one that he had already used at the end of the first part of the introduction, which described the supreme and transcendent being of God. The second term is *Sarveśvareśvaraḥ* (Lord of all lords), which expresses God's essential or ultimate sovereignty or "overlordship." These two ideas of supremacy and lordship are both present in the later usage of paratva.

The third phrase is *jagad-upakṛti-martyaḥ* (becoming a mortal, or taking mortal form, for helping the universe). The "mortal" (martyaḥ) here contrasts sharply with the "highest" (uttama) and "overlordship" of the two previous phrases. This contrast is still further heightened by the fourth phrase, *āśrita-vātsalya-vivaśaḥ* (overpowered by forgiving and protecting love toward those who have sought refuge with Him). This seems to mean that in God's redemptive action, His vātsalya becomes His dominant characteristic, dominating, that is to say, over His lordly justice and His transcendent inaccessibility. We shall be concerned with the precise meaning of this side of the divine nature and its relation to the other side in later chapters. Here we want simply to note once again that the contrast between these two sets of phrases corresponds to the dramatic contrast in Divine attributes and Divine actions described in the two parts of the introduction. It is this contrast within the clearly established unity of the Divine nature and the Divine Person that provides the subject for this study.

RĀMĀNUJA'S USE OF THE TERM PARATVA AND OTHER RELATED WORDS

Rāmānuja does not himself use the terms *paratva* and *saulabhya* with the significance that they have in the thought of Sudarśana Sūri and Vedānta Deśika, namely, as technical terms or general concepts to classify the Divine attributes into two distinct groups. Indeed, he appears never to have used the word *saulabhya* and only in a few instances the word *paratva.* Nevertheless, these two abstract terms of his commentators do succeed in focusing attention on important aspects of his theology that he expressed in other terms.

The term *paratva* does occur three times in *Śrībhāṣya* 3.2.35 and once in 3.2.37, but the first three instances are quite clearly the use of the abstract form ending in *-tva* to construct a sentence without the use of any finite verb, a very frequent practice in the scholastic Sanskrit of Rāmānuja's time. The point under discussion in this adhikaraṇa (group of sūtras) is the refutation of the view that there is a being higher even than the highest Brahman. So in 3.2.35, Rāmānuja says, "This means that this Person is Supreme and it is not possible for anything else to be supreme." This may be literally translated, "which means the supremacy of the Person and the impossibility of the supremacy of what is other than He" (iti-puruṣasya-paratvam, tadvyatiriktasya-paratvāsambhavañca-pratipādya). Similarly, he says at the end of the same paragraph, "Therefore the 'supreme' is the Supreme Person who is omniscient and possesses such qualities as invisibility, for it is certainly only He who is higher than the high [parātpara]. This may be stated thus because He is higher than the 'aggregate-soul' [samaṣṭi-puruṣāt-paratvena]."[4]

The usage two sūtras later might be interpreted as an abstract concept, but it is probably meant as a nominal clause in place of a clause with a finite verb, just as above.

> For the sake of arousing the desire to meditate it has been stated that the finite self in all its states is connected with imperfections [jivasya-sarvāvasthāsu-sadoṣatvam] and that the Supreme Person who is to be attained [by meditation] is without imperfections, is a rich mine of auspicious qualities, and is supreme over everything [else] [*sarvasmāt-paratvam*].

Translated literally, the passage would read as follows,

> the connection with imperfection in all states of the jīva and the lack of imperfections of the Highest Person who is what is to be attained, as well as His being a rich mine of auspicious qualities and His supremacy over all.

Interpreting the passage as a nominal clause would seem to be confirmed by the fact that the comment on the previous sūtra ends as follows: "Therefore this Supreme Brahman alone is supreme over all" (literally, higher than all, *sarvasmāt-param*). The *sarvasmāt-paratva* in the following paragraph seems to be a recapitulation, with the abstract ending *-tva,* of this statement in the simple form, itself the conclusion of the six sūtras called collectively "the adhikaraṇa concerning 'para'," just as the other two phrases sum up the twofold characteristics (ubhayalingam) of Brahman discussed in previous sūtras.[5]

If, on the other hand, we were to understand paratva here as an abstract concept, we would have a use by Rāmānuja himself of the concept of supremacy which is in accord with its later meaning but which has not yet been generalized to include all other Divine attributes relating to Divine lordship or Divine transcendence.

These passages in any case indicate how easily the style of scholastic Sanskrit lends itself to the transition from a simple adjective to an abstract noun. The adjective *para* is used thousands of times by Rāmānuja in the sense of "high," "higher than," or "supreme" and, less frequently, with the sense of "other than."[6] The terms *parama* (highest) and *paratara* (higher) also occur occasionally, with a meaning identical with para in the sense of "high." The root meaning of para is "far," with which English word it is cognate.[7] The later concept *paratva* is the abstract of para in the sense of "supreme." Its primary meaning is therefore "supremacy," not "otherness," but the concept of Divine supremacy itself includes within it the notion that God is distinct in character (visajātīya) from all "lower" beings.

Sometimes in using the comparative form *paratara* (higher than, or superior to) or its abstract noun *parataratvam* (superiority to, or supremacy over, something else), Rāmānuja rather clearly indicates one or more dimensions of the Divine supremacy. This is particularly true of his comment on the statement in *Gītā* 7.7: "There is nothing higher than I" (mattaḥ-parataram).

> Because I am the cause of the two "natures" [material nature and the higher prakṛti consisting of finite selves] which are the causes of all things, and because I am the Śeṣī even of the intelligent beings who are the śeṣins of the nonintelligent entities [material objects], I am superior [paratara]. Likewise, because I possess such qualities as universal knowledge, creative power, and untiring strength, I am superior, and there is nothing whatsoever distinct from Me which could be superior by possessing such qualities.[8]

In the *Vedārthasaṃgraha,* Rāmānuja uses the term *paratva* a number of times in the section establishing the supremacy over all other gods, notably Brahmā and Śiva. Here again, it is difficult to know whether to keep the abstract noun *supremacy* when translating into

English the sentences in which the term *paratva* occurs or to translate as "He is supreme over . . ." It does not make too much difference for our purpose here, for the whole discussion implies the concept of Nārāyaṇa's "supremacy," whether or not the abstract noun *paratva* is literally translated. This concept is not quite so general as in its use by Rāmānuja's commentators, but the meaning is not far removed from the later category, since this "supremacy" is the most general qualification of the Supreme Deity. The question here at issue is: who is this particular Being, this particular Person, who is supreme, or higher than all other entities? Rāmānuja replies that He is not Brahmā, the fashioner of the cosmos, or Śiva, revered by so many as the Supreme Lord (*Parameśvara*), but the Lord God (Bhagavān), whose proper name is Nārāyaṇa or Viṣṇu, who is not a general principle but a specific concrete Person with a particular bodily form. At the end of this section Rāmānuja rejects the suggestion that there could possibly be any being above this One who is the material and the efficient cause of creation, and he refers to the place in the *Vedānta Sūtras* where the same question is discussed, the point in the *Śrībhāṣya* where, as we have just seen, he uses the term *paratva* (in the phrase *sarvasmāt-paratvam*).[9]

THE ABSENCE OF THE TERM SAULABHYA IN RĀMĀNUJA'S WRITINGS

It is a surprising fact that Rāmānuja never uses the word *saulabhya.* It is the abstract noun of the adjective *sulabha,* which means "easily obtainable or attainable." In the context of the personal relation of the devotee to His Lord, *sulabha* means "easily approachable or accessible." Even the adjective *sulabha* is seldom used by Rāmānuja, and apparently never as a description of God.

Does it not then involve a distortion of Rāmānuja's thought to attempt to fit some of the Divine attributes into the general category of saulabhya? The full answer to this question can only be given through the fuller discussion in later chapters of this aspect of the Divine nature. However, a partial answer can be given by examining Rāmānuja's comment on *Gītā* 8.14, where the word *sulabha* appears. This verse reads, "For the one who constantly remembers Me and never lets his thoughts stray to any other object, for this disciplined yogī, I am easily attainable [sulabhaḥ]." Rāmānuja's comments bring out the very deepest level of the mystery of Divine accessibility: the inability of either God or the devotee to live without fellowship with one another. We shall consider this doctrine in detail later. Here it is enough to note that the doctrine is emphatically stated in commenting on this particular verse. This might lead us to conclude that there is a real connection between the word *sulabha* and the aspect of the Divine nature that later Śrī Vaiṣṇavas designated as saulabhya.

However, Rāmānuja's comments seem to imply a criticism of two ideas inherent in the ordinary meaning of sulabha, which is literally "easily gained." Viewed from man's side, Rāmānuja holds, the attainment of God is anything but easy, for it implies the very difficult achievement of perfectly disciplined meditation on God. Even more important is the fact that this intimate communion with God is not something that man can gain; not even the advanced devotee who yearns desperately for this communion can gain it by his own effort. Salvation is God's election and God's gift. It is in this special sense that it is easy:

> and I am easily attained [suprāpaśca], for unable to bear separation from him (the highest kind of devotee who cannot live without Me), I Myself choose him [aham-eva taṃ vṛṇe], and it is I Myself who grant [aham-eva-dadāmi] him the fruition of His meditation.

Moreover, it is a gift of such magnitude as to stagger human comprehension: "I Myself am the one who is to be attained, not merely some aspect of My nature, such as My sovereignty."[10]

It may well be that Rāmānuja avoided the words *sulabha* and *saulabhya* because they could lead to a misunderstanding of God's nature and of the way to attain Him. By the time of the later commentators, the doctrine of Divine grace was so widely accepted among Śrī Vaiṣṇavas and so fundamental to their theology that they would not have felt it necessary to safeguard against "easy attainability" leading to the misunderstanding that attainment of God is a human achievement. They may also have been less concerned to qualify the meaning of "easy" than Rāmānuja himself was.

We can, of course, do no more than speculate on why the later Śrī Vaiṣṇavas chose as the name for a general category a word which Rāmānuja had not used himself. It would not seem difficult to have expanded slightly the meaning of one of the terms which Rāmānuja did use. For example, Śrī Vaiṣṇavas had restricted the meaning of *sauśīlya* (good conduct) to refer specifically to God's "gracious condescension" in treating His inferiors as equals. Rāmānuja often uses this term to describe God's gracious nature. He does not, however, include under it all the other attributes pertaining to God's gracious nature and His action to accomplish men's salvation. For whatever reason, the following generations of Śrī Vaiṣṇavas left this and the other Divine attributes with their particular meanings and chose the term *saulabhya* to denote this whole group of qualities.

Modern Śrī Vaiṣṇavas have sometimes used the English word *love* to indicate both the fundamental divine attribute in relation to the worshiper (or even to all creatures) and the worshiper's response to that Divine love.[11] As an interpretation of Śrī Vaiṣṇava concepts in terms of modern Western thought influenced by Christian ideas, such a choice has much to commend it, but this use of one generalizing term is foreign to Rāmānuja. He uses a number of more particular terms with distinct shades of meaning. The human response to God's loving and redemptive action is sometimes designated by words meaning "love" but more typically by the term *bhakti* (devotion toward, communion with, participation in), and the Divine qualities which provoke this human response are several and distinct.

THE POLARITY OF SUPREMACY AND ACCESSIBILITY IN THE DIVINE NATURE

While the terms *paratva* and *saulabhya* thus do not appear in their later usage, there is considerable evidence that the later commentators have correctly designated a crucial polarity in Rāmānuja's theology. A hint in this direction may be given in the paragraph from the *Śrībhāṣya* just considered. After summing up the previous sections of the sūtras with nominal clauses (or abstract terms) indicating Brahman's freedom from imperfection, abundant store of auspicious qualities, and supremacy over all else, Rāmānuja takes up the sūtra that is to introduce the main topic of the chapter: the means to attain Brahman.

> Being about to investigate the nature of meditation, the author of the Sūtras now declares that the meditating devotee receives the reward of meditation, i.e., release, which consists in attaining the Supreme Person, only from that Supreme Person Himself. . . . Why so? . . . "Because only that is possible!" For it is only He, who is omniscient, omnipotent, and very generous, who having been worshiped . . . is pleased to grant different forms of enjoyment and final emancipation, which consists in attaining His own essential nature.[12]

The phrase of particular interest here is "who is omniscient, omnipotent, and very generous" (sarvajñas-sarvaśaktir-mahodāraḥ). Sudarśana Sūri comments on this: "The concept of great generosity is mentioned here to signify that the [other] two [qualities] serve no purpose to a person who is miserly."[13]

As frequently happens in the Śrī Vaiṣṇava tradition after Rāmānuja, the attributes expressing the Divine saulabhya are emphasized as most essential—especially in the worship of the devotees. The very passage on which Sudarśana Sūri comments shows the distinctive difference in Rāmānuja's own emphasis. This is one of several transitional passages between the first part of the *Śrībhāṣya,* dealing with Brahman as the primal cause, and the second, dealing with the means to attain Brahman: the various disciplines of meditation and devotion. Here Rāmānuja remarks again that Brahman is both the goal to be reached and the means to reach that goal, for He alone is the one who is able to grant the supreme end, the attainment of Himself, as well as all lesser gifts, to His worshipers. This conclusion is based on three attributes of Brahman: His omniscience, His omnipotence, and His great generosity. The first two are of a different kind from the third, but all are equally important, and all are equally "necessary" in the objective process of redemption and "useful" in the subjective experience of the worshiper.

The relation between attributes of these two types is not always, however, a simple conjunction, an "and." In certain crucial passages it is more like a "yet nevertheless also." These abstract terms, *paratva* and *saulabhya,* though they were not used by Rāmānuja, do capture a real distinction between two groups of more concrete attributes in Rāmānuja's concept of God. Sometimes the distinction seems to be between two halves that complement each other harmoniously, but at other times this distinction, though never becoming a separation, does indicate a certain tension between two poles in the Divine nature, a tension that not only makes possible the reconciliation of seemingly divergent and contradictory traditions but also provides the inner dynamic and liveliness in Rāmānuja's thought. This is a liveliness that makes his followers turn again and again to his own writings even though they have the more scholastically precise formulations of his later followers.

6 Svarūpa and Svabhāva: Two Kinds of Divine Essence

Rāmānuja's Distinction between Different Kinds of Divine Attributes

Rāmānuja is much less inclined than later Śrī Vaiṣṇava teachers to organize his teaching in the form of schematic classifications, especially with respect to the attributes or qualities belonging to the Divine nature. The simplest distinction he draws is referred to as the *ubhayalingatva:* the fact of God's possessing two kinds of characteristics—on the one hand, His positive perfections; on the other hand, His freedom from any kind of imperfection.

A more important link with the later scholastic schemes is provided by the distinction Rāmānuja draws between what might be called primary and secondary qualities of the Divine nature.

> Those other qualities which are "equal to the thing," i.e., which are attributes determining the essential nature of the thing [svarūpa-nirūpaṇa-dharma] and therefore necessarily entering into the idea of the thing, must be included in all meditations, no less than the thing itself. To this class belong qualities such as true being, knowledge, bliss, purity, infinity, and so on. For the essential definition of Brahman—which had been suggested by texts such as "that from which all these beings," etc., as the cause of the world—is given in texts such as "the True, knowledge, infinite is Brahman," "bliss is Brahman," and others; and hence, in order that a true notion may be formed of Brahman as the object of meditation, such qualities as true being, bliss, and so on, have to be included in all meditations on Brahman. Such additional qualities, on the other hand, as, for example, compassion, which indeed cannot exist apart from the subject to which they belong but are not necessary elements of the idea of Brahman, are to be included in those meditations only where they are specifically mentioned.[1]

> As truth, knowledge, bliss, infinity, and purity . . . are characteristics that determine the essential nature of Brahman, meditation upon the essential nature of Brahman is impossible without them.[2]

It is important to keep in mind that this distinction is not drawn at the beginning of a systematic discussion of the Divine attributes but is prompted by the question of whether all the qualities mentioned as objects of meditation are essential qualities and hence should be included in all meditations. Rāmānuja explains sūtra 3.3.12. to mean that "mere elements in a figurative representation of Brahman under the form of an animal body" such as "having joy for its head" are not qualities of Brahman.

> Otherwise, i.e., if Brahman really possessed different members, such as head, wings, and so on, He would be liable to increase and decrease, and this would be in conflict with texts such as "the True, knowledge, infinite is Brahman"—but if this reasoning holds good, then all the infinite qualities belonging to Brahman such as lordship, profundity, generosity, compassion, and so on—all of which are incapable of existing apart from the subject to which they belong—would have to be comprehended in all those meditations on Brahman when they are not expressly mentioned; and this could not possibly be done, as those qualities are infinite in number. This difficulty the next sūtra removes.[3]

The passage from the *Vedārthasaṃgraha* on the reconciliation of apparently contradicting texts also uses the term "defining attribute" (svarūpa-nirūpaka-dharma) in order to explain how, when there are innumerable Divine qualities, it can be said that Brahman is only (eva) knowledge and bliss. This is possible, Rāmānuja says, because these defining attributes are identical with the essential nature of Brahman, and therefore it can be said that He is "only" knowledge and bliss.[4]

It appears from these two contexts that Rāmānuja accepted as well known the idea that the five qualities of Brahman mentioned in the defining Upaniṣadic texts are "defining attributes" distinguished from other less essential qualities in the Divine nature. Yet this well-known distinction does not seem to affect the description or the ranking of the Divine attributes, except that the svarūpa (essential nature) is often mentioned before the kalyāṇaguṇas (auspicious qualities). Moreover, the term *svarūpa* with reference to God is sometimes used to mean more than simply what is defined by the five essential attributes. Even the comment on 3.3.13. has the expression *ādi* (and so forth) after the five qualities. Rāmānuja several times uses the expression *jñānānandaikasvarūpa* (whose essential nature is wholly knowledge and bliss), but the preceding phrase in the compound is usually "opposed to all evil," and this Rāmānuja certainly intended to include in the essential nature of Brahman. It is indeed the equivalent of *amalatva* (purity or stainlessness), which is one of the five defining attributes.

On a number of occasions, however, Rāmānuja speaks of the svarūpa of God in a more general way.[5] These usages may be classified according to their increasing generality.

The term *svarūpa* with reference to the Deity is used—

1. to express the Upaniṣadic definition of the Self;
2. to qualify the first definition in such a way as to make clear the distinction between the Supreme Self and the finite self by (*a*) emphasizing Brahman's uniqueness, or distinctness from all other entities, and (*b*) emphasizing that the nature of Brahman is fundamentally and essentially free from and opposed to all impurity;
3. to include all the auspicious qualities of Brahman, both the qualities expressing His Lordship and all other qualities, but to exclude all the spiritual and material entities which, though "parts" of Him as His body (śarīra) and His mode (prakāra), are subject to modification;
4. still to exclude all the material universe and the souls attached to the bodies within it but to include in God's essential nature His eternal realm and all the persons (divine attendants) and objects of enjoyment within it, and preeminently the immaterial (aprākṛta) bodily form (rūpa or vigraha) of the Supreme Person.

In certain passages in the *Gītābhāṣya* and in the introductory description of God in the *Vedārthasaṃgraha,* Rāmānuja uses the terms *svarūpa* and *svabhāva* in a way that may correspond to the later scholastic distinction. These apparently synonymous terms, both of which may be translated "essence," "essential nature," or "inherent nature," are clearly used to refer to different aspects of the Divine nature.[6]

The adjective *svābhāvika* is often used by Rāmānuja to qualify some of the Divine qualities or attributes. The usual meaning of svabhāva is simply "nature," and the adjective can usually be translated "natural" (to Him) or "innate." But what is the distinction between svarūpa and svabhāva?

The later commentators take svabhāva to mean "attributes," namely, qualities other than the five essential and defining attributes. Sudarśana Sūri goes even further and identifies svarūpa and svabhāva with īśitṛtva (lordship) and saulabhya (easy accessibility to His devotees) respectively. Svabhāva also accompanies svarūpa in reference to the finite self (jīvasvarūpa, tatsvabhāva),[7] in reference to Brahman's form, attendants, and abodes (rūpa-parijana-sthāna . . . svarūpa-svabhāva-mahāvibhūti),[8] and in reference to the difference between Brahman, on the one hand, and finite selves and material things, on the other.[9]

Principal N. S. Anantha Rangachar has suggested an explanation of Sudarśana Sūri's differentiation between the two terms that would be of general application. He suggests that in both cases svarūpa refers to the unchanging nature and svabhāva to the part of the nature that can change. The lordship of Īśvara (which includes the five defining attributes of the Self) and the essential nature of the finite self (essentially consisting of the five qualities of knowledge, bliss, and so on) never change, but the mercy of God indicated by His svabhāva may change in the sense that it is checked by the soul's transgressions, and the svabhāva of the finite self, which he takes to be its *śeṣatva* (its subservience to the Lord), might change if the soul does not recognize it and becomes subservient to another.[10]

This explanation is useful but not totally satisfactory—in the case of the Supreme Self, because the usage of svarūpa itself is so fluid; and in the case of the finite self, because Rāmānuja repeatedly declares the quality of śeṣatva to be of the very essence of the jīvātman. Yet, the interpretation of svabhāva as "attributes" does seem quite reasonable. We shall perhaps do best to think of svabhāva as indicating the distinctive nature of an entity in a slightly broader sense than svarūpa. It is therefore identical with the svarūpa of Brahman when that is used in senses three or four, as outlined above, but indicates the other Divine attributes when svarūpa is used in sense one or two.[11] This, however, still does not explain the phrase in *Gītābhāṣya* 18.55: *svarūpa-svabhāva-guṇa-vibhūti,* where a distinction is made between *svabhāva* and *guṇa* (quality). For this usage I can offer no explanation.[12]

A POSSIBLE EXPLANATION FOR THE DISTINCTION BETWEEN SVARŪPA AND SVABHĀVA

The dimensions of Rāmānuja's concept of God are substantially what are suggested by the four relevant mangalaślokas, but the variety in the descriptions makes it difficult to arrange this material precisely according to the later schemes of Rāmānuja's followers. It is especially difficult to draw a hard and fast line between the defining attributes of Brahman and others which also belong to Brahman, but not essentially or necessarily so. The term *kalyāṇa* (auspicious) is sometimes identical with the Divine svarūpa, but sometimes indicates auspicious qualities (kalyāṇaguṇāh) in addition to the defining attributes. The kalyānaguṇas which are often mentioned are the so-called ṣaḍguṇas (six qualities), which are stated in the *Viṣṇu Purāṇa* to define the nature of Bhagavān and which play an important role in the doctrine of the Vyūhas in the *Pāñcarātra Āgamas.* These six are jñāna, bala, aiśvarya, śakti, vīrya, and tejas.[13] The first would seem to be identical with the jñāna of the Upaniṣadic definition; the other five have meanings that shade into each other, centering around the ideas of power and majesty. The later commentators define jñāna as "omniscience" in order to distinguish it from the essential attribute of knowledge or consciousness.

Are these six qualities, then, less essential to the nature of Brahman than the five defining attributes (jñāna, ānanda, ananta, satya, and amalatva)? If so, what becomes of Sudarśana Sūri's interpretation that īśitṛtva is the svarūpa of the Supreme Lord? This is possible only if the ṣaḍguṇas are included in the svarūpa of Brahman, and this is sometimes done in the later tradition by including them all under the essential attribute of jñāna. Rāmānuja's own writing does not give us much warrant for this kind of solution, for the ṣaḍguṇas are often taken as the representatives of the whole group of kalyāṇaguṇas, which according to the later school, following Rāmānuja's statement concerning the five defining attributes, all belong to nonessential attributes of Brahman.

Moreover, this question of the ṣaḍguṇas is but one aspect of our perplexity. Why should Rāmānuja state that two large groups of qualities, one pertaining to creation and sovereignty, the other to redemption, are not part of the essential nature of Brahman? To understand this we must pay close attention to the *text* that Rāmānuja is interpreting and to the *context* of this statement.

Rāmānuja is commenting on the *Vedānta Sūtras,* and the third pāda of the third adhyāya is concerned with the vidyās, the different forms of meditation on Brahman which are taught in the Upaniṣads. These sūtras are interpreted to mean that one and the same Brahman is the object of all these various meditations, but the meditations themselves are distinct, since different qualities of Brahman are mentioned in each. That raises two questions that lead to the distinction between different classes of Divine attributes: which qualities are so essential to the nature of Brahman that they must be included in all meditations upon Him even when they are not specifically mentioned, and what is the function of the other qualities in the meditations? Leaving aside metaphorical qualities and purely rhetorical ascriptions, there is still an infinite number of auspicious qualities that "cannot exist apart from the subject to which they belong" (guṇy-apṛthak-sthitatva-mātra) and that "are only connected with Brahman" (brahma-sambandhinām-eva). Practically speaking, they cannot all be included in every meditation; therefore, only those must be included which are "equal to the thing" (artha-sāmānya). Other qualities are to be included only where they are specifically mentioned.

Rāmānuja gives four of these other qualities as examples: *aiśvarya* (lordship, sovereignty, dominion, or wealth), *gāmbhīrya,* (profundity, inscrutability, dignity, or grandeur), *audārya* (generosity), and *kāruṇya* (mercy or compassion). In the following paragraph kāruṇya alone serves as the example of this countless number of Divine attributes. These examples are not chosen at random, and they are certainly not meant to indicate qualities that are not important in Brahman's nature. Quite the contrary, these four qualities are representative of those aspects of the Divine nature which Rāmānuja repeatedly remphasizes: His Lordship over His creation and His love toward His worshipers. Why then does he say that these "are not included in the definition of Brahman" (pratītyanubandhitvābhāva)? He does so because he is following the tradition of Upaniṣadic interpretation epitomized in the *Vedānta Sūtras,* which by combining certain texts arrive at this list of defining attributes of the Self: *satya* (truth or abiding reality), *jñāna* (knowledge or consciousness), *ānanda* (joy or bliss), *amalatva* (stainlessness or purity), and *anantatva* (infinity).[14]

Rāmānuja believed that this is the Upaniṣadic definition of the Self applied to both the Supreme Self (Paramātman) and the individual finite self (pratyagātmā or jīvātmā), but with some important differences. One difference is that in the case of the finite self all of this divine nature can be obscured by the ignorance caused by bondage of karma. Hence the quality of amalatva has a special importance for Rāmānuja in his definition of Brahman and is often indicated first, with one of several characteristic phrases.

Another important difference is that anantatva, strictly speaking, belongs only to the Supreme Self. Finite selves after liberation from saṃsāra attain an "infinity" of knowledge but not the essential infinity of God.[15] Nevertheless, Rāmānuja does accept the Vedāntic conception that in one important sense the finite self has the same essential nature as the Supreme Self, and he maintains that it is precisely the knowledge of this common nature that must be intuitively realized by the finite self through following one or another of the disciplines of meditation given in the Upaniṣads. Although Rāmānuja makes several important qualifications of this general Vedāntic doctrine in order to make clear the dissimilarity between the Supreme Self and the finite self, the doctrine as such remains. This can be seen not only at many places in the *Śrībhāṣya* but also in the *Bhagavadgītābhāṣya,* which in general puts more emphasis on *dāsyabhakti,* the devotion of a servant to his master. Thus he paraphrases *Gītā* 6:30, "who sees Me in all, and sees all in Me," as follows:

> One who has reached the highest stage of yoga approaches My nature, as is declared in the text, "Stainless, he attains supreme equality [sāmānyam]" [*Iśa Upaniṣad* 6]. Seeing that all ātmā-nature in its pure state beyond good or evil is equal to Me, he will see that I am in all ātmās and all ātmās are in Me, and in virtue of this equality, if he knows the nature of one ātmā, he knows the nature of all ātmās. I do not veil Myself from the man who knows his own ātmā in its proper nature, for My nature is the same as his. Indeed, I consider him as My own Self [ātmā], as equal to Myself, and I always reveal Myself to him.[16]

God in Himself, and God in Relation to Finite Beings

How then was it possible for Rāmānuja to think that some of the Divine attributes that were most important for him did not define the svarūpa of Brahman; that is, were "outside" His svarūpa in the narrower sense, consisting of the five defining attributes? Any answer is admittedly guesswork, but this is one point where some speculation is essential if we are to succeed to any degree in entering into Rāmānuja's mind and sympathetically understanding his darśana: both his "view" and his "vision" of the Supreme Person.

We can say that Rāmānuja took the Upaniṣadic definition seriously, both its conception of the Self and its teaching of the way to meditate on the Self. This is undoubtedly true; Rāmānuja took the scriptural texts seriously and literally.[17] But he did not just accept them blindly. His whole theology is an effort to understand the Śruti, the Smṛti, and the authoritative commentaries, preeminently the *Vedānta Sūtras,* all included together in the term *śāstra.* He wished to understand them as one whole with a single meaning, and to this end he sought to reconcile the apparent contradictions among their texts. There is no evidence that he saw such an apparent contradiction in leaving so many important attributes outside the svarūpa of Brahman.

One explanation might be that he simply did not give too rigid a definition to svarūpa. He expanded it when the qualities he wished to emphasize were other than the five defining attributes. There is some evidence that this is true; he could even include God's transcendent bodily form and the whole eternal abode within svarūpa when he wanted to emphasize how essential these were to our knowledge of Brahman, how inseparably linked to the Supreme Person, and how utterly different from everything in the phenomenal world. Nevertheless, the differentiation between *jñānānandaikasvarūpa* (whose essential nature is solely, or wholly, knowledge and bliss) and *kalyāṇaguṇagaṇah* (who has a host of auspicious qualities) occurs too frequently for us to conclude that the clear distinction drawn at one point in the *Śrībhāṣya* (and the *Vedāntadīpa*) is only a necessary concession to the text of the *Vedānta Sūtras* or to the tradition of Vedāntic interpretation, which is then tacitly ignored elsewhere.

There is one episode in the traditional biography of Rāmānuja that may shed an oblique light on this question of the definition of the essential nature of God. It is said that Rāmānuja was dictating the *Śrībhāṣya* to his disciple Kūraṭṭāḻvān (Kūreśa), to whom he had given permission to stop writing if he heard anything with which he did not agree. When Rāmānuja defined the finite self (jīvātmā) as *jñānaikasvarūpa* (whose essential nature is wholly consciousness, or that which has cognition alone as its distinguishing attribute),

> Kūreśa ceased writing, for to him such a definition, though valid, was as good as no definition, inasmuch as the most essential characteristic of the soul, namely its *allegiance* or *liegeship to God, śeṣatva,* was a serious omission; . . . for no basis for true religion was raised by merely apprehending the soul as *that which is characterised by consciousness,* unless the soul is also the *sole property* or possession of the Universal soul, God. Defining soul as *that which has consciousness merely without* any reference to its being essentially related to God, as quality is related to things, or as property to a base, or as mode to substance, as light to the sun or scent to the flower, amounted to tacitly ignoring such essential relationship; and that without this relation to God first emphatically asserted and defended, anything said of the soul was ineffective, inasmuch as a soul without God is non-existent, in the same way as without the sun, light is non-existent. . . . But Rāmānuja was absorbed in his thoughts; and continued dictating further but Kūreṣa had come to a full stop. This incensed Rāmānuja, who cried;—"Sir, if *you* wish to write the commentary on the *Vyāsa-Sūtras* (*Brahma Sūtras*) you may do so," and kicked him and ceased dictating. . . . Rāmānuja by the time, reflected over the whole position in his retreat; and it flashed on him that his omission to define the soul as *that which is belonging of God* was a grave mistake inasmuch as the essentiality of soul was the very foundation of theology.[18]

As the accurate report of a historical incident, this story raises a number of problems, especially since the *Vedārthasaṃgraha,* which was definitely written earlier than the *Śrībhāṣya,* is dominated from start to finish with the doctrine of the śeṣī-śeṣa relationship. Yet it is quite possible that this story is based on an actual incident, or perhaps on the memory of numerous discussions between Rāmānuja and other Śrī Vaiṣṇavas concerning this point in the first few years after Rāmānuja came to Śrīrangam. It would seem rather curious for the subsequent tradition simply to have invented an incident that reflects so little credit on either the sagacity or the behavior of its greatest teacher, who was worshiped by his followers as a veritable reincarnation of Rāma's brother Lakṣmaṇa and who was also called Yatirāja, "the prince among ascetics."

If the substance of this account is historical, it is a further piece of evidence that Rāmānuja started out as a young man with a primarily Vedāntic training and only gradually learned and accepted the emphasis of the Śrī Vaiṣṇava tradition. By the time of what is presumably Rāmānuja's first extant work, the *Vedārthasaṃgraha,* he had evidently thoroughly assimilated these traditions and constructed his own synthesis.

According to this incident, Rāmānuja had to be reminded by one of his followers of the second relational definition of the finite self, which in the Śrī Vaiṣṇava doctrine of the soul must accompany the first definition drawn from the Upaniṣads. This story reveals more than a preference of Rāmānuja for the Upaniṣadic teaching or a result of his long training in Vedānta; it also shows that his first thought about svarūpa was as a distinct essence or substance, not as a definition of a relation to other entities. The first definition is the same for the finite self and the Supreme Self; they both have the nature of consciousness, whose knowledge of itself is sheer joy. For the finite self, however, this definition has to be supplemented, since it owes its very existence to the Supreme Self, for whom and in whom it exists. In the case of the Supreme Self, on the other hand, who is completely self-subsistent, *His essential nature can be defined without reference to His relation to any other entity.*

It is true in Christian theology, also, that God's creatorship, however important it may be in the believer's conception of Him, is not part of His essential nature but a continuing act of His will, for God could have chosen and could choose not to create at all. Christian theologians can include love in the essential nature of God, not because of God's love for His creatures, for there might not have been any creatures to love if God had willed otherwise, but because of the love within the Godhead itself among the three Persons of the Trinity. Since *kāruṇya* (mercy or compassion) is a Divine quality in relation to finite beings, it can be understood why Rāmānuja says that this quality and innumerable others are not essential to the definition of the Infinite Being, in and for Himself. This no way implies a lack of importance ascribed to the Divine mercy or to any other qualities expressing or implying relations to the cosmos.[19] In fact, Rāmānuja spends most of his time talking about these relations, because for him Reality does not consist solely of Infinite Being (as for Śankara); it consists of the Infinite Being in relation to finite beings, which are independent realities, yet parts of God's own Reality.

7 The Five Defining Attributes of God's Essential Nature

The Divine Svarūpa as the Central Aspect of God's Supremacy

The concept of paratva is sometimes used by Sudarśana Sūri and Vedānta Deśika to indicate one group of the *nirūpita-svarūpa-viśesaṇas,* the other group of such "nonessential" attributes expressing the Divine saulabhya. Elsewhere, however, especially with Sudarśana Sūri, paratva—or its equivalent, īśitṛtva (essential lordship)—is taken to include, or even to be identical with, the svarūpa of God.

The first classification might seem to be more logical, since both paratva and saulabhya refer to groups of qualities expressing God's *relation* to other entities, whereas the Divine svarūpa in the strict sense is the Divine "whatness," which does not imply a relation to any other entity. However, it is the definition giving Brahman's relation to the universe that Rāmānuja most emphasizes, a definition that emphasizes Brahman's supremacy, the fact that He is higher than any other entity. The fact that Brahman is superior to the finite self must be brought out in defining Brahman's essence, as well as His relation to the existence of these entities, for He is an ātmā or puruṣa like the finite selves. It is therefore imperative to define His essential difference from them, as well as His existential relation to them.

Rāmānuja's concept of the Divine supremacy includes the five defining attributes of the Supreme Self, as well as all other secondary or nondefining qualities that express God's supremacy over all other entities. The other groups of qualities expressing God's accessibility (saulabhya) are separated from or contradictory to the essential nature of God; they are further qualifications of the essential nature already defined, but these five defining qualities taken as a group already imply supremacy (paratva), since they all are defined in such a way as to contrast distinctively with finite selves. The five defining qualities would not seem logically to imply īśitṛtva (essential lordship), which concerns a *relation* to other existing entities. Rāmānuja's own usage, however, supports Sudarśana Sūri's classification, for Rāmānuja deals at the same time with both the essential nature of Brahman and His relation to other entities. We see this in the opening paragraph of the *Vedārthasaṃgraha* as well as in the comments on the second sūtra in each of his three commentaries on the *Vedānta Sūtras.*

In the *Vedārthasaṃgraha* Rāmānuja first defines the essential nature of the finite self as being free from the distinctions of the material bodies in which it resides and as being in essence wholly characterized by knowledge (jñāna) and bliss (ānanda). Then follows the definition of the Supreme Self (Paramātmā), who is described as the Inner Ruler (Antaryāmī) of the finite self. His essential nature is defined as follows:

> the sole cause of the origination, continued existence, and dissolution of the universe . . . and of the cessation of saṃsāra. His essential nature is distinct from all other entities because He is opposed to all evil and is wholly infinite perfection [kalyāṇatā]. He has a host of such auspicious qualities [kalyāṇa-guṇas] which are countless and of matchless excellence. He is known throughout the Upaniṣads by various terms such as "the Self of all," "The Supreme Self," and "Being." He is the Lord [Bhagavān], Nārāyaṇa, the Supreme Person [Puruṣottama].[1]

It is interesting that following a definition of the finite self in terms of its essential qualities of knowledge and bliss, these same essential qualities are not mentioned in the definition of the Supreme Self, but the emphasis is on His being the sole cause (kāraṇa) of all the changes in the state of finite beings, both souls and material objects. It is quite clear that the qualities of knowledge and bliss are simply assumed for the Supreme Person, since He, too, is a "self," though one of a unique nature. Being the cause of creation, and so on, is regarded as the fundamental distinction between the Supreme Person and other beings, but the term *distinction* or *distinctive nature* (vilakṣaṇa) is reserved for the second part of the definition. He is distinct from all other entities because of His perfection, both in the negative sense of being the antithesis of everything which is defiling (that is, inauspicious) and in the positive sense of being wholly auspicious in nature, possessing a plentitude of unsurpassably excellent attributes.

The third part of the definition gives the most important names by which Bhagavān-Nārāyaṇa, the Supreme Person, is known in the Upaniṣads, which are regarded as the very source of the knowledge of Him. These names indicate three essential points: He is the ultimate Reality (sat, tattva); He is *the* "Self" (ātmā); and He is Supreme (para, parama, uttama). It is this last quality, in particular, which defines His distinctiveness from all other entities. Para here means "higher than," not "other than"; but it is being immeasurably higher than all other beings, utterly surpassing them in excellence, that constitutes His "otherness" from finite beings. At the same time He is also "under" and "encompassing" all other entities.

The *Vedārthasaṃgraha* then continues with a detailed examination of the passage in the *Chāndogya Upaniṣad* called the *Sadvidyā,* "the knowledge concerning Being," which is taken to prove that the One who is infinite Being produces the variety of finite beings out of Himself, sustains and directs them, and finally terminates their phenomenal existence.[2]

The interpretation of the second sūtra, "from whom is the origin etc., of this universe," is quite different in the *Vedāntasāra,* where it forms an introduction to the work as a whole, than in the *Śrībhāṣya,* where it is a relatively brief comment. (The comment in the *Vedāntadīpa* abbreviates the first part of the comment in the *Śrībhāṣya.*) In both comments, however, there is the same connection of ideas that we have just seen in the *Vedārthasaṃgraha.*

The *Vedāntasāra* first notes the text on which the sūtra is based: "From whom all other beings are born; by whom when born, they are all preserved and to whom they go back when they perish—do you desire to know that well, that is the Brahman" (*Taittirīya Upaniṣad* 3.1.1). That Brahman is this cause is proved by the text from the *Chāndogya Upaniṣad* just referred to (6. 2.1 and 3): "Being alone, my dear boy, this was in the beginning: one only without a second. . . . It thought 'May I become many and be born.'" The next question dealt with is how a perfect Brahman can create an imperfect universe. We are referred to later sūtras for the answer to this question, but the question itself introduces the main topic in this comment: the demonstration by citing the relevant texts that Brahman is superior to and distinct from the finite self. The three passages from the *Śvetāśvatara Upaniṣad* and the one from the *Bhagavadgītā* all make the same point: Brahman is the cause of the universe and is distinct from both the two other types of reality, finite selves and matter, over which He rules. It is the passage from the *Bhagavadgītā* (15.16-18) which is perhaps most important, because the *Gītā* here mentions three of Rāmānuja's favorite metaphysical designations for Brahman: Puruṣottama, Paramātmā, and Īśvara. It is He who "supports the three worlds, having entered them." "Because I transcend the destructible beings and am also higher than the indestructible finite self, I am celebrated in the world and in the Veda as the Supreme Person."[3]

"That from which" or "from whom" (yataḥ) is defined in the *Śrībhāṣya* as

> that Supreme Person who is the Lord of all, whose essential nature is opposed to everything defiling, whose will is ever accomplished; who possesses an infinite number of auspicious qualities, first among which are knowledge and bliss; who is omniscient, omnipotent, and supremely merciful; from whom the creation, continued existence, and reabsorption of this world proceed—He is Brahman. That is the meaning of this Sūtra.[4]

The rest of the comment is taken up with answering a double objection: first, that the passage referred to by this sūtra does not, by means of the characteristics (lakṣaṇas) it mentions, make possible a knowledge of Brahman, since each of the different attributes could indicate a different Being; and second, that these attributes of creatorship, and so on, are not capable of defining Brahman as secondary characteristics or initial pointers (upalakṣaṇas) to His nature, since secondary characteristics are only useful if the thing to which they refer is already known in some other aspect. Rāmānuja answers the second part of the objection first. The "cause of creation," "cause of continued existence," "cause of dissolution," and so forth, serve as upalakṣaṇas pointing to a Being already known, for the very name "Brahman" indicates something about His nature. As was stated at the beginning of the comment on the first sūtra, the word itself indicates one possessing essential greatness (bṛhattva) and power of growth (bṛṃhaṇa). Moreover, the relative pronoun *which* or *whom* refers to something already known from the *Sadvidyā* of the *Chāndogya Upaniṣad* referred to above. The one principle denoted as "being" (sat) is the material and efficient cause of all. The first part of the objection is also refuted, since Brahman's being the Creator, and so on, can also be regarded as His distinguishing characteristics (lakṣaṇas), for these three statements characterize the same single Being (not three different deities).

THE FIRST FOUR DEFINING ATTRIBUTES: SATYA, JÑĀNA, ANANTATVA, AND ĀNANDA

The comments in the second sūtra noted thus far are also presented in an abbreviated form in the *Vedāntadīpa.* Only the *Śrībhāṣya,* however, has an additional paragraph defining three of the essential attributes of Brahman.

> [This text] teaches us that Brahman is the cause of the origination, etc., of the world, and of this Brahman thus known, the other text "True Being, Knowledge, Infinite is Brahman" tells us that His essential nature marks Him off from everything else. Here the word "true being" [satya] describes Brahman as possessing unconditioned [nirupādhika] being, thus distinguishing Him from nonintelligent matter, which is subject to change, and from intelligent beings, which are linked with such matter in the created world, for since both souls and matter are capable of entering into various states called by different names, they are excluded from the possibility of unconditioned being. The word "knowledge" or "consciousness" [jñāna] describes the state of permanently uncontracted knowledge, thus distinguishing [Him] from released souls, whose knowledge was at one time contracted. The word "infinite" [ananta] describes [His] essential nature as free from all limitations of place, time, or particular substantial nature. Since this essential nature possesses qualities, [His] infinity is grounded in both [His] essential nature and [His other] qualities. By this [qualification of infinity] the eternally free souls [nityas], who are distinct from the two classes of souls excluded from this definition of Brahman by the two previous terms [satya and jñāna], are also excluded, for their essential nature and qualities are not [like Brahman's] of unsurpassable excellence.[5]

Rāmānuja interprets this Upaniṣadic definition of Brahman in such a way as to exclude one after another of the three kinds of finite selves, as well as the matter in which the first group of souls are embodied. Since this is the case, the properly differentiating attribute is the last, since its definition shows that even those fortunate souls who have never been enmeshed in saṃsāra and have always enjoyed God's transcendent realm do not, in the strict sense, share Brahman's essential attribute of infinity.

Following the Sūtras, Rāmānuja also describes the finite self as *aṇu* (atomic or tiny), as contrasted with Brahman, who is *sarvagata* (omnipresent).[6] This distinction between the "atomicity" of the finite self and the pervasiveness (vibhutva) of the Supreme Self is taken by Rāmānuja's followers as one of the primary distinctions between the two.[7] Rāmānuja himself seems more interested in the more basic difference in nature underlying such distinction in "size."

Rāmānuja brings this out by his comment on the *Bṛhad-Āraṇyaka Upaniṣad* (2.3.6).

> There is no other substance higher [para] than that Brahman who is designated by the phrase "not so," which means that there is nothing more exalted [utkṛṣṭa] than Brahman either in essential nature or in attributes. . . . Finite selves [prāṇas] are "true" or "real" [satya] because, unlike the material elements, they do not undergo changes which alter their essential nature. The Supreme Person [Paramapuruṣa] is the reality [satya] of these souls, because while they undergo contraction and expansions of consciousness in accordance with their karma, He who is free from all sin knows no such alteration. Therefore, He is indeed their reality [satya—namely, more real than they].[8]

The essential quality of ānanda is dealt with separately because it does not occur in the primary text discussed above, *satyam-jñānam-anantam-Brahma,* but it is regarded as equally essential. Ānanda is also an essential attribute of the finite self, but Rāmānuja insists that the title "Ānandamaya" (*Taittirīya Upaniṣad* 2.5), which he takes to mean, "full of bliss," refers specifically to Brahman, not to individual souls. This is, in the words of the sūtra (1.1.13), "on account of multiplication":

> This section [*Taittirīya Upaniṣad* 2.8] . . . by multiplying each succeeding bliss by a hundred, reaches that bliss which is the very summit of an unsurpassable excellence [niratiśaya-daśāśirasko' bhyasyamāna]. Such bliss is not possible for the finite self, which enjoys only a small share of limited happiness mixed with infinite unhappiness. Consequently it clearly indicates as its abode the Supreme Self alone, who is opposed to everything defiling, composed entirely of what is auspicious, and distinct in character from all other beings.[9]

AMALATVA

The fifth of the defining attributes is *amalatva* (purity; literally, stainlessness). Every description of Brahman by Rāmānuja, however brief, includes (and usually begins with) such a phrase as *nikhila-heya-pratyanīka* (opposed to everything defiling), or *nirasta-nikhila-doṣa-gandham* (free from all trace—literally, scent—of evil or imperfection). The importance of this quality in differentiating the Supreme Self from the first self is indicated in the following passage:

> To comprehend a certain substance [vastu] is to comprehend its distinctive character [asādhāraṇa-ākāra]. But bliss and the other essential attributes without further qualification [kevala] do not suggest Brahman's distinctive character, since they also belong to the finite self. What are distinctive or peculiar [literally, uncommon (asādhāraṇa)] to Brahman are bliss and the other essential attributes which are of such a nature that they are [fundamentally] opposed to what is evil or defiling [heyapratyanīka]. The finite self, on the other hand, although in its proper nature it is free from evil, is capable of connection with what is evil. To have the nature of being [fundamentally] opposed to evil means to have the character which is the opposite of grossness and all similar qualities that belong to the empirical world, in both its material and its intelligent aspects.[10]

Immateriality, however, is only the negative and more superficial definition of amalatva. Earlier in the *Śrībhāṣya,* Rāmānuja defines it as follows:

> To be free from evil [apahata-pāpmatvam] is to be free from karma [apahata-karmatvam], which means to be free from even a trace [gandha] of subjection to karma. Finite selves are subject to karma since they experience pleasures and pains determined by [obedient to] their karma. . . . Therefore the quality of being free from evil is the attribute of the Supreme Self alone, who is different from the finite self. Based upon this [quality] and conditioned by His essential nature are certain other scriptural designations: His being "the Lord of the world and the desires," "the One whose purposes, etc., are ever realized," and "the One who is the inner Self of all." All these are attributes of Him alone.[11]

So far we have seen that the fact that the Supreme Person is free from and essentially opposed to evil shows one basic distinction between the Lord and the individual soul. There are at least three other reasons for Rāmānuja's emphasis on this doctrine. First, there is his desire to provide an alternative interpretation of a term that was the favorite of his most powerful philosophical adversaries, the Advaitins. This Upaniṣadic term is *nirguṇa,* and it is interpreted by Advaitins to refer to the absolute nature of Brahman grasped only at the higher level of knowledge, a nature devoid of any qualifications or distinctions whatsoever; hence nirguṇa (without qualities). Rāmānuja, however, denies that there is any being higher than the Lord possessing infinite auspicious qualities, who is Himself the Supreme Brahman, and he therefore applies both terms, *saguṇa* (with qualities) and *nirguṇa,* to the Supreme Person. "Those texts stating that He is without qualities [nirguṇa] are also well established, since they pertain to the negation of the defiling qualities of material nature [prākṛta-heya-guṇa]."[12]

The second reason for Rāmānuja's emphasis is his desire to show that it is possible for Brahman to be embodied in, and to be in contact with, imperfect and sinful beings, both material and spiritual, without detracting from or contradicting His perfection. Rāmānuja denies that embodiment proves dependence on karma (and hence contact with evil), since a being who has the power of realizing His will can simply will to assume a body. Nor is the body of the Supreme Self subject to the defects of material nature (prakṛti), for it is not an effect of prakṛti but a body that is in accordance with His own desire and suited to His own nature.[13]

In this sūtra (1.1.21) Rāmānuja applies this principle to show that God's bodily form is pure, both in the transcendent realm and in the particular bodily shapes that God assumes for the benefit of His worshipers. In sūtra 1.2.8 he applies it to a different kind of "embodiment": the presence of the Supreme Person within the heart of the devotee, to further his meditation. The Supreme Self dwelling within the finite self does not experience the pleasure or pain of the latter's body, for such experience is brought about by the karma of that self. This subjection to karma is impossible for the Supreme Self, who is free from evil.[14]

In sūtra 3.2.20, the same conclusion is reached about the general embodiment of Brahman in the universe.

> Although ether [ākāśa] is separately contained in each one of a number of objects such as jars and pots that undergo increase and decrease, it is not itself touched by their imperfections. So also the sun, although it is seen reflected in a number of bodies of water of unequal size, is not touched by their in-

> crease and decrease. Likewise the Supreme Self, though dwelling within various shaped beings some material, like the earth, and others intelligent, remains untouched by their imperfections, such as increase and decrease, remains one though present in them all, and keeps His store of auspicious qualities untouched by even a trace of imperfection. The sun reflected in the water is not affected by any of the imperfections of the water because it is not itself in the water. The Supreme Self does really dwell within the earth, but still there is an analogy with the sun's reflection, for His nature is so essentially antagonistic to all imperfection that there is as little reason for Him to participate in the faults of others as for the sun to be involved in the imperfections of the water into which it shines.[15]

The final and most important reason for Rāmānuja's emphasis on God's purity and radical opposition to evil is that this was a deeply held conviction. This is one half of the *ubhayalingatva,* the fact of God's possessing dual characteristics, the second half of which is His possession of a host of auspicious qualities of matchless excellence. There is nothing which is more characteristic of Rāmānuja's theology, as it is reflected in the memories of his followers as well as in his own writings, than this emphasis on the perfect nature of God, meaning both "without imperfection" and "full of all possible perfections."

The words which Rāmānuja uses for absence of evil convey something of his feeling about the evil being opposed and thus, indirectly, about the One who is its complete antithesis. In addition to the Upaniṣadic terms, *pāpman* (evil), *doṣa* (fault), and *mala* (dirt, filth, impurity), there is the word *heya,* appearing in the frequent phrase *heyapratyanīka* (opposed to evil). Heya is used as a synonym for the previous terms, but it seems to have the same overtones as mala, for its literal meaning is "what is to be shunned or avoided." Therefore, "abhorrent" might seem the best literal translation, but I have usually translated it as "what is defiling," since this is part way to the more abstract and general term *evil,* indicates the close relation in meaning to mala, and forms a proper opposite, in cultic terminology, to *auspicious.*

In South Indian religion of both village and temple town—as indeed in many other religious cultures in most parts of the world—these opposite concepts of the auspicious and the defiling play a most important role, not only in temple worship but in all the rituals of the life cycle and the changing seasons performed in the home. On the one hand, there are powers that promote the growth and well-being of creation, while on the other, there is all that is connected with death and decay and with the unfriendly powers working for man's destruction.

One of the contrasts between Vaiṣṇavism and Śaivism in South India is that the latter has absorbed more of the mysterious daemonic elements, apparently abhorrent and opposed to human welfare, into the concept of Deity itself, whereas Vaiṣṇavism has tried to make a clear distinction, to restrict itself to what is pure, *sāttvic*—having the nature of *sattva,* the purest of the three constituent attributes of prakṛti.[16] This is a possible explanation of one of the earliest names of the Vaiṣṇava sect, the Sātvatas. The Vaiṣṇava emphasis on pure materials is reflected in the strong preference of Rāmānuja and his followers for sāttvic scriptures and sāttvic worship.

Something of this feeling can be seen in the words Rāmānuja has the opponent speak at the beginning of the adhikaraṇa discussing Brahman's dual characteristics (ubhayalingatva).

> Therefore even if a being is not subject to karma, its connection with various kinds of impure [aśucita] bodies is defiling [apuruṣārtha]. Hence even when a being voluntarily enters into such bodies in order to rule them, connection with imperfection is unavoidable, for immersion in pus and blood, even if done voluntarily, is nevertheless surely defiling.[17]

There can be little doubt that Rāmānuja shares the feelings of his opponent (Pūrvapakṣin) about defilement, and it is therefore of special interest to note that he does not simply identify impurity with dirt in the literal sense, namely, with the earth and its material constituents. In his comment on the next sūtra he directly answers the Pūrvapakṣin.

> Not so, we reply, for not even material things are defiling by nature. However, according to the nature of the deeds of these beings who are subject to karma, one thing, solely by virtue of the will of the Supreme Person, causes pain to one man at one time and pleasure at another, or pain to one man, and at the same time pleasure to another. . . . Therefore, because of the finite self's subjection to karma, its connection with this thing or that may be defiling, if so determined by

> its particular karma, but for the Supreme Person, who is subject only to Himself, this very same connection may indicate only His delight in His sport [līlārasa] which takes the form of His rule of each of these various things.[18]

It is this understanding of the Divine "purity" that makes possible the more celebrated doctrines of Rāmānuja, that the cosmos is God's body and that it is—if we only have pure enough eyes to see—like His transcendent realm, a manifestation of His glory (vibhūti).

RĀMĀNUJA'S EMPHASIS ON GOD'S PERFECTION

This concern for God's unsullied perfection is evident in Rāmānuja's explanation and defense of the important Vedāntic doctrine that the knowledge of Brahman can be gained only from the Scriptures.

> Hence only the Śāstras [Scriptures in the broadest sense] are the authoritative source of knowledge concerning the Supreme Person, the Lord of all, who is the Supreme Brahman. There is no possibility for even a trace of any imperfection due to His similarity in nature to the things known by the ordinary source of knowledge, since the Scriptures declare Him to be entirely distinct in character from all the substances known by these other means of knowledge, to be an ocean of bountiful qualities, which are immeasurable and of matchless excellence, such as possessing universal knowledge and having His will ever accomplished, and being in essential nature radically opposed to everything defiling.[19]

The defense of God's perfection is also one of the recurrent themes in Rāmānuja's sharp attack on the rival schools of the Vedānta, the Kevalādvaita or Māyāvāda of Śankara and the two varieties of Bhedābheda. It is, to be sure, not the only one. There are two others which are emphasized in the long comment on the first sūtra: first, the existence of the finite self as a knowing subject, a real entity, and an independent center of consciousness, which can know and love the Supreme Self; and secondly, the reality of the world that God has made and the reliability of the means of knowledge that He has provided to know that world.

Since many of the Western studies of Rāmānuja's thought have concentrated on the mahāsiddhānta of the first sūtra, they give the impression that Rāmānuja's impassioned attack on the Advaita is principally motivated by his concern for man and the universe in which man is living and that the doctrine of God enters only indirectly, to the extent that Rāmānuja is trying to defend the path of devotion as a means of attaining communion with God. Such, however, is by no means the case. There is a specific theological objection to both Advaita and Bhedābheda: they do not properly acknowledge God's perfection. This is also dealt with in the comment on the first sūtra, but not so prominently, probably because it does not bear directly on the question at issue, which is there epistemological rather than theological in the narrow sense; that is, establishing the proper steps in order to arrive at a knowledge of Brahman. Moreover, this point has been dealt with, explicitly and extensively, in the first part of the *Vedārthasaṃgraha,* to which in fact Rāmānuja refers us for a fuller interpretation of the *Sadvidyā.*[20]

The fundamental criticism of the other schools of the Vedānta is made clear right at the beginning of the *Vedārthasaṃgraha,* in the second mangalaśloka in praise of Yāmuna. It is said that Yāmuna has dispelled the darkness of delusion consisting of these (alternative) doctrines, all contrary both to revealed Scriptures and to logic. These are: (1) that "the Supreme Brahman is subject to ignorance and afflicted with illusion and hence undergoes transmigration [saṃsarati]"; (2) that "He is connected with limiting adjuncts [upādhis] and thus is overwhelmed [by the power of karma]"; and (3) that "He is the abode of evil or imperfection [aśubha]."[21]

These three brief characterizations and implied criticisms of the three rival schools are worked out in detail, in the brief summaries of the three schools[22] and in the course of interpreting this passage from the *Chāndogya Upaniṣad,* arguing at length with the Advaitins and afterward briefly with the two varieties of Bhedābheda. Rāmānuja's severest stricture is actually reserved for the third position, that Brahman is at once both different and nondifferent from finite selves, with whom He is identical in one part of Himself. Rāmānuja ridicules this view by comparing this "Brahman" to a man who has one arm adorned with bracelets and rings and anointed with sandal paste, while the other arm is pounded with a hammer and put in deadly flames. How could such a person, happy in one part but miserable in another, be the Lord (Īśvara)? This variety of Bhedābheda is even more blasphemous than Advaita, which ascribes ignorance to Brahman, for at least the immeasurable sorrow with which Brahman is connected is ultimately unreal for the Advaitin, but for this Bhedābhedin it is quite real, and there is no possibility that the state of saṃsāra in which Brahman is suffering will ever cease, since there is an infinite number of souls that remain to be freed from it.[23]

According to later commentators, this third view was that of Yādava Prakāśa, Rāmānuja's guru in Kāñcīpuram. There is a story from Rāmānuja's biography that is quite relevant here, though it would appear from that story and other items in the biography that Yādava was a follower of Śankara. That actually makes little difference either to this critique in the *Vedārthasaṃgraha* or to the story from the biography, for the basic criticism of all these systems is precisely the same: with all their supposed emphasis on the oneness of reality they do not escape the reality of ignorance and the realm of ignorance, and they necessarily involve Brahman in that realm.

Before turning to the story, we should note that the same criticism of the other schools is made in much briefer form in the introduction to the *Vedāntadīpa,* in the conclusion of the important second sūtra of the *Vedāntasāra,* and also in the *Śrībhāṣya* in the comments on both the first sūtra and sūtra 2.3.28. The additional point that is made in the latter reference in the *Śrībhāṣya* and in those in the *Dīpa* and the *Sāra* is that the other schools cannot escape an admission of difference between Brahman, souls, and matter, even in the state of *pralaya* where the three are so inextricably connected that they cannot be distinguished by name and form, and that they thus agree with the orthodox position (of Rāmānuja) in this respect, as well as in their positing of a fundamental nonduality (advaita), which the Scriptures teach concerning Brahman. Rāmānuja's position, however, is the only one that does not involve Brahman in the imperfection of finite beings, since though united to Him as His body and His modes, their imperfections do not affect Him who is the inner Self of that body and the fundamental substance underlying those modes.[24]

The story in Rāmānuja's biography is that one day Rāmānuja was performing his duty as a disciple to massage his guru (or, according to the other account, anoint him with oil) while Yādava was commenting on certain verses of Scriptures. He interpreted the term *kapyāsam* of *Chāndogya Upaniṣad* 1.6.7 to mean: "Brahman has his eyes red like the posteriors of the monkey." Rāmānuja was so grieved to hear this interpretation that he shed a hot tear, which dropped on Yādava's body and startled him. Asked what was the matter, his pupil replied, "I am so grieved that beautiful Vedic lines are so awkwardly construed." When Yādava angrily demanded Rāmānuja's interpretation, the young student gave two alternatives:

> God in the Sun is He whose eyes are like the "lotus which blooms under the balmy beams of the sun" or "lotus which rests on its stalk below." It is to repudiate God to deny Him Person; and when Vedas postulate such a Personality, it is doubly to repudiate Him by reading blasphemous similes into the Vedas, where reverential gravity and grandeur are intended. Such constructions betoken nothing short of heresy.[25]

Yādava was here following Śankara's interpretation, which is possible linguistically but which pointedly raises the question of why Śankara or Yādava would accept an interpretation offensive to the pious reader. Śankara notes that this illustration is not meant in derision, but the question still remains. It seems likely that Śankara did not feel constrained to give a more respectful interpretation because the Person here described is not the Absolute Brahman but only the Īśvara with form and qualities, apprehended by those who have not attained the higher knowledge (paravidyā).

If this Yādava Prakāśa did expound the system of Bhedābheda that bears his name, then his motivation might have been slightly different. While Brahman in one part of Its essence does have the bodily forms of the individual souls with which it is identical, in its original and absolute state Brahman is entirely without form. Hence any description of Brahman with a bodily form must refer to the individual souls, not to the absolute and perfect Brahman.

This story brings out in a striking way, not only Rāmānuja's concern for the spotless purity of God but also his conviction that the transcendent bodily form of the Supreme Person shares in this perfection. There is no objection, it is to be noted, to analogies with the material world as such, but it must be with some beauty, virtue, or excellence of this imperfect world that the Divine Person or the Divine Form is compared.[26]

THE ONE ESSENCE DEFINED BY THE FIVE ATTRIBUTES

The five defining attributes of Brahman just described are not meant to be considered as five qualities of the same order. Jñāna is the fundamental attribute indicating the "whatness" of Brahman. Indeed, it not only is an attribute but may be said to be identical with the essential nature of Brahman, hence the frequent expression, *jñānaikasvarūpa* (whose essential nature is solely consciousness). Ānanda is simply another way of describing the conscious nature of Brahman and may therefore, like jñāna, or along with jñāna, be understood as identical with God's essential nature itself, as in *jñānānandaikasvarūpa* (whose essential nature is solely knowledge and bliss) or when the Supreme Person is occasionally called "Bliss."[27]

In the mahāsiddhānta of the first sūtra, Rāmānuja, addressing the Advaitin, describes the relation of jñāna and ānanda as follows:

> For bliss means an agreeable state of consciousness. Such passages as "Brahman is consciousness and bliss" therefore mean: Brahman is just this consciousness, the essential nature of which is bliss. Now this [the identity of these two qualities] is precisely the homogenous character [ekarasatā] [of Brahman], on which you so insist. We have already said that hundreds of texts teach that Brahman, whose essential nature is knowledge, is at the same time the knowing subject [underlying that knowledge]. In the same way, other texts show that Brahman is not mere bliss, but a subject enjoying bliss. To be a subject enjoying bliss is, indeed, the same as to be a conscious subject.[28]

This same theme has been taken up in the context of bhakti near the end of the *Vedārthasaṃgraha.* There devotion is described as a kind of love (prīti) and this love as a kind of knowledge.

> Knowledge that has a pleasing object and is pleasurable, is itself pleasure or happiness [sukha]. . . . The pleasure associated with the knowledge of objects other than Brahman is limited and impermanent, but in the case of Brahman, this knowledge, which is of the nature of happiness, is infinite and permanent. This is the meaning of the text, "Brahman is bliss." . . . Since Brahman is "delight" [rasa], one is happy when He has attained Brahman. The Supreme Person, who is happiness of matchless excellence by Himself and in Himself, also becomes happiness to others, since He is unqualifiedly of the nature of happiness.[29]

Here we find an analysis of one of the essential attributes of

Brahman which compares it with the happiness of finite selves. For our study of paratva it is important to note that this quality of Brahman is an infinite magnification of what is purest in *all* objects, not only in other (finite) selves; but, on the other hand, any true happiness of the finite self is derived from the source of supreme happiness. When we consider the relations of the Supreme Person to other entities in chapter 11, we shall return to the end of this paragraph (omitted from the above quotation), where Rāmānuja emphasizes the doctrine of *śeṣatva,* the essential subservience of the finite self to its Master and Owner, who is God.

8 The Supreme Creator

Brahman as the Material and Efficient Cause of the Universe

In many of his descriptions of the Deity, Rāmānuja has put first the fact of His being the cause of everything (sarva-kāraṇatva). In commenting on sūtra 1.1.21, he gives examples of three kinds of texts describing God. The first group declares that the Supreme Brahman is the sole cause of the entire universe. The second group defines His essential nature as true being, knowledge, infinity, and bliss. The third group first denies that He has any of the defiling qualities of material nature (prākṛta-heya-guṇān), that He is connected with a material body, or that He is associated with the condition of being subject to karma, which is itself the root of connection with matter; then these texts affirm that He has auspicious qualities and an auspicious (bodily) form.[1]

In this analysis of Divine attributes mentioned in different texts, Rāmānuja does not mention purity (amalatva) along with the four defining attributes of Brahman, as he does when he lists the essential attributes to be included in all meditations under sūtra 3.3.13. Instead he includes it, without using the word *amalatva,* as the first half of Brahman's dual characteristics (ubhayalinga). His comment on sūtra 3.2.15 similarly distinguishes the dual characteristics from the essential nature of Brahman. There he is following the line of the objector's distinction. The Pūrvapakṣin understands the text, "True being, knowledge, infinite, is Brahman," to mean that the nature of Brahman consists only of undifferentiated illumination (nirviśeṣa-prakāśa) and contrasts this nature with attributes which are subsequently denied by the text—"Not so, not so" (neti, neti)—and must thus be known to be false (mithyā). These are such qualities as being all-knowing, having His will ever accomplished, being the cause of the universe, being the Inner Self of all, and having His desires eternally realized. To this objection Rāmānuja replies as follows:

> Just as we must acknowledge that the essential nature of Brahman is illumination [namely, consciousness], so that such texts as "True being, knowledge, infinite, is Brahman," will not be deprived of their meaning; so likewise [we must admit that] Brahman certainly has the dual characteristics;

> otherwise the texts teaching the qualities of omniscience . . . etc. [which you just mentioned] and also freedom from such imperfections as ignorance, would lose their meaning.[2]

What Rāmānuja is saying to the Advaitin might be paraphrased like this: we are quite prepared to grant that God's essential nature is infinite and eternal self-consciousness, but that fact is established only on the basis of scriptural texts, and there are many other scriptural texts just as authoritative and on no account superseded by the ones you cite; these other texts tell us about many other qualities of Brahman, which make clear His perfection and His supremacy over the universe. We shall admit that there are different kinds of texts describing different kinds of attributes, but the essential thing to remember is that they are *all true.* If you admit even one to be true, then they must all be true, for they all rest on the same authority of Scripture.[3]

We are justified, then, in differentiating the subject matter of this chapter from that of the preceding chapter, but we may not consider it of secondary importance, since it is equally part of the Divine nature about which the Scriptures teach.

Rāmānuja's understanding of causality (kāraṇatva) is affected by his acceptance of the doctrine of *satkāryavāda,* which, in brief, is the view of the transformation of the causal substance into a new form, but not into a new and different substance. (Rāmānuja here accepted the Sāṃkhya view, along with most Vedāntins, as against that of the Nyāya-Vaiśeṣika school.) Consequently, the causal relation in the strict sense is not, as we might expect, between God as cause and world as effect but between Brahman in His causal state as the cause and Brahman in His effected state as the effect. In both states, souls and matter form part of Brahman as His body and His modes. Causation is what is responsible for the universe in its present state, not for its absolute origination, since finite selves and the fundamental nonintelligent substance underlying material objects are coeternal with Brahman. While, strictly speaking, it is Brahman with His cosmic embodiment who is the effect, the essential nature of Brahman is unchanged in the latter state. It is finite beings whose state (in the case of souls) or nature (in the case of material objects) is radically changed, since they are brought out of the darkness called pralaya into the ordered universe (sṛṣṭi) that the Supreme Person has created or projected.[4]

Brahman is the material cause, since He is the primordial Being (sat)—albeit eternally differentiated into Self and body, out of which this manifest universe (prapañca) has come forth. He is also the intelligent (efficient) cause who orders and directs each new creation. Rāmānuja often refers to the *bahu-syām* (May I be many!) of the *Sadvidyā* as indicating the Supreme Person's fundamental resolve to create a variegated universe. It is true that all this variety was already potential in the causal state of pralaya preceding creation. In that state, however, the intelligent entities and nonintelligent matter were pressed so closely together and so inseparably united with the Supreme Self that their distinctions from one another and from Him, though real, could not be expressed by name and form. Therefore in this state one can speak of Brahman as *ekam-eva* (one only), whereas in the state of creation the differences have become manifest; the souls have been projected into manifestation in material bodies through which they can enjoy the material objects of enjoyment that God provides for them. One of Rāmānuja's briefer expositions of the *Sadvidyā* puts this as follows:

> That which is called "Being" [sat], i.e., the Supreme Brahman, free from any trace of evil, possessing a host of countless auspicious qualities of matchless excellence together with the power ever to accomplish His will, who is the cause of everything, willed thus: "May I be many!" After He had created [or projected, sṛṣṭvā] the entire universe consisting of the elements of fire, water, etc., He caused the whole mass of individual souls to enter into this universe existing in the form of a magnificent variety [vicitra] of material bodies such as those of the gods, etc., each intelligent soul [jīva] into a body befitting its own particular karma where it became the self [ātmā] of that body. Then He Himself, wholly of His own accord [svecchayaiva] entered these souls as their Inner Self and thus evolved names and forms in these bodies which hitherto were mere aggregates of matter; i.e., He made each aggregate a particular thing or substantial object [vastu] that could be designated with a word or name [śabda].[5]

For Rāmānuja, a discussion of Brahman as the cause leads very quickly, as in this passage, to the doctrine of Brahman as the Self within the finite selves. This central metaphysical doctrine will be discussed in the following chapter.

Rāmānuja takes universal causality as a fundamental mark of the Divine supremacy, and since that universal cause is the one Supreme Person, he does not follow the tendency that is so strong in the Purāṇas, and also in the *Pāñcarātra Āgamas,* to interpose a number of intermediate causes or powers between a transcendent Creator and an imperfect universe. Rāmānuja accepts the traditional Vedāntic cosmogony, strongly reliant at this point on the Sāṃkhya philosophy, which describes the various states in the creation of the world. Van Buitenen quite rightly remarks that "Rāmānuja is not particularly interested in the circumstances of world origination beyond the fact that it is a causal process by which the qualified, subtly embodied God as the material cause evolves into the phenomenal world of souls and matter constituting a modus of God as the immanent guiding spirit."[6]

This lack of interest, I believe, is explained by Rāmānuja's absorbing interest in the One who is the supreme cause, which means: He who is the cause in a quite different and more fundamental sense than all finite causes. Thus Rāmānuja holds that the initial resolve to become many is repeated at each stage of the creative process. Such an act of will and intelligent reflection cannot belong to the particular nonintelligent element that is said to originate the following element in the series. Therefore "such thought can only belong to the Supreme Brahman embodied in the mahat, ahaṃkāra, etc." Thus each new effect in the causal process of creation is really from Brahman Himself, and "everything originates from Brahman directly."[7]

Further on in the *Śrībhāṣya,* Rāmānuja applies the same principles to the second main stage in creation, its discrete aspect (vyaṣṭi-sṛṣṭi), which is the differentiation of the names and forms of individual beings. He maintains that this creative act, also, is that of the Supreme Brahman, not of Hiraṇyagarbha (the collectivity of finite selves), which means that in this action, Hiraṇyagarbha simply serves as the body of Brahman.[8]

THE DIVINE SPORT (LĪLĀ)

There is a major objection to the doctrine of Brahman as universal cause which Rāmānuja must answer. Brahman is Himself capable of creating the universe, but *why* should He do it?

> This magnificently variegated creation looks like something which was made for some purpose [prayojana], and there is no possible purpose which the Lord could have had. There

are two kinds of purposes which motivate those who undertake some action after having previously considered what they may thereby accomplish; their own interest, or the interest of others. Since the Supreme Brahman is one whose inherent nature is such that all His desires have already been attained, by creating the universe He does not accomplish any purpose which has not already been achieved. Neither could He have created in the interest of others, for a Being whose desires are all attained would only work for the interest of others, by bestowing favor upon them, and He would not be the cause of a universe like ours, filled with infinite misery of so many kinds, such as pregnancy, birth, old age, death, and hell. If He were to create, He would make a world which was entirely happy. Therefore, since Brahman has no possible purpose, He cannot be the cause [of the universe].[9]

Having thus stated the objections as convincingly as possible, Rāmānuja comments on the answer given in the two following sūtras. The first answer refers to the important Hindu conception of Divine sport (līlā). The sūtra reads: "But it is mere sport, as in ordinary worldly life," and Rāmānuja comments as follows:

The purpose of the One, all whose desires are attained and who is [already] altogether perfect [paripūrṇa], in creating the universe . . . is nothing else than mere sport [līlā-eva-kevalā]. "As in ordinary life," . . . i.e., as we see some great king, who already rules the whole earth and thus has no further opportunity to exhibit his perfect courage, valor, and conquering prowess, engaging in some recreation, like a game at balls, with the purpose merely of sport. So likewise there can be no objection to the view that the Supreme Brahman's purpose in causing the origination, existence, and destruction of the universe, which He does by a tiny act of His will, is only sport.[10]

The comment on this sūtra in the *Vedāntasāra* is slightly different.

For Him who is self-satisfied [ātma-tṛpta] "having attained all His desires" means the availability at all times of all the instruments necessary for giving Him all the enjoyments which He desires. Self-satisfaction is different from the satisfaction derived from enjoyments. Matter and finite selves are indeed the instruments of that very delight in His sport [līlā-rasa] which is distinct from His self-satisfaction [ātma-tṛpti].[11]

The next sūtra is itself unusually long and clear, and Rāmānuja only slightly expands its meaning in his brief comment. The charge to be refuted is this: if Brahman actually created the universe, He would be partial, since He has created beings of such different status, all the way from gods to minerals, and He would be cruel, since He would thus be causing His creatures dreadful suffering. The very brief answer given here is that Brahman is not responsible for either the different rank or the sufferings of created beings, since they are determined by the karma of these finite selves, both in each new embodiment of a soul within the same creation and in the type of body it receives at the beginning of a new creation.[13]

If we put together the objection in sūtra 32 and the twofold answer given in the following two sūtras, we may get some insight into Rāmānuja's understanding of the Divine creative action. God's action in "sport" is both for His own sake (sva-artha) and for the sake of others (para-artha), but not in the sense in which those alternatives are understood by the objector. All purposive human action, except that in a game, is done to gain or accomplish something that one wants but does not yet have. There is nothing that God desires that He does not have eternally at His disposal. This is why He is "self-satisfied." This does not, however, mean that He may not engage in activity that He finds enjoyable in itself and that has no end beyond itself. This is His delight in His sport (līlā-rasa). For such Divine action the material and spiritual substances making up the universe are not the goal but only the instruments (upakaraṇa) or materials (parikara).[13] It is the Divine sport itself which is the purpose of God's creation. In this sense we may say that this universe was not primarily created for the sake of or in the interest of finite beings, for God's spontaneous self-expression in creation is an end in itself.

There are two important qualifications that must be made here, however. First, finite beings cannot complain that creation is against their interest or that God has been partial or cruel, for both the inequalities in status and the sufferings to which the objection referred are the result of the souls' own previous actions in previous embodiments. To this extent God has limited His creative action, since He creates each soul in a body appropriate to the fruit of its previous deeds. This very fact shows that līlā does not mean "aimless" in the usual sense of wandering to and fro without any fixed course.

In the *Vedārthasaṃgraha,* Rāmānuja quotes the statement from the *Viṣṇu Purāṇa,* "Hear the exploits of Him who sports like a boy," and he seems to understand this as referring to the cosmic līlā of God, as well as to the pranks of the boy Krishna.[14] He can understand the text as referring to both, since he also regards the avatāras as descending "in sport," but in the case of avatāras he adds, "so as to help the world." Later in the *Vedārthasaṃgraha,* furthermore, in the middle of the section on the supremacy of Nārāyaṇa, he refers to the avatāras of Viṣṇu as instances of the Supreme Cause entering into His own effects.

When Viṣṇu himself is given the status of an effect (created and finite being) by scriptural texts describing Him as on the same level with

> Brahmā and Śiva . . . this must be understood as a descent [avatāra] by His own will [svecchā], in order to help the universe [jagad-upakārāya] and for the sake of His own sport [svalīlayā]. Thereby He brings to its complete number the number of effects [creatures] of a particular category.

Rāmānuja then gives three examples of this descent to complete the number in a class. It is only in the first example that he uses the word *līlayā;* this refers to the incarnation Upendra, "younger brother of Indra," which may be not only a title of the Vedic deity Viṣṇu, or of the dwarf-avatāra Vāmana, but also a name given by Indra to the youthful cowherd Krishna (the avatāra) after one of his boyish pranks. Rāmānuja is not averse to a play on words when it suits his purpose, so here we may understand, "as a prank" or "just for fun," as well as, "in exercise of His cosmic sport." The second avatāra mentioned is Rāma, and here the qualification repeated is svecchā (voluntarily). The third example is Krishna, and here Rāmānuja states both "voluntarily" and "to relieve the earth of its burden" (bhūbhāra-avatāraṇāya).[15] There is no *or* indicated between these three terms, so it would seem that they are neither synonymous nor mutually exclusive. Thus the term *līla* can be applied to God's actions both in His cosmic creation and rule and in His descent into the phenomenal realm, but action for the welfare of creatures is generally thought of especially in connection with God's avatāras.

There are a few places in his writings, however, where Rāmānuja suggests that even the linking of souls with bodies is a gracious act of God, inasmuch as it is only in this way that they can enjoy this world and eventually attain eternal bliss. This is the second and even more important qualification to be made to the general statement that creation is not primarily for the sake of creatures. Rāmānuja develops this thought in his comment on *Gītā* 3.10.

> Long ago at the time of creation, Prajāpati [by which is meant the Supreme Lord, Nārāyaṇa] reflected that creatures were unable to function because of their entanglement with beginningless matter, that they were without the distinctions of name and form and were submerged in Himself. They were incapable of attaining any of the goals of human life [puruṣārtha] and were fit only for nonintelligent things. In order to resuscitate them, being supremely compassionate [parama-kāruṇika], He created them [or caused them to emanate (sṛṣṭvā)] along with sacrifice [yajña], which He instituted for the worship of Himself, and He said, "By this sacrifice make yourselves increase. Let this sacrifice fulfill your aspiration to the highest human goal of salvation [mokṣa] and all other desires that are in accordance with that highest goal."[16]

Bharatan Kumarappa calls attention to this passage and rightly links this thought with Rāmānuja's statement in the *Śrībhāṣya* that prakṛti is "the means for the experience of pleasure and pain, and for the final release of all intelligent souls." Kumarappa also points to the following sentence in Rāmānuja's defense of the Lord's destruction of wickedness: "What the Lord Himself aims at is ever to increase happiness to the highest degree."[17]

Rāmānuja's comments on the verses of the *Gītā* following 3.10 make quite explicit this connection of sacrifice and material nature, and also the Divine purpose of promoting universal welfare in creating men along with sacrifice. There is meant to be a continual exchange between gods and men: divine gifts to men and the return of these gifts as human offerings to the gods. Thus are gods and men to prosper one another. For men this prosperity includes their eternal salvation as well as worldly blessings, provided that they recognize that it is the Supreme Person who—acting through the lower gods—has granted material gifts so that they may be used in His worship. Rāmānuja emphasizes in his paraphrase that it is the Supreme Lord Himself who has set this wheel of sacrifice in motion. He also emphasizes the teaching of the *Gītā* that the aspirant after eternal salvation, whether he follows the discipline of action or that of contemplation, falls into sin if he does not eat only such food as has been consecrated by first having been offered in sacrifice.[18]

Rāmānuja has presented the general Hindu conception of līlā in such a way as to redefine the idea of Divine purpose in creation. He rejects the objector's identification of both prayojana and artha with "gain," the aim of gaining a desired object not presently possessed. Since sheer sport is itself the purpose of the Divine activity, there is no object that must be gained by that activity. Nevertheless, this activity serves to provide God with enjoyable experience (bhoga), which is in addition to His utter perfection and self-completeness (ātma-tṛpti) and is in this sense "for his own sake" (sva-artha). In the *Gītābhāṣya,* Rāmānuja clearly suggests that the creation is also "for the sake of others" (para-artha), since the manifest state of creation gives finite spirits the opportunity to use their material bodies and material things, by means of sacrifice, to attain release from the transient realm of saṃsāra and to attain eternal communion with the Lord. If we bear in mind that sṛṣṭi is not absolute creation, we can see that there is no contradiction between the Divine prayojana of līla, which affords Him delight (rasa), on the one hand, and the welfare of creatures, on the other. God projects souls and matter into the manifest state at the end of each period of cosmic night (pralaya), but both souls and matter are as such eternal. They are thus not created by God but are the eternal instruments of God's cosmic activity. However, their "creation" in the limited sense of sṛṣṭi (projection into manifestation) is done with the aim of enabling souls to use matter in such a way as both to enjoy the finite realm and to work out deliverance from it to the eternal realm of abiding joys.[19]

THE UNIQUENESS OF THE SUPREME CREATOR

Rāmānuja's central metaphysical doctrine of the body-soul relationship between the universe and God supplies most of the content of this first doctrine enunciated in the Sūtras, that Brahman is the universal and fundamental cause. Therefore the details of God's exercise of creation and control can best be considered in the following chapters, which are concerned with the positive side of God's supremacy, the fact that He is not simply "other" than the universe. Before turning to this next chapter, however, there is one passage in the *Vedārthasaṃgraha* that should be noted, since it most emphatically states God's difference from all other beings and at the same time indicates what is His positive relation to everything else.

> It is impossible for any other entity than Brahman to have another form, kind of nature, or capacity to act added to its own form, nature, and capacity. But this Supreme Brahman, because He is radically different from all other entities, possesses every kind of nature and all possible capacities. This means that it is not contradictory for this one Being to have an infinite and magnificent variety of forms and still to have one single form, since He possesses infinite, immeasurable, and amazing powers. It is true that Brahman is similar to other entities simply by virtue of being an entity [vastu], but this should not lead us to worry that this [possession of a variety of nature, forms, and powers], which would indeed be contradiction for any other entity, involves Him in even the slightest contradiction.[20]

To put this point as sharply as possible: it is precisely because Brahman "is" all things—insofar as He possesses all their distinctive (bodily) forms, their inherent natures, and their various capacities for action—that He differs from all other entities. We can, however, put this same idea the other way round: the difference between God's nature and that of all finite beings is that He includes all finite beings with their infinite variety of distinctive natures in His own infinite Being. He can do this because He is the Inner Self, both of the universe collectively and of each individual being within it. What that means we shall see in the next chapter.

9 The Supreme Self Ensouling The Cosmos

Brahman as Śarīrī and Prakārī

In the course of explaining the *Sadvidyā,* at the beginning of the *Vedārthasaṃgraha,* Rāmānuja states his distinctive metaphysical doctrine as follows:

> The finite self [jīvātmā] has Brahman as its Self, for it is His mode [prakāra] since it is the body [śarīra] of Brahman. . . . All things having one of the varieties of characteristic physical structure, such as the divine form or the human form, are the modes of finite individual selves, since they are their respective bodies. This means that these physical objects, too, are ensouled by Brahman. Therefore all words naming these objects . . . first signify the objects they name in ordinary parlance, then, through these objects, the finite selves dwelling in them, and finally these words extend in their significance to denote the Supreme Self [Paramātmā] who is their Inner Controller [antaryāmī]. Thus all terms do indeed denote this entire composite Being [samghāta]. Thus [this section of Scripture] explains in detail that this entire created universe [prapañca] of intelligent and material entities has Being [sat] as its material cause, its instrumental cause, and its support [ādhāra]; it is controlled [niyāmya] by Being and is the śeṣa of Being.[1]

Rāmānuja then applies this understanding of the passage as a whole to the famous text that is its climax, declaring identity between the cosmic principle (Brahman) and the self (ātmā): *tat-tvam-asi,* "That [Brahman] art thou!"

> Indeed, both the terms *that* and *thou,* when put in a predication of identity [sāmānādhikaraṇya] signify Brahman alone. The term *that* refers to Brahman, who is the cause of the universe, the abode of all auspicious qualities, the flawless and the changeless One; whereas the term *thou* signifies that same Brahman who, because He is the Inner Controller of finite selves, has these selves, along with their bodies, as His modes.[2]

The doctrine that the most significant meaning (mukhyārtha)

of all names is the Supreme Self is a corollary of both of the fundamental relationships here propounded. Rāmānuja frequently expresses this, as in the passage above, by saying that the meaning of all words extends up to or culminates in (paryanta) Brahman. This corollary can be derived from either relationship: the name of a body can properly be applied to the self ensouling that body, and the name of an attribute or mode belongs also to its underlying substance, for this is the significance of coordinate predication (sāmānādhikaraṇya). This corollary, or restatement of the two basic relationships in terms of language, is important for Rāmānuja in his task of reconciling the apparent contradictions of various scriptural texts.

The two basic doctrines are best understood as different conceptions of the same relationship, which in the Śrī Vaiṣṇava tradition has usually been entitled the "body-self relationship" (śarīra-śarīri-bhāva). Kumarappa, however, believes that the substance-mode relationship is "Rāmānuja's own distinctive view of the relation in which Brahman stands to the world."

> The effect, we found, was nothing but a mode of the causal substance; the body also, we have just seen, is nothing but a mode of the self. Hence it follows that all Scriptural teaching with regard to Brahman as cause and world as effect, or of Brahman as soul and the world as body, imply in the end that Brahman is Substance and the world is His mode.[3]

Rāmānuja often says that the body is only a mode, but it is a mode of self or soul. He frequently indicates some causal sequence, and this almost always has the form: "By virtue of being a body [in the instrumental case, śarīratayā] this substance is a mode." Occasionally there is a statement that seems to reverse the sequence: "By virtue of being a mode of a soul, a material body is a definite thing or substance [padārtha]." This means, however, that any material substance has intelligible and substantial reality only when it is a mode of a soul or self, which is the same as saying: only when it is the body of a self.[4]

Bodies have a relation to their ensouling selves analogous to that of generic characteristics and qualities to their respective substances, for the self is the sole ground (āśraya) and the sole purpose (prayojana) of the body, and the body is its mode (prakāra). Rāmānuja defines each of these three qualifications more closely as follows:

> Bodies are altogether dependent on souls as their ontological ground, since they perish as soon as they are separated from a soul. Bodies exist only to enjoy the fruits of their respective karma. Bodies are modes of their respective souls, since they are attributes qualifying these souls.[5]

The same relationship that exists between material bodies and finite selves is also present between finite selves or souls and the Supreme Self. Thus Rāmānuja goes on to say, "Because the finite selves are the body of the Supreme Self, they are modes of that Self; therefore words denoting finite selves extend in their meaning to signify the Supreme Self."[6]

The reason why the soul-body relationship is considered even more fundamental than that of substance-mode is brought out in the answer to an important objection raised in *Śrībhāṣya* 1.1.13.

> It is objected that only generic characteristics and qualities can be predicated of substances [i.e., not one substance predicated of another]. If one substance is the mode of another, that is expressed [not by a predication of identity between the two substances but] by a special grammatical form, in which the suffix *-in* is added to the name of the substance which is the mode, as in *daṇḍin,* "staff-bearer," and *kuṇḍalin,* "earring-wearer." However, this objection is not correct. It is not whether a thing is a generic characteristic [jāti], a quality [guṇa], or a substance (dravya) that determines whether it is possible for it to be predicated of [as identical with] a certain substance, for these categories tend to merge into one another. It is rather its being a mode [prakāra] of some substance that makes it possible for *A* to be predicated of [as identical with] *B,* and being a mode of something else means to have its existence, persistence, and conception inseparably connected with the substance of which it is the mode. The cases where a special grammatical form [root plus suffix] is used are thus [not because two substances are involved but] because the second substance is really independent and only occasionally functions as the mode of something else.[7]

A first reading of this passage might give the impression that the fundamental category being discussed here is "mode." As is frequently the case in Rāmānuja's dialectic, one needs to begin with the objection if he is rightly to understand Rāmānuja's conclusion.

The question here at issue is this: is it possible for one substance to be predicated of another, apart from the recognized exceptional case where the possessor or user of some object like a stick or an earring bears its name? There is no argument about whether generic characteristics or other qualities are modes that can properly be identified with their underlying substances. Of course they are. The question is: are there any substances that are invariably modes of some other substance, namely, are completely dependent on some other substance for their essence and existence? Yes, Rāmānuja replies, bodies are precisely such substances as exhibit a mode's utter dependence on a more fundamental and underlying reality. To say that something is a mode is just a brief way of stating its relationship of utter dependence, but to state that something is a body is to state an irreducible and fundamental fact. Therefore it is this category which is primary. If a material thing is the body of some intelligent self, then it is a mode. Rāmānuja's belief that finite selves constitute the body of the Supreme Self is for him, not the conclusion of a rational argument, but a fundamental fact vouched for by Scripture. It is thus because of this fact that finite selves constitute the body of Brahman that we can say that these souls or selves are modes of Brahman.[8]

THE TRIPLE RELATIONSHIP BETWEEN THE SELF AND THE BODY

What, then, is a "body"? Rāmānuja rejects several possible definitions as not applying to all the different types of entities described as "bodies" in Scripture. Not all bodies are physical bodies made up of the material elements and animated by the life-breath (prāṇa); nor are they all places in which pleasures can be enjoyed. The definition must also apply to all substances, such as the earth, which Scripture describes as the Lord's body, to the bodily forms that released souls may assume, and to the bodily forms that the Lord Himself assumes at His own wish. Rāmānuja therefore defines the body as follows: "Any substance [dravya] that an intelligent being [cetana] is able completely to control [niyantum] and support [dhārayitum] for his own purposes, and the essential nature of which is entirely subservient [śeṣatā] to that intelligent self, is his body." All beings, both intelligent and material, are in precisely the relation to the Supreme Person indicated by these terms, and they therefore together constitute His body.[9]

There is a similar definition given in the *Vedārthasaṃgraha:*

> The relationship between the self and the body is: (1) that between the support and the thing supported, which is incapable of separate existence [pṛthak-siddhi-anarha]; (2) that between the controller and what is controlled; and (3) that between the master or owner and what is subservient to him [or his disposable property].[10]

In the *Gītābhāṣya,* Rāmānuja occasionally makes use of these fundamental concepts to describe both the relation of the Supreme Self with finite selves and the relation of the finite selves with their bodies.

> In the heart of all beings who constitute My body, I am seated as their Self [Ātmā], for to be the "Self" means that I am entirely their support [ādhāra], controller [niyantā], and owner [śeṣī] . . . . Thus, because it controls the body [deha-niyamanena], supports the body [deha-bharaṇena], and owns the body [deha-śeṣitvena], the finite person [puruṣa] is the "great lord" in compari to its body, senses, and mind.

> When one perceives that the selves who are in the bodies of gods, men, etc., by virtue of their being the owners, supports, and controllers of those bodies, are equal because they all have a form entirely of consciousness . . .[11]

In two other passages in the *Gītābhāṣya,* Rāmānuja draws an important distinction between the body-soul relationship on the finite plane and that relationship when God is the Self.

> Know that they all originated from me. They abide in Me, they are My body, but I am not in them, which is to say, I do not depend on them. In other cases, the self, though to be sure the one on whom its body depends, also derives some benefit from its body, but know that there is no benefit in them for Me. This means that My purpose is only and entirely sport.

> I pervade the universe as its Inner Controller [antaryāmī], in order to support it, and by virtue of being its Owner [Śesī]. . . . I am the supporter of finite beings [bhūta-bhṛt], but I derive no benefit from them.[12]

The following chapters will take up in more detail these three descriptions of God's relation to the universe, namely, ādhāra (support or ontic ground); niyantā (controller or ruler); and–most difficult to translate–śeṣī, (owner or master).

THE PERFECTION OF GOD AS EMBODIED SELF

Rāmānuja had to meet the charge that if God were in such a soul-body relationship with the universe, He would be affected by the imperfections of His cosmic body. To refute this objection, Rāmānuja advances a number of related arguments in different contexts. These can be summarized under the following four headings:

1. In the composite being of Brahman, each substance retains its distinctive nature.
2. The imperfections of a body do not affect the self that ensouls it.
3. The Supreme Self is not subject to karma, which is the cause of experiencing pain and other evils, but is Himself the Lord of karma.
4. Not only is possessing bodies no defect for God, but these bodies add to His lordship.

The first argument is that the combination of the material things that are objects of enjoyment (bhogya), the finite selves who are the experiencers of enjoyment (bhoktā), and the Lord, all in one complex being, does not confuse their differing natures, for each retains its own nature. This is analogous to a piece of cloth woven with threads of three or more different colors; each thread retains its own color, and each particular point in the cloth has only the one color of the thread present at that point. The analogy is limited, since the different colored threads can exist separately before being woven together in the cloth, whereas matter and finite spirits constitute the body of Brahman in the causal state before creation as well as in the present world and hence their existence is always as modes of Brahman, never as independent substances.[13]

> It is impossible that material objects, such as sticks and stones, clods of earth and blades of grass, which are subject to constant mutation and are utterly despicable [literally, excessively defiling (atyanta-heya)], should be identical in essential nature with Brahman, who is flawless, immutable, opposed to everything defiling, entirely auspicious, distinct in character from all other entities, essentially infinite consciousness and bliss, and the possessor of various infinitely great realms manifesting His glory. So also it is impossible for the finite spirit, which can

> be connected with infinite misery and which is as inconsequential as a firefly, to have the nature of Brahman, who is known from such texts as "Removed from evil" to be opposed to everything defiling and to be a treasure store of countless auspicious qualities of matchless excellence. . . . In all states [the state of cause before creation and the state of effect afterward] Brahman has spiritual and material entities as His body. . . . There is no confusing the distinctive natures [svabhāva] of material things, finite selves, and Brahman; they are, respectively, being subject to change, being liable to suffering, and possessing a treasure store of auspicious qualities.[14]

Elsewhere, after making the same statement as in the concluding sentence here, Rāmānuja adds, "But because the Supreme Self is their Inner Ruler and Self, He is not touched by their imperfection [apuruṣārtha] and mutation [vikāra]."[15] A very general statement of this second line of reasoning is given in the last adhyāya of the *Śrībhāṣya.* "The conclusion that there is distinction (as well as non-difference) is safeguarded because the Supreme Self is as superior to the finite self as the latter is superior to its body."[16] The point is made more specific in the following comment: "As the attributes of the material body, such as its particular condition at various ages, do not affect the finite self ensouling that body, so the [imperfect] attributes of the finite self do not affect the Supreme Self."[17] This is also very succinctly put: "The Lord of all is not touched by the imperfections of what is [only] His body."[18]

One of the primary tasks, in most schools of Indian philosophy, was to demonstrate theoretically and realize personally the distinction between the material body and the soul within. This principle of the Sāṃkhya was taken over and continued to be emphasized by all the schools of the Vedānta, including Rāmānuja's. It might therefore appear that this single argument would be quite sufficient and, indeed, that the whole doctrine of the body-soul relationship is but a thin disguise for a thoroughgoing dualism. Such, however, is not the case. Rāmānuja takes the unity of the body with its ensouling subject just as seriously as he takes the difference between them. While he thus uses the second argument (the difference of the soul from its body), he does not rest his whole case upon it. Van Buitenen puts this understanding of Rāmānuja's doctrine a little too emphatically, but I believe correctly, in the following comment:

> It is this microcosmic harmony of the soul, as the consciously directing agent and the body as its perfect instrument, which Rāmānuja has elaborated into an analogy for a macrocosmic harmony. It is remarkable that the conception of the body as the defect of the soul has hardly any significance for Rāmānuja: the marvellous utility of the body is for him its most significant function.[19]

Next we come to the third argument, to which Rāmānuja refers many times but which he develops systematically in commenting on sūtra 2.1.14, which tries to answer the objection raised by the Sāṃkhya philosophy that "if the Lord possesses a body, He necessarily experiences all pain and pleasure due to embodiedness, no less than the finite self." Rāmānuja answers:

> It is not because a soul is connected with a body, but because of its karma, the fruit of its good and evil deeds, that it experiences pleasure and pain caused by various bodily states. There are other kinds of bodies than those originated by karma. Other texts . . . show that [the released self] . . . , although he has a body, is not touched by even a shadow of evil [apahatapāpma], although He has the entire universe in both its gross and subtle forms as His body, does not have any trace of connection with karma, which certainly means that He has no trace of evil. The Sūtra states, "As in ordinary life in the world." As in ordinary life those who either observe or transgress the ordinances of a ruler experience pleasure or pain according as the ruler shows them favor or restrains them, it does not follow from the mere fact of the ruler having a body that he himself also experiences the pleasure and pain due to the observance or transgression of his commands.[20]

Rāmānuja then quotes the illustration given in the ancient commentary, the *Dramiḍabhāṣya.* As in ordinary life a prince, even if staying in an unpleasant place, avoids all its discomforts by using a fan and other means of comfort and continues to rule the countries under his sway, enjoying all possible pleasures, so the Lord of creation, whose power serves Him as a constantly moving fan, is not touched by the evils of that creation but rules the world of Brahman and the other worlds and continues to enjoy all possible delights.[21]

The difference between the two illustrations is instructive. The ancient Vedāntic teacher represents God's freedom from evil in a merely negative way: God, he says, has the power to keep the evils of the world over which He rules away from Himself and thus enjoy the pleasures of a ruling prince to the utmost. Rāmānuja, on the other hand, has here interpreted ruler to mean, not enjoyer, but the one who determines the rewards (and hence enjoyments) and the punishments of His subjects. There is no question, for Rāmānuja, of the Lord having to ward off evils which would otherwise afflict Him, since He is by nature such that He cannot catch even a whiff (gandha) of them. This means positively that He dwells in a higher realm, or exists on a higher plane of reality, but at the same time He undergirds, pervades, and controls the transient realm afflicted with evil and marked by imperfection.

The fourth argument that Rāmānuja advances gives further expression to this thought.

> By stating the truth that Brahman is the Self of finite beings, we have not contradicted the truth that He is the very home of auspicious qualities and the antithesis of everything evil and defiling, for the imperfections [doṣa] adhering to the bodies, which are modes, do not affect the Self who is the underlying substance [prakārī] of these modes. On the contrary, it has already been stated that this [embodiment of Brahman] is possible by virtue of the quality which proves His unsurpassably excellent lordship [niratiśaya-aiśvarya].[22]

Similarly, in discussing *pariṇāma,* the "modification" which Brahman undergoes in changing from the state of cause to the state of effect, Rāmānuja explains, "The pariṇāma we teach is not of such a nature as to ascribe imperfections to the Supreme Brahman. On the contrary, it ascribes to Him unrestricted lordship [niraṅkuśa-aiśvarya]."[23]

The word that Rāmānuja often uses to express the fact that the universe is a positive perfection of God is *vibhūti,* the "manifestation of His lordship" or the "realm which He controls." This concept will be discussed in the next chapter.

Rāmānuja has thus tried to demonstrate that the scriptural attribution of embodiment to Brahman is an expression of His oneness with His creation, His lordship over it, and therefore also His distinction from it, and he has tried to show that this concept is thus the key for the understanding of the diversity and apparent contradiction between various passages of Scripture. So Rāmānuja concludes one important discussion of the subject by saying,

Thus the entire group of intelligent and nonintelligent entities, which are different from Him, constitute His body, and He alone is the unconditioned Self ensouling that body [nirupādhikaś-śārīra-ātmā]. For this very reason competent authorities call this doctrine [śāstra] concerning the Supreme Brahman by the name "Śārīraka": the doctrine of the "embodied" Self.[24]

10 The Supreme Ruler and His Realm

Brahman as Ādhāra

There are three pairs of terms used in the definition of the "embodied self" and the "body." The first pair is *ādhāra* and *ādheya*. Ādhāra means support, substratum, or container (of a fluid), and ādheya, though from a different root, is taken to mean that which is supported or contained.[1]

The meaning of ādhāra and its occasional alternative, āśraya,[2] as it concerns the present topic of paratva, the Divine supremacy, has largely been brought out in the two previous chapters. God is the ground of all finite being because He is Being itself, and all beings have come forth out of Him. Rāmānuja uses the familiar Vedāntic analogy of the clay that remains the sole reality in all the things made out of clay.[3] This is only an imperfect analogy, however, for it may lead to Yādava Prakāśa's view that Brahman is as such both the original impersonal substance *and* its subsequent transformation.

Rāmānuja accepts the underlying metaphysical doctrine that the effect is simply a transformation of the cause (satkāryavāda), not a really new reality. This means that both cause and effect have to be interpreted as complex realities consisting of a substance qualified by (and possessing) modes. In both states this primary substance or grammatical subject (prakārī) has the same significance that the material cause had had in the simpler Sāṃkhya conception of causality that Rāmānuja took as his starting point. God as Prakārī is the fundamental reality. In Rāmānuja's usage, causation refers to the transformation in the state of the universe. Brahman qualified by His modes of finite selves and material nature is both the cause (kāraṇa) and the effect (kārya). Therefore the concept of "first cause" cannot for Rāmānuja by itself express God's ontological primacy. It is the concept *ādhāra* that does express that God is the ontic ground of finite being, as well as the cause (both material and efficient) of its periodic transformations of state.

All finite beings are completely dependent (āyatta) on God for their essential nature (svarūpa), continued existence in the phenomenal realm (sthiti), and actual functioning or activity (pravṛtti).[4] Therefore ādhāra is one of the three concepts used in defining

Brahman as the embodied Self (Śarīrī). Finite selves are also the support (ādhāra) of their respective bodies, which could not continue in existence without their support. In their turn, however, these finite selves are supported by a more fundamental Reality, for they are also themselves bodies or parts of the body of the Supreme Self, and He alone is therefore the ultimate ground (ādhāra) of all beings, the self-subsistent Person.

The concept of ādhāra is used to convey one of the most fundamental facts about God's relation to the universe, yet Rāmānuja usually refers to this notion in conjunction with other related ideas. This is partly because ādhāra is an auxiliary concept used to clarify the meaning of the more fundamental categories of "self" and "substance" and partly because some of its meaning is conveyed by the more traditional category of "cause." A third reason for the lack of separate attention to this concept may be that the word *ādhāra,* like the English translations *support* or *ground,* is fundamentally impersonal. It may be, therefore, that Rāmānuja prefers to link this impersonal term with the two other terms used in the definition of the embodied self, *niyantā* and *śeṣi,* both of which have a much more personal connotation for him.

There is one context where Rāmānuja strongly emphasizes the idea of Divine support for His creatures, but we shall delay consideration of that to a later chapter, for that is in the context of God's accessibility (saulabhya). In that context it is especially the word *āśraya* that is used, in the sense of "refuge." In a sense, the "support" that the devotee receives from God is nothing other than the general Divine ādhāra, but in another sense it is different, and certainly the devotee experiences his utter dependence on God in a very special way. The other two concepts, *niyantṛtva* and *śeṣitva,* also have a general meaning in the context of God's supremacy over His creation and a special and in some ways different meaning in His revealing and saving encounter with His devotees.

BRAHMAN AS NIYANTĀ AND ANTARYĀMĪ

The second aspect of the self-body relationship is that between the ruler or controller (niyantā) and that which is ruled (niyāmya). This conception clearly expresses the personal and dynamic character of God's relation to the universe. This relation of ruler to what is ruled also exists between finite selves and their bodies, as we have already seen, but it is most clearly exemplified when God is the Self. The control of souls over their respective bodies is sometimes obstructed and may not be perceived if those bodies are injured or paralyzed.[5]

The verb *niyam* has the basic meaning of "stopping" or "holding back" and the derived meanings of "restraining," "controlling," and "governing." The form of the word that Rāmānuja applies to God, *niyantā* (the one who restrains), was in ordinary parlance applied to a charioteer, who guides his chariot by restraining and thus controlling his horses. (It is perhaps only a coincidence, but God incarnate, in the *Bhagavadgītā,* takes the role of a charioteer.) The noun *niyama* was the word used to designate the second of the eight steps or "limbs" of yoga, that of the "restraint of body and mind." As Ramanuja uses the word, however, the emphasis is less on control in the negative sense than on the positive action of governing or ruling, and niyantā may therefore be translated either "controller" or "ruler." The former may be slightly preferable as indicating the original denotations of the word and as distinguishing it from the many other words that may be also translated "ruler." The word *niyantā* thus approaches the meaning of Īśvara (Lord), but it has a narrower meaning and lacks the devotional associations of the latter word, as well as of the closely related terms, *pati* and *svāmī.* Rāmānuja rarely uses the word as title; it is rather his precise name for one of the essential aspects of God's essential lordship (īśitṛtva), which means, also, of His supremacy (paratva) over His creation.[6]

Since this rule or control is that exercised by the self within its body, God in this aspect of His relation to finite beings may be called the antaryāmī, the "controller within" or the "inner ruler." This name is, in fact, Rāmānuja's favorite name for God in His nature of the Self within the body. He discusses the name first as it appears in the passage from the *Bṛhadāraṇyaka Upaniṣad* (3.7), known as the *Antaryāmi-brāhmaṇa.* There are two versions of this passage, in the Kāṇva and Mādhyandina recensions. Rāmānuja begins with a text common to both versions: "He who dwelling in the earth is within the earth, whom the earth does not know, whose body the earth is, who rules the earth within, He is thy Self, the Ruler within, the Immortal." The passage goes on to apply this teaching, first to celestial bodies and then to the material elements.

The Mādhyandina text has three additional sections, namely, "He who dwells in all worlds," "He who dwells in all Vedas," and "He who dwells in all sacrifices"; and instead of the "He who dwells in knowledge (vijñāna)" of the Kāṇva text, it reads, "He who dwells in the Self." This "controller within " (antaryāmī) is not the finite self (jīva) but the Supreme Self free from evil, Nārāyaṇa. He is the only one who rules all worlds, all Vedas, all divine beings, and so on. He who thus abides within them rules them from within and constitutes the Self of which they are the body. None other than the Supreme Person could occupy such a position, He who is all-knowing and whose will is ever accomplished. A similar passage in the *Subāla Upaniṣad* shows that it is only the Supreme Brahman who has everything for His body, is the Self of all, and rules all (sarvasya-niyantṛtvam). Moreover, the essential immortality (*svābhāvikam-amṛtatvam*) that these texts ascribe to the Antaryāmī can only be an attribute of the Supreme Self. Both versions of the *Antaryāmī-brāhmaṇa* definitely distinguish the Antaryāmī from the (finite) embodied self (śārīram), together with all nonintelligent entities like speech, because it (the finite self) is that which is ruled or controlled (niyāmyatvena).[7]

The meditation which this and other scriptural passages enjoin with the Self as the object is meditation on the Antaryāmī, for they have clearly stated that the life-breath and all other entities originate from the Supreme Self, who abides within the self of the meditating devotee as his Inner Controller.[8]

At the beginning of each complete new creation (at the end of a total dissolution), the Supreme Person remembers the constitution of the previous universe and causes the entire universe present in its potential form to go out from Himself. He first remanifests the Vedas and then teaches them to the cosmic fashioner, Hiraṇyagarbha, whom He entrusts with the creation of the particular classes of beings, just as they are ordained in the Veda and just as they existed in the previous world order. However, He does not then withdraw from this world; He Himself abides in it as its inner Self (antarātmā).[9]

One of Rāmānuja's arguments against the Sāṃkhya philosophy is that the positing of nonintelligent primordial matter (pradhāna) makes it impossible to explain how the state of creation would come to an end.

If there is a Lord to give intelligent guidance to primordial

> matter, then the alternating states of creation and dissolution can be explained by the Lord's power to accomplish all His purposes [satyasaṃkalpatvena]. . . . The Sāṃkhya proponent might well retort that the theory of an intelligent Being guiding creation has faults of equal gravity. (1) He cannot be the cause of either creation or dissolution since all His desires are already attained and He possesses perfect and unsurpassable joy and He would therefore have no reason to create anything. (2) He would be implicated with mercilessness [nirdayā] for an unequal creation. But these objections are not correct. (1) A king who is perfect or complete [paripūrṇa] may still engage in activity for the sake of sport. (2) A particular creation may be due to the omniscient Lord's realizing that the state of material nature requires a new creation, while the unequal status of creatures is caused by their respective karma. . . . [Prakṛti is not, however, an independent agent in creating according to karma], for the essence of good and evil deeds is their pleasing or displeasing the Supreme Person, thus giving rise to His favor or His wrath. . . . The Supreme Person, who is the Lord [Bhagavān] . . . engages in sport befitting His greatness [māhātmya], determine that certain deeds are good and others are bad, and gives finite selves bodies and sense organs and the power of controlling them [tan-niyamana-śakti]. He enters these souls as their Inner Self [antarātmā] and abides within them, controlling them as the One who permits them to act [anumantṛtayā]. . . . When the finite selves . . . have performed good or evil actions according to their respective wishes, the Lord recognizes the one who performs good actions as the one who obeys His commands, prospers him with the four goals of human attainment, righteousness, prosperity, fulfillment of physical desires, and salvation, while He causes the one who transgresses His commands to experience just the opposite of these blessings.[10]

Rāmānuja holds that the finite self is not only a knower but also a doer, an agent. To the objection that the self must be independent of the Supreme Self in its actions if commands and prohibitions can meaningfully be addressed to it, Rāmānuja replies that we must acknowledge that the activity of the soul is caused by the Supreme Self, for this is what Scripture teaches. Nevertheless, the soul is responsible for its good or evil actions, for the Supreme Self, who is the Inner Controller, causes this action (pravartayati) by giving

His assent or permission (anumati) when He has taken note of the soul's volitional effort (udyogam). This is analogous to the permission a man must get from his partner before he can sell jointly owned land to a third person. That permission must be obtained, but he himself is responsible for obtaining it and hence is also the one who must take the consequence, good or bad, of his action in selling. In some exceptional cases, the Lord, when pleased with good actions, engenders a tendency toward further good actions, and when very displeased with evil action, He punishes the agent by giving him a delight in further evil that leads him downward, away from God.[11]

In the *Vedārthasaṃgraha,* Rāmānuja combines these items in a single passage.

> Here another objection may be raised. "You have stated that the Supreme Self is the Inner Controller [antaryāmī] of all creatures and that everything is controlled [niyāmyam] by Him. But if so, no one would be qualified [adhikārī] to obey the injunctions and prohibitions . . . since one is only then qualified if he is capable of acting or abstaining on his own mental initiative. There can be no such person, since you say that the Supreme Self is the one who directs [preraka] all activity and causes all action to be done, which means that He is controlling [niyamanam] everything. . . . Causing both good and bad action to be done would mean that God is cruel." We reply to this as follows: The Supreme Self has endowed intelligent beings in general [or equally (sāmānyena)] with the equipment [parikaram] needed either to perform or abstain from action. In order to enable these selves actually to carry out their actions, He who is their support [ādhāra] enters into them, exercises control [niyamana] as the one who permits them to act [anumantṛtayā], and abides in them as their owner and master [śeṣī].[12]

Elsewhere in the *Vedārthasaṃgraha,* Rāmānuja comments on the passage from the *Manusmṛti* (12.122) which begins, "He who is the ruler [praśāistā] over all," as follows: "This means the controller [niyantā] is the 'ruler over all,' since He enters within [all things] as the Inner Controller [antaryāmī]."[13]

When Rāmānuja's view of God's relation to man's religious action and specifically to man's efforts to attain salvation is discussed in chapter 14, I shall note some of the passages in which the

Antaryāmī or God, present as the "small ether" within the heart, is described as promoting the meditation of the devotee.

VIBHŪTI: THE REALM OF FINITE BEINGS UNDER GOD'S RULE

In understanding Rāmānuja's conception of the nature of God's rule or control, we must study his view of the realm over which that control is exercised. The most important way of describing this realm is that it is the body of God. There was also another important concept in the tradition which Rāmānuja was able to use in explaining God's rule: *vibhūti.* The word itself has a considerable variety of associations. Its etymological meaning as an adjective is taken to be "penetrating" or "pervading." In the *Ṛg Veda* it is used to mean "abundant" or "plentiful" and also "mighty" or "powerful." The noun may mean "development or "expansion" or "abundance" and also "manifestation of might" or "superhuman power." This last meaning is that which the word connotes in Śaivism: those powers of the Lord that the devotee can attain by worshiping Him. The noun also may mean "sovereign power," "splendor," "glory," "prosperity," or "opulence." In Śrī Vaiṣṇavism the word means the manifestation of Divine power and rule. In some of *Pāñcarātra Āgamas* the thought is elaborated that there are two vibhūtis: the manifestation of God in this world is the *līlāvibhūti* (the realm of His sport) or *ekapādvibhūti* (the realm of one quarter of His glory); and His transcendent manifestation is the *nityavibhūti* (the eternal realm), also called the *tripādvibhūti* (the realm of three quarters of His glory).[14]

This is one of the terms that Rāmānuja has defined more than once. This is because the word occurs several times in the tenth chapter of the *Gītā* and is incorporated in the traditional title of the chapter included in all texts: "Vibhūtiyoga." The first definition (verse 7) begins with equating the term with aiśvarya and goes on to explain, "that which is dependent on Me [Krishna] for its origination, existence, and activity" (mad-āyatta-utpatti-sthiti-pravṛtti-rūpam). In verse 19 he defines vibhūti as the state of being controlled or ruled (niyāmyatvam). The other comments on verses in which the term *vibhūti* is used are also instructive. On verses 15 and 16 he comments that as the supreme sovereign who transcends even the gods, just as they do the lower creatures, God alone is entitled to reveal His uniqueness and His vibhūti by means of which He controls (niyamana) and pervades (vyāpya) the world as its

Controller (niyantṛtvena). In verse 18 he interprets yoga to mean creating and so on, and vibhūti to mean controlling (niyamanam). Introducing the section dealing with these most excellent manifestations of God (verses 21-38), Rāmānuja says:

> Because the Lord [Bhagavān] abides as the Self in all beings, which are His own vibhūtis, He may be called by the names of these beings in coordinate predication (sāmānādhikaraṇya), just as the words denoting particular bodies extend in their significance to the souls dwelling in those bodies. . . . Therefore He will expatiate on the various kinds of vibhūtis using such coordinate predication. This enumeration of vibhūtis will include only the most excellent [or eminent (utkṛṣṭa)].

After concluding the list, Rāmānuja sums up its significance: God is the core of all beings, whatever their condition. The totality of beings, both active and inert, cannot exist apart from God their inner Self. There is no end to God's auspicious vibhūtis; the discussion has not been exhaustive. "Whatever pertains to God's vibhūti" in verse 40 means: the whole group of beings that are subject to His lordly rule (īśitavyam). These beings, along with everything bountiful or prosperous and all auspicious enterprises, "originate from a fraction of My splendor [tejas], which is the capacity to prevail over others, which means that they all originate from one fraction of My inconceivable power of ruling or controlling [mama-acintya-śakter-niyamana-śakti]."

There are two comments on the list of excellences that make it clear that Rāmānuja regards vibhūti as the finite creation or mode of God, for when the names of Rāma and Vāsudeva appear (verses 31 and 57 respectively) he comments that the finite selves previously mentioned, like the sun, are attributes, because they constitute the body of Bhagavān. Therefore it must be Rāma's great bowmanship and Krishna's human sonship to Vasudeva which are the vibhūtis in these instances. The unexpressed assumption behind this reasoning is that Rāma and Krishna, in their own persons, are not vibhūtis of God but God Himself.[15] Commenting on *Gītā* 15.6, Rāmānuja says that the light (self-consciousness) of the finite ātmā belongs to God because it is "My vibhūti and My aṃśa (part)."[16]

In the introduction to chapter 15 of the *Gītā,* Rāmānuja says,

> The souls bound to material bodies and the emancipated souls constitute the vibhūti of the Lord [Bhagavān]. The Supreme

> Person who is the Lord, however, is quite distinct in nature from this vibhūti of His . . . since He utterly surpasses it in excellence [atyanta-utkarṣana], for He is radically opposed to everything defiling, and of an entirely auspicious nature.[17]

This same idea is repeated in the summary of the previous chapter given in the introduction to chapter 16. In 16.1, Rāmānuja comments that those who possess a divine nature believe that the entire Veda deals with the Lord (Bhagavān) and His vibhūti and with how to worship Him.[18]

In the *Vedārthasaṃgraha,* Rāmānuja also uses the term *vibhūti* in a number of important contexts, as well as the related word *vaibhava,* which is a more general expression for the manifestation of Divine glory and rule. In one of the opening paragraphs he says:

> Scriptures are meant to set forth God's manifestation [vaibhava] and therefore they use such expressions as śakti [power], aṃśa [part], vibhūti, rūpa [form], śarīra [body], and tanu [embodiment] to express the fact that He controls all intelligent and all material entities, all of which are different from Himself.[19]

This statement is repeated almost verbatim in the *Śrībhāṣya.*[20]

There are two references to vibhūti in the *Vedārthasaṃgraha* in connection with proving Nārāyaṇa's (Viṣṇu's) supremacy over Brahmā and Śiva. "Brahmā and Śiva are likewise His creaturely manifestations [vibhūtis] because they have the same status as such gods as Indra."[21] "The creator and the destroyer are vibhūtis of Janārdana [Viṣṇu-Nārāyaṇa]. The vibhūti comprises Brahmā, Viṣṇu, and Śiva together as a class. . . . Thus it is said that God exists by His own will and for His own sport, within the vibhūti."[22] The term *vibhūti* here clearly denotes the creatureliness of all the many gods who exist within (not above) the cosmos, which is ruled by the Supreme God, Nārāyaṇa.

In a later passage, he uses the expression *ananta-mahā-vibhūti,* which he qualified as "untouched by modification [pariṇāma] caused by time," and follows this with a clause, "an infinite number of intelligent beings, both bound and freed, and the nonintelligent objects for their enjoyment, which are His sport and a part of Himself [sva-līlā-sva-aṃśa]." Rāmānuja's followers have understood "infinitely great realm" to refer to the *nityavibhūti,* His "eternal realm," and have taken the second clause to refer to the *līlāvibhūti,* "the realm of His sport." The presence of the phrase "untouched by pariṇāma" in the first clause contrasting with the ascription to matter of "the power of pariṇāma" in the second clause makes this interpretation possible, but it is to be noted that Rāmānuja does not follow the later terminology of mentioning two vibhūtis; the term appears only once in the passage. Following this paragraph Rāmānuja gives a number of quotations from the *Mahābhārata* and the *Viṣṇu Purāṇa* to support his description of Brahman. These indicate that līlā is connected with the Lord's activity in the changing universe, and they seem to relate vibhūti to His transcendent nature or transcendent state that is not subject to change. This would very well support the traditional view that Rāmānuja is here referring to two vibhūtis, but it is not conclusive evidence, since Rāmānuja may be understanding the term in its more general sense of "glorious manifestation."[23]

Though the terms *līlāvibhūti* and *nityavibhūti* frequently occur in the three later commentaries on the *Gadyatraya,* they are not found in the Gadyas themselves, where the word *vibhūti* is used a few times but without any special prominence. In the *Śaraṇāgatigadya, mahāvibhūti* is used once in the vocative case, meaning, "Thou who possessest the great realm manifesting Thy rule." It does not seem to refer to the heavenly realm, since the title, "Lord of Vaikuṇṭha," follows shortly afterward. Later on, in the sentences explaining what is included in the intuitional experience of the Lord, "My vibhūti" is included in the statement, "My essential nature, form, attributes, vibhūti, and instruments of sport (līlā-upakaraṇa)." In this second case, vibhūti could be interpreted as referring to the eternal realm, since "instruments of sport" include all the souls and material bodies in the temporal realm.[24] In the opening paragraph of the *Vaikuṇṭhagadya* the term *māhavibhūti* occurs as a title of the Lord, but it does not recur in the later paragraphs specifically describing Vaikuṇṭha.[25]

Rāmānuja also uses the term *vibhūti* in commenting later in the *Vedārthasaṃgraha* on the last verse of the "Vibhūtiyoga," the tenth chapter of the *Bhagavadgītā.* (In the *Gītābhāṣya,* he follows the terminology of the text and does not mention vibhūti in his comment on *Gītā* 10.42, since the word itself does not appear in that verse.)

> This [verse] means "Having entered into this infinitely varied and amazing universe as its Self by an infinitesimal part of Myself and supporting everything by My will, by virtue of this form

> possessing an infinitely great realm [ananta-mahā-vibhūti], I remain an ocean of immeasurably generous qualities, for I am incomparably amazing." [The Lord] says the same thing in the verse, "Who can comprehend the incomprehensible form of Brahman, who being one, is many and being many, is one?" By being its ruler, He is One. He enters into the magnificent variety [vicitra] of intelligent beings and material things as their inner Self, and in their several forms He has a variety of modes and causes a variety of actions. Thus He shares in the plurality of forms. In thus entering and supporting the universe of varied forms containing all amazing things—doing this with an infinitesimal part of Himself—He who is the Lord, the Supreme Brahman, the Supreme Person, Nārāyaṇa . . . though He exists in plurality, remains nevertheless essentially *one.*[26]

In this passage, the expression "infinitely great realm" seems definitely to refer to this temporal "universe of varied forms containing all amazing things." It is clear from Rāmānuja's usage in the *Vedārthasaṃgraha* that the term *vibhūti* may apply to God's eternal realm as well as to the phenomenal universe but that the expressions *mahāvibhūti* and *anantamahāvibhūti* are not exclusively reserved for what the later commentators call nityavibhūti, the "eternal realm." The usage in the *Gadyatraya* (whether or not written by Rāmānuja) agrees with the rather fluid meaning of vibhūti in the *Vedārthasaṃgraha.* It makes little difference whether Rāmānuja refers to God's eternal realm as a vibhūti in the same sense in which he applies that term to the finite world, since it is axiomatic for him that God is in full control of His own supreme abode. This passage clearly shows both God's infinite superiority to the universe and its revelation of His wondrous power to create and enter into (pervade) such an amazing variety of forms.

VIBHŪTI: THE FINITE REALM MANIFESTING GOD'S GLORY

The term *vibhūti* occurs much less frequently in the *Śrībhāṣya,* but two of the passages where it does occur are very significant, for they bring out the second important aspect of the meaning of this concept.

> The liberated soul [mukta] experiences [enjoys (bhogyatvam)] the Supreme Brahman, who is free from change, who is of an entirely auspicious nature and is radically opposed to everything

> defiling, and who is unsurpassably excellent joy, along with all His auspicious qualities and that which constitutes His vibhūtis. The mukta thus enjoys even the worlds that are subject to change, since they come within God's vibhūti.[27]

The nature of this finite world, when experienced as the vibhūti of the Lord, is described in a comment on the text beginning, "where one sees nothing else, hears nothing else, knows nothing else, that is fullness [bhūman]" (*Chāndogya Upaniṣad* 7.23). Rāmānuja first explains the context of this passage and concludes that the teacher encourages his student to take up meditation by telling him that the nature of Brahman is bliss that is extremely large and full (bhūman). The text just cited gives a definition of Brahman, and its meaning is as follows:

> When Brahman is experienced as superlative bliss, there is nothing at all to be seen apart from Him, since the totality of beings is included within the essential nature of Brahman and the realm manifesting His glory [vibhūti]. Therefore he who intuitively experiences Brahman as superlative happiness qualified by His attributes and His vibhūti—which may also be called His lordly dominion [aiśvarya]—sees nothing else at all, since it is impossible for any entity to exist apart from Brahman. Nor does he "see" [experience] any sorrow, since all the objects he can experience in that intuition are of the nature of happiness, for happiness is just that which while being experienced is agreeable to man.

At this point the objection is raised that this universe is actually experienced as other than Brahman and as being of the nature of sorrow or only limited happiness. Rāmānuja replies that such ordinary experience is that of souls under the influence of karma. "To him who is liberated from the ignorance in the form of karma, this very same universe, being included in the experience of Brahman qualified by His attributes and His vibhūti, becomes sheer happiness." Rāmānuja compares the experience of the world affected by ignorance to the taste of water to a man with jaundice. Water has an entirely good taste to one in good health, but to this sick man it will taste either quite unpleasant or at best only moderately pleasant. A second example is that of a king's son who has a plaything (līlā-upakaraṇa) but does not know that it is meant to amuse him: he does not care for it. If he learns that it is meant to give him pleasure, however, he becomes very fond of it. "Likewise the world becomes the object of unsurpassably excellent love to one who recognizes that it is ensouled by Brahman and is a plaything or an instrument of the sport [līlā-upakaraṇa] of Brahman, whose essential nature is unsurpassably excellent bliss."[28]

Rāmānuja considered the term *vibhūti* to express the fact that finite being is related to God as a manifestation of His lordship or glory. Vibhūti can therefore be equated with aiśvarya, which means sovereign dominion, but generally it is "dominion" in the sense of being ruled (niyāmya) rather than "dominion understood as the power of rulership or control (niyamana-śakti) that Rāmānuja wants to emphasize about vibhūti. It is always a description of the body (śarīra), not of the self within the body (śarīrī); of the mode (prakāra), not of the underlying substance so qualified (prakārī). This distinction implies no separation, however, and the passage from the *Śrībhāṣya* (1.3.7) makes clear that when our minds have been freed from the false view of things produced by karma we shall experience God's realm manifesting His lordship as having a nature that is good and productive of happiness, like the nature of God Himself. The concept in Christian theology that most nearly conveys the meaning of vibhūti, insofar as it expresses both the finitude and the essential goodness of God's universe, is "Creation": "The heavens declare the glory of God and the firmament showeth His handiwork" (Ps. 19:1).

11 The Supreme Owner and Master

The Definitions of Śeṣa and Śeṣī

We have already noted the curious anecdote from Rāmānuja's biography, which relates that when he was dictating the *Śrībhāṣya* to his disciple and scribe Kūraṭṭāḻvān, Rāmānuja forgot to give the second definition of the soul, that it is the śeṣa of God, which is to say, subservient to God and His own property (see above, chapter 6). Whatever the explanation of that anecdote may be, it is certain that this concept of the śeṣa-śeṣī relationship is one of the most important and characteristic ideas in Rāmānuja's theology. Rāmānuja does not use the terms *śeṣī* and *śeṣa* as often as he does some other central concepts, but without them his definition of the soul-body relationship would be seriously incomplete.

The original meaning of the word *śeṣa* is "remainder," from the root śiṣ (leave remaining), a meaning reflected in the adjective and adverb *aśeṣa,* "without remainder" and hence "entire" or "entirely."[1] One of the derived meanings of śeṣa is "subordinate part" or "subsidiary," and it was used in this sense of "accessory" in the Karma Mīmāṃsā to describe any subordinate part of the sacrifice which was intended to serve the principal purpose, called śeṣī. The śeṣa is thus defined in the *Karma Mīmāṃsā Sūtras:* "One constituent is accessory when it is subservient to another."[2] The śeṣī is that which possesses or is characterized by a śeṣa and hence is "the principal element to which other elements are accessory." Krishna Datta Bharadwaj expresses this Mīmāṃsakā understanding thus: "Śeṣa is a thing which exists for another, and that for which it exists is the Śeṣī."[3]

In both the *Vedārthasaṃgraha* and the *Śrībhāṣya* Rāmānuja defines these terms in the course of a debate with one school of the Karma Mīmāṃsā. Therefore he takes the commonly accepted meaning of these terms in the Karma Mīmāṃsā as his starting point and then goes on to dispute the application or specific meaning that they had been given by the Prābhākara school. His definitions themselves, however, show that he also had in mind another widely understood meaning of śeṣa that had moved further away from the original meaning of "remnant." One of the Sanskrit grammarians defines the terms as follows: "Śeṣa is an object possessed, whereas the possessor is śeṣī."[4]

In the course of the discussion on the meaning of words in the *Vedārthasaṃgraha* Rāmānuja challenges the Prābhākara view that the meaning of words consists in their being commands and that the thing to be done (kārya or niyoga) is the principal element in sacrificial rites. He insists that words refer to *what is,* not to what ought to be done, and that the meaning of action itself (including sacrificial action) lies in the goal to be achieved, not in the action itself. It is in this context that he defines what is the principal point and what is subordinate.

> The śeṣa-śeṣī relationship in any situation means just this: the śeṣa is that whose essential nature consists solely in being useful to something else by virtue of its intention to contribute some excellence to this other thing, and this other [paraḥ] is the śeṣī. Thus sacrifice [or other work] and the effort it entails are undertaken by virtue of the intention of obtaining its meritorious result [phala], while everything else [all the accessories to the sacrifice] is undertaken with the intention of bringing the sacrifice [or other work] to a successful conclusion [siddha]. In the same way, the essential nature of born slaves [garbhadāsa] and other servants is solely that they are beings who have value for their masters [puruṣa] by virtue of their intention to contribute some particular excellence to him. Likewise, the essential nature of all entities, eternal and noneternal, intelligent and non-intelligent, is solely their value for the Lord by virtue of their intention to contribute some excellence to Him. Thus everything is in the state of being subservient [śeṣabhūtam] to the Lord, and He is the master and owner [śeṣī] of everything, as is declared in texts like, "He is the ruler [vaśī] of all and the Lord [īśānaḥ] of all," and "the master [pati] of the universe."[5]

Rāmānuja appears to have borrowed the analogy of the master and the born slave from the view he is criticizing. Van Buitenen translates this reference as follows: "Just as a master benefits a born slave by making use of him for his own purpose, so the niyoga (the thing to be done and its potential for future effects after it is done) benefits the niyojya (the one who desires karmic benefit of the action): but this does not mean that the niyoga loses its status of principal term (pradhāna)."[6] When discussing the identical point in *Śrībhāṣya* 1.1.1. Rāmānuja seems to have the same passage in mind, but he makes quite a different use of it. Whereas in the *Vedārthasaṃgraha* he has tried to turn the tables on the Prābhākara position and reverse the application of śeṣa and śeṣi, in the *Śrībhāṣya* he contents himself with proving that his opponent is not able to make a sensible use of these concepts (in calling the niyoga the śeṣī and the niyojya the śeṣa). In both cases, however, his use of the master-slave relationship as an analogy for the śeṣī-śeṣa relation is his own extension of the citation above, and in both cases he makes a use of this analogy (a different use in each case) that extends its meaning beyond the point at issue.

In the *Vedārthasaṃgraha* he applies the analogy specifically to God and the universe: God is the owner and master, and all His creatures are in the position of slaves. His comment in the *Śrībhāṣya* is as follows:

> Moreover, the śeṣī may not be defined as what is correlative to an action in the interest of something else, for it is just this "being in the interest of" that needs to be defined. Furthermore, we see that the chief person [pradhāna] is capable of action aimed at his servant or dependent [bhṛtya]. If it is objected that in keeping his servant fed the chief person acts in his own interest, we reply, No, for the servant also acts in his own interest when he keeps his master fed.[7]

There is no application here to the relation between God and the world, but what is said about the śeṣī and the śeṣa sheds some additional light on that subject. Rāmānuja points out that the principal object, compared to a proprietor or landlord, is not simply the beneficiary of the action of his servants; he also acts for their benefit. The fact that this action may be in his own interest is irrelevant, for the servant acting for his master's benefit may also be acting in his own interest. In the *Vedārthasaṃgraha,* his definition of the śeṣī was only as the one who is served by the śeṣa and for whose benefit the śeṣa exists. Here in the *Śrībhāṣya* he brings out that the śeṣī also benefits the śeṣa.

In the thought of Rāmānuja's followers, this second idea becomes of major importance. The confidence of the prapanna in his salvation hinges on the fact that it is the function of the śeṣī (the master) to look after his śeṣa (the servant or slave). For example, Vedānta Deśika first defines the Lord as śeṣī, the one for whose purposes material things exist and the master (svāmī) whom intelligent beings are obligated to serve. That is to say, finite selves, in addition to being śeṣas in the general sense of existing to serve the Lord's purposes, are also śeṣas in the special sense of being His servants (dāsāḥ). The general goal of usefulness to the Lord becomes for selves the goal of service (kainkarya), since the self is His servant (dāsa). In consequence of being the śeṣī and the svāmī, the Lord attains a unique glory: the enjoyment of service. Then Vedānta Deśika goes on to the second implication of the Lord's śeṣitva.

> Iswara is responsible for the protection of His servants and has also the power to do so, whereas the *jīva* or *chetena* is not responsible for his own protection nor has the ability to protect himself. This is due to Iswara being the unconditional (nirupādhika) *śeshī* and the unconditional Director and Ruler. Owing to their being the unconditional śeshas and their being subject unconditionally to His control, it becomes, indeed, the responsibility of the owner to protect what belongs to Him and of the strong to protect the weak. Iswara, however, makes up his mind to protect the *jīva* only after making him adopt some means or *upāya* for winning His protection.[8]

The key word in this passage is "responsible," for if the Lord is responsible for the salvation of His servants, it would seem that He is morally obligated to save them. Principal Anantha Rangachar does not believe that Vedānta Deśika intended the doctrine of śeṣitva to be understood as putting the Lord under "obligation" to His creature He suggests that the word *prāpta,* which Rajagopala Ayyangar has translated as "responsible" can better be understood as "function."[9]

This part of the passage above might be rephrased as follows to bring out the concept of "function": "The Lord can protect and save finite selves, and it is His proper function to save them, whereas the finite self is incapable of saving himself by his own effort, nor is it his proper function to do so." Rather than saying that the Lord is "responsible" for the salvation of His servants, therefore, it might be better to say, "Of course the Lord will save His servants." The Śrī Vaiṣṇava tradition, though it does not "obligate" God to save His dependents, has tended to assume that God is by nature such that He certainly will save those who surrender themselves to Him and that He will eventually save all His creatures, who are essentially

His śeṣas. There are some statements in Rāmānuja's writings that also tend in this direction, but what is missing in Rāmānuja's own theology is the "of course." The passage cited from the *Śrībhāṣya* makes it quite probable that Rāmānuja, like his followers, connected God's nature as Savior (Rakṣaka) with the fact that God is the Supreme Master and Owner (Śeṣī), but for Rāmānuja, God's saving action is not so much a corollary of a metaphysical doctrine as a mysterious act in which God breaks through His essential inaccessibility to His creatures.

THE CENTRALITY OF ŚEṢITVA IN THE *VEDĀRTHASAṂGRAHA*

The implication of the relation between śeṣī and śeṣa that is stressed in the *Vedārthasaṃgraha* is that it is the essential nature of the creature to serve God. This is a doctrine that is present in all of Rāmānuja's writings, but nowhere is it more stressed than in the summary of his theology in the *Vedārthasaṃgraha.* There it forms a major theme running through his work.

It is therefore not accidental that the definition of śeṣa and śeṣī and the application of these terms to the relation of creatures to their creator should be found in the *Vedārthasaṃgraha,* even though the definition seems to be given as a parenthesis in a discussion of a quite different subject. This "parenthesis" may not have been planned, but the rest of the work makes clear that Rāmānuja had this conception of God as Seṣī constantly in mind at the time he wrote the *Vedārthasaṃgraha.* It is the most important point made in the mangalaśloka: "Obeisance to Viṣṇu, who is the Master and Owner of all beings, both material and spiritual, without exception."[10]

In the process of discussing the *Sadvidyā,* Rāmānuja defines the relation of the manifest universe (prapañca) of matter and finite spirits to being as follows: "This universe . . . has Being [sat] as its material cause, its instrumental cause, and its support [ādhāra]; it is controlled [niyāmya] by Being and is the śeṣa of Being."[11] The śeṣī-śeṣa relationship is always mentioned along with the ādhāra-ādheya and niyantā-niyāmya relationships, sometimes as defining the fundamental soul-body relationship and sometimes, as in the sentence just cited, as an independent qualification of God and His relationship to the universe.[12]

There are two other paragraphs in the *Vedārthasaṃgraha,* in addition to the definition quoted above, that deal specifically with the significance of the soul's being a śeṣa of the Lord. One is a brief statement in the middle of the work, in which Rāmānuja gives the second scriptural definition of the soul or finite self. The first definition is that the soul is essentially uncontracted knowledge or consciousness, but this knowledge is subject to contraction according to the particular karma of each soul, and in consequence souls are surrounded by ignorance and display only that limited amount of knowledge that is compatible with the various bodies in which they dwell. The conclusion of the first point is that all the souls are equal (with each other, not, in this context, with Brahman) "by virtue of their consisting entirely [or solely] of knowledge devoid of the differences of various kinds of bodies." Then Rāmānuja gives the second part of the definition: "the essential nature of this [finite self] is itself ensouled by Bhagavān."[13] The synonomous word *rati* is used in the introduction to the *Gītābhāṣya* describing the Lord's eternal attendants (sūris) as those whose sole essence and joy is to be His śeṣas.[14]

This thought is developed and defended against objection in the final section of the *Vedārthasaṃgraha.* We have noted above (chapter 7) the passage in which Rāmānuja describes devotion as a kind of love (prīti) and a kind of knowledge (jñāna), knowledge which is bliss because its object is Brahman, who is Himself absolute and eternal bliss. This thought is summed up in the sentence, "All this means that the person who has Brahman as the object of his knowledge becomes happy." Rāmānuja then continues as follows:

> The Supreme Brahman—who is a treasure store of countless superlatively [anavadhikātiśaya] auspicious qualities, is flawless, possesses the infinitely great realm manifesting His glory [anantamahāvibhūti], and is an ocean of superlatively gracious condescension, beauty, and forgiving love—is the principal entity [śeṣī], and the self is the subordinate entity [śeṣa]. Therefore, when the Supreme Brahman is meditated upon as thus related [to the finite self], and when He is the object of superlative love [prīti], He causes that self to attain Him.

Here an objection is raised:

> What you have said would mean that the state of being nothing but an absolutely [atyanta] subordinate entity [śeṣa] is the soul's superlative happiness, but that is a conclusion opposed to all the world's experience, for we see that what is most de-

sired by all intelligent beings whatsoever is nothing else than independence or self-dependence [svātantryam-eva], and that dependence on someone or something else [pāratantryam] is more painful [than independence]. Moreover, there is the text from [*Manu-*]*Smṛti*: "All dependence on others [parāvaśam] is unhappiness; all self-dependence is happiness," and likewise, "Service is called a dog's life, so abandon it."

Rāmānuja replies that this attitude is really a desire for the independence, not of the soul, but of the body, with which the soul is wrongly identified. This desire for independence, moreover, is simply the desire to experience what is pleasurable for the particular kind of body that a particular finite self ensouls. "The proper nature of the soul, however, is solely of the form of consciousness, a form that is quite distinct from all the different kinds of bodies, and its own proper or essential nature is also to be a subordinate entity to some other being [para-śeṣatā-svarūpam]." Both these definitions of the finite self are based on a host of scriptural texts, and since everyone agrees that it is the nature of the self that determines what are the proper goals of human life (puruṣārtha), it follows that the idea that the soul is self-dependent is a misconception of the nature of the self caused by karma, just as is the identification of the self with some body, such as that of a lion or tiger. The true meaning of the text, "All dependence on others is unhappiness," is that the self is in the relation of a subordinate entity (śeṣa) *only* to the Supreme Person; hence subservience to anything or anyone else than God is unhappiness. Likewise, "Service is a dog's life" refers to the service rendered to one who is unworthy to be served. Only the Supreme Person is worthy to be served by all who know the true nature of the self. The Scripture describes this service that has the form of devotion as "knowing" (vedana). It is this knowing of God that has the form of supreme devotion, which is the way to attain Him, for God must elect a man to salvation, and He chooses those who are most dear or beloved (priyatama) to Him: those in whom superlative love (anavadhikātiśayaprīti) for the Lord has been generated (jāyate).[15]

There is a similar criticism of the soul's desire for independence in Rāmānuja's gloss on *Gītā* 18.59, where he three times uses the term *svātantrya* to express the word *ahaṃkāra*: egotism, or the misconception that one is by himself the doer of actions.

> When you are under the delusion that you know independently what is good for you and what is not, and, disregarding My command, decide not to fight, then your independent decision will be in vain, for your physical constitution [as a member of the warrior caste] will make you submit to My command, even though your ignorant mind grieves that [only] I am independent.[16]

THE MEANING OF WORSHIP IN THE *GĪTĀBHĀṢYA*

At a few points in his commentary on the *Bhagavadgītā*, Rāmānuja uses the term *śeṣī* to bring out one aspect of God's supremacy (paratva or superiority (parataratva) over all other entities. At the beginning of chapter 7 of the *Gītā,* Lord Krishna speaks of having two "natures" (prakṛti): a material nature and a higher prakṛti which consists of souls (jīvabhūtam). Verses 6 and 7 represent the Lord Himself as superior to both His "natures." On this Rāmānuja comments that all entities, both material and spiritual, all the way from the cosmic fashioner Brahmā to a blade of grass, originate from the two natures of God and are thus of God.

> These two natures are certainly Mine. As everything originates from them, even so they originate from Me and belong to Me. I alone am their origin; I alone am their dissolution, and I alone am their Śeṣī. . . . Because I am the cause of the two natures which are the causes of all things, and because I am the Śeṣī even of the intelligent beings who are the śeṣins of the nonintelligent entities [material objects], I am superior [paratara].[17]

Rāmānuja comments similarly on Arjuna's statement in *Gītā* 11.2 that he has now heard from Lord Krishna concerning the origin and dissolution of all beings and also concerning the Lord's eternal greatness. He paraphrases the second half of the verse as follows:

> I have heard of Thy immeasurable greatness [māhātmyam], which consists in Thy being eternally the Śeṣī of all intelligent and nonintelligent entities, in Thy being superior to all [parataratvam] because the host of auspicious qualities such as universal knowledge and untiring strength are Thine alone, in Thy being the ground and support of all [sarvādhāratvam], and in Thy being the One who causes all things to function.[18]

The other context in which the concept of śeṣatva is important is in the interpretation of religious action, or worship. Rāmānuja interprets the "Surrendering all actions to me" of *Gītā* 3.30 to indicate the second sense in which the *Gītā* declares the self not to be the doer. (The first sense is that actions are really performed by one's material nature, not by the intelligent self dwelling within the body.) It is God who is the real doer and the owner of all actions, since all selves constitute His body, and their essential nature is defined by their being controlled by Him. To do all acts as though they were done by God is to do them as acts of worship to Him. In worshiping, one should reflect that God causes the acts which belong to Him (svakīya) to be performed by the self, which belongs to Him, and the purpose of these acts is the worship of Himself. Therefore, it is the Supreme Person, the Lord of all, and the Śeṣī of all, He Himself, who causes His own acts (svakarmāṇi) to be done.

> This truth of God's being the Lord of all [sarveśvara] and the principal person or owner of all [sarvaśeṣī] is declared in a number of Scriptural texts. . . . To be the Lord means to be the controller or ruler [Īśvaratvam-niyantṛtvam], and to be the principal person or owner is to be the master of the estate (śeṣitvam-patitvam).[19]

In *Gītā* 9.27, Lord Krishna exhorts Arjuna to do all acts as offerings (*arpaṇam*) to Him. Rāmānuja comments at some length on this verse. God is to be offered both the self which performs the sacrifice or worship and enjoys its meritorious results and also the object which is worshiped (one of the lower deities to whom the Vedic sacrifices are addressed). This offering of both the subject and the object of worship to the supreme Lord consists in realizing that both the worshiping self and the deities worshiped belong to Him.

> Since all this belongs to Me and since all is dependent on My will for its essential nature, existence, and activity, offer everything to Me who am the Supreme Śeṣī and the Supreme Agent —everything, which includes yourself who are the actor, the enjoyer, and the worshiper; the groups of deities who are worshiped; and the groups of acts which make up worship. You should engage in reflection conjoined with fervent love [atyartha-prīti], reflecting that since you are controlled by Me, your sole essence and joy is to be My śeṣa and that the deities you worship are of a similar nature. Thus while directing your mind to the yoga of renunciation, reflect that the self is such that its

> ṣole essence and joy is to be My śeṣa and under My control, and consider all acts to be My worship: therefore perform both secular and Vedic acts.[20]

At a number of other points in the *Gītābhāṣya,* Rāmānuja refers to the ātmā as a śeṣa of God.[21] He concludes his comments in chapter 7 on the highest kind of devotees, the "knower" or "sage" (jñānī), as follows:

> Resorting to Me [mat-prapadanam] presupposes the knowledge that it is the sole essence and delight [eka-rasa] of self to be My śeṣa, knowledge which is the fruit of numerous meritorious births. It is even more difficult to find someone in this world who after many meritorious births has come to know that "It is my sole essence and delight to be Vāsudeva's [Krishna's] śeṣa: my essential nature, existence, and activity depend upon Him, and He is superior to all else [paratara] by virtue of His countless hosts of superior qualities." With that knowledge this rare soul resorts to Me, that is to say, worships Me, reflecting, "Vāsudeva alone is my supreme goal [prāpya] and the means to that goal [prāpaka]."[22]

The act of surrendering to God as one's sole refuge seems to be understood by Rāmānuja as both the initial act of worship and the underlying attitude to the devotee throughout worship. Like worship, therefore, it presupposes a knowledge of the soul's essential subservience, and it may well be understood as a joyful acknowledgment of that metaphysical fact, which was previously hidden from the devotee. In the Gadyas, the concept of surrender to or taking refuge in the Lord (śaraṇāgati or prapatti) becomes of crucial importance, with the same presupposition as in the *Gītābhāṣya*: the soul is the śeṣa of God, who is the Śeṣī of all things, including the worship leading to Him.[23]

THE MEANING OF ŚEṢA AND ŚEṢĪ

Govindacharya often translates śeṣa as "liege" or "vassal."[24] Liege, in particular, conveys something of the meaning of śeṣa that is missed in other translations. Both the etymology of the word and its medieval usage capture a great deal of the significance of the word *śeṣa* as Rāmānuja uses it. Unfortunately for the translator, both the word *liege* and the feudal social system in which the term had had significance have passed beyond our immediate acquaintance as speakers of contemporary English and dwellers in a no longer feudal society. Moreover, the concept of the liege (and to an even greater extent that of the vassal) suggests more relative an authority of the liege lord over his lieges than Rāmānuja intends by the śeṣa-śeṣi relationship. It is true that the finite self is in turn the śeṣī of its body, but insofar as it constitutes the body of God it has more than the limited obligation of a vassal or liege toward his lord; it is absolutely the disposable property or the bond slave of God.

Otto has laid stress on śeṣa as meaning "insignificant remnant,"[25] but this is to go too far in the other direction. God is absolutely superior to the soul, as to all His Creation, but the soul nevertheless has a high destiny and can manifest God's glory. Its essential subservience is also its joy, a point that Rāmānuja makes by playing on the double meanings of the words *rasa* and *rati*, both "essence" and "delight." When this is realized, its subordinate or subservient state gives it the possibility of rendering service to God Himself.

Even though it is not possible to give adequate one-word translations of śeṣī and śeṣa, the foregoing makes fairly clear what Rāmānuja wants to convey by using them. He once paraphrases śeṣī with pati. In itself this does not help us very much, since pati is a rather general term for lord or master, which can be applied to a god, a king, or a husband. The comparison to the lord of the manor or the head of the household does, however, convey a meaning that adds to the conception of controller or ruler. The Śeṣī not only rules; He rules by right over what belongs to Him. His superiority over His creation is not only by virtue of His power; it is what is eminently fitting or appropriate. Because it is appropriate, it is a joy for the enlightened self to recognize its subservience to the Lord and render Him service. The other metaphysical relations of support and supported and controller and controlled have a somewhat different meaning in the special context of devotion and worship. In the case of the śeṣī-śeṣa relationship, however, the special meaning is very close to the general one. Since God is the Śeṣī, His supremacy as the owner and master is also the basis of His concern for the creatures who belong to Him.

12 The Supreme Names of God

The Significance of the Divine Names

The Vaiṣṇava tradition has always maintained the importance of the "name" of God, or rather, of the names and the "Name." In a sense, all the auspicious qualities are names describing God, each celebrating a particular excellence and each suitable for a particular mode of devotional address. There are, however, certain names in the stricter sense that may appropriately be applied to the Deity, names hallowed by their use in Scripture and fraught with the emotional associations of their use in worship. Each sect of Vaiṣṇavas has usually chosen one name as the Divine name par excellence, and the very utterance of this name in the sacred formula of the sect is regarded as a sacred act. For Śrī Vaiṣṇavas, this supreme personal name of God used in the cultic formula is Nārāyaṇa, considered as a synonym for the more common supreme name of Viṣṇu. The sect derives its name from the expanded form of the name, also enshrined in a sacred formula, Śrīman-Nārāyaṇa: Nārāyaṇa united with (or accompanied by) His Divine Consort, the Goddess Śrī (also called Lakṣmī).

The use of auspicious names for the Deity is a practice common to all sects of Hindus. What is distinctive in the doctrine of the Śrī Vaiṣṇavas, as well as of many of the other theistic sects, is the insistence that the supreme name properly refers to ultimate reality and that this reality is not an impersonal principle but the personal God. Śankara's school of Advaita restricts all name and form (nāma-rūpa) to the ultimately unreal phenomenal realm and declares the ultimate reality, the Supreme Brahman, to be beyond all name and form. Just as Rāmānuja must protest the Advaitin's denial of auspicious qualities to the Supreme Brahman, so also he must establish that "name and form" are not limited to objects in the phenomenal world but are part of the distinctive nature of all entities, including the Supreme Entity, God Himself. Moreover, name and form are linked so that the most specific name of an entity is inseparable from a particular bodily form. The Supreme Entity, too, has His own specific name and form.

God who possesses a specific name and form also possesses many other important names of varying degrees of generality. The most important of these general names in the Vedāntic tradition is Brahman.

It is one of Rāmānuja's constant polemical objectives to establish that this Supreme Brahman defined in the Upaniṣads is none other than Viṣṇu-Nārāyaṇa. There are two main propositions to be proved: (1) the one ultimate principle or reality of the Vedānta is the personal Lord, and (2) the proper name of the Lord is Nārāyaṇa. At many points Rāmānuja simply assumes both of these propositions as proved, but at many points in his comments on the *Vedānta Sūtras,* he deals either explicitly or implicitly with the demonstration of the first proposition. In the *Vedārthasaṃgraha,* where he feels much freer in his choice and arrangement of topics, he deals quite systematically with demonstrating both the first and the second propositions.

There are a number of Divine names that are less general than Being, Supreme Entity (Paratattva), and Brahman but less specific than Viṣṇu and Nārāyaṇa. These may be divided into those that indicate that God is the supreme intelligent spirit and those that point to His lordship over the universe. All these names have both philosophical and devotional connotations, but those of the first group usually convey more of the meaning of God's essential nature, while those of the second group connote God's active relation to the universe. We can arrange the four most significant names in an order of increasing specificity: Brahman, Puruṣottama, Bhagavān, and Nārāyaṇa. Brahman, as it is used by Rāmānuja, has already frequently been taken up for scrutiny, so we turn now to the second important Divine name, Puruṣottama.

Puruṣottama, the Supreme Person

Puruṣottama is both a Divine name and a metaphysical definition of God. The word means "highest (or supreme) person," as does the alternative form, Paramapuruṣa. Closely related in meaning is the term Paramātmā, the Supreme Self. Rāmānuja seems to prefer Puruṣottama to Paramātmā as a name for God, though at times he uses them interchangeably. This is partly because of the close association between the terms Puruṣottama and Nārāyaṇa in the scriptural texts that were important in the Vaiṣṇava tradition. The later forms of the "Puruṣa hymn" in the *Ṛg Veda* identify Nārāyaṇa with this first "Man" or primodial Person (Ādi-puruṣa), who by dividing Himself created the universe. Moreover, in the *Bhagavadgītā* the term Puruṣottama is used to designate the Supreme Being who possesses both matter and finite spirits but is superior to both.

Puruṣottama is therefore a scriptural designation that seems clearly to imply that God is the inner Self or Person in His body the cosmos. Everything said thus far about the relation between God and the universe may therefore be understood as a definition of Puruṣottama. Rāmānuja's specific comments occur in his interpretation of *Gītā* 15.17-19, where this term occurs.

The entire fifteenth chapter of the *Gītā* bears the name of "The Yoga of Puruṣottama," and Rāmānuja therefore begins his comment in his introduction to that chapter:

> This present chapter will describe how the realm [vibhūti] of the Lord [Bhagavān] who is worthy of worship, consists of *kṣara,* souls bound in the transient world, and *akṣara,* souls who have been released from it, and how the Lord differs from his vibhūti consisting of these two kinds of souls. This is the Lord who is the Supreme Person [Puruṣottama], the Lord distinct from all else, since He is utterly preeminent [atyanta-utkarṣa] by virtue of being the antithesis of everything defiling and being of an entirely auspicious nature.[1]

Gītā 15.16 refers to two kinds of puruṣas: kṣara and akṣara. Rāmānuja interprets kṣara-puruṣa here to mean, not transient being (matter), as it is taken in most modern translations, but rather: those souls who are in contact with this transient world because of their material bodies.

> But the highest Puruṣa is of a different nature from both the bound and the liberated puruṣas, and in all Scriptural texts He is spoken of as the Supreme Self [Paramātmā]. Because of this very designation of Paramātmā, He is known to be of a different nature from both the bound and the liberated puruṣas. How? Because He penetrates and thus supports the three worlds; matter, intelligent beings joined to material bodies, and intelligent beings liberated therefrom. Because He pervades and sustains them, He is of a different nature from them. He is also distinct from them because He is eternal [avyaya] and is absolute Lord [Īśvara].

> Since I transcend both the kṣara-puruṣa and the akṣara-puruṣa, I am known both in Śruti and in the "world," which means in Smṛti . . . as the highest Puruṣa [Puruṣottama].

> He who knows that I am the Supreme Person of an entirely distinct nature [visajātīyam] because My nature is eternal—in contrast to both kinds of puruṣas—and because of My pervasion and support of them and lordship over them, knows everything that can be known as a means of attaining Me.[2]

Herein, then, lies the supremacy of the Supreme Person over finite persons, that He is eternal or imperishable in a more significant sense than souls who still are or once were connected with perishable bodies and that He pervades and supports these finite persons and is their Lord.

BHAGAVĀN, THE SUPREME LORD WORTHY OF WORSHIP

The general term for Lord in Rāmānuja's writings is Īśvara, often used in compound terms such as Sarveśvara (Lord of all) and Sarveśvareśvara (Lord of all lords). There are a number of other terms that function virtually as synonyms, such as Pati and Nātha. The word Īśvara was in common use in the systems of different schools and sects to denote the supreme personal spirit transcending both matter and finite spirits.

The name Bhagavān (root form, *bhagavat*) has the same general meaning of "Lord," but in Rāmānuja's usage, as in that of the Vaiṣṇava tradition generally, it comes much closer to being the specific personal name of Viṣṇu, both in His supreme state and in His incarnations. It is this name of the Deity that is used in the title, *Bhagavadgītā,* and it occurs frequently in the text of the *Gītā*, as well as in Rāmānuja's commentary. Rāmānuja uses the term as an honorific when mentioning the great sages and venerable figures of the past, such as the authors of the *Mahābhārata* and the *Viṣṇu Purāṇa,* and in the same capacity before the personal name of God: Bhagavān-Nārāyaṇa. Rāmānuja seems to regard this name as the closest possible general term that can substitute for that most specific name of God: Nārāyaṇa.

Rāmānuja does not define the word *bhagavat* himself, but he twice quotes the definitions given in the *Viṣṇu Purāṇa* (6.5.72-75, 76-77, and 79), once in the *Vedārthasaṃgraha* (omitting verses 73-75) and once in the mahāsiddhānta of the *Śrībhāṣya.* In both cases the citations make up a significant part of a list of quotations from Smṛti that are meant to refute decisively the Advaitic definition of Brahman as the sole reality (all else being unreal) consisting solely of undifferentiated consciousness (that is, not, as Rāmānuja maintains, the supreme personal Being *possessing* consciousness as well as other attributes).

There are two kinds of definitions of the name Bhagavān given in these verses in the *Viṣṇu Purāṇa.* One is based on the common usage of the term and defines the Lord as the supreme and only truly worthy object of worship. The other gives a metaphysical definition of the Lord's qualities.

The first kind of definition (given second in the text) is as follows: "This great word 'Bhagavān' denotes Vāsudeva, who is the Supreme Brahman, and no one else. The general meaning of the word is 'worthy of worship' (pūjya]. To Him it applies directly, but only indirectly to others.[3] At the beginning of his comment on the first sūtra, when he defines the word "Brahman," Rāmānuja refers to the definition of bhagavat as an analogy to his primary and proper application of the word Brahman (meaning "greatness") to the Supreme Person alone, while the application to other persons or things possessing greatness is only secondary or derived.[4]

The metaphysical definition (or definitions) quoted in the *Vedārthasaṃgraha* states that the term *bhagavat* is applied to "the Supreme Brahman, who is pure, possesses great realms manifesting His glory [mahāvibhūtyākhya], and is the Cause of all causes." The word signifies the six qualities, jñāna, śakti, bala, aiśvarya, vīrya, and tejas, without any defiling qualities (heya-guṇa). In the *Śrībhāṣya,* Rāmānuja also quotes the intervening verses (73-75), where from an analysis of the syllables *bha-ga-vat* the following meanings are derived. The Lord is the provider and the sustainer, the leader (preserver), mover (destroyer), and creator. Moreover, He is the universal Self who dwells in all, and all beings dwell in Him. A somewhat different list of the six qualities is also given here: aiśvarya, vīrya, yaśas, śrī, jñāna, and vairāgya.[5]

The first list of six qualities is the one Rāmānuja very often refers to in his writings, either listing all six or indicating that they are meant by giving the names of two or three qualities. These are the six qualities which are so important in the Pāñcarātric doctrine of the Divine form and of the emanation of the Vyūhas. Rāmānuja frequently refers to the six qualities as the examples of the entire ocean or treasure of auspicious qualities in the Divine nature, but he never defines them. Even to translate them into English, therefore, we must have recourse to his commentators. They give definitions of the qualities practically identical with those found in the *Pāñcarātra Āgamas.* Since these qualities are taken by the later tradition as indication of the Lord's essential lordship and supremacy, there is no tendency to transform their meaning in such a way as to emphasize the Divine accessibility. We therefore are reasonably safe in assuming that the later Śrī Vaiṣṇava definition for these six qualities represents Rāmānuja's understanding of them, though it is doubtful whether he assigned them such semi-independent functions in the creative process as was done in Pāñcarātric thought.

The six qualities are defined as follows. Jñāna (knowledge) is direct and simultaneous knowledge of all things. Bala (strength) is the capacity to support everything without even being fatigued (or, by His mere will). Aiśvarya (sovereignty or lordship) is unchallenged rule over all. Vīrya (valor) is the quality of immutability in spite of being the material cause of the mutable creation (vīrya may alternatively be given the above definition of bala). Śakti (power) is given two alternative meanings: (1) the power of being the material cause of all, or (2) the power to make possible what is impossible for others. Tejas (splendor) likewise has been given two definitions: (1) self-sufficiency, not requiring any external aid, or (2) the quality of overpowering others by His splendor.[6]

It was possible for Rāmānuja to bear in mind both the general meaning of the words and the more esoteric meaning attached to them in his own religious tradition. It is not always possible to combine the exoteric and esoteric meanings in a single English translation. The translation I have adopted—knowledge, untiring strength, sovereignty, immutability, creative power, and splendor—deviates from the common meaning of these terms only when that is necessary to give some idea of their esoteric significance.

The fact that Rāmānuja always refers to these "six qualities" as a group would seem to indicate that he was less concerned with their individual meaning than with their collective testimony to the lordship and supremacy of the Lord (Bhagavān).

At the same point in the mahāsiddhānta, Rāmānuja goes on to comment on a passage two chapters later in the *Viṣṇu Purāṇa* (6.7) concerning the "pure object" (śubhāśraya) of meditation. He states that it is the peculiar bodily form of Bhagavān that is this pure object (bhagavat-asādhāraṇam . . . mūrtaṃ-rūpam-śubhāśraya). All other deities, such as Brahmā, live within the realm afflicted with ignorance and are therefore incapable of serving as a proper object of devotion.[7] Only the One who stands above creation as the Lord, yet who possesses a distinct form, is the Lord worthy of worship: Bhagavān. In the following section, we shall see how Rāmānuja proceeds along the same line of reasoning with respect to the specific identity of the Supreme Lord possessing name and form: from the Supreme Cause to the only worthy object of worship.

THE SUPREMACY OF NĀRĀYAṆA

It is one of Rāmānuja's major polemical objectives to prove that it is Nārāyaṇa, synonymous with Viṣṇu, who is the Supreme Lord, not Brahmā or Śiva or any impersonal principle that is claimed to transcend all three.

Rāmānuja's line of argument is given briefly in the *Śrībhāṣya* (1.1.15), but it is presented much more fully in the *Vedārthasaṃgraha*. There is also a hint of it in the passage in *Śrībhāṣya* 1.1.21 listing three different kinds of texts. The last of the four texts declaring Brahman to be the sole cause reads, "Indeed then there was only Nārāyaṇa, not Brahmā or Īśāna (Śiva)" (*Mahā Upaniṣad* 1).[8]

Rāmānuja argues in the *Vedārthasaṃgraha* as follows. Brahman is first defined as the cause of creation, and so on, and therefore He is to be known only by a study of the sections of the Scriptures dealing with His creation and rule; which is to say that we are to consult the texts stating *how* we are to meditate only after we definitely know on *whom* we are to meditate, the particular name and character of the universal cause. In determining this name, we begin with the most general name given to this cause and move to more and more particular names until we reach the proper name of a concrete individual. This succession is: Sat (Being), Brahman (Extreme Greatness), Ātmā (Intelligent Being), and finally Nārāyaṇa, who is the one particular Self or Person who is supreme. There can only be one such supreme cause (parama-kāraṇa). Hence Nārāyaṇa is the One denoted by the more general terms just mentioned; He is the particular Being who is the universal cause. His supremacy over all (sarvasmād-paratva) is established in a passage, "Hrī and Lakṣmī are His consorts." This is made more explicit in the section dealing with Nārāyaṇa where all the words used in the different Scriptures to denote the Supreme Reality, along with their inherent qualities, are applied to Nārāyaṇa. The section then goes on to show that all other entities different from Him are dependent (āyatta) on Him, pervaded (vyāpya) by Him, supported (ādhāra) by Him, and that Brahmā and Śiva also are parts of His glorious realm (vibhūti), since they have the same status as Indra and the other Vedic deities. The importance of this text is that it has no other purpose than to expound exactly who the Supreme Reality is.[9]

Rāmānuja also argues the supremacy of Nārāyaṇa because He is denoted by the letter *A*, which is the root of the sacred syllable *Auṃ* (or *Oṃ*). The root of all the Vedas is the sacred syllable, and its root is the letter *A*. Hence, He who is named by the letter *A* is the Supreme Deity, and this is Nārāyaṇa. Moreover, Scriptures declare that all language is *A* and that Brahman is *A*. All language evolves from the letter *A*, and all the entities denoted by language evolve from Brahman. Since Brahman is thus affirmed to be the meaning of the letter *A*, it is established that the one who possesses the name *A* is the Supreme Being, and that one is Nārāyaṇa.[10] There are two reasons why passages mentioning other deities as supreme ought properly to be applied to Nārāyaṇa. First, terms referring to Śiva have a general meaning; śiva means "pure" and śambhu means "auspicious." Thus they can be applied as adjectives to Nārāyaṇa.[11] Secondly, however, even those passages that definitely refer to Brahmā or Śiva as entities ultimately refer to Nārāyaṇa, since He is their inner Self, as He is of all finite selves. Consequently, the supremacy ascribed to them really is that of Nārāyaṇa, of whom they are only creaturely manifestations (vibhūti), like Indra and other lower deities.[12]

Rāmānuja then quotes extensively from the *Viṣṇu Purāṇa*, which he says is universally accepted and which he previously has stated is to be accepted in case of conflict with other Purāṇas which accept some other deity as supreme, since following the *Matsya Purāṇa*, only the Purāṇas extolling Hari (Viṣṇu) as supreme are sāttvic (pure), that is, exhibit constituent of material nature that reveals rather than conceals the spiritual realm.[13] This appeal to the superior authority of the *Viṣṇu Purāṇa* is a secondary argument that does not affect the first argument that Śruti teaches Nārāyaṇa as the Supreme Cause, but it is also of interest to our topic, since the emphasis on sattva brings out an aspect of paratva already briefly noted: God's supreme nature includes all the excellent qualities of His creation, both of matter and of materially embodied souls.

An objection, however, is presented on the basis of the *Viṣṇu Purāṇa* itself. Does it not tell us that the members of the Trimūrti are equal in the passage, "That same Bhagavān-Janārdana assumes three names, Brahmā, Viṣṇu, and Śiva, to create, sustain, and destroy"? No, Rāmānuja replies, the passage means that Janārdana (Viṣṇu) is the inner self of the whole phenomenal world consisting of these three deities and all other beings. The Viṣṇu with the same status as Brahmā and Śiva is a descent or incarnation (avatāra) of the Supreme Viṣṇu into the created world, by His own choice and for His own sport (līlā).[14]

Rāmānuja's final paragraph on this subject refers to *Viṣṇu Purāṇa* 6.7 in the same way already noted in the *Śrībhāṣya.* He reiterates that Brahmā and the other gods are only finite selves (kṣetrajña) and creatures (visṛṣṭa) created (projected into the universe) by the Creator, who is the Supreme Person. Brahmā and other gods are mere finite selves, not fit to be pure objects of meditation (śubhāśraya), inasmuch as they are impure (aśuddha) because of their association with the three bhāvanās.[15]

As noted in chapter 5, it is in this section establishing the supremacy of Nārāyaṇa that Rāmānuja makes a number of his rare uses of the abstract noun *paratva.* Although the immediate sense of the word in this context is the supremacy of Nārāyaṇa over Brahmā and Śiva, its presupposition is a more general notion of Divine supremacy, a conception of the kind of relation, both in distinction of nature and in exercise of lordship, which obtains between God and His creatures.

Rāmānuja believes that there is a scale of created beings. Although the souls are all of the same rank, in the bodies that they ensoul they cover a vast range of beings, beginning with Brahmā, as he so often says, right down to motionless things. There is only one Being who is apart from and above this scale of creatures, and that is the Supreme Person, Nārāyaṇa. The first reason for this, and the one that Rāmānuja repeatedly emphasizes, is that Nārāyaṇa is the cause of the periodic origination, continuing existence, and dissolution of the universe. The most exalted deities are in this essential respect as far below Him as is the smallest blade of grass, for they are bound by the law of karma; and even apart from the fact that they are bound to material bodies, they are only finite selves like all other souls. The second reason is hinted at in this closing paragraph on the supremacy of Nārāyaṇa. They are not worthy objects of meditation for those who wish to be freed from the bondage of karma, since they are themselves caught up in it. As there is only one supreme cause, so there is only one worthy object of meditation. He alone is above the world ordered according to karma, and He alone controls that karma instead of being controlled by it, since it is simply the expression of His pleasure or displeasure.

13 The Supreme Form and Abode

The Defense of the Divine Form

To say that God has a particular name, Nārāyaṇa, implies for Rāmānuja that God has a particular bodily form about which the Scriptures inform us, a form not only in His phenomenal manifestation or descents (vibhava or avatāra) but also in His supreme state. Bharadwaj points out that Rāmānuja's conception of God agrees with that of other theistic religions, including Christianity, Islam, Zoroastrianism, and Sikhism, in holding that God possesses personal qualities—all of them differing in this respect from Śankara's Advaita. The Vaiṣṇava view is unique, however, in maintaining that God is not formless but possessed of a personal form, indeed the most beautiful form.[1]

It may be that Rāmānuja's defense of the Divine form is only a part of his defense of the conception of a personal God against the Advaitic denial that ultimate Reality has any qualities and its insistence that all name and form (nāma-rūpa) are only part of empirical reality and thus ultimately unreal. However, Rāmānuja devotes several paragraphs of the *Vedārthasaṃgraha* to this topic, long after he has refuted the views of the other Vedāntic schools and soon after his arguments for the supremacy of Nārāyaṇa and his refutation of the Prābhākara theory of language. From this we may infer that there were those who accepted the doctrine that God is personal but not the idea that He has a transcendent bodily form.

Rāmānuja's argument is a direct appeal to Scripture.

> There are thousands of scriptural texts that declare the following truth about Nārāyaṇa, who is the Supreme Brahman. Just as His essential nature consists of indefinable knowledge, bliss, and purity; just as He has countless auspicious qualities of matchless excellence, the first six of which are knowledge, creative power, untiring strength, sovereignty, immutability, and splendor; and just as He causes all other entities, both spiritual and material, to function by an act of His will; so also He has one permanent celestial form which is agreeable and appropriate to Him; He has an infinite variety of superlatively auspicious ornaments that suit His form, and immeasur-

> able, infinite, and amazing weapons of various kinds which are appropriate to His might; He has a consort of matchless glory with respect to Her essential nature, beautiful form, qualities, manifestation, dominion, and gracious conduct, which are pleasing and appropriate to Him; He has an infinite retinue of attendants and accessories suitable to Him whose immeasurable virtues include auspicious knowledge and actions; He has an infinitely great realm manifesting His glory which includes all objects and instruments of enjoyment; and He has a celestial abode [divya-sthāna], the essential and inherent nature of which is beyond the grasp of speech or thought. All this is eternal and flawless.[2]

Rāmānuja then quotes a number of texts that support and elucidate one or more of the points he has made.

In the concluding paragraph of the section he makes the additional point that all of these qualifications of Brahman are distinct from worldly reality and ordinary experience. Just as there are texts that declare that Brahman's essential nature is essentially different from everything else and beyond definition and there are other texts that declare that His countless superlative qualities are essentially different from everything else, so also the text beginning "who has the color of the sun" declares that "His form, attendants, abode, and so on, are essentially different from everything else, are unique to Himself and have an indescribable essential and inherent nature."[3]

For Rāmānuja, the idea that God has a transcendent bodily form is inevitably connected with His having a suitable celestial abode where He dwells with His consort (or consorts), is attended by His celestial ministers, and enjoys every possible pleasure which is appropriate and agreeable to Him. Rāmānuja goes to some length to prove—with the evidence of scriptural texts and the application of the Karma Mīmāṃsaka rules of exegesis—that there is a class of beings known as *nityasūris,* who have never been involved in saṃsāra but have always been watching the Lord and waiting upon Him. He also seeks to demonstrate that the term *paramapadam,* the "supreme place" of Viṣṇu, does refer to the transcendent "place" in which God dwells, as well as, in other passages, to His own essential nature and, in still other contexts, to the realization of the soul's essential nature when it is released from all the bonds of karma.[4]

Not only does Rāmānuja assert that there is as much scriptural authority for God's form, abode, and so on, as for the defining attributes of His essential nature and His other auspicious qualities but he is also willing to expand the concept of God's essential nature (svarūpa) to include God's form and abode. The inclusion of the attendants and the abode in the Divine svarūpa refers specifically to their coeternality with God. Like the "six qualities" and other auspicious attributes, they are part of the one Being who exists before creation takes place: "Being alone there was in the beginning."

In this connection Rāmānuja defines the terms *satyakāma* and *satyasaṃkalpa*—taken from the *Chāndogya Upaniṣad* (8.1.5)—which he very often includes in his definitions of descriptions of the nature of Brahman. By distinguishing between these two apparently synonymous terms, Rāmānuja wishes to show that this basic scriptural definition establishes the eternal reality of God's transcendent realm and all that it contains. The text reads, "That is the Self, free from sin, ageless, deathless, griefless, free from hunger and thirst, whose desires are satya and whose will is satya." Rāmānuja interprets the five negative qualifications to deny that Brahman has any of the defiling nature (heya-svabhāva) of material nature and the souls connected with it, though these material objects and materially embodied souls are instruments of His sport. The term *satyakāma,* on the other hand, means "He who possesses objects of His desire, which are eternally real," for the word *desire* (kāma) here means "Those things that are desired." The word *satya* here is used in the strong sense, meaning "eternally real." It is true that the objects in the phenomenal universe that exists for God's sport are "real" (satya) in the sense that they are objects which can validly be known, but they are impermanent and hence less "real" than the attendants (sūris) and other entities in God's supreme abode, who are permanent or eternal (nitya).

The term *satyasaṃkalpa* applied to the Supreme Person has a different meaning from that of *satyakāma. Will* (saṃkalpa) also means "objects accomplished [siddhim] by His will," but the word *satya* here applies primarily to the Divine will rather than to the objects that it achieves. This has two important implications: (1) in addition to the permanently real objects serving for His enjoyment, God can create an infinite number of new objects in the phenomenal world by His mere will; and (2) both the permanent (sthira) objects that are instruments of His enjoyment (bhoga-upakaraṇa) and the impermanent (asthira) objects (namely, subject to change) that are instruments of His sport (līlā-upakaraṇa) have their essential nature, continuing phenomenal existence, actual functioning, and differentiations dependent (āyatta) on His will.[5]

Rāmānuja also finds support in the view of one of the ancient masters of the Vedānta, referred to as the author of the *Vākya,* who refutes the view that the form of the Supreme Person is only temporarily assumed in order to favor His worshiper. Rāmānuja explains this quotation from the *Vākya* with the same argument he has already used: "even as such attributes as knowledge have been stated to constitute the essential nature of the Supreme Brahman, likewise His bodily form [rūpa] belongs to His essential nature [svarūpa], for the Scriptures declare that His essential nature is such."[6]

THE NATURE OF THE DIVINE FORM AND THE DIVINE ABODE

In the same section of the *Vedārthasaṃgraha* just noted there occurs a paragraph that gives a detailed description of the Divine form.

> He who is always gloriously visible is the pre-eminent Person who dwells within the orb of the sun. His splendor is like that of a colossal mountain of molten gold and His brilliance that of the rays of hundreds of thousands of suns. His long eyes are spotless like the petals of a lotus that, sprouting forth from deep water on a soft stalk, blossoms in the rays of the sun. His eyes and His forehead and His nose are beautiful, His coral-like lips smile graciously, and His soft cheeks are beaming. His neck is as delicately shaped as a conch-shell and His bud-like divine ears, beautifully formed, hang down on His stalwart shoulders. His arms are thick, round and long and He is adorned with fingers that are reddened by nails of a most becoming reddish tinge. His body, with its slender waist and broad chest, is well-proportioned in all parts, and His shape is of an unutterably divine form. His color is pleasing. His feet are as beautiful as budding lotuses. He wears a yellow robe that suits Him and He is adorned with immeasurable, marvelous, endless and divine ornaments—a spotless diadem, earrings, necklaces, the Kaustubha gem, bracelets, anklets, belt etc.—and with the Conch, Disc, Club and Sword, the Bow Śārnga, the curl Śrīvatsa and the garland Vanamāla. He attracts eye and thought alike of all by the measureless and boundless beauty that is His. He overflows the entire creation of animate and inanimate beings with the nectar

> of His comeliness. His youth is exceedingly wonderful, unimaginable and eternal. He is as delicately tender as blossoming flowers. He perfumes the infinite space between the cardinal points with the odor of holiness. His profound majesty is forever encompassing the entire Universe. He looks upon the hosts of His devotees with loving eyes, filled with compassion and affection. His sport is to evolve, sustain and dissolve all the worlds. All evil is foreign to Him—He is the treasury of all beautiful qualities and He is essentially different from all other entities. He is the Supreme Spirit, the Supreme Brahman, Nārāyaṇa.[7]

A similarly detailed description of the bodily form of Nārāyaṇa and a far more detailed account of the Divine abode and its residents, including His consort Śrī and the chief attendants of the Lord, are presented in the *Vaikuṇṭhagadya.* A much briefer description, but of the same kind, is given in *Gītābhāṣya* 9.34. All of them describe the particular beauties of different parts of the Divine body, beginning with the amplification of two phrases from the *Chāndogya Upaniṣad* (1.6-7). We have already noted the story in Rāmānuja's biography about his dispute with Yādava Prakāśa over the interpretation of this second phrase. This passage actually incorporates the three alternatives which Sudarśana Sūri says were those allowed by the author of the ancient *Vākya.*[8]

The clause in the introduction to the *Gītābhāṣya* about the divyarūpa is much more abstract:

> Whose one permanent celestial form is a treasure store of infinite qualities such as radiance, beauty, fragrance, delicacy [tenderness], charm, and youthfulness, which are inconceivable, celestial, wondrous, eternal, flawless, and supremely excellent a form, agreeable and appropriate to Him.[9]

This clause is repeated verbatim in *Gītābhāṣya* 6.47 and in *Śaraṇāgatigadya,* paragraph 5. It also appears with the insignificant addition of one word (gaṇa) in *Śrībhāṣya* 1.1.21 ("infinite host of qualities" instead of just "infinite qualities"), but instead of appearing as an independent clause in a description of the deity (nominative in the introduction to the *Gītābhāṣya,* accusative in *Gītābhāṣya* 6.47, and vocative in *Śaraṇāgatigadya,* paragraph 5), it is the second part of a sentence: "Likewise, even His celestial form . . . is natural to Him [svābhāvikam]."

In the *Vedārthasaṃgraha,* Rāmānuja had already quoted this sūtra 1.1.21 in the course of his defense of God's having a bodily form. What he stresses in his treatment of it in the *Śrībhāṣya* is that the Divine form is affirmed, not denied, by Scripture. What the Scriptures deny of Brahman is any connection with qualities or bodily form connected with defiling material nature (prakṛti) and dependent upon karma, but they definitely enunciate that He has auspicious qualities (kalyāṇaguṇān) and an auspicious form (kalyāṇarūpam). The key word here is the one that was noted in chapter 4: svābhāvika. This may mean simply "natural" (by its own nature), since the *sva-* is an integral part of the word, or the *sva-* may retain a reflexive meaning, "natural to Him," which in turn may mean "being part of His own inherent nature," similar to Rāmānuja's inclusion of the Divine form and abode within God's svarūpa, in the section in the *Vedārthasaṃgraha* just discussed. The conclusion of the comment would seem to support this interpretation: "Hence the Supreme Brahman Himself possesses such a form [as we have just described], so this [form] is nothing else than His own attribute [tasya-sva-dharmaḥ]." It is possible that Rāmānuja may here also be indicating the substance of which God's celestial form consists, since he has definitely stated that it is not material (aprākṛta).[10]

Bharadwaj has pointed out that Rāmānuja does not seem to hold the view of later Śrī Vaiṣṇavas that God's transcendent auspicious form and transcendent abode are composed of śuddhasattva, whether this be regarded as the pure quality in matter completely separated from the two base qualities or as a different substance altogether which is not inert like matter but which is conscious, yet distinguishable from God's own essential nature. Rather, Bharadwaj maintains, Rāmānuja states that "God's form is His own nature or essence just as His attributes are." Since six of the Divine attributes "are held to be most prominent," God is described by the *Pāñcarātra Āgamas* as having a form consisting of the six qualities defining Bhagavān, and Rāmānuja adopts this view. Bharadwaj is here referring to the section in the *Śrībhāṣya* in which Rāmānuja defends the orthodoxy of the Pāñcarātra or Bhāgavata doctrine and maintains its usefulness in revealing the true meaning of the Vedas. The puzzling thing about this section is that while Rāmānuja here declares that the Āgamas were composed by Nārāyaṇa Himself, he nowhere outside this section quotes from them, and he does not take up into his system doctrines which are peculiar to the Pāñcarātra. Moreover, he is exceedingly selective in the views of this system that he mentions, ignoring several which came to have considerable prominence among his followers. It is quite possible that Rāmānuja has adopted the Pāñcarātric view at this point; to wit, that the bodily form of God in His supreme state prior to any manifestation, there called the "subtle" (sūkṣma), is composed of the group of six qualities particularly indicating the Divine lordship. Bharadwaj may therefore be right in stating that, according to Rāmānuja, "God's form is made of omniscience, strength, sovereignty, constancy, power and lustre." All that we can definitely state is that Rāmānuja regarded the particular bodily form of God as just as integral to His nature as are God's personal qualities and that this transcendent body is quite different from all material bodies.[11]

In *Śrībhāṣya* 1.2.2, Rāmānuja comments on several scriptural appellations which, he holds, can belong only to the Supreme Self. These indicate, among other things, that God's form is of superlative splendor, because His celestial form (divyarūpa) is immaterial (aprākṛta), unique to Himself (svāsādhāraṇa), superlatively excellent (niratiśaya), and auspicious (kalyāṇa). God is the One to whom all pure (pariśuddha) objects and means of enjoyment belong, among which are all kinds of odors and tastes which are uniquely for Him (svāsādhāraṇa), flawless, superlatively excellent, and auspicious.[12]

SUPREMACY AND ACCESSIBILITY IN THE DIVINE FORM

There are two themes running through the passages dealing with the Divine form that correspond to our interpretive concepts of supremacy and accessibility. On the one hand, Rāmānuja vehemently insists that the Supreme Deity Himself has a real and permanent personal bodily form, in addition to His having the entire universe as His body. The various beauties and excellences of this bodily form, as of the entire transcendent realm in which God dwells in this form, have the names of various aspects of beauty at the human level. It is made quite clear, however, by all the adverbial phrases which are applied to these adjectival qualities that these excellences of the human body are raised to an incomparably higher level when they are applied to the body of Nārāyaṇa, the Supreme Person. The same is true of the aspects of human personality which are ascribed to God, but because these aspects of beauty apply directly to the body, not to the indwelling personality, it must be made even more evident that these qualities of the Divine form are quite distinct from and entirely superior to the qualities that can be applied to a defiling material body (prākṛta-heya-deha).

Just as there is no qualityless Being at a higher level of reality than the Lord possessing all auspicious qualities, so there is no formless Absolute that transcends the Deity with a bodily form. The Supreme Person who is the Supreme Brahman is none other than Nārāyaṇa, who always dwells in His unique transcendent form in His transcendent abode, accompanied by or united with His Divine Consort Śrī and waited upon by celestial ministers and attendants, as well as by the hosts of liberated souls, who may assume bodies or not, as they wish, but in any case exist in the Lord's supreme abode. In the section on the Pāñcarātra system just noted, Rāmānuja does not distinguish between the supreme state of the Lord described as "subtle" (sūkṣma) and Vāsudeva as the first of the four "divisions" or "emanations" (vyūhas), who possesses all six qualities (ṣāḍguṇya) to constitute the body of Vāsudeva, and it is for him axiomatic that Vāsudeva with such a body must be the supreme form of God.[13]

The Supreme Person in His transcendent or celestial bodily form (divyarūpa) dwelling in His transcendent abode (divyasthāna) is inconceivable (acintya) and beyond the grasp of speech or thought, even to the lower gods or to accomplished ascetics. He is utterly inaccessible in this transcendent form, and yet He makes Himself accessible to His creatures by manifesting His form. The only quality that is applied to God in both the first and the second halves of the introduction to the *Gītābhāṣya* is saundarya (beauty). Both in His supreme inaccessibility and in the accessibility that He brings about by His grace, the Lord is characterized by His beautiful form. In the description of God's beautiful form in the *Vedārthasaṃgraha* just quoted, Rāmānuja states that God attracts all His creatures by His beautiful form.[14] The same understanding of the attractiveness of the Divine form as it appears among men is presented more poetically in the introduction to the *Gītābhāṣya* (see above, chapter 5).

In the key passage on this subject in the *Śrībhāṣya* (1.1.21), the existence of the Divine form is immediately linked with its use: the satisfaction of God's worshipers.

> In order to favor His worshipers [upāsakās], the supremely compassionate Lord, solely by His own will, causes this same form, which is definitely part of His own inherent nature [svābhāvikam-

> eva], to assume that particular generic structure, such as that of a typically divine or human body, which will be a shape [ākāra] suited to their particular understanding.

Rāmānuja then explains this further with reference to the phrase in *Bhagavadgītā* 4.6: "Taking up my own prakṛti, I am born again and again." *Prakṛti* here means "inherent nature" (svabhāva), so this means: "Taking up His own inherent nature [svabhāva] but not the nature [svabhāva] of those in saṃsāra."[15] The function of this Divine form in the process of God's gracious work of protection and redemption will be taken up in the next chapter.

14 The Merciful Protector and Savior

The Rewarder of Good and Evil

In the thought of Rāmānuja, God seems to have two somewhat different relationships to man's religious activities. In the first relationship, He presides over the working of the law of karma. Here He does not interfere with the moral decisions and the religious activities (or absence of such activities) on the part of the finite self. Only in certain exceptional cases does He cause individuals to perform good or bad actions, and this is only when the individuals already have a strong disposition in one direction or the other, so that the Lord's encouraging them to go further in the direction they have already chosen is only a special means of rewarding unusual goodness, or punishing incorrigible evil-mindedness and evildoing. Apart from this special case, the Lord simply gives permission or approval (anumati) for souls, which He has endowed with the power to act and the capacity to discriminate between good and evil, to perform whichever course they themselves desire.

God's second relationship to man's moral and religious action is quite different from the first. In this second relationship, He actively intervenes, both in the life of individuals and in the affairs of the world as a whole. He manifests Himself in the empirical universe or, in other terms, descends periodically from His perfect and eternal realm of bliss to the constantly changing world filled with misery or, at best, only limited happiness.

There is not, in Rāmānuja's mind, any contradiction between the first relationship of Law and the second relationship of Grace, but there is a clear distinction between the two relationships. Indeed Rāmānuja's followers found it difficult completely to reconcile the two, precisely because of the prominence that Rāmānuja gave to the second relationship, in which God intervenes in the affairs of the world. Before turning to this second relationship, the activity of God in presiding over the law of karma needs to be understood, since Rāmānuja regards the activity as the indispensable presupposition for everything he says about God's protective and redemptive action toward those who worship Him.

First of all, Rāmānuja makes it quite clear that the power for future effects, present in good or bad action, is not a myterious power immanent in the cosmos, which the followers of the Karma

Mīmāṃsā called apūrva or niyoga. It is, on the contrary, nothing other than the Lord's pleasure or displeasure which then brings either happiness or suffering, as the case may be, to the individual who has done this action. The works that please God and thus cause Him to grant appropriate rewards are primarily acts of worship, namely, sacrifices and other religious duties prescribed in the Vedas or in other sacred Scriptures. Though the Vedic sacrifices are directed to the deities to whom the Vedic hymns are addressed, they are all actually enjoyed by God Himself, since He is the inner Self of all these deities. In this respect there is no essential difference between ordinary religious works and the higher forms of meditation and devotion. Both works and meditation achieve their results by pleasing the Supreme Person, who alone is the one who bestows all the goals of human desire: pleasures in this life, the attainment of the lower and transitory heaven after death, and the attainment of permanent bliss by being liberated from the bonds of karma that keep one in an endless cycle of rebirths. The difference lies in the end that a man wishes to reach by his religious act. Meditation or devotion to the Supreme Person is usually undertaken in order to secure man's supreme goal of release from this transient and painful world. However, rites enjoined by the Scriptures or even forms of worship that are ordinarily performed to gain some worldly benefit may help in winning the favor of God, which will bring permanent salvation, provided they have been done without any desire to earn merit to be used for worldly results.

Meditation, like action, achieves its effect only by winning the Divine favor or grace, but it is distinguished in this respect, that it can so please the Lord that it nullifies His displeasure at the mass of sins accumulated by the soul in an endless series of lives. The effect of the Lord's displeasure is His condemning the soul to ignorance of its true nature and destiny and His causing it to identify itself with its material body and the worldly pleasures experienced through that body. When the Lord's displeasure at accumulated sin is nullified by his delight in the meditation and devotion of the worshiper, He destroys the ignorance He has caused and grants the soul knowledge of its own nature and of Himself. Such knowledge leads to the attainment of God and, at the cessation of this life or some future life, to the attainment of communion with the Supreme Person and release from the bondage of saṃsāra.

Rāmānuja gives the following analogy to show how the Supreme Person bestows rewards.

> It is also observed in human society [loke] that men earn wealth of various kinds by such occupations as farming, and by means of this wealth, they pay homage [arcayanti] to the king, either directly or through his ministers. When the king has thus been honored, he bestows rewards [phala] appropriate for each gift or act of homage [arcana].

Rāmānuja goes on to say that sacrifices, gifts, and oblations are indirect aids toward propitiating the Supreme Person, while praise, worship, and meditation directly propitiate Him. When propitiated —offered pleasing worship (ārādhita)—God, like a king, bestows appropriate rewards, namely, temporal happiness and final release.[1]

This is a very significant analogy, for it makes it appear that God's relation to men is comparable to that of a king who bestows his favor on his subjects in proportion to the value of their gifts and services to Him. This suggests something very important about the nature of God and also about man's motivation in serving God: he serves God in order to win God's favor and receive His blessing in return. This is quite precisely the conception of sacrifice and worship found in the celebrated Latin phrase, *do ut des*: "I give in order that Thou wouldst give."

This theme of pleasing God in order to win His favor certainly runs throughout Rāmānuja's theology, and it is sometimes taken as so characteristic of his thought as to set him apart from his followers, who more and more stressed the unconditional character of Divine grace (nirhetuka-kṛpā). However, there is another line of thought that runs through all of Rāmānuja's writings, though it is less prominent in his commentaries on the *Vedānta Sūtras* than in his other works. The other thought also has its human analogy in the relation between a king and his subject or, perhaps more accurately, between the head of a household and his servant or slave. This is the śeṣī-śeṣa relationship discussed in chapter 11 above. In this relationship the service of the subordinate to his superior is not done in order to win some favor; it is done simply as his duty. As this relationship applies to God and the soul, this is a joyful duty, so that subservience and service to God is man's real happiness.

Rāmānuja's followers have stressed that God's relation to the soul is also quite different from that of the ruler who bestows his favor according to the merit of his followers. It is the proper function of the master or owner to take care of his servants, and this is all the more true when a servant has acknowledged his inability to care for himself and his utter dependence upon his master. Rāmānuja himself never suggests that God "must" save men or even that He certainly will, by virtue of His nature, for to say this would be to limit God's complete lordship and supremacy. Since God is the master and owner (Śeṣī) of all His creatures, it is quite fitting that He should protect and save them, but there is no question of any responsibility or necessity forcing Him to do so. He is impelled to save men only by His own supreme compassion (parama-kāruṇya). Such Divine mercy or compassion does not imply for Rāmānuja that God must abandon His strict justice and His treatment of men according to their moral deserts. He deals with this point specifically in the *Śrībhāṣya* in refuting the charge of "mercilessness" in God's creating a world in which there is suffering. He defines mercy (dayā) as "a disinterested concern in the welfare of others, which is incapable of enduring their suffering." Mercy that causes one to transgress the law in order to help someone else is not a virtue but weakness. The Lord's mercy or compassion is certainly not such weakness. The Lord is always endeavoring to increase superlative (niratiśaya) happiness, and in order to do this He must subdue the accumulated mass of sins and check the tendency of creatures to disobey His laws.[2]

GOD'S DESCENTS AND MANIFESTATIONS (AVATĀRA)

The Pāñcarātra system as it was accepted by later Śrī Vaiṣṇavas maintains that there are five forms of the Deity, but in his defense of that system in the *Śrībhāṣya* Rāmānuja mentions only three: the "subtle" form (sūkṣma), the fourfold "division" of the supreme reality (vyūha), and the "manifestations" in incarnations such as Rāma and Krishna (vibhava).

> The Supreme Brahman, called Vāsudeva, whose body consists of the complete group of the "six qualities" [saṃpūrṇa-ṣāḍguṇya-vapus] divides itself into the different forms of sūkṣma, vyūha, and vibhava, and He is attained in His fullness [samyak-prāpyate] by the devotees who, according to their qualifications, worship Him by means of works guided by knowledge. They teach that "From the worship of the vibhava one attains to the vyūha, and from the worship of the vyūha one attains to the sūkṣma, the Supreme Brahman, called Vāsudeva."[3]

Rāmānuja states that the Pāñcarātric teaching concerning the vyūhas is that the supreme Brahman, called in that system Vāsudeva, loving His devotees (āśrita-vatsalam), voluntarily abides in a fourfold form in order to become a refuge for those who resort to Him (sva-āśrita-samāśrayaṇīyatvāya). At the end of the same paragraph Rāmānuja mentions that the three subordinate vyūhas, Sankarṣaṇa, Pradyumna, and Aniruddha, are the presiding deities ruling over the finite selves, their minds, and their egocentric principles, respectively. The charge that Rāmānuja is refuting is that each succeeding vyūha originates from or is born of the previous one, which would be contrary to the orthodox doctrine that each individual soul is eternal. It may be for that reason that Rāmānuja is silent about what may be the most important function of the vyūhas in the Pāñcarātric system, their being successive forms of the Supreme Creator in the process of creation.[4] It seems more likely, however, that he does not wish to accept any alternative theory to the general Purāṇic doctrine that Brahmā is the agent of the supreme Deity in creation. Moreover, he believes in the direct causation of each succeeding stage in creation by the supreme Deity Himself, and he does not want to introduce any division into the Supreme Cause. The function he assigns to the vyūhas is the same one he most frequently mentions in connection with the avatāras of God, namely, that they are forms God assumes to enable His creatures to reach Him. Nowhere does Rāmānuja refer to these vyūhas again.[5]

The two forms of the Deity that he does not mention at this point where we would expect them are the Inner Controller (antaryāmī) and the Consecrated Image (arca or arcāvatāra). As we have already seen, the concept of the antaryāmī is a central one in Rāmānuja's theology, and his failure to mention it here is thus all the more puzzling. One possible explanation is that he believed his conception of the antaryāmī was different from that in the Pāñcarātric system. The *Pāñcarātra Āgamas* also called this form of God *hārda,* meaning "God dwelling in the heart," and this was conceived as a veritable incarnation of God in the hearts of those specially devoted to Him. The antaryāmī, on the other hand, may be understood as the general immanence of God in all His creatures. Another explanation is advanced by K. C. Varadachari, who suggests that Rāmānuja is following his usual practice of confining himself strictly to the point at issue. The Divine forms of vyūha and avatāra might be confused with finite individual selves, and it was therefore necessary to assert that they were not such, but manifestations of God Himself.

Thus Rāmānuja states that the three subordinate vyūhas are mere bodily forms which the supreme Brahman voluntarily assumes. Since neither the antaryāmī nor an arca would be mistaken for an individual self, it was not necessary to mention them here.[6]

Still another possible explanation is that Rāmānuja assumed that the forms of the Lord as antaryāmī and arcāvatāra were included under the more general concept of vibhava. This is the case in a discussion of the subject by his disciple and successor, Parāśara Bhaṭṭar, who begins by stating that "it is the established conclusion of the Bhāgavatas that the Supreme Being has three aspects, Para, Vyūha, and Vibhava." When he comes to a detailed explanation of the third category, vibhava, he mentions four kinds of incarnation: (1) direct incarnation of the Lord, (2) entering into the soul of distinguished sages, (3) the Lord's lending His strength temporarily for the occasion, and (4) the Lord's entering "any form by his devotee for worship. This is known as arcāvatāra."[7]

These explanations may indicate why the other two Pāñcarātric forms are not mentioned in the section of the *Śrībhāṣya* defending the orthodoxy of the Pāñcarātric system. We are left with the question, however, as to why Rāmānuja has nowhere mentioned the concept of arca specifically. It might be that he could not find sanctions in the Vedas for the Pāñcarātric idea that God was fully incarnate in the consecrated image. It is quite certain that he himself participated in worship to the image form of the Deity, both in temples and at home. It is possible that he regarded the images as aids to meditation on the other forms of the Deity, but his comment on *Gītā* 4.11, which speaks of the Lord manifesting Himself to men in other shapes than those of His incarnations, suggests that he regarded consecrated images also as Divine manifestations for the benefit of the worshipers. There Rāmānuja paraphrases Lord Krishna's statement as follows: "Although My nature is beyond the grasp of speech and thought even for yogis, I adapt Myself to those who follow My ways, in such a way that they may not only see Me but may enjoy Me with all their senses."[8] Even if Rāmānuja did accept consecrated images as real incarnations of the Divine Presence, it is obvious that his interest was in the supreme form of the Deity portrayed by the image. Even with respect to incarnation, his emphasis is not on the particular characteristics of Rāma or Krishna but on their identity with God in His essential nature and supreme form.

Rāmānuja gives remarkably little of the kind of information about the avatāras with which the various Purāṇas abound and which has been summarized in such later Śrī Vaiṣṇava manuals as the *Yatīndramatadīpikā*. He does not discuss the number of Divine incarnations or whether they are primary or secondary incarnations.[9] Usually he mentions only the names of the two most prominent human incarnations, Rāma and Krishna, and once, in the *Vedārthasaṃgraha*, he also mentions an incarnation of Viṣṇu among the deities as the younger brother of Indra (Upendra).[10] Indeed, we find the same few fundamental notions repeated in most of the passages in which Rāmānuja discusses the concept of avatāra. However, these are basic concepts, not only in the doctrine of incarnation but also in Rāmānuja's entire theology.

As might be expected, the most frequent references to avatāra occur in the *Gītābhāṣya*, and the most detailed comment is on the verses of the *Gītā* where Lord Krishna explains the purpose and nature of His incarnation or, more literally, "descents." In *Gītā* 4.4. Arjuna asks Lord Krishna to explain how He could have taught this discipline to the sage Vivasvant at the beginning of creation, if His birth were later than that of Vivasvant. Rāmānuja assumes that Arjuna knew that Krishna is the Supreme Person and being eternal could easily have taught Vivasvant, so he paraphrases Arjuna's question as several distinct questions.

> Is the birth of the Lord of all . . . in a body of the same character as that of beings subject to karma, false [mithyā] like a magical trick? If it is real [satya], of what manner is His birth, and of what nature [ātmaka] is His body? What is the cause of His birth; when does His birth occur, and what is its purpose?

In his comments on the following verses, Rāmānuja interprets Lord Krishna's answer to Arjuna to contain the answers to these questions, and we can therefore, following van Buitenen, arrange Rāmānuja's comments under four headings.

First, the fact that the Lord has had many births in the past proves their reality, and these births are comparable to Arjuna's own birth.

Second, the Lord comes into finite existence by His own will and in His inherent nature; without giving up His inherent nature of Divine lordship, His opposition to evil, and His possession of auspicious qualities, He causes His nature to assume the form pertaining to a god, a man, or some other being.

Third, there is no fixed time appointed for the Lord's birth. Whenever the Vedic dharma is declining and its opposite is on the increase, then of His own free will He manifests Himself in incarnations.

Fourth, the purpose of the Lord's coming is as follows: from time to time He observes that the virtuous (sādhus), who are the eminent Vaiṣṇavas, are seeking Him out as their refuge, but they are not attaining Him, for His name and wonderful deeds are beyond the grasp of speech and thought. Since they cannot perceive Him, they are unable to sustain their souls, and they suffer vast confusion. At those particular times God comes into existence in our world in order to save (protect) them by allowing them to behold His essential nature and His deeds and to listen to His words. God has two other purposes in descending to earth: to destroy the wicked and to restore the declining Vedic religion, which is worship of Him, by revealing His essential nature, which is worthy of worship.[11]

Rāmānuja comments on the next verse (4.9) as follows: the man who knows that the Lord's birth and deeds belong to Him and have no connection with material nature and that they are intended for the salvation of the good, himself experiences no further births and attains God.[12]

Several times later in the *Gītā,* Rāmānuja comments on passages which state that there are those who see Lord Krishna's body as an ordinary body.

> I am the one who is to be worshiped [ārādhya] by all acts. I am the Lord of all. My essential nature and inherent attributes [svarūpa-svabhāva] are beyond the grasp of speech or thought. Because of supreme compassion [parama-kāruṇyāt] and because of love for My devotees [āśrita-vātsalyāt] in order to become a refuge for all [sarva-samāśrayaṇīyatvāya], I have descended [become incarnate (avatīrṇa)] as the son of Vasudeva without abandoning My inherent nature [svabhāva]. Yet not knowing the imperishable and unsurpassable nature of My supreme state [param-bhāvam], fools think that I have become manifest from a previous manifest state. They think that as an ordinary king's son with a material body I was forced into the manifest world by the necessity of karma. Therefore such people do not take refuge in Me; nor do they worship Me with their acts.

These deluded people do not recognize the Incarnate Lord because He is concealed by māyā (which here means the conjunction of souls with material bodies), for He only appears to have the characteristic nature of a human being or other finite being. "They do not recognize Me, who am the cause of the entire universe and the Lord of all, who have taken up existence in the characteristic form of human being [manuṣyatva-saṃsthānam-āsthitam] in order to become a refuge for all."[13]

Two chapters later the *Gītā* returns to this thought. Rāmānuja makes the same comment as before and goes on to say that the opposites of such deluded people are those whose good karma enables them to take refuge in God. Having been released from bondage and assumed a divine nature, they know that "He is the beginning of all creatures, the imperishable One. His name, acts, and essential nature are beyond the range of speech or thought. Because he is supremely compassionate, He has descended as a human being in order to protect the good [sādhu-paritrāṇāya]."[14]

When Arjuna is beholding the terrifying universal form of the Lord, he addresses the Lord thus: "In Thine avatāras, one of which is this present incarnation, Thou art the protector of the everlasting Vedic dharma."[15] Frightened of this form, He prays for the return of the Lord's human form to which he was accustomed. When that familiar four-armed body returns, Arjuna says, "Now I have come to my senses again, now I behold once more this lovable beautiful body of Thine, peculiar to Thee, which has the characteristic structure of an ordinary human being and is most benevolent."[16]

The references to avatāra in the *Śrībhāṣya* in general lay more stress on the nature of the incarnate Lord's body and somewhat less emphasis on the redemptive purpose of God's descents, a quite understandable difference considering the different nature of the two works, but the doctrine enunciated is precisely the same. *Śrībhāṣya* 1.1.21 was referred to in the previous chapter in connection with the supreme form of the Lord. In the comment there on *Gītā* 4.6-8, it is stated that the principal object of the Lord's repeated births is the "protection of the good," and "the good" means His worshipers.[17] In *Śrībhāṣya* 1.3.1, Rāmānuja states this same conception of the nature and purpose of the avatāra as follows:

> In order to be a refuge for gods, men, and other creatures, the Supreme Person, without at all abandoning His very own nature

> [svakīyam-svabhāvam] associates Himself with the characteristic form, structure, qualities, and actions of the different classes of beings, and then is born in many ways.[18]

Rāmānuja's discussion of avatāra in the *Vedārthasaṃgraha* contains a few ideas not found elsewhere. He brings in the ideas of the divine sport in connection with God's descents from the infinite to the finite level or, as he puts it there, from the level of cause to that of effect. This idea of līla in connection with avatāras is not found in Rāmānuja's own words in the *Śrībhāṣya* or the *Gītābhāṣya,* though it appears in a passage from the *Viṣṇu Purāṇa* that Rāmānuja quotes twice in *Śrībhāṣya.*[19]

The other idea peculiar to the paragraph of the *Vedārthasaṃgraha* is that God descends in order to complete the appropriate number of beings in each particular class of beings in His creation.[20] Though the term *avatāra* is not used, the presence of Viṣṇu as one of the Trimūrti may be similarly regarded, for He also exists as one of a class of finite beings (along with Brahmā and Śiva) within the created realm (vibhūti). By the time Rāmānuja wrote the *Gītābhāṣya,* it appears that he was even more anxious to safeguard the Divine nature of the incarnation, for as we noted above, He explains that Rāma and Krishna (Vāsudeva), whom the *Gītā* includes in chapter 10 among the vibhūtis, are not in their own persons vibhūtis, which seems to imply that they are solely Divine. It may be, however, that there is not even such an apparent difference, for Viṣṇu is also included among the vibhūtis in *Gītā* 10 as the most excellent of the ādityas, and Rāmānuja makes no such exception for Viṣṇu as for Rāma and Krishna. It seems that Rāmānuja accepted Viṣṇu as the name of one of the created deities as well as a synonym for the Supreme Cause, and this may be one of the reasons why he generally prefers Nārāyaṇa as the proper name of God.[21]

In a later paragraph of the *Vedārthasaṃgraha,* Rāmānuja briefly enunciates the same doctrine of avatāra which he presents more fully in the *Gītābhāṣya.* The Supreme Lord Viṣṇu voluntarily descends into the world of gods, men, and animals where He dwells in the midst of creatures who are really under His rule, in order to be a refuge (āśraya) for all the different classes of creatures. All other beings, including the gods, are forced by their particular karma to enter into a particular material body, but the Lord is born many times among the different classes of beings by His own free will, in His very own form which is superlatively auspicious (svena-eva-niratiśaya-kalyāṇa-rūpeṇa) in order to help the universe (jagad-upakārāya).[22]

THE INNER CONTROLLER IN THE HEART OF THE DEVOTEE

Whether or not Rāmānuja accepted the Pāñcarātric idea of hārda (a special incarnation of God in the heart of certain great souls), he certainly assigns a special function to the omnipresent Inner Controller (antaryāmī) in the context of meditation and devotion. In commenting on several sūtras in the *Śrībhāṣya,* he maintains that the Supreme Person is present as the Inner Controller within the heart of the meditating devotee to aid in that meditation or even to cause it.[23]

In *Śrībhāṣya* 1.4.1 Rāmānuja says that as the universal Inner Controller, the Supreme Self also brings about the meditation of the devotee, for a later sūtra (2.3.41) "will state that the fact that the finite self can act [kartṛtvam] depends on the Supreme Person. Being the means for bringing about the meditation and the goal of meditation, He Himself is the highest object to be attained."[24]

God's most intimate control of the finite self is thus both an expression of His supremacy over that self and of His will to prepare that self for a state of uninterrupted communion with Him, a communion of which there may be some foretaste in this life for one whose devotion is animated or encouraged by the indwelling Ruler. Here supremacy and accessibility meet without paradox.

The following chapter will be concerned with that profounder relationship in which the soul's awareness of both God's supremacy and His accessibility is first intensified and then God's supremacy, though never denied, is sometimes momentarily forgotten.

15 The Inner Mystery of God's Love

The Two Aspects of Divine Accessibility

The previous chapter was concerned with the first aspect of God's accessibility to His creatures: His intention and action to become a refuge (āśraya) for His creatures.

Rāmānuja usually distinguishes between the creative action of God, for His sport (līla), and His redemptive action, which in general is to aid or benefit (upakārāya) the universe and specifically is to provide a refuge for all in the universe.[1] This distinction is not so sharp as in some other schools of Hinduism. An important part of the creative activity of God is the maintenance of the order of the universe, both natural and moral. Correspondingly, the task of the avatāras most directly stated in the *Bhagavadgītā* is the upholding of the moral order (dharma) and the punishing of immorality.

Rāmānuja believes that the main purpose of God's descents is to make Himself available for communion with men, especially the good men (sādhus). He interprets sādhus to mean those who fervently desire release from saṃsāra and eternal communion with God. Yet he certainly does not wish to minimize the importance of God's role as a protector of the moral order in the universe, for he has a very positive conception of the value of the world and of its relation to God. He believes that God is not only the supporter of dharma but also the one who bestows all blessings upon His creatures, material as well as spiritual. Final salvation is by no means simply the negation of life in this world, though it is the highest end of man and it must take precedence over all wordly aims and ambitions. The performance of one's moral and religious duties in this world is so indispensable that it must continue even after one has renounced ordinary worldly life and has become an ascetic. These duties in themselves, however, are not synonymous with man's highest goal. Their performance should both precede and continue to undergird man's pursuit of his true destiny, eternal communion with his Lord. It is precisely the close connection between God as Moral Governor and God as Savior that constitutes the special problem of later Śrī Vaiṣṇava theology, but this problem of the relation of unmerited grace to meritorious effort does not seem to have concerned Rāmānuja.

The other distinction between God's creative and redemptive activities is connected with Rāmānuja's understanding of the nature of the avatāra. Whereas God's creative activity is performed by God working as the inner Self of various entities that constitute His body, God's redemptive activity is carried on directly by the Lord in His own unique body, which does not consist of material nature but appears to be just like the bodies of the particular class of beings among whom He has descended.

It is striking that in precisely those passages in which Rāmānuja is discussing avatāra, he emphasizes the supreme attributes of God: His lordship, His possession of all auspicious qualities and freedom from all inauspicious characteristics, and His transcendence of the mental grasp of all finite beings. The passages in the *Gītā* which speak of fools being ignorant of the Lord's true nature give him the fullest scope to elaborate this theme. In fact, the great majority of Rāmānuja descriptions of God are chiefly concerned with the attributes which his commentators placed in the category of paratva. For this reason, a disproportionate number of chapters have been devoted to topics relating to God's supremacy and essential lordship.

This does not mean that Rāmānuja considers the fact of Divine accessibility of less than fundamental importance. He wants to emphasize that it is the Supreme Person Himself who has descended to us. If it were not so, our worship of Him would not lead us to the desired goal of liberation from this finite realm marred by evil and misery. It is essential for the worshiper that God be both supreme and accessible. Raghavachar discusses this while commenting on the beauty or aesthetic perfection of Brahman.

> Ramanuja describes Brahman as the aesthetic Absolute for the reason that it is "subha" and "asraya." "Subha" means that which elevates, sublimates and raises the contemplating soul to perfection. "Asraya" means that which is accessible, available for experience, an object of immediate experience. Brahman is immediate as well as transcendent. It is nearer than the nearest and can lead the soul to the highest *summum bonum.* The finite entities are accessible but are not elevating. The infinite nature of Brahman as sat, chit, nirmala, ananda and ananta, is what invests the contemplating soul with perfection, but is not accessible to common consciousness. It is Brahman, as beauty in its aesthetic aspect, that combines this twofold

> perfection of utter saulabhya and utter paratva, "intimacy" and "ultimacy" to borrow the terms of Prof. Webb. This aspect of Brahman is the final justification for ascribing beauty to Brahman.[2]

There is a further explanation of Rāmānuja's emphasis on God's supremacy when he is speaking of His incarnations. The dramatic effectiveness of the introduction to the *Gītābhāṣya* and of many other briefer descriptions of God's nature hinges on the contrast between "beyond the range of speech or thought" and "within the range of the vision of His devotees"—a contrast drawn in the mangalaśloka of the *Vedāntadīpa* that is somewhat similar to that in verse 21 of Yāmuna's "Stotraratna."[3] The frequent use that Rāmānuja makes of this contrast may well be a reflection of his own sense of wonder that the essentially inaccessible God has made Himself approachable and available to men. This is also the first aspect of the meaning of all the four attributes that Rāmānuja so frequently uses in referring to God's making Himself available as a refuge: mercy or compassion (dayā or kāruṇya), generosity (audārya), gracious condescension (sauśīlya), and protecting and forgiving love (vātsalya).

God's intention to save men and the initiative He takes to do so are particularly expressed by the only one of these concepts that Rāmānuja himself defines: dayā (synonymous with kāruṇya). The meaning he gives this attribute is more than his rather negative definition would indicate. This concise definition is "inability to endure [asahiṣṇutā] the suffering of others [para-duḥkha] and disregard of one's own advantages [or without consideration of one's own gain (svārtha-nirapekṣā)]." Rāmānuja follows this with the assertion that the Lord "is trying to increase superlative [niratiśaya] happiness" or, as Thibaut translates, "to increase happiness to the highest degree."[4] This desire to remove the unhappiness and increase the happiness of His creatures, not for His own sake but for their good, is the Lord's mercy or compassion.

In all God's descents or manifestations in the finite realm, in all His efforts to make Himself available to men so that they may worship Him and thus attain their goals, He remains the Supreme Person, the Lord of all. His compassionate concern for men is not a weak pity; it does not contradict but rather requires His strict justice. In His compassionate dealings with men, God is both accessible and supreme. There is one situation, however, in which God not only makes Himself accessible to the experience of His creatures but also seems to forget His supremacy. This is in the special relationship He has with His most excellent devotees.

THE SPECIAL RELATIONSHIP BETWEEN GOD AND HIS EXCLUSIVE DEVOTEE (THE JÑĀNĪ)

In the *Bhagavadgītābhāṣya* Rāmānuja describes a relationship between God and those who are exclusively devoted to Him, the highest class among all His devotees. They are called the wise (jñānīs) or the great-souled ones (mahātmās). "Other yogīs are like a handful of mustard seeds compared to Mount Meru; their relative rank pales into insignificance compared to the superior yogīs, the jñānīs."[5] Whereas the devotion of others to God is only in order to please Him so that He will enable them to gain their own ends, the exclusive object of the jñānī's devotion is God Himself. "Even though I am omniscient and omnipotent, I cannot tell how dear I am to the jñānī, for such affection is beyond measurement. . . . In the same manner he is also very dear to Me."[6] These jñānīs are also described as those who have no other objective, because their sole objective, necessary to sustain their souls, is meditation on God Himself.[7] These supreme devotees worship God from the sheer joy of experiencing Him in devotion and also with the consciousness that they are His śeṣas and are therefore obligated to render Him all that a servant should do for his master.

From the side of the devotee, this relationship with God is one of utter dependence and reliance on God for support. There is, in the first place, the intellectual realization that all intelligent and material entities, in all conditions whatsoever, are dependent on the Supreme Person with respect to their essential nature, existence, and activity (svarūpa-sthiti-pravṛtti). The highest kind of devotee applies this knowledge also to himself: "I am a śeṣa of Vāsudeva. My sole joy consists in being a śeṣa of Vāsudeva, with my essential nature, existence, and activity under His control, knowing that He is superior to all others because He possesses countless auspicious attributes."[8]

The devotee's sense of dependence, however, goes far beyond the recognition of God as the universal Ground and Lord, for the support of which he feels in need is the experienced presence of God. "The jñānī is one for whom happiness consists only in union with Me and sorrow only in separation from Me. No one is born with such a nature."[9] The superior yogī has an intense desire to find God and to remain in communion with Him. This yearning love is so intense that the superior yogī is unable to tolerate a moment's separation from God. "Without Me he is unable to sustain his soul [ātmā] so he merges his mind in Me."[10] The same emphasis is evident in Rāmānuja's paraphrase of Lord Krishna's words in *Gītā* 7.1. "'With the mind attached to Me because it is turned toward Me' means: his love for Me is so great that if he were to be separated from My essential nature, qualities, actions, or glorious realms, even for an instant, his nature would fall to pieces. Therefore he keeps his mind closely bound to Me."[11] The great souls (mahātmās) are defined as "those possessing a great mind, who understand Me as I am indeed, who because they love me so much are unable to sustain their souls without Me." "Their minds are attached to Me, they have taken refuge with Me and meditate on Me; thus they obtain Me, the supreme goal."[12] The same idea is brought out in the definition of exclusive devotion in *Gītā* 9.13., and in the comment on the following verse, this communion is interpreted as continual worship. "Because of their intense love for Me, they discover that it is impossible to support their souls [ātmadhāraṇam-alabhamānaḥ] for even an infinitesimal part of a moment without being engaged in singing My names, or in holy exercise, or in obeisance to Me."[13]

It is the second side of the relationship between God and the devotee that is somewhat surprising. Rāmānuja understands Lord Krishna to be teaching in the *Gītā* that He is similarly dependent upon His exclusive devotees. There is no question in Rāmānuja's mind of denying the one-sided ontological dependence of the universe on God. Indeed, it is precisely in the *Gītābhāṣya* that Rāmānuja makes a distinction between the finite self's relation to its body and God's relation to His cosmic body. In the former case, although the soul is superior to the body, there is some mutual dependence, for the soul also depends on the body to accomplish its purposes. In the case of God, however, there is no such dependence on the cosmos. "My existence [sthiti] is not under their control, which means that they are not helping in any way in My existence. . . . I am the supporter of all beings; they are no help at all to Me at any time. What I will in My mind itself causes the existence of all beings and also supports and controls them."[14]

Nevertheless, God's love for the devotee is so great and His longing for the devotee is so intense that He declares that He also needs the devotee to sustain His soul or self (ātmā).

> I am easy to attain by that yogī . . . who desires eternal union with Me and who bears Me constantly in mind from the moment of starting this meditation. He is unable to sustain his soul without extreme affection for Me and without thinking about Me. My very self is the object he desires to obtain, not a mere aspect of My being such as worldly power and wealth [aiśvarya]. I am easy to be obtained [suprāpaśca] because, unable to bear separation from him, I Myself select him. I grant him that perfection in meditation appropriate for obtaining Me, destroy the obstructions in his path, and grant him the state of being most affectionate to Me.[15]

Rāmānuja puts this mutual dependence between God and his favorite devotees very emphatically in his comment on *Gītā* 7.18.

> I consider that the jñānīs are My very soul. This means that the support for My existence is under their control. Why is this so? Because the jñānī does not have even the possibility of sustaining his soul without Me. He takes Me alone as his incomparable goal. Therefore without him, I cannot sustain My soul. Therefore he is My soul.[16]

In two passages in the ninth chapter, Rāmānuja goes even further in describing God's reversal of the ordinary metaphysical relationship between Himself and His creatures.

> Those who worship Me out of intense love because they cannot sustain their souls without worshiping Me, which worship is their sole aim, whether they are born in a high caste or a low caste, exist within My very self provided with every happiness as though their qualities were equal to Mine. "I, too, am in them" means: I treat them as if [iva] they were My superiors."[17]

This statement is somewhat explained by a comment earlier in the same chapter. "Even when I have given Myself to such a worshiper, it appears to Me that I have done nothing for him."[18]

This paradoxical reversal of values can only be understood on the basis of God's generosity (audārya). Rāmānuja paraphrases

Lord Krishna's words in 7.18 to mean that all the classes of devotees are generous (udāra) in that they favor God by accepting any gift from Him. God considers that by accepting His gift they have given Him their all.[19] The devotees can only be called "generous" here in the light of God's own generosity, which is so great that He considers their accepting His gifts more important than His having given them. This same idea of the divine generosity underlies Rāmānuja's paraphrase of 9.26: "Whoever presents to Me with devotion, a leaf, a flower, a fruit, or water, that offering of devotion I accept from the devout-souled giver."

> This verse means: My devotee loves Me so much that he is unable to sustain his soul unless he offers Me one of these easily available objects like a leaf, keeping the offering itself as his sole aim. . . . Even though I am the Lord of all and My desires are ever fulfilled . . . I consume such an offering as if I had received something unimaginably dear.[20]

In this light the later commentators' definitions of the Divine generosity seem quite likely to convey what Rāmānuja himself had in mind when he ascribed this quality to God. Vedānta Deśika defines audārya as follows:

> It is the quality of ignoring the receiver's inferiority or the giver's superiority, giving with pleasure, not expecting any repayment because the recipient is treated as one with a right to a share. In addition, generosity means not being satisfied even when one has given on a large scale. Therefore, the generous giver, like Lord Krishna, says that all the petitioners are themselves "generous."[21]

This same conception of God's generosity is evident in a verse addressed to the Goddess Śrī in one of the hymns of Rāmānuja's disciple and successor, Parāśara Bhaṭṭar.

> Thou dost feel embarrassed to grant no more than worldly wealth [aiśvarya], liberation of the soul from the bonds of matter [kaivalya], or even Thy supreme estate [paramapada] to one who folds his hands in reverent salutation [añjali] before Thee, for Thou thinkest, "I have done nothing fitting for him." O how great is Thy generosity![22]

These commentators also define the quality of "profundity"

(gāmbhīrya) as expressing God's generosity, namely, the fact that His generosity and favor toward His devotees is unfathomable: it is immeasurably great, and it is incomprehensible how God could give as though He were ignorant of the unworthiness and insignificance of the recipients. Along the same lines is one of their definitions of the term *kṛtajñatā* as Rāmānuja applies it to God. This is usually translated as "gratitude," its literal meaning being "the recognition of something done." Sudarśana Sūri gives as a second alternative: "He recognizes only the good which has been done by His dependents, even though it is very little, and He does not remember their faults or all the good which He Himself has done [for them]."[23] This is similar to one of Parāśara Bhaṭṭar's definitions of kṛtajñaḥ as a name of Viṣṇu: "He recognizes the small favors [done for Him] by creatures in saṃsāra, who have forgotten that they are only servants and that nothing belongs to them, and who because of their ignorance behave as though they were independent."[24]

In the case of gāmbhīrya the commentators' definitions may be affected by the tendency of later Śrī Vaiṣṇavas to reinterpret Divine qualities originally indicative of God's supremacy so that they also will point to His accessibility. Rāmānuja himself does not define gāmbhīrya, so we do not know for sure whether it was its original meaning of "depth" or "profundity" which caused him to use it so frequently as a Divine attribute or whether it was some derived meaning which was most important for him, such as "inscrutability" or "majesty." For many of the Divine attributes the commentators give various alternative meanings, and it is quite possible that Rāmānuja may also have given somewhat different meanings to the same term in different contexts. What is more important to note, however, is that the concept of generosity itself contains a combination of supremacy and accessibility. This quality is one that finds its clearest expression in someone with the resources to bestow gifts: the king or the great landowner, who for Rāmānuja frequently furnishes the human analogy for the position of the Supreme Person. It is especially the lavish generosity that Rāmānuja seems to have in mind, which is a royal prerogative. Although the presupposition of this generosity is wealth or greatness, the most prominent feature of the definition is the self-forgetfulness of the giver motivated by his desire to give.

This notion of self-forgetfulness is even more prominent in the commentators' definitions of *sauśīlya,* another important Divine attribute that Rāmānuja frequently mentions but never defines. This term has the common meaning of "good conduct," as does the simpler form *śīla,* but at some point it acquired a much more specific meaning in the Śrī Vaiṣṇava tradition. Sudarśana Sūri gives two related meanings, the second really an application of the first to the Divine Person.

> Śīla is the quality whereby superiors mix intimately with inferiors, not as a strategem, but as a genuine expression of their nature. Or it means such behavior of the Lord's that His dependents will not be frightened, remembering that He is God [Īśvara]. He Himself does not make any distinction between Himself and His devotees, not thinking of His supremacy [paratva].[25]

Parāśara Bhaṭṭar interprets a number of the names of Viṣṇu as expressing this quality of sauśīlya, which he understands to include the Lord's allowing Himself to be at the disposal of His devotees: under the control of those who submit themselves to Him.[26] Like audārya, sauśīlya can only be exercised by one who is essentially superior. That is why this concept may properly be translated by the English word *condescension,* but it must be qualified as "gracious condescension," not only because of the unfavorable associations of the noun by itself but because that unfavorable connotation of condescension is inherent in the situation of a superior dealing with an inferior, unless the conduct of the superior is so gracious that his inferiors are not frightened or embarrassed, indeed are so charmed by his gracious presence that they temporarily forget his superiority. This equality is not real but only "as it were" (expressed by *iva* in Sanskrit), yet it is essential to the situation of intimate communion between the Lord and His servants. It is the attitude and the behavior of God as avatāra that furnish the background for the understanding of all these qualities indicating the Divine saulabhya, and it is from the lives of the avatāras that illustrations of a particular quality are often drawn by the commentators. It is the present situation of the serious worshiper, however, that furnishes the most important context for Rāmānuja's thought about these qualities, as well as for that of his followers. Rāmānuja was concerned about the present communion of the devotee with the Supreme Lord, and it is about that communion that he is thinking when he says that the Lord treats His chosen devotees as His equals, or even as though they were superior to Him. The possibility of such an ontologically impossible situation is the "gracious condescension" of the Lord.

The other important Divine attribute that underlies this paradoxical relation is *vātsalya,* which may perhaps best be translated in its Śrī Vaiṣṇava usage as "protecting and forgiving love." The word originally denoted the love of a mother cow for her calf, but it came to be used much more generally to indicate affection, especially the urge to protect and succor. When Sītā suggested that Rāvaṇa should seek the mercy of her husband Rāma, she called Rāma "śaraṇāgata-vatsalaḥ." Parāśara Bhaṭṭar refers both to the original meaning of the term and to the famous passage from the *Rāmāyaṇa* in his interpretation of Vatsalaḥ as a Divine name.

> Though God has been acquainted with His śaraṇāgatas [those who have taken refuge with Him] for a long time, for some reason He wanders about (seeking to do some favor for His devotees) like a cow that has just delivered a calf, bellowing because her teats are irritated by the fulness of her udders and perplexed as to what she should do. This state of God is known even in the case of Rāvaṇa.[27]

In his definition of vātsalya, Sudarśana Sūri draws a further important consequence from the analogy of the relation of the cow to her calf. "Vātsalya means considering even a fault as a virtue, as does the mother cow immediately after the delivery of her calf. This state is the extreme limit of *kṣamā* [patience, forbearance, or forgiveness], and that quality is therefore not mentioned here separately."[28] Sudarśana Sūri is thus taking the Tengalai side in one of the important controversies between the Tengalai and Vaḍagalai schools. The Tengalai position is still more succinctly put by Periya Āccān Piḷḷai: "Because of His love [prema], even the defects of His dependents appear as virtues."[29] The Vaḍagalai teacher Vedānta Deśika gives the following definition.

> God has been described as "śaraṇāgata-vatsalaḥ." This means that His vātsalya is His affection for those souls whom He has promised to save, and this affection [prīti] goes to the extent of ignoring [screening off from vision] their faults. However,

> the view that the faults are considered as virtues is an exaggeration [ativāda].[30]

As in the case of the other two attributes just discussed, a kind of Divine self-forgetfulness is implied in this conception of vātsalya, a fact obscured by the later controversy, for there is something even more important here than the ignoring of the sin of the creature; there is the forgetting of the sinless perfection of the Creator and Judge, the doctrine dearest to Rāmānuja's heart. It might be argued on the basis of Rāmānuja's definition of mercy (dayā) that he would not have accepted either of the later definitions of the schools. In that case, Rāmānuja would have understood vātsalya along the lines of the later definition of *mārdava* (inner softness): "inability to bear separation from his devotees."[31] Once we recognize the longing for communion with His devotees as an attribute of the Divine nature, however, the essential problem returns. Why should God desire, let alone intensely yearn for, fellowship with sinful creatures? It can only be because of a fundamental impulsion in the Divine nature, a quality which at times takes precedence over everything else in God's Being. This is not a general setting aside of Divine justice. Because of His supreme compassion, God has established Himself (through His incarnations and other manifestations) as a refuge for *all,* but His vātsalya is expressed only toward those who have taken refuge (āśrita) in Him. For those, however, and more especially for the few who have shown their worthiness for His special favor, God is an "ocean of vātsalya," and Rāmānuja almost certainly understood this protecting love to include "the extreme limit of forgiveness." The result of that contact in intimate communion is the destruction or the burning away of sin, so that the devotee can look forward to liberation from this sinful world and eternal communion with his Lord, but that cleansing action is only possible because the Lord, free from the slightest trace of anything defiling, so yearns for communion with His creatures that He disregards their sinful state. This is what Rāmānuja expresses with the last of the four phrases at the end of the introduction to the *Gītābhāṣya: āśrita-vātsalya-vivaśaḥ* (overwhelmed by His love for His sinful creatures who have come to Him for refuge).

The quality of compassion discussed in the previous section

seems to have less relevance to this intimate sphere of God's communion with His devotee, yet that general concern for the happiness of creatures and distress at their misery is the basis of these more specific and dramatic Divine qualities. In the definition of mercy or compassion, too, there is a Divine self-forgetfulness: the forgetting of His own interest or gain (svārtha-nirapekṣā), the forgetting of His eternal delights and His cosmic sports, in His compassionate concern for His finite creatures.

16 Rāmānuja as a Hindu Theologian

The Term Theologian as Applied to Rāmānuja

Most of the interpretations and translations of Rāmānuja in Western languages at the beginning of the twentieth century tried to correct the prevalent Western impression that Śankara's Advaita is identical with the Vedānta, and indeed with all of Hinduism. This effort was only partially successful, but insofar as it did succeed, it gave rise to another impression: that Rāmānuja's chief significance as a thinker was his effort to refute Śankara. A corollary of this focus on the metaphysical debate with Śankara has been an almost exclusive concentration on the *Śrībhāṣya* and, more than that, on the commentary on the first sūtra.[1]

A. Govindacharya of Mysore City was an outstanding exception to the general trend. He translated into English two of the more devotional works of Rāmānuja, the *Bhagavadgītābhāṣya* and the *Śaraṇāgatigadya,* as well as much Śrī Vaiṣṇava devotional material, including the lives of the Āḻvārs and the Ācāryas (the latter book especially concerned with Rāmānuja).[2]

Hindu interpreters of this century have laid varying stress on the metaphysical and the devotional aspects of Rāmānuja's thought. In the case of Hindu scholars outside the Śrī Vaiṣṇava community, the difference in stress may reflect their differing degrees of respect for Rāmānuja as a philosopher. Śrī Vaiṣṇava scholars have continued both the traditional emphasis on Rāmānuja as the authoritative expositor of the Vedānta and the emphasis on Rāmānuja as the saintly leader of the community.[3] Most of these Hindu interpreters have a broad knowledge of Indian philosophy. In many cases they have themselves been teachers of both Western philosophy and Hindu thought in Indian universities. Understandably, therefore, they have compared Rāmānuja's thought with various systems of Western metaphysics and philosophy of religion, as well as with classical and modern expressions of other schools of Hindu thought.

The Indian Christian, Bharatan Kumarappa, writing in 1933, regards Rāmānuja's work as the "loftiest philosophical expression" of Indian theism and a significant contribution to a universal theistic metaphysics that is based on experience and is "not willing to dismiss the world of values as illusory."[4] Kumarappa presents

Rāmānuja as a theistic philosopher paying lip service to the authority of Hindu Scriptures, which he freely interprets in order to bring them into agreement with the truths "which came to him from his own sectarian religion, Vaiṣṇavism."[5]

Among non-Hindu interpreters of Rāmānuja there has been a gradual shift away from exclusive preoccupation with his metaphysics and a growing recognition that if he is to be described by a Western term, "theologian" is a more appropriate word than "philosopher." This shift can be seen in the writings of Rudolf Otto. In his translation of Rāmānuja's lengthy comments on the opening sūtra of the Brahma Sūtras, Otto was concerned primarily with Rāmānuja's battle against Śankara, which he regarded as a metaphysical debate but one whose outcome was of fundamental religious significance. Otto took Śankara and Rāmānuja to be representatives of two great antagonists (which may possibly also be regarded as two poles of religious experience): "theopanistic mysticism" pitted against "the Lord, the feeling, willing, personal, rational, loving and beloved God of the heart and conscience."[6] Thirteen years later, after a trip to India during which he had met the Śrī Vaiṣṇava scholars of Mysore (including Govindacharya), Otto wrote a book on the Śrī Vaiṣṇava religion, in which he compared its doctrine of Grace with the Christian doctrine of Grace. Here he expanded his earlier comments about Rāmānuja's dispute with Śankara. He described this as

> a battle for God, for a real God, such as not philosophical speculation, but as the heart and feelings desire and need Him: A God of personal commitment, love, adoration, and self-surrender. . . . He is basically not concerned with "philosophy," but with an apologetic for a religious inheritance which he will not allow to be stolen away. Not theistic cosmology but religion is his interest. The battle is for the God who is the supreme and only "salvation"[heil] for His believers. Not as a philosopher but as a theologian is Ramanuja interesting for us.[7]

More recently, the Dutch scholar J. A. V. van Buitenen has tried with his translations of the *Bhagavadgītābhāṣya* and the *Vedārthasaṃgraha* to present a more balanced picture of Rāmānuja's thought to the world of Western scholarship. He differs from Otto's emphasis on the *Śrībhāṣya* and the dispute with Śankara, preferring to stress Rāmānuja's positive contribution, but he extends Otto's thesis still further in maintaining not only that Rāmānuja should be understood as a theologian but also that the whole of the Vedānta is, in Western terms, "theology."

> The increasing tendency among historians of Indian philosophy to study the systems of Indian thought, particularly Vedanta, with special reference to and in comparison and juxtaposition with Western philosophies has created an unfortunate misunderstanding of the typically theological character of Vedantic speculation as a whole. . . . On the Western side there is often apparent a certain aversion to theology as such and an inability to keep in mind that the soteriology of Vedanta is not "philosophic" in purpose, but religious, inspired and borne out by scripture and revelation. The fact that the results of scriptural exegesis do not conform to conclusions of historical philological research does not mean that therefore scripture plays a subordinate role, as a handmaiden to the philosopher who cannot hope to put across his original views without the authority of revelation, and so makes it fit in with his own doctrine. This view fails to take into account the importance of the tradition of exegesis, of its method and rules.[8]

Bharadwaj's recent thesis, *The Philosophy of Rāmānuja,* which itself attempts to study Rāmānuja's thought "from a devotional point of view," quotes with approval the following statement of A. A. Macdonell: "His chief claim, the reconciliation of the doctrines of the Upaniṣads, the Bhagavadgītā, the Mahābhārata and the Purāṇas, with his own religion and philosophy, was theological rather than philosophical."[9] Bharadwaj himself concludes that "the greatness of Rāmānuja really lies in the success of his effort to elucidate canonical scriptures."[10]

Dr. S. S. Raghavachar of the University of Mysore objects to Dr. Radhakrishnan's alluding to Rāmānuja as "the Hindu Theologian" in his *An Idealist View of Life,* because

> unfortunately the term "theological" carries the associations of a dogmatic formulation of a system of thought on the authority of Scripture. It means a creed fashioned out of dogmas, not pursuing truth for its own sake and not employing methods of free, rational and philosophical investigations. It is reason fettered by faith.[11]

Raghavachar insists that Rāmānuja's thought is not "theological" in this sense, since Rāmānuja admits both perception and inference as valid modes of knowledge, and his acceptance of the primacy of Scripture is not more pronounced than that of such other Vedāntic teachers as Śankara and Madhva. Moreover, Rāmānuja adopts on rational grounds the Mīmāṃsaka view that "all knowledge is intrinsically valid" unless it contradicts itself or contradicts other "unimpeachable facts ascertained by observation and reasoning." Thus Rāmānuja states that "even for supporting the Śruti, what is against reason and is contradictory of the evidences should not be postulated."

> Lastly, the supremacy of the scripture, its role as the revelation of the supreme, is itself based upon its satisfactory fulfillment of the criterion of truth and validity settled by empirical intelligence. It satisfies its claim to truth by conforming to a standard that is not set up by itself.[12]

Raghavachar rightly points out the importance of perception and reason in Rāmānuja's thought, but even if there was a decision to accord Scripture primacy as a source of knowledge concerning the nature of God and the way to salvation, the fact remains that this was a decision reached by all schools of the Vedānta, a decision which seems to me to justify van Buitenen's view that *theological* is a more appropriate term than *philosophical* for the entire Vedānta, including the school of Rāmānuja. Such translation is never entirely adequate, and both philosophy and theology not only have a wide range of intellectual connotations but also summon a wide range of emotional response. It is true that there is a pronounced philosophical content in many of the Hindu Scriptures themselves, particularly the Upaniṣads and the semicanonical summary of Upaniṣadic teaching, the *Vedānta Sūtras.* This fact may give Hindu thinkers who interpret these Scriptures a better claim to the title of "philosopher" than that of Christian thinkers who have interpreted the Bible, but I would suggest that in the case of both Hindu and Christian exegetes of sacred Scriptures the manner of interpretation is at least as important as the nature of the material being interpreted.

My concern here, in any event, is not to deny that Rāmānuja is also in some significant sense a philosopher but to maintain that he is certainly a theologian, as that term is used in Christian circles. I suggest that considering his thought as "theological" may make its specific character clearer, at least to Western students of religion.

When I describe Rāmānuja's thought as "theological," I mean that it grows out of a tradition of religious devotion that it seeks to defend (Otto) and that it tries to reconcile the different types of Scriptures (Macdonell). What is even more important, however, as van Buitenen has rightly emphasized, is that these Scriptures are considered to be transhuman and hence authoritative and that a serious attempt is made to conform the interpretation to the content of the scriptural texts. It is, of course, always debatable to what extent any theologian, of whatever religion, really conforms his mind to his sacred texts; there is always a process of interaction with a resultant "reading into" the text of what is really not there, but there is also a "reading out" of meaning that is really there but has not previously been clearly brought to light. In this phenomenological study I am not concerned to determine the proportions of reading in and reading out but only to recognize the serious intent in Rāmānuja's mind to make his thought conform to the meaning of the texts. He believes that there is a consistent meaning to be found in all sacred Scriptures, but he is prepared to suffer apparent and temporary inconsistency, or at least incompleteness, in order to remain faithful to the meaning of the particular text on which he is commenting. This by no means implies a lack of a metaphysical position or of interest in ontological problems. It simply means that this is not "philosophy" in the sense in which that term has been used in the West since the Renaissance: inquiry determined by the canons of human reason without the influence of supposed "revelation."

Rāmānuja is a "theologian" both in the sense that he believes that the knowledge of God is given in the sacred Scriptures, indeed only therein, and in the sense that he attempts to extract the real meaning, which for him means the literal meaning, of these Scriptures. He is also an "orthodox theologian" in the sense that he does not set out on his interpretation of the Scriptures independently but relies as far as possible on the previous tradition of interpretation of those Scriptures in his own religious community. He is a "systematic theologian," since he attempts to demonstrate that the Scriptures can be understood as a harmonious whole if we but recognize certain truths about God and His universe, and these fundamental doctrines are elucidated and applied with relation to the various aspects of his teaching.

RĀMĀNUJA'S INTERPRETATION OF SCRIPTURE

Whether or not we call Rāmānuja a theologian, we have to recognize that he shares in an Indian intellectual tradition that has many philosophical elements, notably a concern with epistemology that is nearly as great as that of post-Renaissance Western philosophy. Yet in the particular tradition of philosophical-theological inquiry to which Rāmānuja belonged, the Vedānta, this inquiry has the form of an exegesis of the Vedas and the later Hindu Scriptures. If we are to understand the thinking of Rāmānuja, we need to note his own conception of his task as an interpreter of Scripture. A full-scale study of Rāmānuja's principles and practice of exegesis would be most rewarding. While that is not possible here, one widespread misunderstanding of Rāmānuja's approach, of which Kumarappa is a spokesman, needs to be discussed.

Much of this study has been concerned with Rāmānuja's treatment of the attributes belonging to the Divine nature. For those educated with the historical conceptions of the modern West, it is natural to interpret Rāmānuja's holding together of different groups of Divine attributes as an important aspect of his effort to reconcile divergent religious traditions. This suggests itself the more readily in the case of the Divine attributes, since Rāmānuja finds textual support for the five "defining attributes" of the Supreme Self in the Śruti (the Upaniṣads), whereas for evidence of the relational attributes of God not considered part of His "inner essence" (svarūpa), he generally cites texts from the second level of Scripture called Smṛti (especially from the *Bhagavadgītā,* which is a part of the great epic, the *Mahābhārata,* and from the *Viṣṇu Purāṇa*). Kumarappa maintains that Rāmānuja

> at any rate found in the Viṣṇu Purāṇa a description of the blessed qualities of the Deity, which descriptions he failed to find except in very meagre form in the Upaniṣads. He accordingly depends chiefly on the Viṣṇu Purāṇa for an enumeration of the attributes which belong to the Divine nature.[13]

Kumarappa finds in Rāmānuja's quotations from the *Viṣṇu Purāṇa* two ideas "not to be found in the Upaniṣads, and hence . . . to be regarded as distinctly sectarian. . . . One of them is the enumeration of six qualities—glory, strength, dominion, wisdom, energy and power—as belonging to Brahman. . . . The other . . . is the description of the Deity as assuming various forms for the benefit of the world." He also holds that there is a much clearer and more consistent formulation in the *Viṣṇu Purāṇa* than in the Upaniṣads of the doctrine that "the Deity is a Perfect being, in whom there is no evil."[14] Kumarappa maintains that "Rāmānuja . . . does not hesitate to read his own view into texts . . . even in his Śrībhāsya. [And in] his commentary on the Bhagavadgītā dealing . . . with a literary work of his own sect, he is at liberty to give expression to sectarian ideas without let or hindrance."[15]

If Rāmānuja were simply reading his own sectarian views into his interpretation of the texts, however, it is difficult to understand why he often uses the narrower Upaniṣadic definition of Brahman's essential nature, which does not include aspects of the Divine nature that are fundamental to Śrī Vaiṣṇavas: all the qualities expressed in God's relations to the world as creator, ruler, and redeemer. While this restriction of the "essential nature" of God can be understood as a distinction between the Divine aseity and other aspects of the Divine nature, it remains true, I believe, that Rāmānuja uses the narrower Upaniṣadic definition because that is what he finds in the Upaniṣadic texts.

If one were to attempt a historical analysis of the influence of the various religious traditions on Rāmānuja's thought, he could demonstrate that there has been a real interaction among these traditions and a significant synthesis of Upaniṣadic, Purāṇic, and Dravidian concepts. But such an interpretation, however carefully documented, would remain an "outside" view of Rāmānuja and his thought. For this particular study it is of more concern to understand what Rāmānuja himself thinks he is doing. On the question of the relation of the Upaniṣads and the Purāṇas in the proper interpretation of Scripture, he is quite explicit.

Rāmānuja refers to a rule of the *Karma Mīmāṃsā Sūtras* (1.1.3): "Smṛti is to be disregarded whenever it contradicts Śruti." He first states that when a matter can definitely be settled by reference to Śruti, as in the case of the rules for conducting sacrifices, Smṛti need not be consulted. The Upaniṣads, however, are concerned with truths beyond the competence of perception and inference, and students with only an elementary knowledge of this scriptural revelation require some help to understand the meaning of the Vedānta. Such corroboration is provided by many Smṛtis composed by trustworthy persons in accord with Śruti. But where the Smṛti disagrees with Śruti and with many other Smṛtis, it cannot furnish such corroboration and hence does not furnish authoritative knowledge.[16] In the *Vedārthasaṃgraha,* too, Rāmānuja states that the Epics and Purāṇas corroborate the Vedas, thus establishing the same meaning.[17] "Since the Vedas are endless and difficult to understand, the great seers have been ordered by the Supreme Person to transmit the sense of the Veda in every age in order to help all the worlds, and they have composed the Dharmaśāstras, Epics, and Purāṇas."[18]

Most of Rāmānuja's quotations from the Purāṇas are from the *Viṣṇu Purāṇa,* which he says is accepted by scholars from the four corners of the land as adequate for both ethics and theology. He accepts all the Purāṇas as inspired by the cosmic fashioner Brahmā (whatever sage may have compiled them), but they are of four different types, because they were composed on different "days" when a particular strand of material nature was dominant. Only those like the *Viṣṇu Purāṇa* that were composed when the strand (quality) of sattva (purity) was preponderant are fully authoritative, and they prevail in case of conflict with other Purāṇas in whose composition the other qualities of rajas (passion) or tamas (dullness) predominated or which were composed under the influence of a mixture of all these qualities (guṇas). As far as theology is concerned, the *Viṣṇu Purāṇa* has the "exclusive purpose of setting forth a certain aspect of Brahman's essence" (not simply a phenomenal projection), namely, "Viṣṇu, who represents Nārāyaṇa's character of omnipresent pervader and savior-god of incarnations."[19]

Van Buitenen's reply to the criticism of Rāmānuja's use of the *Viṣṇu Purāṇa* is worth quoting:

> Not infrequently Rāmānuja is opposed to Śankara as the "first sectarian commentator," by which is meant that he was the first to introduce into *Vedāntamīmāṃsā,* so far kept pure, external and deteriorating elements which made his system a parochial *manifesto* rather than a universally valid system of thought; or it is said that he fabricated scriptural evidence, that is to say, made room within the Vedānta for a great many śrutis and smṛtis that Śankara either ignored or delegated to the rank of relative truth. It is clear that those who pass these criticisms take Śankara's selections and treatment of scriptures as normative, in other words, believe on speculative grounds that Śankara is more right than Rāmānuja. Rāmānuja's citations of the Viṣṇupurāṇa are only illustrative and corrobora-

> tive. His justification of these citations would be acceptable to his fellow Vedāntins. It is for all Vedānta that he claims to speak.[20]

He compares Rāmānuja's sparing use of Smṛti with Madhva's practice. The latter "not only quotes Purāṇas and Tantras much more frequently than śruti, but treats their evidence as decisive for Vedānta."[21] It should be added that Śrī Vaiṣṇavas in the generations following Rāmānuja also made much greater use in their doctrinal works not only of Smṛti but of the *Pāñcarātra Āgamas* and the Tamil hymns of the Āḻvārs.

THE CONTRAST BETWEEN RĀMĀNUJA'S STYLE AND LATER SCHOLASTIC STYLE

One of the most popular summaries of doctrine among contemporary Śrī Vaiṣṇavas is the *Yatīndramatadīpikā* of Śrīnivāsadāsa, who lived in Tirupati about the beginning of the seventeenth century A.D.[22] The title may be paraphrased as "A Guiding Lamp to the Theology of Rāmānuja," and the introductory verse says that it was composed for the instruction of beginners (bālabodhārtham).[23] It is subdivided according to nine logical-metaphysical categories. The information concerning the nature of God is succintly presented under the eighth category, Īśvara, but some topics are dealt with in the chapters on Nityavibhūti (the eternal realm), Dharmabhūtajñāna (attributive consciousness), and Jīva (the finite self). The chapter on Īśvara first gives a definition of Īśvara and then defines what is meant by His being the material and efficient cause of the universe. Then comes a proof that this Sole Cause is not Brahmā or Śiva but only Śrīman-Nārāyaṇa. After refuting various false views of Īśvara, the author describes the nature of God according to the different classes of attributes (each attribute carefully defined) and the five forms of God. The chapter ends with a brief paragraph on the Divine consort.[24]

The work of Rāmānuja's that is closest in structure to the *Yatīndramatadīpikā* is his *Vedārthasaṃgraha,* but if one compares the two, it becomes very quickly obvious how much less schematic Rāmānuja's presentation is. In this work, as well as in his commentaries, he does not treat topics with logical exhaustiveness but confines himself to questions that bear directly on the topics at hand and to points of past or current dispute between Śrī Vaiṣṇavas and others. Sometimes the questions raised are so fundamental that it is necessary to go into great detail and to treat topics that seem far afield. The outstanding example of this is *Śrībhāṣya* 1.1.1; yet even in that section, which is so long and so comprehensive that it has been regarded as an independent treatise, the same characteristic of his thought stands out very clearly: every topic taken up is necessary to prove Rāmānuja's case, and no topic is taken up simply for the sake of logical completeness. The topics are determined by Scripture and tradition; the specific questions are framed in accordance with the burning theological, philosophical, and practical religious issues of the day. Every paragraph and every sentence is very much to the point. This concern for relevance in Rāmānuja's thought is not, however, the same as the anxiety over wasting a single word that has characterized Hindu grammarians, which may be reflected in the care to avoid any repetition shown by his own followers. Rāmānuja can be prodigal with words when it serves his purpose, and his use of terms is not nearly so precise as that of the later Śrī Vaiṣṇava scholastics. He uses many important terms repeatedly without defining them, and certain key terms seem to be used with a wide range of meaning. This makes a study of his thought more difficult, but it is precisely this that makes Rāmānuja such an interesting thinker. He is always debating with his opponents, exhorting his followers, or praising his Lord; he is never simply writing a textbook.

RĀMĀNUJA'S DISTINCTIVE STYLE: DEVOTION EXPRESSED IN PROSE

Everything that Rāmānuja has written is in prose. Even the Gadyas, which resemble poems or hymns in their content, are written in prose. Since most of these writings are in the form of commentaries, traditionally written in prose, this may not seem surprising. Yet there is a strong poetic strain in the bhakti tradition, including the South Indian Vaiṣṇava tradition. Many of the Sanskrit Scriptures are in verse, and the entire Tamil scriptural tradition of the Śrī Vaiṣṇavas consists of a collection of hymns. Many of the Śrī Vaiṣṇava teachers, moreover, have written hymns (stotras) or poems (kāvyas) in addition to commentaries or doctrinal treatises in prose. This is strikingly true of Rāmānuja's predecessor Yāmuna, who has written two hymns as well as a brief summary of the *Bhagavadgītā* in verse.[25] The only work of one of Yāmuna's disciples that has survived is an eight-verse hymn in praise of Lord Varadarāja (the form of Viṣṇu in Kāñcīpuram) by Kāñcīpūrṇa, the non-Brahmin devotee who was Rāmānuja's first spiritual guide, though not formally his ācārya.[26] Rāmānuja's able assistant Kūraṭṭāḻvān has compositions in both prose and verse;[27] the same is true of his son, Parāśara Bhaṭṭar, whom Rāmānuja appointed as his successor in Śrīrangam.[28] A number of Śrī Vaiṣṇava teachers in the following generations have contributed to the collection of hymns. The versatile teacher Vedānta Deśika has composed many hymns and a drama in verse, in addition to many commentaries and treatises in prose.[29]

More important than the fact that Rāmānuja writes in prose is the fact that he thinks "in prose," not prosaically but with an emphasis on rational consistency. Yet "thinking in prose" does not lead him to expound his system in terms of a scheme of logically exhaustive categories. He remains primarily a commentator of sacred texts, some of them in verse, and many of them expressing the poetry of devotion. The poetic flavor of the *Gītā* is not altogether lost in Rāmānuja's prose commentary, especially since he makes his comments in the form of a paraphrase, keeping the form of a conversation between Lord Krishna and Arjuna.[30] The meaning of each verse, however, is fitted into a comprehensive theological scheme, with the consistency appropriate to prose. In his commentaries on the *Vedānta Sūtras,* Rāmānuja is elaborating and defending a tradition of prose commentary on the Upaniṣads. A large number of verses from the Upaniṣads and other Sanskrit Scriptures are commented on in the course of his writings. Rāmānuja does not simply lift out proof texts; he tries to pay attention to the context, but it is a context of rational discourse, and Rāmānuja demands that each word be considered literally.

It may be his insistence on literal precision as well as on rational consistency that leads Rāmānuja to stay away from poetry. Both the secular and the sacred use of the poetry of praise was regarded by some contemporaries as flattery not to be taken literally. Praise (stuti, stava, or stotra) was for them virtually synonymous with exaggeration. Rāmānuja's disciple Parāśara Bhaṭṭar takes pains in his commentary on the "Thousand Names of Viṣṇu" to explain that the recitation of the names of the Lord (nāmasaṃkīrtana) is not such poetic exaggeration.[31]

The Āḻvārs use the various techniques of Indian poetry to express their strong feelings. Their verses display a variety of moods, including unsatisfied longing, jealousy, and disappointment, as well as gratitude, humility, and joyous fulfillment. Their techniques include exaggeration and what is called *nindastuti* (praise through abuse). This latter poetic form assumes that the person praised must be very great indeed if he can stand being insulted.[32] In any case, as this nindastuti is used in addressing Lord Viṣṇu, it implies a great familiarity between the Lord and His devotee, and it involves both irony and paradox.

There is no reason why irony and paradox cannot be incorporated in a "prose translation" of such poetry. Yāmuna recognizes some of the different moods present in the different verses. This at least is the impression one gains from the commentary tradition on the most philosophical of the Tamil Vaiṣṇava hymns, the *Tiruvāymoḻi* of Nammāḻvār. Rāmānuja, on the other hand, according to these same commentaries, opposes Yāmuna's interpretations at such points and attempts to formulate an alternative that demonstrates Nammāḻvār's logical and theological consistency.[33]

One such instance is recorded in the biographies of Rāmānuja: his instruction in the *Tiruvāymoḻi* by Yāmuna's disciple Tirumālai Āṇḍān (Mālādhara). Āṇḍān started his lessons, following the interpretation he had learned from Āḷavandār (Yāmuna). Uḍayavar (Rāmānuja) gave some special meaning to each stanza, to which Āṇḍān's standard response was, "We never heard [this interpretation] from Āḷavandār." When Āṇḍān came to stanza 2.3.3, he interpreted it as follows: "Oh God, when my knowledge was not matured, Thou gavest me the knowledge of my relation to Thee, yet Thou has also given me a connection with this body, which is capable of destroying the knowledge already born." He then added in comment, "With this feeling of loss [of the Divine gift of knowledge] the Āḻvār starts this stanza." To this interpretation Rāmānuja objected.

> When the Āḻvār was pleased with God in the previous and the following stanzas, it is not proper for him to express his displeasure with God here in between. Therefore the meaning must be like this, "In this saṃsāra full of illusion and ignorance, when I was completely ignorant, Thou madest me to have affection for Thy service."

Āṇḍān was not convinced by this ingenious shift of the order of words in the stanza in order to show that Nammāḻvār was here, too, expressing his gratitude (upakāra-smṛti). In fact, he stopped his lessons, saying to Rāmānuja, "This interpretation [of yours] is the creation of Viśvāmitra [sheer invention without any basis]. We have not heard this from Āḷavandār."

At the end of the story Rāmānuja was vindicated, for Tirukoṭṭiyūr Nambi came and convinced Tirumālai Āṇḍān to resume his lessons, explaining that he (Nambi) had indeed heard such an interpretation from Yāmuna and that Rāmānuja had the power intuitively to divine Yāmuna's profoundest meaning. Yet the other instances in the commentary tradition where Rāmānuja differs from Yāmuna's interpretation make clear that Āṇḍān had grounds for his complaint. Rāmānuja's interpretation is an innovation, made in the interests of logical consistency and of a uniform mood of grateful praise. Complaint against God has little or no place in Rāmānuja's notion of devotion, which should be an unremitting remembrance of the perfections of the Divine nature.[34]

Rāmānuja's great achievement and great contribution to his religious community is the filling out of the outline provided by his predecessors, possibly Nāthamuni and certainly Yāmuna, into a complete theological system. It is not surprising that some of the poetry of the devotional tradition is lost in the process. What is more remarkable, considering the differences in personality as well as in background, is that Rāmānuja has incorporated and elaborated so many of Yāmuna's insights in his own thought and has, at least with respect to God's accessibility and inaccessibility, retained a touch of the poetic paradox of Yāmuna and the Āḻvārs.

17 Rāmānuja's Relation to His Successors: The Problem of the Gadyas

Implications of the Question of the Authenticity of the Gadyas

By two centuries after Rāmānuja the Śrī Vaiṣṇava community had split into two subsects that looked to Vedānta Deśika and his older contemporary Piḷḷai Lokācārya, respectively, as their formative teachers, though the final hardening of sectarian lines did not occur until a generation later, when Lokācārya's successor Manavāḷamāmuni gave a definitive form to the Tengalai doctrine and sectarian organization. Vedānta Deśika seems to have regarded himself as a reconciler of divergent views, but he is regarded by some of his Vaḍagalai followers as a more gifted teacher than Rāmānuja and as the virtual founder of a new religious community bearing his name. The Tengalais on the other hand, have long regarded Manavāḷamāmuni (two generations after Piḷḷai Lokācārya) as a veritable reincarnation of Rāmānuja. Both subsects regard themselves, however, as faithful to the teaching of Rāmānuja and his predecessors. They differ as to whom Rāmānuja appointed as his successor and as to how the succession proceeded from that time on.

The writings that have survived during the period between Rāmānuja and the definitive split indicate the presence of different points of view but not of the fully developed positions of the later schools. Both schools accept the commentaries on Rāmānuja's works of Sudarśana Sūri, who was a generation older than Piḷḷai Lokācārya and Vedānta Deśika, but neither school claims Sudarśana Sūri as one of its line of ācāryas. Meghanādāri Sūri was another teacher of about the same time, but his views found favor with neither school.

An understanding of Rāmānuja's own theology should make it possible to estimate how closely his thought has been followed by the two schools of Śrī Vaiṣṇavas. This study has been concerned with only a part of Rāmānuja's theology, his doctrine of God (Īśvaratattva), and most of the points of controversy between the two schools touch only obliquely on the doctrine of God. In terms of the divisions of Vedāntic theology, the dispute over the nature of Divine grace concerned the definition of the means to attain salvation (hita). Yet the connection of this dispute with Rāmānuja's conception of God, however indirect in terms of the formal theological system, is clearly important. Has one of the later schools shifted from Rāmānuja's own conception of the Divine nature, or have they both diverged from Rāmānuja's own position?

Here, I believe, lies the major significance of Pandit Agnihothram Rāmānuja Thatachariar's thesis that Rāmānuja was not the author of the three Gadyas and the *Nityagrantha,* a significance that has been grasped and elaborated by Professor Robert Lester. Pandit Agnihothram is suggesting far more than just that Rāmānuja did not write certain small devotional works attributed to him. He is suggesting that Rāmānuja's total teaching and total religious stance were quite different from that of the later Śrī Vaiṣṇavas of both schools. He suggests that Rāmānuja was a Vedic Brahmin who upheld the Śrī Vaiṣṇava community in his defense of a theistic interpretation of the Vedānta but whose relation to the sectarian doctrines and practices of the community was extremely tenuous. Pandit Agnihothram cannot altogether deny the sectarian teachings in what he himself accepts as Rāmānuja's genuine writings, but he regards them largely as concessions to popular religious sentiment.

The detailed arguments of Pandit Agnihothram and Professor Lester are given in the notes to this book.[1] What concerns us in this chapter are the general issues this challenge raises concerning the relation of Rāmānuja to subsequent Śrī Vaiṣṇava history. I believe that these problems should be faced, even though in some cases their solution lies far beyond my competence, and certainly beyond the scope of this book.

Pandit Agnihothram has viewed his own tradition in a Western historical perspective, and he has seen something that seems evident to the historian but unacceptable to the orthodox Śrī Vaiṣṇava, namely, that there are important differences between Rāmānuja's thought and the subsequent tradition. He emphasizes something that is hinted at in Rāmānuja's biography as well as in his own writings: that Rāmānuja came from a much more Vedic-oriented background than many Śrī Vaiṣṇavas and was less imbued with the Vaiṣṇava sectarian tradition than most of his followers or his predecessor Yāmuna.

Pandit Agnihothram has also, however, some very nonobjective prejudices of the kind that sometimes lurk behind the "objectivity" of historians. He reads the texts in the light of his own Vedic predilections, which to some extent reflect his particular family traditions within the Vaḍagalai subcommunity, and therefore he pushes Rāmānuja too far in the other direction from the developments in the Śrī Vaiṣṇava community.

Both Rāmānuja's admittedly genuine writings and certain episodes in the biography show that Rāmānuja did not remain simply a Vedic-oriented Vaḍama Brahmin. Though he was never an uncritical convert to sectarian Vaiṣṇavism, he certainly tried to learn from it, both intellectually and personally. According to the biographies, the beginning of this learning process was carrying a pot of water every day to the temple in Kāñcīpuram for the worship of the Supreme Lord in His image form of Varadarāja.

Even if the evidence from the biographies is ruled out as too uncertain, the fact remains that in his first major work, the *Vedārtha-saṃgraha,* Rāmānuja stresses that the human soul is the servant (dāsa) or disposable property (śeṣa) of God and concludes the work by refuting a Vedic Brahmin who quotes from the *Laws of Manu,* "Service is a dog's life."[2] Equally important is Rāmānuja's dependence, at a number of points acknowledged, on the thought of Yāmuna, who both personally and through his family had a much closer connection than Rāmānuja with the sectarian Śrī Vaiṣṇava traditions.

PRAPATTI AND BHAKTI

The question that has usually been central in any discussion of the *Gadyatraya* is its doctrine of prapatti. Later Śrī Vaiṣṇavas have held that Rāmānuja in those works clearly expounds the doctrine that is so important in their own thought: that a person will be saved if he simply surrenders himself to God, even though he has not practiced any of the recognized means to salvation: karma, jñāna, or bhakti. The Vaḍagalais maintain that it is only in the Gadyas and the *Nityagrantha* that prapatti is unambiguously expounded as an independent means to salvation, for in his other writings Rāmānuja teaches the more difficult path of repeated devotional meditation, called bhakti or upāsanā. Pandit Agnihothram accepts this traditional Vaḍagalai distinction concerning the doctrines of salvation propounded in these two groups of writings, but he breaks sharply with his tradition in denying that the same man could have taught such a different doctrine in a second group of writings. Therefore this second group of writings, in his view, cannot have been composed by Rāmānuja himself.

If the Gadyas contained a doctrine of prapatti identical with that of the later schools, we should certainly be confronted with a contradiction that is difficult to imagine existing in the mind of Rāmānuja. However, the actual concept (or concepts) of prapatti found in the Gadyas differs both from that of the later schools and from that in Rāmānuja's undisputed works. Indeed, in some ways, the notion of surrender to God in the Gadyas forms a link between the undisputed writings of Rāmānuja and the later developments in the two Śrī Vaiṣṇava schools. It is this intermediate position that makes it difficult to determine definitely whether or not Rāmānuja himself wrote the Gadyas and the *Nityagrantha*.

Rāmānuja's two alternative interpretations of the chief prapatti text in *Bhagavadgītā* 18.66, called the *caramaśloka* (the last word), are not used by Vedānta Deśika to support the doctrine of prapatti as he understood it, because they do not clearly state that "surrender" is an alternative path to salvation from that of "devotion." Rāmānuja's two interpretations of the caramaśloka, however, reveal an understanding of "surrender" that is not so different from the position of the Gadyas. *Gītā* 18.66 is as follows:

Abandoning all duties,	sarvadharmān parityajya
Adopt me as thy sole refuge;	mām ekaṃ śaraṇam vraja
From all sins I thee	ahaṃ tvā sarvapāpebhyo
Shall rescue: be not grieved!	mokṣayiṣyāmi mā śucaḥ[3]

In his first interpretation Rāmānuja takes "all dharmas" to mean all the paths to mokṣa previously taught—karmayoga, jñānayoga, and bhaktiyoga—but he does not take *parityajya* literally. These disciplines are not to be abandoned but to be performed as a worship pleasing to God and entirely in the spirit of love, in a manner accordant with the devotee's own position in society and spiritual qualifications. Those things that should be abandoned are the karmic "fruit" of such actions, the idea that the actions are one's own, and the idea that one is their real author. Correspondingly, adopting the Lord as one's sole refuge means that one recognizes that He is both the actor and the One worshiped through the action: He is both the goal (upeya) and the means (upāya). If the Lord is thus worshiped, He will deliver His devotees from the accumulated sins that prevent the devotee from reaching Him.

In his second and alternative interpretation, Rāmānuja interprets "dharmas" to mean expiatory ceremonies to remove sins. Since there is an infinite weight of such sins, since the ceremonies designed to remove them are also countless and difficult to perform, and since life is short, the Lord counsels Arjuna not to practice such expiatory rites but instead to take refuge in Him, and He will remove the sins that prevent Arjuna from undertaking bhaktiyoga.[4]

Vedānta Deśika comments that Rāmānuja is not so clear about the deeper meaning of this verse (the doctrine of prapatti) here as he is in his later work, the *Śaraṇāgatigadya*. There is a hint, Deśika says, contained in the second interpretation, for it shows that just as a man may give up expiatory ceremonies and surrender to the Lord in order to be able to begin bhaktiyoga, so one who considers that he cannot perform bhaktiyoga at all may give up bhakti-, jñāna-, and karmayoga and may surrender to attain Him directly; that is, to secure mokṣa.[5]

A different interpretation of Rāmānuja's comment was given by Meghanādāri Sūri, a Śrī Vaiṣṇava scholar somewhat earlier than Vedānta Deśika, who had a number of views of prapatti that differed from those subsequently adopted by either of the two schools. One of these distinctive views was that Rāmānuja's view of prapatti was the same in all his works, in the *Śrībhāṣya* and the *Gītābhāṣya* as well as in the Gadyas. It is, he holds, an independent means, and it is this prapatti as an independent means that Rāmānuja propounds in the *first* of the two interpretations of the caramaśloka. The second, he says, is concerned with bhakti, with surrender as a means to clearing away the obstacles to the commencement of bhaktiyoga.[6] Meghanādāri Sūri's comment rightly focuses attention on the first interpretation as the one that is in accord with Rāmānuja's teaching in the *Śrībhāṣya* as well as in the Gadyas. It is this first interpretation that seems to me to be at the basis of the later developments of the doctrine of prapatti as an independent means to salvation.

In this first interpretation, Rāmānuja is following the summary of the meaning of the eighteenth chapter of the *Gītā* given in verse 22 of Yāmuna's *Gītārthasaṃgraha*. "The last lecture deals with the knowledge in virtue of which all agency is attributed to God" (Īśvara-kartṛtā-buddhiḥ). All through the *Gītābhāṣya,* Rāmānuja has been emphasizing this point, but here he extends it from its initial application to ritual action (karma) to include all human efforts to attain salvation. All of these forms of worship should continue, but it is only in a secondary sense that they are means to salvation, for God Himself is the true means (upāya) as well as the goal (upeya), the One who enables the worship to be done (the doer) as well as the One who is worshiped. Śaraṇāgati or prapatti is here, not an alternative to bhakti, but its true meaning, though in devotional expressions where the emphasis is on the all-sufficiency of the Lord's action and the unworthiness of the devotee, bhakti, jñāna, and karma seem to fall into insignificance. This is certainly a long way from the later understanding of prapatti as a particular cultic act by means of which one's salvation is assured. It is even further away from the later practice of having prapatti done on one's behalf by the ācārya or the later doctrine that it had already been performed on one's behalf by Rāmānuja. Nevertheless, it certainly provides some basis for these later developments, for Rāmānuja has followed Yāmuna in radically extending and deepening the teaching of the *Bhagavadgītā* in such a way as to relativize (though not to make any the less necessary) all human religious effort as a means of gaining salvation. Once it is recognized that it is fundamentally God who accomplishes man's salvation, the joys of mystical communion and humble service, which might previously have been considered part of the human path to reach God, are understood to be part of the divine estate into which the devotee enters by the grace of God.

It is important also to note Rāmānuja's comment on the previous verse (18.65). Having said that God is now going to speak his final word to Arjuna concerning the bhaktiyoga, Rāmānuja interprets the sixty-fifth verse to mean that Arjuna is instructed to practice that continuous representation or calling to mind that is synonymous with knowledge, worship, and meditation, which is contemplation most dear to the worshiper. God should be worshiped with excessive love (not simply by rituals without accompanying emotion). The worship that is pleasing to God is the performance of the entire round of services that are incumbent on a śeṣa, services that a liege or serf should perform for his master or owner.[7] Here the entire life of devotion is interpreted, not, as sometimes in Rāmānuja's writings, as particular actions that please the Lord and elicit an appropriate reward, but as that which is in accordance with one's essential nature, which is both one's duty and one's joy.

THE GADYAS AND THE LATER COMMENTARIES

One of the striking differences in terminology between the Gadyas and the undisputed writings of Rāmānuja is the use of the expression, "parabhakti, parajñāna, and paramabhakti." (Pandit Agnihothram has noted these terms but has not based on them a separate objection to the authenticity of the Gadyas.) In the other writings *parabhakti* (higher or supreme devotion) is equated with the true knowledge of God produced by repeated meditation upon Him and is contrasted with ordinary devotion (sāmānyabhakti) toward God to gain worldly ends from Him. In the Gadyas, however, there seem to be two further stages in spiritual growth beyond parabhakti: *parajñāna* (higher knowledge) and *paramabhakti* (the highest devotion). These terms are nowhere defined in these works; they are interpreted by later commentators to mean the following: parabhakti, the devotee's longing (before its accomplishment) to have an everlasting vision of the Lord; parajñāna, the achievement for a brief period of such a vision of God; and paramabhakti, the desire to have the experience of this vision continue forever.[8]

If such was the meaning for the author of the Gadyas (whether Rāmānuja or someone else) there is a distinctiveness in terminology but no conflict in basic ideas between this notion of bhakti and that in the undisputed works of Rāmānuja. These three stages seem to describe especially the Āḻvārs' devotional experience: periods of intense and anguished longing for communion with God alternating with periods of enjoyment of the Divine fellowship. The state of continuous communion with the Lord comes only after the end of this earthly life.

In terms of basic doctrine and fundamental point of view the Gadyas and the *Nityagrantha* seem much closer to Rāmānuja's undisputed writings than they are to the developing Śrī Vaiṣṇava scholasticism of a century and a half after Rāmānuja, whose representatives we may see in the three commentators on the *Gadyatraya*: Sudarśana Sūri, Periya Āccān Piḷḷai, and Vedānta Deśika. Sudarśana Sūri regards prapatti as an independent means to salvation, which is distinct from bhakti. Periya Āccān Piḷḷai teaches that prapatti, surrender to God, is the only way to reach Him and that it must replace a way of devotion in which one relies on one's own efforts. Vedānta Deśika, on the other hand, insists that Rāmānuja taught bhakti as the means to attain God in all his works except in the *Gadyatraya* (and the *Nityagrantha*), where prapatti was taught as an easier means open to all, including women, Śudras, and outcastes, instead of being limited to men of the three higher castes (which in South India limits it almost entirely to Brahmins), who alone are privileged to study the Vedas and perform Vedic rites, the prerequisites to the practice of pious meditation on Brahman.[9]

The understanding of prapatti in the Gadyas is clearly different from the views of the later commentators, and there seem to be some differences, as least in emphasis, among the three Gadyas themselves. The obvious interpretation of śaraṇāgati in the Gadya bearing this name is that it is an act of surrendering to or taking refuge with the Lord in order to be freed from the sins that prevent one from taking up the path of devotion and in order to be given the grace to follow that path. This would mean, however, that the author is only teaching "surrender" as a necessary condition of commencing the path of devotion (which Rāmānuja has done several times in his undisputed works), not as an independent path in its own right. To avoid this conclusion, the commentators interpret "parabhakti . . ." to mean the spiritual state of one who has *already* been saved; they are not the upāya (means) but the upeya (the goal). In addition to this interpretation, Sudarśana Sūri gives a slightly different one in which parabhakti is identified with prapatti as the means to salvation (which implies that God Himself is the means, since He saves the one who has confessed his own helplessness), and parajñāna and paramabhakti have the same significance as in the first interpretation, not upāyas but upeyas obtainable just before final release from the body.[10] Similarly Vedānta Deśika comments that the bhakti prayed for here is not an upāya for attaining mokṣa but an end in itself (svayamprayojana).[11]

The appearance of the term *bhaktiyoga* in the mangalaśloka of the *Vaikuṇṭhagadya* presents the later commentators with a comparable difficulty. This dedicatory verse is a tribute to Yāmuna: "Having dived into Śrī Yāmunācārya's ocean of ambrosia to the best of my understanding, I have brought up [from the bottom] the gem called bhaktiyoga and am holding it up to view." It seems to be modeled on the first three verses of Yāmuna's "Stotraratna," which are themselves in praise of Yāmuna's grandfather and spiritual predecessor, Nāthamuni, the founder of the Śrī Vaiṣṇava monastic order at Śrīrangam and the collector of the hymns of the Āḻvārs. In the third verse of the "Stotraratna" it is said that by his words Nāthamuni caused the supremely real and comprehensive (paramārthasamagra) bhaktiyoga to descend into this world.[12]

Vedānta Deśika comments that at the beginning of the *Vaikuṇṭhagadya* bhaktiyoga should not be understood in the same sense as in the *Bhagavadgītā* and Rāmānuja's *Gītābhāṣya,* since this would be inconsistent with the statement a few lines further, "There is no other means [of salvation for me] than prapatti at His two lotus-like feet." Hence, Deśika says, bhaktiyoga is here to be understood as meaning "contemplation of Bhagavān as an end in itself."[13] This is a most illuminating comment, for it shows that it was something of an embarrassment to the later commentators that bhakti could be taken as synonymous with prapatti, since by that time both schools of Śrī Vaiṣṇavas were convinced that there was an essential difference between bhakti and prapatti. It seems to me quite inconceivable that if the Gadyas were written not more than a generation earlier than these commentators, as Pandit Agnihothram suggests, they could have incorporated this far less developed and precise usage, a usage that is indeed strikingly similar to that in the work of Yāmuna which has influenced the Gadyas, namely, the "Stotraratna."

The comments given in the previous paragraphs show to what lengths the commentators had to go to show that the understanding of prapatti in the Gadyas was different from that in the *Gītābhāṣya* and other works of Rāmānuja, because here also the commentators were in agreement that the Gadyas and the *Nityagrantha* were the only writings of Rāmānuja in which he unambiguously taught prapatti, not simply as a condition for the development of bhakti, but as an independent means to salvation. If the idea of śaraṇāgati or prapatti in the Gadyas is much closer to that in Rāmānuja's undisputed works and in Yāmuna's "Stotraratna" than to that of either of the later Śrī Vaiṣṇava schools, then the simplest explanation for this fact is that these works were written by Rāmānuja himself or, if not, at least by a follower standing quite close to Rāmānuja in time and in thought.

Although the later comments reveal the long process of development that had taken place in the intervening century and a half, they do correctly point to those aspects of Rāmānuja's thought that made that development possible: his emphasis on the importance of Divine grace in accomplishing man's salvation, on the one hand, and the necessity of man's acknowledgment of his essential subservience to and dependence on God, on the other. The conclusion of Rāmānuja's earliest work, the *Vedārthasaṃgraha,* specifically answers the objection that it would be degrading for the soul to be in a relation of essential (and therefore eternal) subservience to any other being. Rāmānuja's play on the double meaning of the term *rasa* and *rati,* which can mean both essential nature and delicious-tasting nectar (namely, delight)—somewhat like the French word *essence*—shows that he regarded the worshipful service of the soul to God not only as its duty but also as its proper fulfillment, its abiding joy.[14]

The doctrine of *bhogasāmyam* in the *Vedānta Sūtras* (that the soul after release is in a state of enjoyment equal to Brahman), on which Pandit Agnihothram puts so much emphasis, is always interpreted by Rāmānuja in line with his fundamental doctrine of the subservience of the soul to God. For the same reason, most of Rāmānuja's descriptions of bhakti correspond to what the later manuals on types of devotion referred to as *dāsyabhakti,* the devotion of a servant to his master. This did not, however, necessarily exclude the important Vaiṣṇava idea of the devotion of the human beloved to the Divine Lover, an analogy that was so important for the South Indian Āḻvārs, which was differently developed centuries later in North India by various Vaiṣṇava sects. The latter could be included in the former, since *pati* (husband) never loses its more fundamental significance of "master" or "lord." Certain passages describing bhakti in the *Gītābhāṣya* make it difficult to determine whether any erotic symbolism is intended or not; if so, it is well encompassed within the more comprehensive and fundamental master-servant relationship. However this may be, the emotional fervor and excitement usually associated with such erotically tinted mysticism are preserved in Rāmānuja's description of bhakti.

Rāmānuja frequently states that that devotion which is the means of attaining Brahman is itself "superlatively dear [anavadhikātiśayapriya] to the devotee." This means that devotion, which looked at in one way is a means to an end, is, from another perspective, an end in itself and a proper description of man's eternal destiny. Therefore, the later commentators' explanation of the meaning of bhaktiyoga in the Gadyas has a great deal of truth in it, but we must recognize that this same quality of being worthwhile in itself because it shares in the essentially joyful nature of the God it apprehends is emphasized throughout Rāmānuja's writings. Undoubtedly it receives particular emphasis in the Gadyas, where it is interpreted with the aid of a synonym for service (or readiness to serve one's lord) that was apparently well known in the Śrī Vaiṣṇava stotra literature, though it does not appear elsewhere in Rāmānuja's writings: *nityakainkarya.* The phrase, "I am thy servant in all situations," appears in the anonymous hymn called the *Jitantā Stotra* which apparently predates Yāmuna, another verse of which is quoted by Rāmānuja in the *Vedārthasaṃgraha.*[15] This is similar to the expression in the "Stotraratna" verse 46, *aikāntikanityakinkara,* "the eternal servant (asking, what may I do?) of Thee alone."[16] It is a short step from *servant* to the abstract noun *service* (kinkara to kainkarya), the expression occurring in the Gadyas. In both these earlier stotras, there is the idea of service to the Lord as itself man's supreme goal rather than as simply the means to reach that goal, and this conception of service is related to some kind of self-surrender. In describing this surrender the word *prapanna* is used, which means "one who has surrendered himself," an expression that became very popular in later Śrī Vaiṣṇavism.[17]

It is the *Śrīrangagadya* that most emphasizes service (kainkarya or dāsatā) to the Lord as the goal, and it is in this Gadya that the statements occur that seem most explicitly to diverge from the views of Rāmānuja's other works and to support the later doctrine of *angi-prapatti,* that prapatti is not just a branch (anga) of the tree of bhakti but itself the tree trunk which supports the limbs. Thus each of the three Gadyas might seem to have a different author, whether or not Rāmānuja were one of them. However, the great similarity in style, terminology, and conception makes it much more likely that the three Gadyas have a single author, so we must seek to understand the significance of these apparent differences among the Gadyas by some other solution than that of multiple authorship.

We have already noted that bhakti is sometimes considered by Rāmānuja as the goal of the religious life, as well as the means to that goal, and that he moves easily back and forth from one usage to the other. It is just such fluidity in terminology that is present in the Gadyas. At those points where devoted service to the Lord is emphasized as the goal, the means to that goal is the Lord Himself, and the only human requirement is surrender of oneself and recognition of one's essential subservience (śeṣatva) to the Lord. (Properly speaking, this is not a means but the acknowledgment that there is no human means to salvation without Divine grace.) This is not considered by the author of the Gadyas as an alternative to the bhaktiyoga; it *is* bhaktiyoga considered from the standpoint of man's essential nature of subservience to and helplessness before God, and it is therefore not surprising that it is particularly emphasized in a stotra, which is a praise of God's glory and a confession of one's own unworthiness. There is this same difference of emphasis, but not of fundamental conception, between Yāmuna's *Stotraratna* and his doctrinal works. The Gadyas are considered by Śrī Vaiṣṇavas to be part of their stotra literature, and there is little doubt that their author so intended them as stotras, whether that author was Rāmānuja or one of his early followers.

GOD'S GRACE AND MAN'S SURRENDER IN THE WRITINGS OF RĀMĀNUJA'S DISCIPLES

Relatively little attention has been paid to the thought of Rāmānuja's immediate disciples, especially outside of the Śrī Vaiṣṇava community itself. Apart from the disputed verse biographies, there are extant writings attributed to at least eight followers of Rāmānuja, two of them his most famous converts.[18] While my examination of this literature is still incomplete, it seems rather clear that most if not all of these writings take up doctrinal positions closer to the later Śrī Vaiṣṇava tradition than to the conceptions present not only in the undisputed writings of Rāmānuja but also in the disputed works.

The writings in Tamil verse attributed to Aruḷāḷa Perumāḷ Emberumānār are generally faithful to Rāmānuja's teaching, but there is even more emphasis than in Rāmānuja's writings on the soul being the servant or slave of God. In one place he uses a term meaning "uncaused grace" (āhilaruḷāi),[19] a term with the same meaning as *nirhetuka-kṛpā,* frequently used by later Śrī Vaiṣṇavas but never by Rāmānuja. In line with this term are the references to the total sufficiency of surrender: "Is there any sorrow for you, poor mind, once you have said śaraṇam [refuge], falling at the feet of God?"[20] "If you take any other means [to attain salvation], 'taking refuge' [śaraṇāgati] will not be effective."[21] One verse is reminiscent of the later Vaḍagalai definition of vātsalya (forgiving love), an ignoring of the defects of the devotee: "Even though He sees many thousands of mistakes of His devotee, He does not have the eye to see them."[22] But even more striking is the verse, "Will God speak ill of the defect of His devotee? [No, He] is like the cow that likes [to lick] the wounded part of the calf."[23] This comes very close to the later Tengalai doctrine that God actually relishes the devotee's sins because of the opportunity it gives Him to forgive.

There are also a number of verses that refer to the crucial importance of having a guru or ācārya.[24] This is an important doctrine in both Śrī Vaiṣṇava schools and is emphasized in the biographical tradition, but it is not present as an alternative path to attaining salvation in any of Rāmānuja's Sanskrit writings, including the Gadyas and the *Nityagrantha.*

Rāmānuja's disciple and scribe Kūraṭṭāḻvān is said to have written a commentary on the Gadyas.[25] If this work were extant, it would probably settle the question of the authorship of the Gadyas. Unfortunately, it is not, but there are some other works attributed to Kūraṭṭāḻvān that have survived, and these show a general agreement with Rāmānuja, but with a striking independence in the style and the content of his thought.

Kūraṭṭāḻvān stresses the Lord's great willingness to forgive sinners and grant them salvation, even when they are quite unworthy of such grace.[26] Indeed, it is precisely through such unmerited grace that the Lord displays His greatness.[27] The Lord is in a sense "obligated" to save the sinner, not because the sinner has any claim on God's favor but because God's own nature requires Him to show such grace, and His nature must not be thwarted by human sin.[28]

One difference from his teacher's view is Kūraṭṭāḻvān's denial of any meaningful distinction between the Lord's general compassion for His creatures (dayā or kāruṇya) and His special "affection" or "forgiving love" (vātsalya) for those devotees who are totally devoted to Him.[29] "Thy forgiveness [kṣamā] is great. . . . Then how can we make the mistake of thinking that Thy vātsalya is only for those who are eager to obtain Thee, for Thou naturally showest Thy vātsalya to all creatures without distinction if they approach Thee with folded hands." The collapse of this distinction should not be overemphasized since it occurs in one verse of a hymn, not in a doctrinal treatise, but it may well be an important clue to the difference between Rāmānuja's position and the increasing emphasis on unmerited Divine grace among his followers, an emphasis that was to eventuate in the special doctrines of the Tengalai school. Since this tendency is so marked in Rāmānuja's closest associate, it would be better to regard it, not as a deviation from Rāmānuja's teaching, but as an alternative development from a common fund of Śrī Vaiṣṇava teaching mediated through and developed by Nāthamuni and Yāmuna.

Other verses of Kūraṭṭāḻvān express strikingly the same themes of God's gracious condescension and man's privilege of serving God that are clearly present in Rāmānuja's own teaching.[30] There is one verse of some historical as well as doctrinal interest, "Though I have been accepted by Rāmānuja, worldly confusions still conquer me."[31] This verse suggests that Kūraṭṭāḻvān did accept or "resort to" Rāmānuja in the cultic sense in which later Śrī Vaiṣṇavas "resorted to" their own particular ācārya as well as to Rāmānuja as the human teacher chiefly responsible for salvation. The verse also suggests, however, that being accepted by Rāmānuja did not end the disciple's "worldly confusions" and that continual prayer for Divine grace was needful. Kūraṭṭāḻvān's hymns give the same impression we receive of him from stories in the biographical tradition. He was a gifted man, devoting himself fully to his teacher, yet capable of quite independent thought and action.

The compositions of Kūraṭṭāḻvān's son, Parāśara Bhaṭṭar, who was Rāmānuja's successor at Śrīrangam, reveal the influence both of Rāmānuja's system and of his father's poetic style and more sectarian Śrī Vaiṣṇava themes.[32] One verse expresses his father's emphasis in a stiking image. "O Lord of Śrīrangam, saving those who possess knowledge [jñāna], devotion [bhakti], and detachment [vairāgya] is like pouring water over the fish in the sea. But for Thee to save me is like providing water in the desert."[33]

In Parāśara Bhaṭṭar's major work, the commentary on the "Thousand Names of Viṣṇu" (*Viṣṇusahasranāma*), the same doctrinal tendencies are evident as in his hymns, expressed more soberly in the language of prose. The introduction contains a defense of the chanting of the names of God (nāmasaṃkīrtana) as an easier and universally accessible means to attain salvation, in contrast to the path of disciplined meditation, which is open only to men of the three higher castes (which means in South India, in practice, to Brahmin men) and then only to those who are sufficiently qualified by their spiritual constitution (by the predominance of the quality of sattva, pure matter) and by a regular practice of good conduct. Both meditation and praise are forms of bhakti, which is defined as "the state of servants [dāsya] having strong affection [anurāga] for their master [svāmī]." *Stuvan* (praising) is defined as: "Eager to utter in words the qualities of God and experiencing the same Divine qualities on which he meditates, which experience produces such joy that the hairs of his body stand on end, tears fill his eyes, and a lump comes to his throat." Bhaṭṭar also defines other types of worship, such as obeisance (namasyan) and *yajamāna,* which he takes to mean *devapūjā,* worship of the Deity in the image form. Bhaṭṭar says that precisely because God possesses lordship (aiśvarya), "which is the supreme greatness. . . . He can be worshiped by stotras [hymns of praise] alone without any effort, for great people are pleased by a request for their blessing. They do not want much."[34]

Bhaṭṭar seems to have been impressed by the wonder of communion between the utterly pure Lord and the utterly impure worshiper, specifically, himself. This theme recurs in his hymns,[35] and he deals with it in more rational terms in this commentary.

> Those who have bad qualities, bad character, or low birth can approach God without any fear, because God will consider only their taste for bhakti. Then immediately the devotee becomes extremely virtuous, having all his sins washed away as though by the flood of the river Ganges.[36]
>
> The Lord [Bhagavān] is not affected by contact with persons, whether or not they are making an effort [to worship Him]. Nor is the power of His grace [anugraha] affected by the lack of purity and other subsidiary qualifications on the part of the worshiper. Quite the contrary, God accepts even a person who is not fit to have contact with Him, after purifying him and making him fit, because God is the supreme purifier [paramapāvana].[37]

Parāśara Bhaṭṭar deals specifically with the following obvious objection of the Vedic orthodox Brahmin:

> Surely it goes too far to maintain that the beginning of the knowledge of reality [tattvajñāna], which can be achieved by an ascetic practice [tapas] that is elaborate [or weighty (guru)], time-consuming [dīrgha], and laborious [duṣkara] . . . can also be achieved by using mere words. . . . [If so,] all the elaborate path prescribed by the śāstras [authoritative texts] would be pointless.

Bhaṭṭar replies with equal vigor:

> This statement is made by an inferior Vedic scholar who is, indeed, a demon. He has not understood the greatness of the Lord [Bhagavān]. Though nāmasaṃkīrtana [chanting the names of God] is very light [laghu], it surely bears an unbearable burden. The elaborate śāstric teachings do not lose their point for they can serve those capable of undertaking them. Anyone is eligible for nāmasaṃkīrtana, whether or not he is able to do it, like the fortune that is the outcome of a special disposition of the Lord. Even in the case of elaborate means of worship, the cause of the worthwhile result [literally, fruit (phala)] is the grace [prasāda] of the Lord. Is such grace prevented in the case of a simple means of worship? As in the case of the elaborate means of worship, God is pleased [prasīdati] by the extensiveness of the practice of meditation, so in the case of the simpler means of worship, He is pleased by considering the purity of thought [of the worshipers].[38]

Many statements of Bhaṭṭar's seem very close to the later doctrinal positions of the "pure grace" or southern school (Tengalai) of Śrī Vaiṣṇavas, yet it is clear that the distinction he makes is not between bhakti and prapatti. Surrender to God is for him, as for Rāmānuja, the necessary foundation of any act of devotion. The distinction is between the elaborate form of bhakti, which Rāmānuja has described in his commentaries on the *Vedānta Sūtras,* and simpler forms of worship, which, it seems clear from his commentary on the *Gītā,* Rāmānuja also approved. What is not so clear is whether either Bhaṭṭar or Rāmānuja regarded these simpler and more universally available forms of worship as leading to the full knowledge of God or only to the beginning of that knowledge, through clearing away all the obstacles. This question, however, was not terribly important in the religious life of the Śrī Vaiṣṇava since, as Bhaṭṭar points out, both elaborate and simpler forms of worship depend for their effectiveness on the grace of the Lord. Moreover, praise as well as Vedāntic meditation involves a holding up to mind of the qualities of God, and this very activity is so sweet that the question of a final goal of release from the bonds of existence, to which this process of remembrance leads, fades into insignificance.

Another important disciple of Rāmānuja's was Tirukkuruhai Piḷḷān (Kurukeśa), who wrote the first of the Śrī Vaiṣṇava commentaries on Nammāḻvār's *Tiruvāymoḻi,* called the "Six Thousand" (namely, 6,000 granthas; a grantha is thirty-two syllables). He is regarded by the northern school (Vaḍagalai) as Rāmānuja's first successor, the propagator of both the Sanskrit and the Tamil Scriptures (Ubhaya Vedānta Pravartaka). His work is supposed to incorporate Rāmānuja's oral commentary on Nammāḻvār's great philosophical poem or hymn. A comparison with the later more elaborate commentaries, where Rāmānuja's views on many of the verses are specifically identified, lends support to this tradition. This very fact, however, makes it extremely difficult to identify the distinctive emphases in this disciple's teaching that were not present in Rāmānuja's own oral commentary. A thorough study of the various commentaries from the standpoint of the historical development of Śrī Vaiṣṇavism has not yet been undertaken. It might well help to answer this and other intriguing questions of historical relationships.

Some of the statements in the "Six Thousand" commentary show close affinity to thoughts expressed by Kūraṭṭāḻvān and Parāśara Bhaṭṭar. The abstract noun *saulabhya* does not seem to be used (Rāmānuja also does not use it), but the equivalent forms, *sulabhatva* and *sulabhatā,* occur a number of times, and the Lord's descending as an avatāra is said to be "for the sake of accessibility to His dependents" (āśritasulabhatva).[39] The phrase "affection for His dependents" (āśritavātsalya) occurs frequently.[40] This is in accord with Rāmānuja's usage, especially in the *Gītābhāṣya.* The "Six Thousand" also occasionally uses expressions meaning "subordinate to His dependents," a concept that Rāmānuja occasionally refers to in slightly different words, notably at the end of the introduction to the *Gītābhāṣya.*[41] This concept becomes even more significant in the work of Kūraṭṭāḻvān and his son Parāśara Bhaṭṭar.[42]

Like the other disciples of Rāmānuja, Piḷḷān does not make the later contrast between bhakti and prapatti as another well-defined path to salvation. He does indicate in a number of passages, however, that there is an easier alternative to bhaktiyoga that involves a more direct and total reliance on the grace of the Lord. He says once that if those on their deathbeds remember the Lord with only a single folding of the hands (añjali) or a single word or thought (smṛti), "this is better than bhaktiyoga."[43] He also states that the Lord does not consider the unfitness of the one who approaches Him or his high or low caste status. At some points the commentator paraphrases Nammāḻvār in emphatic terms.

> Thus far I have done no good deed to reach Thy feet, nor have I done anything to remove the evil deeds. . . . I completely lost hope . . . but later . . . I reflected that making me fit to be at Thy feet is a small thing for Thee, who hast created all souls. Even though I have performed no karmayoga, bhaktiyoga, or jñānayoga, I appeal to Thee, desiring to see Thee.[44]

Commenting on the text of 6.10.8, "not performing any vow [nonbu], I came to Thee," the commentator asks,

> Can He be attained by one devoid of means [upāyaśūnya], yet desiring to see Him? Even the lower deities who have knowledge approach Thee devoid of means, saying "We cannot bear even a moment without seeing Thee." Then they saw Thee. Therefore I, too, request to see Thee always, or if Thou wilt not come to me permanently, Thou canst come as Thou didst to rescue Gajendra Ā̱lvān [the elephant caught by the crocodile].[45]

One comment seems very close to Parāśara Bhaṭṭar's defense of nāmasaṃkīrtana.

> If you ask, what is the means [upāya] to obtain this goal [prāpya], he [Nammā̱lvār] answers, "By pronouncing the word *namaḥ* [obeisance] to the Resident of Vengada [Śrī Venkateśvara], which is extremely easy [atyantasukaram] and open to all [sarvādhikāra], all sins that are obstacles to service [kainkarya] as well as sins still to be committed will be destroyed without remainder. After that you can do as you wish."[46]

In general Piḷḷān (Kurukeśa) seems less daring in his expressions concerning divine grace than Bhaṭṭar and stays closer to the characteristic expressions of Rāmānuja, which he introduces in long Sanskrit phrases in the middle of his Tamil sentences. His work is the earliest recorded example in Vaiṣṇava literature of Maṇipravāḷam (Sanskritized Tamil), and it is actually more heavily Sanskritized than the later commentaries, in part because of Piḷḷān's literal retention of Rāmānuja's phraseology. Whatever the accuracy of the Vaḍagalai tradition, there is good reason for placing Piḷḷān first in the Vaḍagalai line of succession after Rāmānuja, just as Parāśara Bhaṭṭar clearly continues the development of theological concepts that were to lead to the full-blown Tengalai position. Nevertheless, it is Piḷḷān who frequently uses a term that was to become a hallmark of the Tengalais: *nirhetuka* (without cause). I have not been able to find this used as an adjective qualifying kṛpā (mercy), as it later appears so frequently. It usually occurs as an adverb qualifying the actions of God, but these are actions clearly expressive of the grace of God or some closely related Divine quality. Thus, in commenting on the very first verse, Piḷḷān paraphrases, "Without cause He has shown Himself to me as He is."[47] The close connection with kṛpā is clear in the following comment: "Thou didst save all kinds of souls sunk in the sea . . . without cause. Thus by Thy mercy [kṛpā] Thou didst become the cause to save those who have no other refuge."[48] Much later in the commentary, Piḷḷān paraphrases Nammāḻvār as follows: "How can I obtain Thee by my own effort? Just as before Thou accepted me without any cause, now again by Thy mercy, graciously accept me."[49]

A DEFENSE OF THE AUTHENTICITY OF THE GADYAS AND THE *NITYAGRANTHA*

The challenge of Agnihothram and Lester to the authenticity of four brief works attributed to Rāmānuja forces us to consider more carefully the nature of Rāmānuja's thought and its relation to the rest of the Śrī Vaiṣṇava tradition. They have done a service by pointing out differences between Rāmānuja's thought and that of his successors, in particular, by showing that the influence of the *Pāñcarātra Āgamas* was less on Rāmānuja than on his followers. It seems to me possible, however, to accept the distinctiveness of Rāmānuja's theology within his tradition but to decide that the objections to Rāmānuja's authorship of the disputed works are unconvincing. Indeed, the recognition of Rāmānuja's distinctiveness is more evident when we see the differences between the Gadyas themselves and the later commentaries. But while there are differences, there is also continuity. The Gadyas, if they are genuine, give us a glimpse of the more sectarian side of Rāmānuja's thought, a glimpse that shows an earlier form of some later doctrines.

Lester holds that the Gadyas are later works containing the Vaḍagalai view of prapatti, whereas the Tengalai view is a distortion of Rāmānuja's interpretation of the caramaśloka (*Gītā* 18.66). He notes "three further points at which we must divorce Rāmānuja from popular Vaiṣṇavism." First, "Rāmānuja makes no direct or indirect reference to the Āḻvārs, the *Prabandha* or the *Bhāgavata Purāna*, and only a single and relatively insignificant reference to the Pāñcarātrāgamas." Secondly, worship of the image form of Viṣṇu-Nārāyaṇa, so important in the Āḻvārs' hymns and *Pāñcarātra Āgamas,* "finds very little commendation in the writings of Rāmānuja." The third point is "the status of Śrī or Lakṣmī."

> Śrī Vaiṣṇavism has given the goddess such status, as mediatrix [puruṣakāra] between the devotee and Nārāyaṇa and thus as an object of worship, that the term is employed to characterize the movement. Rāmānuja gives her bare mention and no essential status in the śeṣa-śeṣī relationship.

Lester therefore concludes as follows:

> Basing our estimate of Rāmānuja's place in the Indian tradition on his writings, as it seems to me we must, there is little if any reason to conclude that he [Rāmānuja] seeks to accommodate the Vedic perspective to popular bhakti developments or popular Vaiṣṇavism in particular. . . . It would appear that Rāmānuja was appropriated by popular Vaiṣṇava development, which development claimed his world view but side-tracked his mokṣopāya, designating him a prapanna. . . . We cannot dispute the tradition's association of Rāmānuja, Yāmuna and Nāthamuni, but the affirmation that any of these three figures considered themselves ācāryas of Śrī Vaiṣṇavism is highly problematic.[50]

Lester's radical conclusion follows from his initial assumptions. He bases his view of Rāmānuja exclusively on the latter's major Sanskrit writings, and he demands rational consistency with the primary data of anything that claims to be in accord with Rāmānuja's thought. He does not find such consistency in the Gadyas or in the sectarian Scriptures, both Sanskrit and Tamil, of the Śrī Vaiṣṇavas.

Lester has not dealt with the works claiming to be written by Rāmānuja's immediate disciples but differing more sharply from both the style and content of Rāmānuja's major works than the Gadyas. It is, of course, possible that these works are also spurious, that Śrī Vaiṣṇavas of later generations wrote these hymns and commentaries and attributed them to their illustrious predecessors. Such a view needs to be taken seriously in any particular case where there is some evidence to support it, as in the case of the two Sanskrit verse biographies claiming to be by contemporary disciples of Rāmānuja,[51] but on the whole the works attributed to Rāmānuja's followers represent early stages in the doctrinal developments that led to the fully crystallized Vaḍagalai and Tengalai positions. It would seem to me reasonable to assume that most of these works are genuine and that they reinforce the evidence from the biographical tradition pointing to Rāmānuja's involvement in and leadership of the Śrī Vaiṣṇava community. This implies that Rāmānuja had views not adequately reflected in his major writings and/or that he tolerated views on the part of his disciples that he did not personally share or at least considered far less important.

The conception of the relation of śaraṇāgati to bhakti in the three Gadyas seems to me to be closer to that in Rāmānuja's undisputed works than it is to the developed doctrines of prapatti in the two later schools and also to the incipient forms of those doctrines in the works of Rāmānuja's own disciples.[52] The clearest indication of the nature of the development is provided in the writings of Parāśara Bhaṭṭar, especially since he has written both a prose commentary and hymns in verse. Like the later Śrī Vaiṣṇava authors, he quotes much more freely from sectarian Vaiṣṇava literature than does Rāmānuja. He does not restrict his quotations from the Purāṇas to the *Viṣṇu Purāṇa,* as does Rāmānuja, and he shares the tendency of both the Āḻvārs and the later Vaiṣṇava tradition to exalt God's availability and willingness to help His devotees at the expense of His transcendence and supremacy. In the definitions of the Divine names in his commentary on the *Viṣṇusahasranāma,* Bhaṭṭar interprets several of the names that obviously point to the Divine supremacy in a way that emphasizes the Divine accessibility.[53]

The extent of Parāśara Bhaṭṭar's emphasis on the Divine accessibility is even more striking when one compares his commentary with the one attributed to Śankara. There is no point where Bhaṭṭar's comments run clearly counter to the conceptions of Rāmānuja in his undisputed works, but he treats some topics about which Rāmānuja is silent, notably arcāvatāra, and he does not maintain the balance between the Divine supremacy and accessibility, which I have tried to show is a characteristic mark of Rāmānuja's theology.

It seems to me that with respect to this balance, as well as its limitation of citation to generally accepted Scriptures, the *Gadyatraya* and the *Nityagrantha* agree with the undisputed writings of Rāmānuja rather than with the work of Parāśara Bhaṭṭar. Even the *Nityagrantha,* concerned with outlining a pattern of daily worship that will in practice be offered to the image form of the Deity (arca), is like Rāmānuja's undisputed works in the absence of an explicit acknowledgment of the Pāñcarātric theory that the arca is one of the five forms of God and is a permanent incarnation of the Lord. More extensive and thorough comparisons need to be made before a definite conclusion can be reached, but this evidence seems to me to support Rāmānuja's authorship of these four brief works that subsequent tradition ascribes to him.[54]

If this is the case, how then are we to explain the undoubted differences from the five longer works of Rāmānuja? At least three explanations have been advanced, the first two of which seem to me quite plausible. The first explanation is that these works were written considerably later than all the others, in Rāmānuja's extreme old age. Some traditional accounts support this idea. According to one, Rāmānuja was carried away in ecstasy while he was watching the movable images of Śrī Ranganātha and His Consort being installed in the "bridal chamber" of the temple at Śrīrangam during the festival of "Panguni Uttaram." Some Śrī Vaiṣṇavas, indeed, consider the *Śaraṇāgatigadya,* not as a composition of Rāmānuja's own mind, but as a report of an actual conversation between Rāmānuja and the Divine Pair. Vedānta Deśika describes it as a dialogue between Lakṣmīpati (Viṣṇu, the husband of Śrī) and Yatipati (Rāmānuja, the master of ascetics). Deśika also refers to the *Śaraṇāgatigadya* as the crown of Rāmānuja's works and as being written later than the *Gītābhāṣya.*[55] The instruction from the Lord to remain at Śrīrangam until his death probably indicates a time shortly before his death and certainly after his return from exile in Mysore. An internal pointer to the relative dates of these writings may be furnished by the fact that they carry further the emphasis on bhakti as the goal as well as the means, an emphasis that is already present to some extent in the *Gītābhāṣya.*

The second explanation of the differences, which is not exclusive of the first, is that they are due to the differences in the literary character or genre of these works. The Gadyas, although they are written in prose, are really hymns of praise, and the *Nityagrantha* is a manual of daily worship. In such works it is not necessary to back up every statement with scriptural support, for they are not primarily works of doctrine, and one's guide is not so much the canonical Scriptures as the living traditions of the sect, especially as they are expressed by the previous line of teachers. There is a connection between Yāmuna's *Siddhitraya* and Rāmānuja's *Vedār-*

thasaṃgraha and his three commentaries on the *Vedānta Sūtras*, and there is an even closer dependence of Rāmānuja's *Gītābhāṣya* on Yāmuna's very brief *Gītārthasaṃgraha*. The Gadyas seem to stand in a comparable relationship to the stotras of Yāmuna, the "Catuśślokī" and the "Stotraratna." Both the terminology and the underlying spirit are strikingly similar.[56]

It is this poetic nature of the Gadyas that has finally convinced van Buitenen of their authenticity. (He does not comment on the *Nityagrantha*, because he has not found it "referred to sufficiently often by Indian authors.")

> The gadyas may be described more precisely as exercises in bhakti as taught by Rāmānuja, an endless and repetitious pondering over and re-memorizing of God's infinite perfections. Large portions are repeated over and over again and many passages are practically identical with such avocations as the introduction to the Gītābhāṣya and comments *ad* Gītā 9:34: and they are strongly reminiscent of Yāmuna's hymns. . . . Though formerly I hesitated, there is no valid reason to doubt the authenticity of this little devotional work: perhaps modern scholars are too apt to suspect lyrics that are ascribed to philosophers and to forget that these philosophers were theologians and officiating priests. The songs of St. Thomas Aquinas, whom nobody would suspect of lyrical aspirations on the basis of his philosophical works, furnish an interesting parallel.[57]

The fact that the tradition recognizes the Gadyas as part of the stotra literature makes it difficult to give too much credence to another traditional suggestion, that in the Gadyas Rāmānuja has revealed the secret doctrine (rahasya) of prapatti that he had concealed in his earlier works. It is not impossible for a "hymn" to serve as a doctrinal work, and certainly this is how the Gadyas have been used by Rāmānuja's followers; but the question is whether Rāmānuja so intended them. The Gadyas and even more obviously the *Nityagrantha* were rahasya in the limited sense that they were intended for the use of Śrī Vaiṣṇavas, not for philosophical and theological debate with those outside their religious community. It seems to me much less likely that the *Śaraṇāgatigadya* could reflect Rāmānuja's mystical experience of conversion with the Lord and His Consort and also have been originally intended as a commentary on the three esoteric mantras of Śrī Vaiṣṇavism. This does not mean that Rāmānuja may not have given instruction to the inner circle of his disciples on the special texts and mysterious formulas of the sect, but if he did so, it seems doubtful that this teaching would have been written down, especially in the form we find in the Gadyas. It seems to me possible that Rāmānuja's teaching in Tamil on the collected hymns of the Āḻvārs, the *Divya Prabandham,* which the Tengalai tradition insists he gave and of which it claims to have preserved some fragments, comes much closer to such "secret teaching."[58]

There is a further consideration of style that seems to me to weigh in favor of the authenticity of the Gadyas. Van Buitenen is quite right that they are in the tradition of stotras or hymns of praise and that they show a conscious dependence on the hymns of Yāmuna. Yet for all that, they are hymns in prose, and the carefully controlled emotion that they exhibit is quite in keeping with the longer works of Rāmānuja, a master of prose theology. As one looks at the early Śrī Vaiṣṇava tradition, one can hardly help but ask: who but Rāmānuja would have composed a poem in prose?

It seems to me probable that Rāmānuja approved and encouraged his disciples in compositions that were more sectarian than his own and that went beyond his own balanced conceptions in their praise of the Divine grace, but he either could not or would not abandon the balanced thought of prose theology for the loftier flights of imagination and emotion characteristic of poetry, with its multiplicity of moods and its use of poetic exaggeration.

Pandit Agnihothram has a right to protest against the later Śrī Vaiṣṇava tendency to relegate to a secondary position the Vedic elements in Rāmānuja's thought, but it would be equally one-sided to do the opposite: to ignore, explain away, or even deny the authenticity of all the non-Vedic aspects of Rāmānuja's writings, for nothing is more characteristic of Rāmānuja's thought than his selective combination of elements from the Vedic and various non-Vedic traditions into a remarkable synthesis. I submit that he maintained both the balance and the inner connection of supremacy and accessibility (paratva and saulabhya) in his concept of the Divine nature in a way that sets him apart, not only from Hindu theologians of other schools but even, to a lesser extent, from his own followers. The *Gadyatraya* and the *Nityagrantha* seem to me to exhibit the balance and unity of paratva and saulabhya that is evident in

Rāmānuja's other works. They do not add anything essential, though they do make some points more explicit, and the evidence from them can therefore be ignored by those unconvinced that they are authentic. If they are not genuine, we can still understand the distinctive character of Rāmānuja's concept of God from his other works, but we are left somewhat poorer in our understanding of Rāmānuja himself, as a theologian and as a worshiper.

With this lengthy justification, then, I conclude the chapter with the prayer of surrender to the Lord in the *Śaraṇāgatigadya*. (The details concerning the Divine form, ornaments, weapons, consorts, attendants, and eternal and temporal realms of glory are omitted.)

> O Thou who art opposed to everything defiling and art entirely auspicious, Thy essential nature is infinite consciousness and bliss, quite distinct in character from all entities other than Thyself. Thy unique celestial form is appropriate and pleasing to Thyself and is a treasure store of infinite qualities such as radiance, beauty, fragrance, delicacy, charm, and youthfulness, all of them inconceivable, wondrous, everlasting, flawless, and supremely excellent. Thou art an ocean of auspicious qualities of matchless excellence that are natural to Thee, countless qualities such as knowledge, untiring strength, sovereignty, immutability, creative power, splendor, gracious condescension, forgiving love, gentleness, straightforwardness, good will, impartiality, compassion, sweetness, profundity, generosity, adroitness, firmness, fortitude, courage, conquering prowess, the eternal possession of all objects Thou desireest, the ability ever to accomplish Thy will, helpfulness in acting for Thy creatures and graciousness in acknowledging what Thy creatures do for Thee. Thou art adorned with celestial ornaments . . . Thou wearest celestial weapons. . . .
>
> O Nārāyaṇa, the beloved Consort of Śrī . . . Thou art [also] the Consort of Bhūmī and Nīlā, who resemble Śrī in these respects. Thy feet are eternally waited upon by countless attendants of various kinds, both male and female . . . such as Viṣvaksena and Garuḍa. . . . Thou art the Lord of Vaikuṇṭha. . . . Thy sport consists in the origination, maintenance, and dissolution of the whole universe. . . . Thou hast eternally realized all objects of Thy desire . . . and They will is ever accom-

plished. Thou art the Supreme Brahman, the Supreme Person, who possessest the great realm of Thy glory.

Thou art the refuge of the whole world without any exception and regardless of all considerations [of class, status, or character]; Thou dispellest the distress of those who offer obeisance to Thee, and Thou art entirely an ocean of forgiving love to those who depend on Thee. Thou knowest always the true nature and condition of all created beings; Thou art engaged in totally controlling all beings without exception, both those that move and those that are stationary.

Thou art the Śeṣī of all spiritual and material entities; Thou art the support of the whole universe; Thou art the Master [Svāmī] of the universe, and Thou art our Master. . . . Thou art distinct in character from everything else.

Thou art the friend of those that are in distress. O Nārāyaṇa united with Śrī, refuge of those without refuge, I have no other resort; I surrender myself and seek refuge at Thy two lotuslike feet.[59]

18 The Divine Consort Śrī: The Problem of the Unity of the Divine Nature

Śrī, the Divine Consort of Nārāyaṇa

Rāmānuja accepts the important Śrī Vaiṣṇava doctrine that the supreme personal God has constantly accompanying Him, or united with Him, His Divine Consort, the Goddess Śrī (another name for Lakṣmī). This qualification of the Supreme Brahman is an important element in the dedicatory verse preceding each of Rāmānuja's three commentaries on the *Vedānta Sūtras*: Śrīnivāsa (in whom Śrī dwells) in the *Śrībhāṣya*; Śriyaḥ kānta (beloved consort of Śrī) in the *Vedāntadīpa*; and Śrīmat (united or associated with Śrī) in the *Vedāntasāra*. However, there is no further reference to Śrī within the body of these works. In Rāmānuja's commentary on the *Bhagavadgītā,* likewise, mention of Śrī is confined to the introduction. It is in the *Vedārthasaṃgraha* that there is the most explicit discussion of the Divine Consort, but there too it is relatively brief, and most of the references are quotations of a few celebrated texts. There are more references to Śrī (and to the subordinate consorts, Bhūmī and Nīlā) in the *Gadyatraya* and the *Nityagrantha,* but even those references are relatively brief and leave the metaphysical status of Śrī somewhat in doubt. This fact is reflected in the doctrinal difference between the two schools of Śrī Vaiṣṇavas. The Vaḍagalais consider Śrī to be infinite, like the Lord, whereas the Tengalais consider Her to be the first among finite spirits.

How are we to understand Rāmānuja's lack of emphasis on one of the most distinctive doctrines of his sect? There is some truth in the orthodox Śrī Vaiṣṇava explanation of this silence on Rāmānuja's part (and of others equally puzzling): that the general philosophical character of his major writings leads him to ignore or to minimize sectarian doctrines. It is precisely such doctrines, they say, which find fuller and clearer expression in Rāmānuja's more esoteric works, the three Gadyas. However, the statements about the Divine Consort (or consorts) in the Gadyas and the *Nityagrantha* do not alter our picture of Rāmānuja's conception of Śrī nearly as much as we might expect from reading the later commentaries on the Gadyas. There is a distinct difference, at least in emphasis, between Rāmānuja's concept of Śrī and that of his followers.

We should not, however, exaggerate this doctrinal difference.

The references in the *Vedārthasaṃgraha,* both Rāmānuja's own words and the texts he cites, should deter us from concluding that the concept of the Divine Consort plays no role at all in Rāmānuja's theology. Rāmānuja takes pains to defend the reality of Nārāyaṇa's Consort at the same time that he is defending Nārāyaṇa's bodily form, ornaments, weapons, eternal ministrants, glorious realms, and celestial abode. All of these, he maintains, are proved by scriptural texts, both Śruti and Smṛti, of the same authority as those that prove the reality of God's essential nature and His host of auspicious attributes. Rāmānuja's primary concern is, not to describe the Divine Consort or any of the other entities which he holds are inseparably linked with the Supreme Person, Nārāyaṇa, but to demonstrate their ultimate and eternal reality (satya). His most detailed description is of the bodily form of Nārāyaṇa, but even here his motivation is at least partially to connect his picture of the Divine form with the authority of certain celebrated and generally accepted scriptural texts.

Embedded in his defense of the Divine form and all the entities which accompany God in that form is a very brief description of the Divine Consort, referred to with the title *mahiṣī* (queen or chief consort).[1] She is "of matchless glory with respect to Her essential nature, beautiful form, qualities, manifestations [vibhava], dominion [aiśvarya], gracious conduct [śīla], and so on, qualities that are pleasing and appropriate to Him [Nārāyaṇa]."[2] Almost exactly the same words are used in describing Śrī in the introduction to the *Gītābhāṣya,* with "auspicious qualities" taking the place of "glory" (mahiman).[3] It is also incorporated, with minor variations, into the two prayers of surrender in the *Śaraṇāgatigadya,* the first to Śrī and the second to Nārāyaṇa.[4] Since Rāmānuja nowhere amplifies or explains this brief definition of Śrī, it is difficult to interpret it precisely, but it seems to imply both a close likeness in nature to Nārāyaṇa and a clear subordination to Him.

The sacred texts that Rāmānuja cites in the *Vedārthasaṃgraha* shed a little more light on his understanding of the Divine Consort. He repeatedly quotes two phrases from Śruti: "Hrī and Lakṣmī are Thy [or His] consorts [patnyau]," and "Viṣṇu's Consort [Patnī], Mistress [Īśānā] of the world."[5] There are also three quotations from Smṛti. One is from the *Rāmāyaṇa*: "On His chest is the śrīvatsa curl, and He has Śrī forever as His Consort." The other two are from the *Viṣṇu Purāna*: "This goddess Śrī, who is the mother of the universe, is eternal and is inseparable [anapāyinī] from Viṣṇu. Just as Viṣṇu is omnipresent [sarvagata], so likewise is She." "When He is [in the form of] a god She has the body of a god; when He is [in the form of] a man, She also becomes a human being. She makes Her own body accord with that of Viṣṇu."[6] The emphasis in these quotations is on the essentially exalted state of Śrī and on Her inseparability from Viṣṇu in His incarnations into the finite realm, as well as in His supreme estate. The only phrase that might indicate a separate function is "mother of the universe," but there is no other quotation from the *Viṣṇu Purāṇa* to indicate what that phrase might mean, and there is nothing in Rāmānuja's own words in the *Vedārthasaṃgraha* to indicate any distinct function for the goddess Śrī.

The later commentators have interpreted the prayer of surrender to Śrī at the beginning of the *Śaraṇāgatigadya* as a clear indication of such a distinct function, one of which is suggested by the title "Mother." One first performs the act of surrender to Śrī and prays for Her blessing on one's act of surrender to the Lord, Sudarśana Sūri suggests, because the Lord is difficult to approach, because He has a father's sternness. Śrī, on the other hand, is full of forgiving love (vātsalya) and is thus the intercessor (puruṣakāra) for approaching the Lord. Sudarśana Sūri also notes an alternative explanation: it is enjoined that we should first approach Śrī and secure Her permission before uttering the sacred formula of surrender to the Lord. It is the first explanation that was generally accepted by the Srī Vaiṣṇavas of his own time and thereafter, and they therefore put a great deal of emphasis on the function of the goddess as the intercessor between men and God, as the forgiving mother who can persuade the sterner father to forgive.[7]

If this traditional interpretation of the prayer to Śrī were correct, it would imply a wide gulf between the conception of Śrī in the *Śaraṇāgatigadya* and that in the definitely genuine works of Rāmānuja. Such an implication might lend support to the view that this Gadya is not written by Rāmānuja. It is unnecessary, however, to assume a distinction between a mother's easy forgiveness and a father's stern justice in order to explain the presence of a prayer to the Divine Consort at the beginning of the *Śaraṇāgatigadya*. It seems more likely that the conception of Śrī here is fundamentally in accord with that in the *Vedārthasaṃgraha*.

It is true that the title "Mother" is applied to Śrī in the prayer of surrender to Her, but it is also applied to Nārāyaṇa, along with "Father," "Friend," and a number of other titles, in the prayer of surrender to Him, which follows directly after the prayer to Śrī. Perhaps even more significant is the fact that the attribute *vātsalya,* with strong "maternal" associations because of its root meaning, the cow's love for its calf, is applied not to Śrī, but to Nārāyaṇa, who is described as an ocean of vātsalya. The later term *puruṣakāra* (intercessor or mediator) does not appear in the *Śaraṇāgatigadya*; nor is there any other term that conveys something of its content. Śrī is called "the refuge of those without refuge," but the same concept, in a variety of forms, is applied to Nārāyaṇa, with even more emphasis.[8]

In the other two Gadyas and in the *Nityagrantha,* there do not seem to be any statements that support the idea that Rāmānuja considered Śrī as the puruṣakāra. There is no other prayer addressed to Śrī, and the reference to the act of surrender in the course of the preliminary instructions for worship given in the *Nityagrantha* appears to refer to the prayer of surrender to Nārāyaṇa in the *Śaraṇāgatigadya*: "One should seek refuge with Him alone with the words beginning with *akhila.*"[9] In the *Śrīrangagadya,* the title "Śrīman-Nārāyaṇa" occurs twice, but there is no description of Śrī.[10] In the *Vaikuṇṭhagadya* there is a brief description of Śrī included in the lengthy description of the supreme heaven.

> Beholding . . . Bhagavān-Nārāyaṇa seated on the body of the serpent Ananta by the side of Lakṣmī, who fills the world of Vaikuṇṭha and all its divine wealth of appurtenances with the splendor of Her form, and gives orders to all the attendants like Adiśeṣa and Viṣvaksena to render the services due to the Lord in various states and situations, and who is in every way worthy of Him by Her nature, beauty, character and charms [śīla-rūpa-guṇa-vilāsa-ādi].[11]

Here there is a special work assigned to Śrī, the supervision of those ministering to the Lord. Since it is the soul's aspiration to become an eternal servant of the Lord, it might be inferred that Śrī supervises all finite spirits in their service to the Lord, but that inference is nowhere drawn in the concluding passage of this Gadya. Moreover, it is quite clear that this supervision is confined to the eternal realm. It is the celestial minister of state, Viṣvaksena, who is said to have been delegated the sovereignty (aiśvarya) of the Lord, which here means the power to will the creation, maintenance, and destruction of the universe. The other reference to Śrī is an indirect one, in the course of the description of the bodily form of Nārāyaṇa, and is borrowed from verse 33 of Yāmuna's "Stotraratna." The Lord's "four arms extending to the knees reveal their contact with the loosened knot of His Consort's hair and with the gems and flowers She wears in Her lovely ears."[12]

The instructions for worship in the *Nityagrantha* call for the worship of Nārāyaṇa and invocation and reverence of a subordinate kind for a large number of celestial attendants, cosmic powers, and other entities. Among these, the goddesses Śrī, Bhūmī, and Nīlā are to be invoked, but their worship seems to be a far less prominent part of the total ritual than the adoration of some of the celestial ministers, especially Ananta and Viṣvaksena.[13]

The counterargument might be advanced that it is natural to interpret the first paragraph of the *Śaraṇāgatigadya* as implying that Śrī is the mediatrix of salvation, since that doctrine had already been clearly set forth by Yāmuna in his hymn in praise of Śrī called the "Catuśślokī," and we have already seen repeatedly that Rāmānuja follows Yāmuna in all his major doctrines. Here too, however, we must carefully distinguish the text itself from the later commentaries (notably that of Vedānta Deśika). The hymn stresses the exalted position of Śrī and Her inseparable connection with the Lord, both in His supreme form and in all His other forms. There is an act of surrender to Śrī which does not appear to be preparatory to the surrender to Nārāyaṇa, as in the *Śaraṇāgatigadya,* but is an efficacious rite by itself. Indeed, the grace (prasāda) of the Goddess is said to be necessary both for worldly prosperity and for the attainment of Viṣṇu's abode.

If we examine the "Catuśślokī" together with the "Stotraratna," then there appears to be a much closer parallel to the form of the *Śaraṇāgatigadya* and to the conception of Śrī sketched in the *Vedārthsaṃgraha.* In the light of the "Stotraratna," the grace and prosperity of the Goddess are seen to be ultimately derived from God Himself: "Who [but Thee] is the Śrī [splendor or prosperity] of [the Goddess] Śrī." Yet this fact has a double significance, for in the "Catuśślokī" Yāmuna addresses the Goddess: "And Thy very name is 'Śrī'." The word *śrī* denotes everything exhibiting splendor, beauty, auspiciousness, prosperity, and royal dignity.[14] The Lord is the *source* of all the excellences, but He is the source of *these* excellences because Śrī is His Consort. The grace of the Lord is indeed such as Śrī bestows, conducive both to well-being in this world and to an even more blessed state in the Lord's supreme abode.

If we return to Rāmānuja's terminology in the *Vedārthasaṃgraha,* we see that he is defending more than the possibility of the Supreme Person's having a Divine Consort. He is trying to establish the fact that the actual Divine Person has that particular Consort who is pleasing to Him and in accordance with His nature. Since Śrī is a separate person, She may also be separately addressed, and that is what is done at the beginning of the *Śaraṇāgatigadya.* Even when She is addressed, however, Her subordination to the Supreme Lord, Nārāyaṇa, is made clear. Whereas Yāmuna uses hyperbole and metaphor, Rāmānuja (or possibly his disciple, in the case of the *Śaraṇāgatigadya*) tries to express both the subordination and the intimacy of relationship in more abstract concepts.

Both Yāmuna and Rāmānuja wanted to guard against the Consort being conceived as the immanent power in material nature who is in some sense over against the transcendent Deity. Their successors in the Śrī Vaiṣṇava tradition remained faithful to their teaching at this point, for they never accepted the Tāntric view that the Consort of Nārāyaṇa was the active creative principle in Her own right, the Śakti. The very fact that Yāmuna and Rāmānuja had effectively excluded this doctrinal deviation, however, made it all the more likely that some other way would be found to differentiate between the Lord and His Consort. The possibility of independent and prior address to the Goddess before praying to the Lord was reinterpreted as a distinction in a function between Nārāyaṇa and Śrī corresponding to a difference in their inherent natures. This difference was drawn along the line which Rāmānuja had felt as the line of tension in the one Divine nature: between God's supreme inaccessibility on the one hand and His gracious accessibility to creatures on the other. In Rāmānuja's own thought, that tension is maintained because no distinct function is assigned to Śrī, for both in the supreme form and in the various incarnate forms, She does nothing but accompany Her Divine Husband and Lord (Śriyaḥ pati), Bhagavān-Nārāyaṇa.

Rāmānuja's disciples gave relatively more emphasis in their writings to Śrī and the other Divine consorts than did Rāmānuja. Kūraṭṭāḻvān and Parāśara Bhaṭṭar both wrote hymns in praise of

Śrī. Both in their writings and in Piḷḷān's "Six Thousand" commentary, the view of the Goddess is similar to that expressed by Rāmānuj in his few brief references, but there are a few references suggesting the importance of the intercession of the Goddess. This is most explicit in some of the comments on Nammāḻvār's verses made by Piḷḷān, notably in the comment on stanza 6.10.10, which reads: "O Thou who hast the Lady of the Lotus shining on Thy chest, I came to Thy feet for refuge, having no other aid." Piḷḷān paraphrases this as follows: "Being without any other refuge and without any other aim, after having taken the Great Goddess [Śrī] as my mediatrix (puruṣakāra), I have taken refuge with Thee." This seems to be the first appearance of the term that both later schools of Śrī Vaiṣṇavas were to use regularly to describe the mediatorial function of the Goddess Śrī. She is the puruṣakāra, the one who recommends the sinful soul to Lord Nārāyaṇa for the bestowal of His grace. In view of Piḷḷān's general faithfulness to his teacher's position, the possibility should be considered that he reflects Rāmānuja's viewpoint on Śrī. It seems to me more likely, however, that this is one of the points where Rāmānuja's disciples were somewhat closer to sectarian Śrī Vaiṣṇava doctrines, especially of the Tamil tradition, than was their master.[15]

TRANSCENDENCE-IMMANENCE OR SUPREMACY-ACCESSIBILITY

Discussing the doctrine of "God as Mother," K. C. Varadachari comments as follows:

> Some theorists . . . granted to God intelligence, consciousness and transcendence, whereas they granted to His power śakti, considered as female, the ability to manifest the universe. Inappropriately enough some of those belonging to this school . . . argued that Consciousness is absolute passivity whereas the power of Consciousness is dynamic but ignorant (unconscious).[16]

The extremes to which this conception sometimes led is illustrated with a line from the *Kubjaka Tantra* (quoted by Arthur Avalon): "Not Brahmā, Viṣṇu, Rudra create, maintain and destroy; but Brahmī, Viṣṇavī, Rudrāṇī. Their husbands are but dead bodies."[17] A similar attitude is expressed in a line of a hymn attributed to Śankara, the *Saundaryalahari*: "Śiva unless cojoined with Thee will not be able even to move; the great Gods therefore worship Thee."

Varadachari suggests that it was in reaction to this tendency that "Vedānta has sternly to revert to the Neuter and the Transcendental (nirguṇa) aspect of the Deity, Brahman."[18] However, the very quotation he gives from Śankara's hymn suggests a different explanation, namely, that Śankara (or, if the hymn is not composed by him, his school) accepted this same Tāntric polarity between Śiva and Śakti but emphasized in philosophical thought the other pole: the transcendent Śiva far removed from the incessant activity and accompanying change of the transient universe. At the lower level of devotion, as in this hymn, the immanent "power" aspect of Deity could be fully and even extravagantly acknowledged.

Varadachari goes on to state that the Vaiṣṇava Āgamas "accept the Motherhood of God along with the Fatherhood of God."

> It can be stated however, that the Motherhood of God has always held a subordinate position to the Fatherhood of God: love has always been subordinated to Law and Sovereign Being. Power was always subordinated to Truth, though the precise ratio or rationale of subordination has remained undetermined. . . . The Mother Śrī is thus the fullest consciousness-power of the Divine Puruṣottama, and in Śrī Vaiṣṇava theology, She is approached as the Mother who leads us as the agent of our ascent to the Lord, which She fulfills through Her illimitable Grace and knowledge.[19]

This distinction in doctrine between Śaivas and Vaiṣṇavas leads to a difference in practice.

> In the Yoga of Śrī Vaiṣṇavism in general, there is no place for dionysiac worships of Kāli in the pure power-aspect. Śrī Vaiṣṇavas make the Mother the agent of our transformation on Sātvik lines as Mahā-Lakṣmī or Śrī who ever resides in the Supreme Puruṣa, Puruṣottama, Nārāyaṇa or Viṣṇu, the omnipervader. God is the means (upāya) and the goal (upeya) and Mother is the agent, the puruṣakāra.[20]

According to Otto Schrader, the Tāntric distinction between the God and the Goddess is also characteristic of the *Pāñcarātra Āgamas.* He regards the distinction that is said to persist between the two even in the great dissolution of the cosmos (mahāpralaya) "as a makeshift for preserving the transcendent character of Viṣṇu: Lakṣmī alone acts, but everything She does is the mere expression of the Lord's wishes."[21]

"However, the transcendent aspect of Viṣṇu (Param Brahma) remains so completely in the background in the Pāñcarātra that we are practically only concerned with the one force (Lakṣmī) which, as Bhūti, appears as the universe and, as Kriyā, vitalizes and governs it."[22]

It will not be possible to determine whether Schrader is correct in this judgment until much more thorough study has been done of the whole Pāñcarātra literature, and especially of those Āgamas which the Śrī Vaiṣṇavas consider most authoritative. The *Ahirbudhnya Saṃhitā,* on which Schrader most heavily relies and which he summarizes at the end of his book, is not one of the three Āgamas generally "considered the most authoritative part of the Pāñcarātra scripture."[23] It is not quoted by Yāmuna and Rāmānuja and is quoted only twice by Vedānta Deśika.[24] In any event, Yāmuna and Rāmānuja did not understand the Pāñcarātra to teach such a Tāntric distinction between the Lord and His Consort. Their non-Tāntric conception of the Divine nature prevailed in subsequent Śrī Vaiṣṇavism.

It would be worth investigating whether in other cases also the dominant polarity in a Hindu conception of the Deity is reflected in the distinction drawn between the God and the Goddess. Both in Śākta and in Śankara's Advaita, that polarity seems to be between transcendent undifferentiated consciousness and the active power immanent in a universe of constant activity and infinite differentiation. Quite opposite evaluations of the two poles are made in the two systems, but the same polarity exists, whether expressed as the distinction between Śiva and Śakti or between Para-Brahman and Māyā. In later Śrī Vaiṣṇavism, on the other hand, the polarity most keenly felt is that between the Divine justice (an expression of God's supremacy or essential lordship) and His mercy (an expression of His accessibility). This polarity is reflected in the ascription of justice to God Himself (Nārāyaṇa), and of mercy to His Consort Śrī.

What is striking about the theology of Rāmānuja, however, is that while the polarity between supremacy and accessibility is clearly present, there is no division of functions between God and His Consort. It is Rāmānuja's concern for the unity of the Divine nature that leads him to guard so carefully against the possibility of any second ultimate cause. It is this same exclusive monotheism that may well account for the fact that in his system the Goddess has no special function different from Her Lord's. She simply accompanies Him in all of His states.

For Rāmānuja the basic paradox is not the combination of transcendence and immanence. That is indeed the paradox for Śankara and his school, and one that verges on absolute contradiction, necessitating the doctrine of māyā. Rāmānuja, however, belonged to an ancient Vedāntic tradition for which there was no paradox in affirming that Brahman was the material and efficient cause of the universe. His transcendence and His immanence in the universe are for this tradition correlative, not the two poles of a paradox.

God, as Śrī Vaiṣṇavas conceive Him, can certainly be described as both transcendent and immanent, but both these attributes may be derived from the same facet of His nature: His pervasiveness. Because He pervades the universe as its Inner Ruler He transcends it, but by virtue of the same pervasion He is also completely immanent within the universe. In Śrī Vaiṣṇava thought, therefore, there is no tension between the concepts of Divine transcendence and Divine immanence, as there is to some extent in Śankara's Advaita and in Śākta.

Rāmānuja expresses this central Vaiṣṇava doctrine of the Divine pervasion of finite existence in a metaphysical analogy that he considers the key to the understanding of the common sacred Scriptures of all Hindus. This is the analogy of soul and body, which is not only given in Scripture but which also provides the basis for reconciling the apparent contradictions in Scripture. The analogy itself and its application to the relationship between God and the cosmos are further defined by three other relationships. All of this definition and elucidation of the soul-body relationship is meant to explain the combination of transcendence and immanence in the Divine nature.

Rāmānuja devotes a great deal of attention to the explanation and defense of this doctrine of *śarīra-śarīri-bhāva,* because it was under attack from non-Vedāntins and from Vedāntins from other schools. There was an intellectual problem that had to be resolved in order to convince others, but it does not seem to have been a continuing source of puzzlement and wonder for Rāmānuja's own faith. The relation of God's supremacy to His specific nearness and openness to men in redeeming them, does, however, seem to have been such a paradox for Rāmānuja—not so much a problem for faith as a source of continuing marvel that the Lord, who is the Supreme Person and the Perfect Being, would condescend to dwell so intimately with finite and imperfect creatures.

This may also be expressed as the tension between the inaccessibility of God in His own proper supreme estate, on the one hand, and His accessibility to His worshipers by virtue of His own gracious will on the other hand. It is precisely this contrast which Rāmānuja's interpreters within his own tradition have pointed out by their division into two distinct groups of his list of the Divine attributes.

For Rāmānuja himself, this is always a tension in unity, but at times in the Vaiṣṇava tradition there has been something of a breach in the unity of supremacy and accessibility in the one Divine Person. A particular avatāra or temple image has sometimes been conceived as partially distinct from the Supreme Nārāyaṇa, or the importance of Śrī has been so stressed that mercy has been described as Her distinctive attribute, and it has been said that She must persuade Her Divine Consort to be merciful to the sinner. It is characteristic of Rāmānuja that at the same time that he is combining into a synthesis elements from various streams of religious tradition he successfully sustains the unity in tension of Divine supremacy and accessibility.

THE MEMORY OF RĀMĀNUJA'S EMPHASIS IN THE TAMIL TRADITION

The largest of the Sanskritized Tamil commentaries on Nammāḻvār's *Tiruvāymoḻi* is called the "Thirty-Six Thousand" or the *Īḍu*. This work is especially loved in the Tengalai school, and the special Tengalai doctrines are indicated in many of the comments on specific verses. The *Īḍu* contains many reports of the comments of earlier teachers, including Yāmuna, Rāmānuja, and some of Rāmānuja's disciples. Since Śrī Vaiṣṇavas consider the hymns of the Āḻvārs as *anubhava-grantha,* a book of mystical experience, they are willing to allow diverse interpretations of the Tamil hymns, something not considered proper with respect to the Sanskrit Scriptures, which are believed to have a single correct interpretation.

In the comments on a number of stanzas, Rāmānuja's interpretation of the stanza is referred to, sometimes along with a different interpretation attributed to Yāmuna. One important instance is in the discussion of *Tiruvāymoḻi* 1.3.1, which all the commentaries agree is concerned with God's accessibility to His dependents, that is, to those who have gone to Him for refuge (the āśritas).

> In the first group of ten stanzas, the Āḻvār says that God is higher than all else [sarvasmāt-paran]. In the second group of ten, he asks people to worship God because He is supreme [para]. The following questions may be raised; "You have said repeatedly that one should worship God. How can a lame man climb on an elephant if you tell him to do so? Likewise how can an insignificant soul in this imperfect world [saṃsāra] approach the Lord of all, all whose desires are fulfilled?" The answer is surely that that the elephant can accomodate itself, lying down so that the lame man can mount. God likewise makes Himself very low so that He can be worshiped by the soul in this imperfect world. When God comes here in His incarnate form [avatāra], the unfortunate people consider that He is simply a human being of equal caste status and therefore miss the opportunity to worship Him. The fortunate people, on the other hand, respectfully approach this avatāra with the thought, "We have with us a very rare person [one who is difficult to attain, *ariyan*]." It is said that Uḍayavar [Rāmānuja] once made the following comment to Embār [Govinda]: "If we say that the Lord of all is difficult or impossible to attain [ariyan], no one will be found here in this imperfect world who can attain Him. Therefore we were explaining His easy accessibility [eḷimai]. The same easy accessibility of the Lord that causes some to leave Him is there in order that you may revere Him." If philanthropists build a village reservoir, some people will commit suicide in it by putting their heads into the mire, yet those affected by the heat come to bathe and cool off. If a lamp is lighted, moths fly into the flame and die, yet some are enabled to live in this world by the light of that lamp. This One is the light of the Vedas. He is the lamp of precious stone that appeared in the cowherd family. He is the light of the sūrya race. When this same Person became incarnate [as Krishna] He destroyed Bāṇāśura, yet by becoming incarnate He also became accessible [easy to attain, sulabha]. As an avatāra He causes Śiṣupāla [and other enemies] . . . to come and fight against Him and destroy themselves, yet for those who favor Him, He becomes the cause of their spiritual welfare.[25]

Since the words attributed to Rāmānuja received written form more than a hundred years after his death, it would seem unlikely to many historians that his actual words would have been preserved. That possibility should not be ruled out, however. The entire comment at least reflects a very accurate communal memory of Rāmānuja's distinctive theological emphasis. Govindacharya has given the entire passage as the teaching of Rāmānuja, which does not seem to be an accurate translation.[26] No indication is given as to who in the tradition conceived the striking illustrations of the ambivalent effects of the Lord's presence in the world in incarnate form. Both Rāmānuja's own words and accompanying illustrations are in striking contrast to the overemphasis on the Divine accessibility in much of the Śrī Vaiṣṇava tradition. This teaching attributed to Rāmānuja maintains the same balance of supremacy and accessibility within the single Divine nature that is characteristic of Rāmānuja's teaching in his Sanskrit writings. It is all the more impressive that this balance is maintained even in this explanation of the Lord's avatāras. The elephant kneeling to be mounted does not lose its greatness in its act of condescension to human weakness; likewise, the reservoir and the lamp, both intended for human welfare, can bring death when they are not rightly approached.

It is in the thought of Yāmuna that we see the closest parallel to Rāmānuja's distinctive emphasis. This could perhaps better be put the other way: in the general spirit of his theology as well as in the specific doctrine, Rāmānuja has faithfully followed the teaching of Yāmuna. In his *Gītārthasaṃgraha,* Yāmuna has summarized the contents of the ninth chapter of the *Bhagavadgītā* in one verse, part of which is as follows: "In the ninth [chapter] is taught His own eminence [sva-māhātmyam] and His supremacy even in His human incarnations [manuṣyatve paratvam]."[27] He is obviously referring with the second phrase to verses 11-13 and especially to verse 11: "Fools despise Me, who have assumed a human body, not knowing My supreme form [param-bhāvam], [for I am] the great Lord of creatures [bhūta-maheśvaram]."[28]

In commenting on this verse, Rāmānuja repeats the phrase *param-bhāvam,* but in his comment on the next verse, he paraphrases this term with *paratva* in the phrase: "causing the concealment of His supreme nature [paratva] consisting of such qualities as supreme compassion." In his comment on verse 11, also, Rāmānuja has described the nature concealed by the human body as consisting of the qualities connected with God's gracious action in saving men: compassion, generosity, gracious condescension, and forgiving love.[29] This makes it plain that Rāmānuja is not contrasting paratva with saulabhya here in the way that is done by his later commentators, and presumably the same is true of Yāmuna. Nevertheless, it is significant that Yāmuna's summary of this chapter brings out the same point that Rāmānuja brings out with emphasis in the introduction to his *Gītābhāṣya* and whenever he deals with the subject of avatāra, that God does not give up His own inherent nature (sva-svabhāva) when He descends to the phenomenal world and takes a creaturely form, even though He temporarily conceals His transcendent form. In other words, God remains God even when in human form. For both Yāmuna and Rāmānuja it is axiomatic that God retains His essential supremacy, an axiom preserved by the subsequent tradition in the image of the kneeling elephant.

19 Questions at the Limits of Phenomenological Understanding

Beyond the Limits of Phenomenology of Religion

This study has attempted to gain an understanding of the Śrī Vaiṣṇava doctrine of God, as taught by that community's greatest theologian, Rāmānuja. For reasons given in chapter 1, I consider it a study in the phenomenology of religion: negatively, in the attempt to refrain from judgments of truth and value; positively, in the utilization of the religious tradition most familiar to the author in an effort to discover and elucidate patterns of meaning in the unfamiliar tradition being studied.

I maintain that such refraining from truth and value judgments is extremely useful in this kind of study, but it is somewhat artificial. A participant in the Śrī Vaiṣṇava community makes such judgments by his very act of taking part in the tradition, while participants in other religious communities, as well as those who have rejected all traditional religious participation, have implicitly or explicitly come to some decision on many of the issues that Śrī Vaiṣṇavas consider vital. To the extent that they have become acquainted with some aspects of Śrī Vaiṣṇava tradition they may have felt called to some personal response, some *yea* or *nay*, with respect to the affirmations of that tradition.

Even when one undertakes a particular religious study with a conscious effort at *epoché*, the choice of subject is frequently determined by specific religious or philosophical concerns, or otherwise by interests that reflect personal and cultural value judgments. The conclusions of such a phenomenological study, moreover, may well be utilized in subsequent reflections beyond the limits of phenomenology of religion. Indeed, it would seem to me irresponsible as well as artificial not to utilize such phenomenological understanding as one has gained in the service of philosophical and theological inquiry. Such inquiry deserves to be pursued systematically. A philosophical or theological wrestling with Rāmānuja's thought is both too difficult and too large a subject to address in a brief appendix to this phenomenological study. Phenomenology of religion began, however, as a transitional chapter in Chantepie de la Saussaye's *Manual of the Science of Religion*, between descriptive history and constructive philosophy: a transition that would be systematic or thematic without making normative judgments.[1] In my opinion phenomenology of religion is best understood as such a transitional or in-between discipline. I have noted how difficult it is to separate this discipline from all matters of history. It is equally difficult to separate it from all the philosophical and theological issues lying just beyond its systematizations.

It seems appropriate, therefore, to raise a few questions in this final chapter that cannot be answered within the limits of this study, both for reasons of method and reasons of space! Two such questions will be taken up after a brief review of the salient features of Rāmānuja's doctrine of God, but there are some more methodological questions that may well be considered first.

POLARITIES IN THE DIVINE NATURE AS AN APPROACH TO THE STUDY OF RELIGIONS

This study has been deliberately confined to Rāmānuja's own thought, yet the analysis of the polarity of supremacy and accessibility has necessitated going beyond the limits of the thought of one Hindu theologian. As soon as we try to determine how our understanding is aided by the interpretations of Rāmānuja by his classical and modern followers, as well as by non-Śrī Vaiṣṇavas, we are led to compare the underlying dynamics of Śrī Vaiṣṇava theology as a whole with those of other Hindu theological systems. It is inevitable that a phenomenological study of even a single mind in a single tradition must eventually consider whether the same structure of ideas and feelings is characteristic of other theologians in the same tradition and of other traditions in the same religion. A study that begins with Kristensen's intention of learning to understand the religion of one particular group of serious believers almost inevitably moves on to a broader kind of "phenomenology of religion" or "comparative religion" more like that of van der Leeuw. The broader comparative survey of religious patterns comes closer to the concerns, and sometimes also to the assumptions, of some kind of philosophy of religion or theology. It is this borderline area that concerns us here: the questions that arise for philosophy of religion or Christian theology from this phenomenological inquiry. There is, however, a general question arising from this study that is more methodological, and that question may well be considered first.

Is it fruitful for the students of other religious systems, both Hindu and non-Hindu, to look for significant polarities in the Divine nature? Is the discovery of such polarities useful in understanding each system in itself (the doctrine of each group of serious believers), and is it also useful in comparing different Hindu systems and thereby increasing our understanding of Hinduism as a whole?

These questions can only be answered completely by trying this approach with other Hindu theologies, but the present study suggests two advantages in focusing on such polarities. Not all religious systems feed on paradox, yet it may frequently be the case that what is an intellectual problem or a point of rational inconsistency for the theologian is crucial for the worshiper's awe and adoration. This religiously significant "inconsistency" is often a direct indication of, or at least a clue to, an effort on the part of the adherents of this tradition to hold together in both thought and worship two different sides of the Divine nature. A second advantage of concentrating on a polarity in the Divine nature is that it enables the student to deal not only with individual concepts but also with the way in which they are held together in the total apprehension of the Deity in that tradition.

The same principle of interpretation might also be applied to the study of non-Hindu religious systems and would apply equally to the analysis of quite different polarities. Yet what is of special interest for this study is that in many theistic systems with a major emphasis on the revealing and saving action of God, this *same* polarity of supremacy and accessibility may have considerable importance. It may be discovered that there is a similar tension in the conception of the Divine nature, and a similar struggle by the orthodox theologian to hold together diverse or even apparently contradictory notions in a unitary view of the Divine nature. Such analysis could lay the groundwork for a comparison of theistic systems in different religions, not so much with respect to particular concepts as with respect to the way in which these concepts are combined.

BASIC DISTINCTIONS IN RĀMĀNUJA'S DOCTRINE OF GOD

The Śrī Vaiṣṇava doctrine of God (Īśvaratattva) taught by Rāmānuja has been analyzed in the preceding chapters in terms of two pairs of concepts. The first pair are *svarūpa* and *svabhāva*: terms that might both be translated as "essential nature" but that are frequently distinguished by Rāmānuja. Although his usage is fluid, he generally differentiates between God's essential nature in the strict sense (svarūpa) and God's nature in a broader sense (svabhāva), which is often identified with the Lord's auspicious qualities (kalyāṇaguṇāḥ) (see chapter 6 above).

The distinction between the Divine svarūpa and everything else belonging to the Divine nature (svabhāva) in no way implies that this "everything else" is unimportant, but it does indicate the metaphysical priority of the five defining attributes of the Supreme Self, which express God's essential nature to be infinite and joyous self-consciousness that is eternally real and flawless. This priority stems from the fact that these five attributes refer to God's nature as He exists in Himself, without reference to any other entity. All the other qualities pertain to God's relations to other entities. In addition to His personal "auspicious qualities," God possesses a unique bodily form, a transcendent abode, and a finite realm manifesting His glory.

Rāmānuja appears to me to have thought of the inner core of God's being as that distinctive essence or substance that God has for and by and in Himself. Surrounding this inner core are a number of other aspects: (1) the various relations of the Infinite Being to the cosmos of finite selves and material objects, all encompassed in the self-body relationship; (2) the qualities expressing both God's lordship over His creation and His loving concern for it; (3) the Lord's beautiful transcendent form, to some extent revealed in (4) His descents into the phenomenal realm; (5) the Lord's presence within finite souls as their Inner Controller, in their participation in the processes of creation and of liberation; and (6) the Lord's eternal heavenly realm, which includes His consort (or consorts), His eternal ministers, and all released souls in communion with Him. While it is possible to distinguish these other aspects of the Divine nature (svabhāva) from the Divine essence (svarūpa), it is not legitimate to try to separate them or put the other aspects on a lower level of reality. When Rāmānuja wants to make this quite clear, he expands the concept of svarūpa to include these other aspects of the Divine nature as well.

There is also a seventh aspect of the "outer being" of God, and this is definitely on a lower level, though inseparably linked with the Lord: the entire phenomenal universe of souls embodied in material bodies and in contact with material objects, all of them subject to the law of karma. This is also a vibhūti, a realm reflecting the Divine glory, but it is the realm of transience and imperfection in which the Lord is engaged in sport (līla), activity that is its own end, or pleasurable in itself, for there is nothing to be done for some other end since God is eternally in possession of all that He desires. The realm of sport and the realm of eternal joy together constitute the body of God.

For a Christian attempting to understand Rāmānuja's theology, certain general comparisons with Christian theology may be helpful, whatever their final theological validity. Thus the Divine svarūpa corresponds to some Christian (and other theistic) notions of God in Himself apart from His creation. The host of infinite-finite relationships and auspicious qualities is likewise comparable to Christian notions of God as Creator and Redeemer. There seems to be no close Christian parallel to Rāmānuja's conception of the superlatively beautiful bodily form of the Lord in His supreme estate, but there are interesting similarities as well as striking differences between the Śrī Vaiṣṇava doctrine of Divine descents (avatāra) and the Christian doctrine (or doctrines) of God's incarnation in Jesus of Nazareth. There are parallels as well as differences between the conception of the Inner Controller (antaryāmī) and Christian notions of the Holy Spirit. In chapter 10 I suggested that Rāmānuja's conception of vibhūti has significant resemblance to Christian understanding of creation as finite but essentially good.

The second and major pair of concepts utilized in this study are supremacy and accessibility (paratva and saulabhya). With respect to these concepts, comparison with Christian doctrines of God seems to me still more fruitful. While the distinction between svarūpa and svabhāva may be intellectually clarified by references to somewhat comparable Christian distinctions, the distinction between God's supremacy and His accessibility is one that a Christian can appreciate emotionally as well as intellectually. He can himself imagine something of Rāmānuja's sense of awe and wonder that God, who is so great and so far removed from the imperfections of temporal existence, should nevertheless *descend* and *condescend* and *commune* with such imperfect creatures. In Christian experience of God in Jesus Christ, there is also the drama, or perhaps even the paradox, of the Heavenly King descending and abasing Himself for sinful creatures.[2]

THE FOUR ASPECTS OF THE POLARITY OF SUPREMACY AND ACCESSIBILITY

In chapter 5 I noted the four phrases at the very end of the long introduction to the *Gītābhāṣya* in which, according to Vedānta Deśika, Rāmānuja has succinctly expressed both the paratva and the saulabhya of God. It is striking how accurately they point, not only to the distinction between supremacy and accessibility, but to a further differentiation in each of those broad categories.

The first of these four terms is *Puruṣottama*—the name that Rāmānuja prefers to use for the Deity when speaking in a philosophical context. The supreme Person is the Personal Spirit who is by nature unutterably superior to all other personal spirits (puruṣas) and to their material bodies. This ontological superiority is expressed not only negatively by accentuating the difference in their status but also positively by expounding the doctrine that He is the in-dwelling Self of all beings.

The second term is *Sarveśvareśvaraḥ* (Lord of all lords). It emphasizes not only the metaphysical supremacy of God over all other beings but also His active lordship. He is the ultimate Lord, for He rules over all lesser lords, even the great divinities who seem from the worldly standpoint to exercise such wide control; their lordship is merely delegated and they are all essentially finite creatures. Moreover, even though God exercises lordship through subordinate lords, He remains directly in control. He alone can be present in this universe without being subject to the rule of karma, for karma itself is simply the expression of His pleasure or displeasure at good or evil. His lordship is not simply a matter of His overwhelming power; He is Lord by right. He is the rightful owner of souls, the Śeṣī of all śeṣins, the universal Owner and Master. He alone is the absolute Lord.

The third and fourth phrases contrast vividly with the first and second, but more than that, there is a distinction between the third and fourth phrases that corresponds precisely to the two levels of accessibility that were discussed in chapter 15. The phrase *jagad-upakṛti-martyaḥ* indicates both the descent of the Lord from His supreme state and His purpose in thus descending: becoming a mortal of benefit the universe. The Lord's compassion for all His creatures is so great that He who is essentially immortal has taken mortal form. As Rāmānuja repeatedly emphasizes, however, the Lord does not really give up His Divine nature in His incarnations. Even in His lowly state, He remains, for those who have the eye to see, essentially supreme.

The fourth phrase indicates the furthest extent of the triumph of the side of the Divine nature described by Rāmānuja's followers as saulabhya. The incarnate Lord, who is about to expound the bhaktiyoga to Arjuna as the means to communion with Him is said here to be *āśrita-vātsalysa-vivaśaḥ* (overwhelmed with protecting and forgiving love for His devotees). Here the scope of the Divine love is narrowed from all creatures to those who have sought refuge with Him, but it is also deepened. The general Divine concern for the welfare of creatures is here transmuted into a fervent longing for communion with His chosen devotees. These are the persons, rare indeed, who not only recognize their metaphysical dependence upon Him but are dependent on communion with Him to sustain their souls. The paradox of Rāmānuja's teaching in the *Gītābhāṣya* is that the Lord is similarly dependent on communion with these souls; without them He cannot sustain His ātmā. Nowhere else does Rāmānuja so emphasize God's metaphysical independence, yet it is precisely here that he most clearly states that the Lord is mystically dependent on His devotees. His vātsalya has overwhelmed the rest of His nature and produced a situation of mutual dependence in which the self of the devotee and His own self draw very near and support one another. This is the deepest mystery of God's nature, but it is a mystery into which only the one who is utterly and exclusively devoted to God can hope to enter, the mystery that the Supreme Person, the Lord of all lords, who is completely self-sufficient and independent, not only takes our mortal form upon Himself in order to benefit the world but allows Himself to become dependent, as it were, on those who utterly cast themselves upon Him.

A QUESTION TO NATURAL THEOLOGY

The first question that Rāmānuja's doctrine of God suggests to Christian theologians falls in the area traditionally called natural theology or philosophical theology. It may be put like this: What is the relation of specific Divine disclosures to general knowledge of God through Creation? The polarity of supremacy and accessibility in the Divine nature characterizes Rāmānuja's doctrine of God. The polarity is comprehensible to Christians because they are acquainted with a somewhat similar polarity in their own conception of God. It may well be that analogues are also present in other theistic systems, especially those that emphasize the revealing and saving action of God. For many theistic systems there is both connection and tension between the supreme majesty of God and His particular acts or utterances of self-revelation. One aspect of this polarity is the inaccessibility of God unless and until He chooses to reveal Himself. Rāmānuja affirms in the introduction to his commentary on the *Bhagavadgītā* that in His proper state God could not be attained even by the Vedic gods or by the masters of ascetic powers. Only if and when God chooses to descend to the finite realm and appear to His creatures may He be attained.[3]

Although Rāmānuja's ontology and his concept of God have many similarities with those of some Western philosophies of religion, his "fideist" view of men's capacity to know God contrasts sharply with the epistemology of most Western philosophies of religion, which are confident of man's capacity to know something of God's nature through the exercise of his native powers of rationality. Whether through inference or intuition, man is considered able to penetrate with his intellect to the Divine nature without a specific Divine self-disclosure. Among the aspects of the Divine nature that philosophers of religion have often considered accessible to the human intellect are God's ontological primacy, His infinite goodness, His creatorship, His sovereign control of all finite beings, and His unity. Over against this, the "fideist" orthodox of many religious traditions have held that these aspects of the Divine nature, or even the very existence of God, can be known only on the basis of some specific Divine revelation.

A phenomenology of religion that goes beyond the attempt to understand the faith of one particular religious community can hardly fail to note this significant contrast between the "orthodox" doctrines of revelation of so many theistic religions and the more rationalist philosophical "theism" of these same religions. It may go further and relate these contrasting views of religious knowledge to certain universal alternatives in human thought and experience, but phenomenology of religion cannot itself answer the question that such divergence in theories of religious knowledge should raise for the philosopher of religion and the theologian. It is precisely such a question that seems to me appropriate at the boundary between a phenomenological and a philosophical approach to the study of religion.

It happens that in the Christian theological tradition the "rationalist" view of the knowledge of God has had a most "orthodox" embodiment: the philosophy and theology of much of the Roman Catholic church for the past seven centuries, based on the teaching of Saint Thomas Aquinas.[4] According to this view there are two levels in the knowledge of God. The lower level is knowledge of God as First Cause, which is available to all men by the natural light of reason, while the higher level is the knowledge of God as Savior, which is given only to those who are saved by Christ in the Church. Thomistic theology has guided much of the massive missionary efforts of the Roman Catholic church since the Counter-Reformation in the sixteenth century. In general it has led to a more sympathetic approach to both the beliefs and the practices of non-Christians than has been characteristic of the more fideist Protestant missions. In order, however, for something in the non-Christian culture to be considered acceptable for continued use by converts or incorporated in apologetic theology, it had to be considered "rational" rather than "superstitious," based on the rational moral foundations of society ordained by God the Creator, or reflecting the knowledge of God the Creator available to all rational men. Rites and beliefs, on the other hand, that clearly derived from non-Christian scripture or were directly connected with the worship of non-Christian deities were considered "superstitious" and had to be rejected by the official missionary theology. This view seems to imply that precisely what was in a non-Christian culture most clearly *religious* in terms of that culture's own norms had to be rejected by Christians as possessing no universal religious value or truth.[5]

Much recent Roman Catholic thinking has moved away from such a sharply two-level conception of the knowledge of God. In part this shift has been due to greater utilization of patristic and other theologies before the time of Saint Thomas that did not so much contrast revelation and reason. In part it has been due to a broader conception of the saving work of Christ, sometimes interpreted so broadly as to include in the sphere of Christ's saving work all those sincerely involved in the sacramental systems of their own religions.[6]

The Thomistic two-level conception of religious knowledge has affected Western philosophy of religion since the eighteenth-century Enlightenment, but with a concentration of attention on what for Thomism is the lower level of religious knowledge: the rational knowledge of God potentially open to all men. Such knowledge was frequently regarded as in principle independent of participation in any cult, Christian or other, and certainly of the reception of any special revelation. Not all Western philosophers of religion have taken this line: Hegel regarded the Divine revelation apprehended and celebrated in the religious community as the unclarified form of the Idea. Many philosophers of religion, however, have had little interest in the study of *religion* or piety. Their interest has been in apprehending rationally, or rationally criticizing supposed apprehensions of, the metaphysical objects of religious knowledge.[7]

It is significant that the focus of both Thomistic natural theology and post-Enlightenment philosophy of religion is on the side of the Divine nature that the commentators on Rāmānuja's theology called paratva: the Divine supremacy. Much less attention is paid to the aspects of the Divine nature we have discussed under the heading of saulabhya: God's accessibility to His creatures and more specifically to His devotees.

The foregoing chapters indicate the extent of Rāmānuja's emphasis on the aspects of the Divine nature subsumed under "supremacy." He certainly stresses a central topic in Western natural theologies: the fact that God is the cause of everything (sarva-kāraṇatva). It is this fact that is decisive in determining that Viṣṇu-Nārāyaṇa, rather than Śiva, is to be acknowledged as truly God, the Supreme Lord.

Yet while Rāmānuja never draws the specific conclusion of Luther and Calvin that the knowledge of God the Creator is not possible without the knowledge of God the Savior, he does reject a rational proof of God's existence similar to Saint Thomas Aquinas's cosmological argument, and he insists quite as emphatically as Luther or Calvin that Scripture is the sole source of the knowledge of God.[8] Furthermore, he maintains that the knowledge of God as infinite consciousness and bliss and as the Supreme Cause is inseparable from the knowledge that Scripture also gives of God's auspicious qualities, beautiful form, exalted Consort, and glorious realms (see chapter 13 above). Apart from this revelation of God in the Vedas and other Hindu Scriptures, not even by the inherent powers of the most exalted creatures (the gods) nor by the acquired power of the most accomplished ascetics can anything be known about the Supreme Lord, who is essentially beyond the capacity of speech or mind.

This doctrine of Rāmānuja's is not a private or sectarian conception of religious knowledge but is the doctrine of Scripture held in common by all schools of Vedānta. All of these systems affirm that God is knowable when He reveals Himself to men (or, when expressed impersonally, is revealed). Although God's supremacy is ontologically prior, it is epistemologically dependent on men's experience of God as He becomes accessible to them, an experience often regarded as limited to those who have studied the Scripture under proper guidance in the midst of the devout community.

In popular Hinduism there is a counterpart to this view of Vedānta philosophy and of the sectarian Hindu theologies. Those deities are worshiped who have manifested their protecting care in the experience of many worshipers, and these worshipers celebrate the paradigmatic protection or rescue of some particular devotee at the very site of the temple or shrine. The popular worship of Viṣṇu and Śiva has much to do with the forms through which these deities are brought closer in time and space to each particular group of worshipers. Whether through their consorts, their incarnations (Viṣṇu), their sons (Śiva), or their temporary appearances to particular devotees (both Śiva and Viṣṇu), they are apprehended as more immediately present than the Lord in His supreme estate (whether conceived as Śiva or Viṣṇu), thus providing an important link between the polytheism of Hindu folk piety and the monotheism of the explicitly sectarian theologies.

The natural theology of Aquinas was the product of a long process of interaction between Jewish, Muslim, and Christian thinkers for which the philosophy of Aristotle provided a language of communication. To some extent those features of the doctrine of God that were common to these three monotheistic faiths were identified with the Aristotelian concept of the First Cause or Prime Mover, even though the disparity between the religious and philosophical conceptions was realized and helped to stimulate continued debate on the precise limits of the natural knowledge of God.

The Hindu equivalent of this "natural theology" was the doctrine of God developed by the Nyāya school, which seems to have had more influence on Rāmānuja's predecessors Nāthamuni and Yāmuna than it did on Rāmānuja himself.[9] This theory of the rational knowledge of God had to contend against a much greater diversity of religious positions than did the natural theology of Aquinas and its Jewish and Islamic equivalents. The Jains and

Buddhists accepted the challenge to argument on rational grounds, but the Jains and the different Buddhist schools had developed somewhat different systems of logic, and they all denied the existence of Īśvara, namely, of a Divine Creator and Lord. The two Vedic schools, on the other hand, which agreed that proof of the nature of reality must be gained from the Vedic Scriptures rather than rational argument, differed radically as to the nature of this reality. While the Vedānta's central affirmation was the reality of Brahman, who seen in personal terms is Īśvara, the ritualist school (Karma Mīmāṃsā) either denied the reality of Brahman outright or simply refused to consider any ontological questions, holding that its authoritative source consisted of injunctions to sacrifice rather than declarations on the nature of being.

Śrī Vaiṣṇava thought brought together Nyāya emphases and previous traditions of the Vedānta. Rāmānuja, leaning strongly toward the Vedānta, denies the sufficiency of any rational argument for the existence of God. He grants that there must be some kind of creator as a sufficient cause for the universe but insists that rational argument does not demonstrate that there would be a single creator or what the nature of that creator would be. Rāmānuja also finds the Nyāya concept of Īśvara inadequate, for it posits a Lord who is only the efficient cause of a universe consisting of unformed matter, whereas Rāmānuja follows the *Vedānta Sūtras* in maintaining that God is the material cause as well as the efficient cause of the universe.[10]

Rāmānuja's conception of religious knowledge is representative of those of a large number of theologians belonging to various theistic schools. He affirms the reality of the created world and the capacity of imperfect men to apprehend its material correctly through both perception and inference. With a mind clarified by the knowledge of God given through Scripture, one recognizes that this real world around us is part of the glory of God. The world adorns God's nature as a bejeweled garment adorns a king. Indeed, Rāmānuja maintains, the finite universe is the "body" of the infinite Lord; God is the world's inner self and its underlying reality. Yet knowledge of the Lord who is the cause of this magnificent universe is to be gained, not by observing the universe and reflecting on it, whether on its order or on its finitude, but by accepting what trustworthy Scriptures state concerning the Lord, Scriptures passed down and interpreted by a trustworthy line of learned and virtuous teachers.

Many religious people in various cultures have denied the possibility of separating a knowledge of God as Creator from a knowledge of God as Protector and Savior, a knowledge derived from specific acts of protecting and saving and/or from participating in a community that is related to His saving action and/or from Scriptures that guide men in availing themselves of His protection and attaining His salvation. Such a denial does not, of course, disprove the assertions of various philosophers of religion that a separate knowledge of God as Creator or Universal Cause is a possibility, and a reality, for rational men, irrespective of the religious cults in which they do or do not participate or the particular soteriology to which they do or do not subscribe. Nor does the widespread position that Rāmānuja articulates disprove the distinction drawn by many Christians of various Catholic traditions between a knowledge of God as Supreme Cause available to all men and a knowledge of God as Savior given only in Christian faith.

Since Rāmānuja's position is in this respect so widespread in human religious communities, however, philosophers of religion and theological advocates of a two-tier conception of the knowledge of God might do well to reexamine the empirical evidence, if any, upon which they have previously relied. The trend of contemporary thinking, both in Catholic theology and in philosophy of religion, is clearly away from such a two-tier view, but the implications of a more adequate conception need further exploration. I should like here, not to attempt to answer, but simply to pose a question that is suggested by much historical and phenomenological study of religion: What is the relation of the knowledge of God as Creator to the knowledge of God as Savior? There may be no general answer to this question, but every philosophical or theological position concerned with the knowledge of God should accept the challenge of the question.

A Question to Neo-Reformation Theology

My second question is addressed to those who would base their theology on specific Divine revelation, in particular to fellow Protestant Christians who share my indebtedness to the Reformation tradition and its recent interpreters. This is the question of the theological significance of the apparent similarities between

Rāmānuja's conception of God and the conception of Protestant Christians. The similarities are apparent, both to Christian students of Rāmānuja's thought and to Hindu students of Christianity. What is the theological significance of these common theological structures in different "religions of grace"?

Conservative Protestant interpreters of Hindu devotional piety have either not recognized these similarities or have attributed them to Christian influence on medieval Hinduism. Liberal Protestants have sometimes made much of the similarities but frequently with sharp criticism of the theological deficiencies and ethical weaknesses of Hindu piety. Neo-Reformation interpreters, however, have recognized important *religious* similarities between Protestant theology and Hindu bhakti but at the same time have denied that such similarities were theologically significant for Christians. This apparently paradoxical position has been most clearly enunciated by Karl Barth.[11] His dialectical critique of religion is intended to establish God's complete initiative in revelation and redemption, an initiative that makes irrelevant men's particular religious forms and the intensity of their piety. Yet it is the same Christian religion so chastised as *Unglaube* (faithlessness) that solely by God's grace (not by the religious efforts of Christians) becomes the "true religion." The critique of other human religiousness is explicitly stated not to be "a preliminary polemic against the non-Christian religions."

> It is our business as Christians to apply this judgement [that religion is unbelief] first and most acutely to ourselves; and to others, the non-Christians, only in so far as we recognize ourselves in them, i.e. as we see in them the truth of this judgement of revelation that concerns us.[12]

Barth's treatment of religion can be understood as a kind of Hegelian dialectic. Unglaube is the antithesis; true religion is the synthesis.[13] The first term of the Hegelian triad, the thesis, is only barely visible. It seems to be hinted at in Barth's recognition of the importance of the religious consciousness, for good or ill, in the Divine-human encounter.[14] Barth is unable, however, to give due recognition to this universal religious consciousness without admitting that his critique of Schleiermacher is too severe. While Barth can assert that Divine grace has transformed the faithlessness of Christians into "true religion," he does not think that Divine grace transforms any non-Christian form of Unglaube into "true religion."

Barth claims that he is making no attempt to show the superiority of the religious content of Christianity. He recognizes the universal character of religious experiences and the similarity of religious forms in different religions, but he considers these similarities theologically irrelevant.

The similarity that concerns us here is much more specific than the common presence of general categories of phenomenology of religion in both Christianity and Hinduism. It is the existence of specific Hindu analogues to the Reformers' doctrine of grace, which for some Christian theologians has been a cause of puzzlement or embarrassment. The explanation of Richard Garbe and others for these Hindu parallels was influence from Christian sources.[15] Barth, on the other hand, seeks to make a virtue of necessity. After pointing out that even Protestantism as a "religion of grace" stands under the same universal Divine judgment against religion, he continues,

> We can regard it as a wholly providential disposition that as far as I can see the most adequate and comprehensive and illuminating heathen parallel to Christianity, a religious development in the Far East, is parallel not to Roman or Greek Catholicism but to Reformed Christianity, thus confronting Christianity with the question of its truth even as the logical religion of grace.[16]

Barth devotes only a long parenthesis to the parallel of Indian bhakti religion, which he regards as "not nearly so forceful as the Japanese one."

> The high or supreme God to whom Bhakti is offered can have any name or character. It is the emotion of love itself and as such which redeems man, which enables him to participate in the answering love of God. . . . The most uncertain part played by the idea of God, the substitution of surrender and love for faith, and the utter and complete formlessness even of the complete concept of love, show that we are in quite a different world from that of the Japanese religion of grace, and an absolutely different world from that of Evangelical Christianity. It would be a very degenerate form of modern Evangelical

> Christianity which felt that the Bhakti religions could claim kinship with it.[17]

There are forms of bhakti, especially in North India, to which Barth's comments about the primacy of the emotion of love and the characterlessness of God may in some measure apply, but Barth's references to a "cat-rule" and a "monkey-rule" indicate he has read something about Śrī Vaiṣṇavism, possibly in Rudolf Otto's book on *India's Religion of Grace,* which for all its limitations certainly does not lend support to this kind of gross misrepresentation of much of Hindu theology, including the position of both Vaiṣṇavas and Śaivas in South India.[18]

It is not important here to find the reasons for Barth's inaccuracies concerning the Indian "religion of grace," but it is of some interest to ask why Barth has embarked on this kind of comparison at all. In order to reinforce his point that any religion of grace remains a religion under Divine judgment, Barth feels compelled to launch into an excursus that might seem unnecessary on his own principles, for he sets forth distinctions between the Buddhist and the Protestant religions of grace as "symptoms, but only symptoms, of the real difference between true and false religion . . . the seal of a truth which we must first receive elsewhere." This truth is that "only one thing is decisive . . . the name of Jesus Christ."

> There can be no question, even in the future, of a real parallelism or coincidence between the doctrine and the life of the Christian and non-Christian religions of grace (however consistent). Instead, certain symptomatic distinctions will be visible here and there, in which the true and essential distinction can always be perceived. But a conviction of this kind can be well-grounded only if it is based exclusively upon faith in the one and only Jesus Christ, for it is only from Him that the relative distinctions can have and constantly derive their relative light.[19]

Barth is thus willing to concede a limited utility to the evidence of doctrinal, ethical, and institutional similarities between different religions of grace, but this utility is quite negative. The similarity is called providential only because it makes clearer the *difference* between any *religion* of grace and the *revelation* of true grace. The distinctions between the Christian religion and other religions of grace are taken as symptoms of the fundamental difference between the Divine revelation that is Jesus Christ and all other purported revelations of deities with all other possible names.

Karl Barth was unable to maintain the paradoxical position he set forth as his intention: to recognize the religious similarity between Christian doctrine and non-Christian theologies, while denying the theological significance of such similarity. The similarity in doctrine is sufficient for him to feel he had to address himself to it, and like many of the liberal theologians whose method he criticizes he find significant differences between the evangelical Christian doctrine and the Buddhist or Hindu doctrine precisely by considering the apparent similarity. Once he concludes, however, that the name of Jesus Christ is the real source of the relative distinctions between religions, he is finding theological significance in the comparison of religious phenomena.

In a world in which names are so often regarded as "mere names," Barth is making a heroic effort to reassert the early Christian confidence in the power of the name of Jesus and is trying to recover for modern Christians a conception of the Divine Name held in many other religious traditions, though not in all. Certainly the Śrī Vaiṣṇava tradition of Rāmānuja emphasizes the particular Divine names that both contain and convey the reality of God. It is true that it is the function of any proper name to identify the uniqueness of the individual bearing it, but human beings also bear family names situating them in their social context. In the religious application of specific names to God, including the early Christian usage, both the unique individuality and the relatedness of God are suggested by His names. When the implications of "no other name" are faced by a theologian, as they are by Barth in the body of his dogmatics, he is forced to draw positive connections, as well as distinctions, between the incomparable Divine Name and every manifestation in our world of Divine truth. While Barth has not done so, it is my conviction that a theologian exploring the implications of the name of Jesus Christ may see in that Divine Name the source, not only of what Barth calls the "relative distinctions," but also of the relative similarities between religions.

Such a step—admitting that there is theological significance in common religious structures—does not solve the Christian theologian's problem in a world in which both great religious diversity and striking similarities between diverse religions exist, but it does accept that there is a problem, a problem that the Christian theologian, as well as the Hindu or Buddhist theologian, must face.

The relative similarities between Rāmānuja's doctrine of God and the conception of God in Christian faith seem to me sufficiently striking and extensive as to call for some theological reflection. The obligation to reflect does not commit the theologian to any particular interpretation of such similarities, but the similarities and the differences should be clearly seen. I would hold that the similarities facilitate the process of interreligious understanding. In recent centuries in India these similarities have served another function: providing a vehicle for communicating the Christian message. Both Roman Catholic and Protestant churches in India utilize a vocabulary in their preaching, teaching, and praying that is drawn very largely from the sectarian theologies of the devotees of Viṣṇu and Śiva. Whatever the failings of Indian Christianity, it is not the "very degenerate form of modern Evangelical Christianity" that Barth has in mind; yet at the level of religion, it surely must "claim kinship" with the Hindu bhakti movements. Not only the official Christian theologies but the personal experience of converts testify to the fructifying influence on Indian Christianity of the Hindu bhakti tradition and sometimes, quite specifically, of the theology of Rāmānuja and his successors.[20] The contemporary interaction in South Indian villages also calls for theological reflection on the apparent closeness between Christian and sectarian Hindu conceptions.[21]

Perhaps some Christian theologians will be willing to speculate that the similarity between Christian and Hindu religions of grace is "providential" in a different sense from Barth's, whether as an indication of God's universal providence, or even as a specific process within God's universal history of redemption, a history that the Christian theologian understands with reference to the name of Jesus Christ.

The peculiar difficulty obstructing communication between adherents of different religions of grace is that they all belong to "religions of revelation" and to "religions of the true name of God." This is true of Hindu theistic movements, both Vaiṣṇava and Śaiva, and of Amida Buddhism (Jodo-shu and Shin-shu in Japan) as well as of Christianity. There are many other religious movements, not emphasizing a doctrine of divine grace, that also base themselves on specific Divine revelations. The very particularity of the theistic conception of deity leads many besides Barth to the conclusion that striking similarities between theistic movements are of no theological importance, since what is decisive is the unique Divine Name disclosed in the unique revelation to the unique community of those whom the Lord has chosen for His own.

This frequent "Barthian" emphasis of many religions of grace presents an ironic difficulty in interreligious communication. The similar doctrines that they hold, doctrines very different from the rationalist universals of many types of philosophical theism, may make it possible for them to understand the meaning of one another's doctrines, but their rival claims to unique revelations and specific salvation histories seem to make any deeper agreement or unity of spirit impossible. It may well appear to the participant in one theistic system that he can appropriate nothing of fundamental value through his study of another theistic system, however close may be the structural similarities. Honesty about such an appraisal to an adherent of the other religious community in question may close the door to scholarly inquiry and dialogue. Even the quest for phenomenological understanding by a student who participates in a different and rival religion of grace may seem to indicate a lack of religious seriousness.

I would suggest that Śrī Vaiṣṇavas and Śaiva Siddhāntins, as well as Christians, will have to live with this problem for some time to come, exercising patience with those who do not belong to their religious community and critical self-awareness concerning their participation in their own tradition. While a religion of grace may well formulate its theological perspective in less fideist terms than Barth's or Rāmānuja's, it is unlikely to rid itself of the offense of theological particularity, nor should it wish to do so. A theist would rather be charged with an obscurantism and an exclusivism unbefitting the modern age than attempt to reduce his faith in the One revealed in a particular body of Scripture to a series of universally acceptable rational principles or to "elevate" his conception of the One possessing the unique name or names of God to the level of a nameless Absolute.

What such patience and critical self-consciousness should mean concretely can be determined only by those within each religious community. My own conviction, beyond the limits of phenomenological *epoché*, is that a Christian student of religion, far from abandoning his faith in the name of Jesus Christ in the interest of universal tolerance and community, should draw on his faith and on the religious experience of his particular Christian tradition in the service of greater interreligious understanding. Certainly he should seek to understand those theistic systems that show important similarities to his own religion. We Christians, who are known in the world at large for the aggressiveness of our approach and the harshness of our judgments, need to learn more caution in judgment and more zeal in understanding. It is also my conviction that, within the Christian community, "rationalist" and "fideist" theologians have still much to learn, assisting one another, concerning the nature of religious knowledge and the content of religious truth.

We can feel in Christian faith the same tension that Rāmānuja senses in his apprehension of the Lord revealed to him in the Vedas and through the Vedānta and the Śrī Vaiṣṇava tradition. That tension is the inner dynamic of supreme lordship and utter availability within the same Divine nature and Divine person. That is why, although Christians stand outside Rāmānuja's tradition, they are able to grasp and to appreciate so much of his thought. The significance of this capacity for understanding poses an important and as yet unresolved question for Christian theology.

Notes

Explanation of Abbreviations

Writings on Rāmānuja are in general referred to by the name of the author or of the modern editor or translator. However, since this would be cumbersome and sometimes confusing in the case of the nine writings ascribed to Rāmānuja, these works are indicated with primary reference to their Sanskrit titles, given in abbreviated form, in works containing the Sanskrit text. Additional or special references to one or more translations other than the one in the book containing the cited text are indicated in the usual way by giving the name of the modern translator. The following list indicates the abbreviations of the titles of Rāmānuja's writings used throughout the notes. The text whose paging or paragraphing is regularly cited in the notes is listed in parentheses after each title.

VedS	*Vedārthasaṃgraha*	(van Buitenen)
SBh 1.1.1	*Śrībhāṣya* 1.1.1	(Lacombe)
ŚBh	*Śrībhāṣya*	(Annangarācārya)
GBh	*Gītābhāṣya*	(Annangarācārya)
VDīpa	*Vedāntadīpa*	(Bhashyam)
VSāra	*Vedāntasāra*	(Narasimha Ayyangar)
ŚarG	*Śaraṇāgatigadya*	(Rajagopala Ayyangar)
ŚRG	*Śrīraṅgagadya*	(Rajagopala Ayyangar)
VG	*Vaikuṇṭhagadya*	(Rajagopala Ayyangar)
NGr	*Nityagrantha*	(Annangarācārya)

CHAPTER 1

1. An outstanding example is Professor Jan Gonda of the University of Utrecht, as can be seen from the breadth of the bibliographical references in volumes 1 and 2 of *Die Religionen Indiens.* Many other Western Sanskritists could also be mentioned. One on whose work I have drawn heavily is a student of Professor Gonda's: Professor J. A. B. van Buitenen of the University of Chicago.

2. The first monograph on Rāmānuja by an Indian Christian was that of Dr. Bharatan Kumarappa. More recent works are those of Dr. F. K. Lazarus, Father John B. Chethimattam, C.M.I., and Father Anthony Manalapuzhavila, O.C.D.

3. The first scholar to give the name "phenomenology of religion" to a specific area within the study of religion seems to have been P. D. Chantepie de la Saussaye, Professor of the History of Religions at the University of Amsterdam. He used this term in the first edition of his work in German, *Lehrbuch der Religionsgeschichte* [1887], which was translated into English under the title, *Manual of the Science of Religion.* I am especially indebted to the work in phenomenology of religion of W. Brede Kristensen, Professor of the History and Phenomenology of Religion at the University of Leiden and his student, G. van der Leeuw, who held the corresponding post at the University of Groningen.

My understanding of Professor Kristensen's thought has been greatly aided by his successors at Leiden, Hendrik Kraemer and K. A. H. Hidding. Professor Hidding introduced me to the Dutch school of phenomenology of religion during my period of study at Leiden (1952-54), by discussing with me his own point of view and the meaning of Professor Kristensen's thought. Both Professor Kraemer and Professor Hidding helped me substantially in this regard through many discussions during the period (1954-57) when I was engaged in translating Professor Kristensen's lectures on the phenomenology of religion, which have been published under the title, *The Meaning of Religion.*

While Kristensen and van der Leeuw have developed phenomenology of religion in different ways, they agree on certain features of this kind of study. That religion is to be studied as a "phenomenon" means that the student is interested in whatever appears to him as an observer. (The Greek term *phainomenon* meant "appearance.") He is trying, not to determine what ultimate truth is embodied in a particular religious belief or practice, but to understand the data that appear to him as he views the religion from the outside. His approach is therefore quite different from that of an actual adherent of a particular religion, especially if that adherent is seeking to understand these same data in the light of his particular faith. Van der Leeuw thinks it is possible for the believer to adopt a phenomenological stance toward the data of his own religious tradition, but to do so he must become for the time being a nontheologian, i.e., he must not interpret that tradition in the light of what it holds to be true. Kristensen is always thinking of a study of a religion other than one's own when he discusses or engages in phenomenology of religion.

In the Netherlands, "history and phenomenology of religion" is considered a single academic discipline, but van der Leeuw, in particular, distinguishes between the historian's concern with a particular set of events at a particular time and place and the phenomenologist's concern with the common meaning in a number of different events, which may be widely separated in space and time. Both scholars agree that the phenomenologist of religion seeks to compare similar phenomena in different religions or different parts of the same religion. Both also agree that the practice of this discipline requires the recognition of religion as a distinctive and important aspect of human life, and they reject interpretations of religious beliefs or practices that explain them on the basis of some social or psychic condition.

The two scholars agree that phenomenology of religion is a discipline distinct from philosophy of religion and from theology, but they differ in the way they define this distinction. Van der Leeuw maintains that phenomenology of religion refuses to pursue the question of the truth or value of the religion under study; it recognizes that this question is all-important for the followers of that religion, but it puts it aside or "within brackets," leaving it to theology and philosophy of religion. It must put aside the questions of truth and value in order to pursue its own goal of understanding the meaning of religious beliefs and practices, for to evaluate them on the basis of one's own religious standards of truth and value would make it impossible to grasp the meaning of such rites and practices that is felt by the adherents of the tradition of which they form a part.

While such refraining from judgment is essential, van der Leeuw holds that it is only the negative side of the phenomenologist's task. This restraint "is never the attitude of the cold-blooded spectator; it is, on the contrary, the longing gaze of the lover on the beloved object, for all understanding rests upon self-surrendering love" (*Religion in Essence and Manifestation,* chap. 109, p. 384). In other words the phenomenologist tries to bring the strange religious belief or practice into his own life. He must therefore pursue the art of the actor in a play, who is able to identify himself imaginatively with the experience of others, or with some experience which he himself has had at some time in the past but no longer feels in the present. "Only the persistent and strenuous application of this kind of intense sympathy, only the uninterrupted learning of his role, qualifies the phenomenologist to interpret appearances" (ibid., chap. 107, p. 675). There is a strong element of feeling in this imaginative reconstruction of the experience of someone in another religion, but this must be part of an understanding that is intellectual as well as emotional, that is, which grasps the fundamental ideas or attitudes animating the outward religious expression of this other person. These underlying ideas are what van der Leeuw calls "ideal structures" (ibid., pp. 672-73).

Kristensen agrees that the historian or the phenomenologist of religion does not try to determine the greater or lesser value of the religious phenomena he studies. For this reason he refuses to consider the so-called "primitive religions" as "lower" forms of religion. "But in another sense evaluation is the soul of our entire labor in the field of the historical religions. If we want to become intimately acquainted with these religions as their believers themselves regarded and evaluated them, we must first of all try to understand their own evaluation of their religion. We must completely discard the view that religions constitute links in a process of historical (or ideal) development, for the believers have never thus conceived of their religion; they have never thought that it only had value in a great historical context. They have always conceived of their religion, not as something relative but as something absolute, as an absolute value. If we wish to understand them, we must comprehend them in this attitude of theirs. We must learn to recognize the autonomous value of each separate religion, for that is how that religion has lived in the hearts of men. Let us not forget that there is no other religious reality than the faith of the believers. If we want to become acquainted with genuine religion, we should direct our attention exclusively to what the believers have said. What we think from our standpoint about the essence or the value of alien religions certainly testifies to our own faith, or our own conception of religious faith, but if our opinion of an alien religion diverges from the opinion and the evaluation of the believers themselves, then we are no longer dealing with their religion. Then we are ignoring the historical reality and are only concerned with ourselves" (*Inleiding tot de Godsdienstgeschiedenis* [Introduction to the History of Religion], p. 22).

4. *Inleiding,* p. 24.

5. Van der Leeuw defines the term *epoché* in *Religion in Essence and Manifesta-tion*, p. 641, n. 1.

6. Van der Leeuw maintains that it would be impossible to enter imaginatively into something that is entirely foreign to our own experience. However, in principle, it is always possible to grasp at least something of the religious experience of another person, even one very much removed from the phenomenologist in time or in cultural setting (e.g., an Egyptian of the First Dynasty), because his experience is also *human*, and there is that in ourselves which makes it possible to understand something of all other human expressions and experience. The fact that we must draw on our own experience of the ideas of the religious tradition in which we participate means that there can be no single objective phenomenology of religion. Van der Leeuw frankly says that his understanding of particular aspects of religion and of the relation of the various religions to one another is only possible on the basis of his total experience as a follower of one particular religion, Christianity. Just as a Buddhist phenomenologist would naturally discover the culmination of religion in Buddhism, so "I regard Christianity as the central form of historical religion." The mutual comparison of religion "is possible only by thus beginning with one's own attitude to life. . . . Surveying the realm of historical religion, therefore, from the point of view of Christianity, I consider that we perceive that the Gospel appears as the fulfillment of religion in general." This does not mean, however, that he here gives up the attitude of refraining from judgments of truth or value, called *epoché*. Buddhism would appear to the Buddhist phenomenologist as the culmination of religions, and the Christian gospel appears to the Christian as the fulfillment of religion. But whether either of these "appearances" is true, i.e., is itself rooted in any ultimate reality, is not a question which can be decided within phenomenology of religion. That is a question for theology (ibid., pp. 645-46).

7. "The historian's standpoint is a different one. There is a distance between him and the object of his research; he cannot identify himself with it as the believer does. We cannot become Mohammedans when we try to understand Islam, and if we could, our study would be at an end: we should ourselves then directly experience the reality. The historian seeks to understand, and he is able to do that in an approximate way, approximate, but no more. By means of empathy he tries to relive in his own experience that which is 'alien,' and that, too, he can only approximate. This imaginative reexperiencing of a situation strange to us is a form of representation, and not reality itself, for that always asserts itself with sovereign authority" (Kristensen, *The Meaning of Religion*, p. 7).

"But it must be said that we cannot possibly achieve such a complete understanding of alien religions. We shall never be able to experience them as powers in life, as their believers have experienced them. We can never learn to carry out their sacred rites. We shall never perform the sacrifices which the believing Greeks, Romans, Egyptian or Hebrews performed, nor their ritual acts, purifications, initiations, etc. And that proves that we shall never completely learn to understand their religion, understand it as they themselves have conceived it. We can only understand them by approximation; we can never make their experience our own" (Kristensen, *Inleiding*, p. 23).

8. H. Kraemer, introduction to Kristensen, *The Meaning of Religion,* pp. xxiv-xxv.

9. *Gitārthasaṃgraha,* 11, 12, and 29, in J. A. B. van Buitenen, *Rāmānuja on the Bhagavadgītā,* pp. 180-81; and *Gītābhāṣya* 7.17-19, 27, in ibid., pp. 104-6.

10. It is particularly Kristensen who has emphasized that the method of the phenomenologist is not a scientific method in the ordinary sense. "A rational and systematic structure in the science of religion is impossible. Again and again a certain amount of intuition is indispensable. . . . The purely logical and rational does not indicate which way we must follow because in phenomenology we are constantly working with presumptions and anticipations. But that is just what makes our labour important. This study does not take place outside our personality. And the reverse will also prove to be the case: the study exerts an influence on our personality. This gives a personal character and value to the research in the areas we have mentioned. An appeal is made to our feeling for the subjects which we want to understand, a feeling which gives us a sureness to our 'touch.' There is an appeal made to the indefinable sympathy we must have for religious data which sometimes appear so alien to us. But this sympathy is unthinkable without an intimate acquaintance with the historical facts—thus again an interaction, this time between feeling and factual knowledge" (Kristensen, *The Meaning of Religion,* p. 10).

"But this informative comparison is not a method which can be mechanically applied in order to secure good results. It is not interested in collecting as much similar data as possible which can be interpreted through statistical analysis. The important thing, rather—to express it most unscientifically—is to have some inkling or presentiment [*vermoeden, voorgevoel*] of which data are essential and which are not, and then with the necessary tact and care to listen to the essential point about which these facts inform us. In studying the variegated material which we have collected, we must intuitively sense what is essential and important. Naturally this is not a method, if we mean by method a manner of working which requires nothing of one's own insight, mental gifts, and intuitive sense of what is essential. But without these gifts nothing important has ever been achieved in the study of the history of religion (or in any other study). That which, in the first place, is necessary is what Schleiermacher . . called *Anschauung* ['vision,' 'beholding'], the capacity to conceive a spiritual reality, e.g. the personality of a man—to fashion for ourselves a total picture of the spiritual being of a person on the basis of a series of outward impressions. . . . Whether we call this capacity intuition, imagination, or whatever we like, it is in any case a creative activity of our mind and spirit. What we are here concerned with is the sense for religious values; that cannot be defined or taught, but it is the precondition [*voorwaarde*] for all religious understanding and is a requirement for every study in the history of religion, most of all for comparative study. . . . I repeat that no method exists whereby important results are reached by a shortcut. It is senseless and fruitless to debate over the greater or lesser usefulness of different methods. Each scientific observer must work in his own way and according to his own method. It will be clear from the results whether he has tackled the subject matter correctly and whether or not his method was well chosen" (Kristensen, *Inleiding,* pp. 20-21).

11. "This limitation of what is attainable lies in the nature of every historical study. We understand in part, and we shall never completely reach the goal. Our historical knowledge and insight are never complete and never can become so, but that is no reason to give up the goal. Yet that is precisely what is done when the very possibility of objective knowledge of the past in the realm of history is denied in principle and it is proclaimed with apparent profundity that every piece of historical knowledge is nothing but a reflection of the conviction of the observers. It is not too much to say that our era's unfortunate tendency to a psychological orientation is the greatest enemy of every healthy study; it distracts our attention and interest from the objective reality and reduces historical knowledge or insight to a product of our imagination. It is true that our historical knowledge is not complete and never can be, but that is just the stimulation we need for a steadily progressing study in the direction of a true conception of the dominant religious forces in the course of history, a conception which is true to reality. Every historian of religion can with his personal gifts make a contribution towards coming closer to this goal" (Kristensen, *Inleiding,* p. 25).

12. *A History of Indian Philosophy,* vol. 3. While a distinct chapter (19) is entitled "The Philosophy of Yāmunācārya," the following chapter (20), running 134 pages, is entitled "Philosophy of the Rāmānuja School of Thought." A few pages in both chapters state Rāmānuja's own position, but his views at most points are supplemented by those of later Śrī Vaiṣṇavas, especially Vedānta Deśika (Venkaṭanātha).

13. The most famous work of Sudarśana Sūri is his lengthy commentary on Rāmānuja's *Śrībhāṣya,* called the *Śrutaprakāśikā.* Sudarśana Sūri's commentary on the *Vedārthasaṃgraha* is called the *Tātparyadīpikā.* The most important commentary on Rāmānuja's *Gītābhāṣya* is by Vedānta Deśika, called the *Tātparyacandrikā.* For definition of the Divine qualities, I have consulted the edition of the *Gadyatraya* giving the Sanskrit commentaries of Sudarśana Sūri and Vedānta Deśika and the Tamil commentary of Periya Āccān Piḷḷai. The definitions of the Divine qualities closest in time to Rāmānuja are those of his successor, Parāśara Bhaṭṭar, in his commentary on the *Viṣṇusahasranāma* called the *Bhagavadguṇadarpaṇa* (see bibliography for details).

14. Krishna Datta Bharadwaj, *The Philosophy of Rāmānuja,* pp. 138-39.

15. The story of Sarasvatī's conferring the title of Bhāṣyakāra is contained in the Teṅgalai "Six Thousand" biography as well as in the later Vaḍagalai biographies. Pinbaḻahiya Perumāḷ Jīyar, *Ārāyirappaḍi Guruparamparāprabhāvam,* Tamil script, p. 208.

16. There are references to at least three lost commentaries on the Gadyas prior to the earliest extant commentary, that by Sudarśana Sūri. These are said to be those by Kūraṭṭāḻvān, Viṣṇu Citta (Engaḻāḻvān), and Nañjīyar. For details see below, chap. 17, n. 25.

17. Compare the comment by Professor Daniel H. H. Ingalls that Śankara and Bhāskara, in spite of their sharp differences, both clearly follow the same earlier commentator on the Brahma Sūtras, though Bhāskara follows "the Commentator" still more closely than does Śankara ("Śankara's Arguments against the Buddhists," pp. 292-93).

18. Compare my "The Importance of History in Indian Religious Movements: One Significance of the Guru Nanak Anniversary Celebration," conference paper delivered at Punjab University, Patiala, Punjab, India, September 1969.

19. In addition to the sayings attributed to Rāmānuja in the various biographies, there is a small "Collection of Sayings" (*Vārttamālai*) of Rāmānuja and other Śrī Vaiṣṇava teachers, most of which can also be found in the "Six Thousand" or one of the later biographies. There are also the comments attributed to Rāmānuja included in the later commentaries on Nammāḻvār's *Tiruvāymoḻi*, especially Vaḍakku Tiruvīdi Piḷḷai's "Thirty-six Thousand."

20. Two modern interpreters of Rāmānuja have responded quite differently to this paucity of definitions. In *The Hindu Conception of the Deity, as Culminating in Rāmānuja,* Bharatan Kumarappa notes some of these qualities briefly but attempts to define only a very few of them. He confines himself almost entirely to Rāmānuja's own writings and devotes most of his attention to the metaphysical relations between the Lord, finite selves, and the material world. The "sectarian elements," which he himself maintains are so central to Rāmānuja's thought, therefore receive rather cursory treatment, and his presentation of Rāmānuja's doctrine consequently suffers from the imbalance. Bharadwaj (*The Philosophy of Rāmānuja*), on the other hand, is aware of the need to define the Divine attributes, but in order to do so he quotes the definitions of these attributes in Śrī Vaiṣṇava later writings without raising the question of whether Rāmānuja's usage corresponds to the later definitions.

21. This is the case with his definitions of *satyakāma* and *satyasaṃkalpa* in *VedS,* para 132, which will be discussed in chap. 13.

22. S. K. Belvalkar, *Vedānta Philosophy,* pt. 1, lectures 1-6, pp. 217-30.

23. Ibid., p. 231.

24. In *The Life and Teachings of Sri Ramanujacharya,* C. R. Srinivasa Aiyengar cites in a footnote (n. 3, pp. 172-73), drawn from the relatively late Tamil biography, the *Rāmānujārya Divya Caritai,* a story about Piḷḷān, said to be the son of Śrī Śaila Pūrṇa (Rāmānuja's uncle and a disciple of Yāmuna). Piḷḷān was already Rāmānuja's disciple when, during a visit to Nammāḻvār's birthplace of Kuruhūr, Rāmānuja conceived the idea of naming a disciple after the Āḻvār. When Piḷḷān volunteered, Rāmānuja adopted him as his spiritual son and henceforth called him Tirukkuruhai Pirān Piḷḷān (Kurukeśvara): "The Lord of Kuruhūr." Piḷḷān's commentary in Sanskritized Tamil echoes both the ideas and the phraseology of Rāmānuja, and many of the interpretations specifically attributed to Rāmānuja in the later "Thirty-six Thousand" are those that Piḷḷān presents in the "Six Thousand" commentary (not to be confused with the later biography of the same length also called the "Six Thousand"). Piḷḷān's specific teaching is discussed in chap. 17.

25. Vasudev Anant Sukhtankar, *The Teachings of the Vedānta according to Rāmānuja,* p. 3.

CHAPTER 2

1. These are *Nyāya Tattva* and *Yoga Rahasya.*

2. Nāthamuni's *Nyāya Tattva* is quoted in Vedānta Deśika's *Nyāya Siddhāñjana.*

3. V. N. Hari Rao, ed. and trans., *Kōil Olugu: The Chronicle of the Srirangam Temple with Historical Notes,* p. 34. It is explained in n. 3, p. 34, that Śrīkāryam "is the supreme office in the temple, referred to in the subsequent pages of this work as the 'Senāpati durantara'."

4. The earliest prose biography, the "Six Thousand," says nothing about a formal position of leadership for Nāthamuni at Srīrangam, or even at Mannanār's temple in Vīranārāyaṇapuram. The brief statement does, however, make clear that Nāthamuni enjoyed the special favor of the Lord, that he and his family were financially supported by the Śrī Vaiṣṇava community, that he performed faultlessly various familiar services of a "lay devotee" (i.e., not an arcaka), that he led the "congregation of the learned" (vidvat-goṣṭi), and that he propagated the śāstras (*Ārāyirappaḍi Guruparamparāprabhāvam,* Tamil script, p. 100).

5. Ibid., pp. 119-20.

6. The traditional accounts vary considerably in the dates given for Nāthamuni; in some he is variously assigned a life span of 330, 340, or 540 years. The *Kōil Olugu* (p. 34) says that he was born after 3924 Kali (equivalent to A.D. 823). In the case of Yāmuna, tradition generally agrees on the date of his birth (A.D. 916 to 918) and considers his life span either 120 or 125 years. See Srinivasa Aiyengar, *Life,* pp. 11-12, 20, 25-26; and Alkondavilli Govindacharya, *The Life of Rāmānujāchārya,* pp. 2, 12-15.

7. My reasons for revising the traditional dating are given later in this chapter. It seems to me that the most probable dates of the important events in Rāmānuja's life indicate that he lived to be at least 80, and he may well have lived to be much older than that.

8. See K. A. Nilakanta Sastri, *A History of South India,* esp. pp. 200-6, 313-38, 377-80, 429-30.

9. This theory has been developed by N. Subrahmanian, Reader in History at the University of Madras, in a long article (still unpublished) entitled "The Brahmin in the Tamil Country (in Ancient and Medieval Times)," especially pp. 40-42, and more extensively in the Ph.D. dissertation of his son, N. Jagadeesan, entitled "History of Śrī Vaishnavism in the Tamil Country (Post Rāmānuja)," pp. 399-406, 411-12.

10. "Six Thousand" (*Ārāyirappaḍi*), pp. 125-29.

11. Ibid., pp. 129-32.

12. Ibid., p. 135.

13. Ibid., pp. 135-47.

14. Ibid., pp. 147-50.

15. Ibid., pp. 150-54. The quotation is Srinivasa Aiyengar's rendering, *Life,* p. 89.

16. "Six Thousand," pp. 154-56.

17. Ibid., pp. 157-58, 160.

18. Ibid., pp. 158-60.

19. Ibid., pp. 160-63. Both Aiyengar (*Life,* p. 105) and Govindacharya (*Life,* p. 76) omit the second phrase from Rāmānuja's instructions to his disciples, after telling them to fetch his personal icon of Lord Varada from his mother: *Matrum-uṇḍāna-sampantangalaịyum,* which would seem to mean "and other

relatives." The "Six Thousand" does not mention other relatives of Rāmānuja by name at this point in the biography, whereas the later Vaḍagalai account (the so-called "Three Thousand") says that in addition to Kūraṭṭāḻvān and Mudali Āṇḍān, Naḍadūrāḻvān (another of Rāmānuja's nephews) was one of the first disciples. Whatever the interpretation of this phrase, Govindacharya is going beyond the text of the "Six Thousand" when he adds that Mudali Āṇḍān was "the only relative whom he [Rāmānuja] retained" (p. 76).

20. "Six Thousand," pp. 163-65.

21. Ibid., pp. 165-66. According to the *Kōil Oḻugu* (pp. 44-45), Rāmānuja first tried personally to manage the temple's financial affairs with the aid of his two disciples: "Āḻvān . . . controlling the religious code, Mudaliyāṇḍān . . . to exercise control over the inner organization of the temple." When the temple retinue "threw many obstacles in the path of Uḍayavar and even tried to poison him," Rāmānuja left Śrīrangam and lived for two years in Tiruveḷḷarai. After he was persuaded to return and once more "took charge of the business of the temple, he appointed a new disciple, Akaḷanga Nattāḻvān (whom Hari Rao thinks was probably a Coḻa chieftain), to manage the temple lands.

22. For the account of the poisoning in the *Kōil Oḻugu,* see n. 21 above. The "Six Thousand" states that the wife of one of the seven householders from whom Rāmānuja regularly begged was coerced into giving him poisoned food, but she managed to hint by her manner that something was wrong. Rāmānuja threw the food in the Kāveri River and started to fast. Finally Tirukoṭṭiyūr Nambi came and appointed one of Rāmānuja's disciples, Kiḍāmbi Āccān, as his cook. "Six Thousand," pp. 184-85; cf. Srinivasa Aiyengar, *Life,* pp. 131-33, and Govindacharya, *Life,* pp. 109-10.

23. *Kōil Oḻugu,* pp. 47-48.

24. This story was told by the present head of the Amudanār family at the Śrīrangam temple, Tiru A. R. S. Rajam Ayyangar, in an interview at his home in the temple precinct with Walter G. Neevel, Jr., and Tiru K. K. A. Venkatachari in June 1968.

25. Tiruvarangattu Amudanār, *Irāmānuja Nūtranḍādi,* with Periya Jīyar's [Manavāḷamāmuni's], *Vyākhyānam,* v.7.

26. Manavāḷamāmuni's commentary (see above, n. 25). Vedānta Deśika's *Yatirājaśaptati* contains no specific reference to the *Nūtranḍādi,* but his modern commentator considers Deśika's statement in v. 12 that Rāmānuja is an incarnation of the Lord's five weapons to be a clear echo of *Nūtranḍādi,* v. 33. See D. Ramaswami Ayyangar, *Yatiraja Saptati of Vedanta Desika,* p. 24.

27. *Kōil Oḻugu,* p. 46.

28. Ibid., pp. xii, 65.

29. *Nūtranḍādi,* esp. v. 49: "When Rāmānuja appeared in the world, the righteous path became straight, the false 'six religions' disintegrated, and cruel Kali died." The poet also says that uttering the name of Rāmānuja will remove Kali (v. 43), that Rāmānuja took steps to remove the darkness of Kali (v. 59), and that Kali will affect those who do not take the wisdom of Rāmānuja.

30. "Six Thousand," pp. 176-77.

31. Ibid., pp. 185-89.

32. Ibid., pp. 202-3.

33. For a discussion of these works, see chap. 17.

34. "Six Thousand," pp. 158-60.

35. Ibid., pp. 207-8. The "Six Thousand," however, does not mention Rāmānuja and Kūraṭṭāḻvān's studying the Bodhāyana *Vṛtti*, which is included in Govindacharya's account (*Life*, p. 141). Srinivasa Aiyengar makes a brief reference to the incident in *Life*, pp. 175-76, n. 2, where he summarizes the account of Rāmānuja's tour throughout India given in the *Divya Sūri Carita*. "He first went to Kashmir to the Śaradāpīṭha, where Sarasvatī gave him the Bodhāyana Vṛitti."

36. This story is not told in the "Six Thousand" about either temple. Govindacharya tells about Rāmānuja's experience at the temple of Lord Jagannātha at Purī (*Life*, p. 142). Srinivasa Aiyengar says this is from the *Prapannāmṛta* (*Life*, p. 173, n. 3a), but he later gives an extended footnote (pp. 178-81, n. 2), about the incident in Purī, which he seems to derive from the *Rāmānujārya Divya Caritai*. Govindacharya gives the Trivandrum story first (p. 138, n. 3) but introduces this with, "Another version has that . . . "

37. "Six Thousand," pp. 209-10.

38. Ibid., pp. 221-30.

39. This story is not in the early sources. The story Srinivasa Aiyengar gives in his text (*Life*, pp. 213-16) is that Rāmānuja defeated 12,000 Sramanas (Jain monks) by assuming his Divine form: the thousand-headed primordial serpent, Śeṣa. When they acknowledged defeat, some accepted Rāmānuja's invitation to join the true faith. In his n. 1 (pp. 215-16), he notes some variants. One, from the *Rāmānujārya Divya Caritai*, is that King Viṣṇuvārdhana, after his conversion from Jainism, "caused the refractory Jains of Padmagiri to be ground in stone mills." Another, from the Vaḍagalai *Guruparamparā-prabhāvam* ("Three Thousand"), is that "the Jains themselves proposed that the defeated party should be ground to powder." However, after Rāmānuja had miraculously defeated them, he interceded with the king to spare their lives. "Many took refuge in the Good Law, and went to swell the ranks of the True Believers." Govindacharya gives virtually the same story (*Life*, pp. 182-83); he states that most of the Jain monks "embraced the Vaishṇava faith by becoming the disciples of Rāmānuja" and goes on to add that Rāmānuja constructed a dam across the Yādava with "the materials of Jain temples pulled down."

40. "Six Thousand," pp. 228, 242. The accounts vary considerably concerning Rāmānuja's role in causing the Coḻa king's fatal illness and death. Srinivasa Aiyengar gives in his text the version that "Rāmānuja afflicted him with a terrible disease that ate into his throat." In *Life*, pp. 209-10, n. 1, he gives some other accounts. According to the Vaḍagalai "Three Thousand," the priests of the Nṛsimhapura temple in Mysore, where Rāmānuja had stopped after his escape from Śrīrangam, "were beside themselves with rage, and performed a magical ceremony to bring about the death of the infamous Chōḻa." The *Rāmānujārya Divya Caritai* has two stories. According to one,

it was the water offered to Nārāyaṇa during the daily recital of the Gāyatrī prayer that "served to turn the Lord against the Chōla." The Lord then met the Coḻa king at night on the king's way to destroy Śrīrangam and stabbed him several times in the neck. The other story given in the same work is that Rāmānuja, while at Nṛsimhapura, directed his disciple Āccān to perform a magical rite to destroy his enemies.

41. "Six Thousand," pp. 243-87.

42. T. A. Gopinatha Rao, *Sir Subrahmanya Ayyar Lectures on the History of Śrī Vaiṣṇavas,* pp. 32-40.

43. "A Note on the Date of Rāmānuja," pp. 145-60.

44. "Six Thousand," pp. 204-5.

45. Ibid., p. 157.

46. Ibid., pp. 212-17.

47. Ibid., p. 297.

48. For a discussion of Parāśara Bhaṭṭar's works, see below, chap. 17.

49. The earliest Vaḍagalai biography is by Brahmatantra Svatantra Jīyar, *Muvāyirappaḍi Guruparamparāprabhāvam* ["Three Thousand"].

CHAPTER 3

1. The objections to the authenticity of this work have been most forcefully put by Professor B. V. Ramanujam of Annamalai University in an article in the *Journal of Indian History,* entitled "Divya Sūri Charitam."

2. Tirukkuruhai Pirān Piḷḷān's commentary is called the *Ārāyirappaḍi* ("Six Thousand") because it contains that number of granthas (groups of thirty-two syllables); see chap. 17.

3. Rāmānuja is specifically cited in Periya Āccān Piḷḷai's "Twenty-four Thousand" and more frequently in Vaḍakku Tiruvīdi Piḷḷai's "Thirty-six Thousand" or *Īḍu.* For a discussion of one significant citation in the "Thirty-six Thousand," see chap. 18.

4. *Vārttamālai* (Saraswati Bandāran, 1887).

5. S. S. Raghavachar, *Introduction to the Vedarthasangraha,* p. 2, referring to the *Tātparyadīpikā.*

6. Ibid.

7. George Thibaut, *The Vedānta-Sūtras, with the Commentary by Śankarācārya,* pt. 1, intro., pp. ix-cxviii; and *The Vedānta-Sūtras, with the Commentary by Rāmānuja,* Sacred Books of the East, vol. 48 (Oxford: Clarendon Press, 1904; reprint, Delhi: Motilal Banarsidass, 1962), intro., pp. ix-xi. V. S. Ghate, *The Vedānta, a Study of the Brahma-Sūtras with the Bhāṣyas of Śaṃkara, Rāmānuja, Nimbārka, Madhva, and Vallabha.*

More recently Raghunath Damodar Karmarkar has published a three-volume text and translation entitled *Śrībhāṣya of Rāmānuja.* In the introduction to vol. 1, he criticizes Rāmānuja's interpretation. He admits that "Rāmānuja appears to have interpreted the Sūtras more correctly than Śankara," but he insists that the words of the Sūtras should be understood in the light of the Upaniṣads, as Śankara maintained, and holds that Śankara's interpretation is therefore the correct one. He concludes, "Rāmānuja's interpretation of the Sūtras, though technically correct, is perhaps incomplete and onesided" (pp. xxxv-vi).

8. *ŚBh* 3.1.1 in Thibaut, p. 587.
9. *ŚBh* 4.1.1 in Thibaut, p. 715.
10. A. Hohenberger, *Rāmānuja's Vedāntadīpa: seine Kurzauslegung der Brahmasūtren des Bādarāyaṇa.*
11. Rudolf Otto, *Siddhānta des Rāmānuja,* German translation of *Śrībhāṣya* 1.1.1, pp. 1-3.
12. Olivier Lacombe, *La doctrine morale et métaphysique de Rāmānuja,* text and French translation, with notes of *Śrībhāṣya* 1.1.1, p. v.
13. M. Rangacharya and M. B. Varadaraja Aiyangar, *The Vedānta-Sūtras with the Śrī-Bhāshya of Rāmānuja,* translation of the first pāda in vol. 1, pp. vii-viii, xi.
14. *ŚBh* 1.1.1, Thibaut, p. 19; Rangacharya, p. 25.
15. *ŚBh* 1.1.1, Thibaut, pp. 38-39; Rangacharya, p. 47.
16. *ŚBh* 1.1.1, Thibaut, p. 147; Rangacharya, p. 215.
17. J. A. B. van Buitenen, *VedS,* intro., p. 32.
18. S. S. Raghavachar, *Vedārthasaṃgraha* of Rāmānuja, text and translation, p. 1.
19. Van Buitenen, *VedS,* intro., pp. 31-32.
20. *VSāra* 1.1.2, pp. 21-22.
21. K. Bhashyam, *Vedanta Deepa* of Rāmānuja, Sanskrit text and English translation, intro., Eng. pp. 6, 12-13; *VedS,* paras. 2, 7-10.
22. Van Buitenen, *Rāmānuja on the Bhagavadgīta,* intro., pp. 12-17.
23. Ibid., pp. 9-12.
24. Ibid., p. 22.

CHAPTER 4

1. Rajagopala Ayyangar, *Vedartha Sangraha* of Rāmānuja, translation with introduction, p. 37.
2. *VedS,* para. 1; Thibaut, p. 3.
3. *ŚBh* 1.1.1, p. 1.
4. *VDīpa,* p. 1.
5. *VSāra,* p. 1.
6. *ŚBh* 1.1.1, p. 2; Thibaut, p. 4.
7. *ŚBh* 1.1.2, p. 106; Thibaut, p. 156.
8. *ŚBh* 1.1.3, p. 111; Thibaut, p. 175.
9. *VDīpa,* intro., p. 1.
10. *GBh* 18.42, p. 163.
11. *GBh* 18.73, p. 171.
12. *ŚBh* 1.4.1, p. 193; Thibaut, p. 354.
13. *VedS,* para. 6.
14. *VedS,* para. 42.
15. *GBh* 3, intro., p. 23.
16. *GBh* 7, intro., p. 62.
17. *GBh* 8, intro., p. 70.
18. *VedS,* para. 43.
19. *VedS,* para. 84.
20. *ŚBh* 4.4.21-22, p. 396; Thibaut, p. 770.

21. *GBh* 6.47, p. 61.
22. *GBh* 9.34, p. 86; van Buitenen, pp. 22-23.
23. *GBh* 10.8, p. 89.
24. *GBh* 12.1, p. 109.
25. *GBh* 12.9, p. 111.
26. *GBh* 11.3, p. 97.
27. *GBh* 11.40, p. 105.
28. *GBh* 11.44, p. 106.

CHAPTER 5

1. *GBh*, p. 1.
2. Sudarśana Sūri, *Tātparyadīpikā,* p. 10, commenting on the first paragraph (para. 4, in van Buitenen's edition).
3. Vedānta Deśika commenting on the introduction of the *Gītābhāṣya* in the *Tātparyacandrikā.*
4. *ŚBh* 3.2.35, p. 316; cf. Thibaut, p. 624.
5. *ŚBh* 3.2.36-37, p. 316; Thibaut, p. 625.
6. "There the word *para* denotes the self which is distinct from one's own self." *ŚBh* 1.1.1 ad *Viṣṇu Purāṇa* 2.13.90; Rangacharya, p. 126.
7. M. Monier-Williams, *A Sanskrit-English Dictionary,* pp. 586-88 (hereafter referred to as MW).
8. *GBh* 7.7, p. 64. The same ideas are expressed a little further on in the comment on *mām ebhyaḥ param* (Me, the one who is higher than they) in 7.13.
9. *VedS,* paras. 97, 101, 104 (three times), and 114 (where in connection with the reference to *Vedānta Sūtras* 3.2.30, some manuscripts have *paratvam* (given by Raghavachar) and others read *parataratvam* (preferred by van Buitenen).
10. *GBh* 8.14, pp. 73-74.
11. Cf., e.g., A. Govindacharya, *The Divine Wisdom of the Dravida Saints,* pp. i-iii, xiii.
12. *ŚBh* 3.2.37, p. 316; Thibaut, p. 625.
13. Dvayam api lubdhasya akimcitkaram iti mahodāratva ukti (*Śrutaprakāśikā* ad *ŚBh* 3.2.37).

CHAPTER 6

1. *ŚBh* 3.3.13, p. 325; Thibaut, p. 638.
2. *VDīpa* 3.3.11, p. 158.
3. *ŚBh* 3.3.12, p. 323; Thibaut, pp. 637-38.
4. *VedS,* para. 84, quoted in chap. 4.
5. Some of these expressions are: *kalyāṇaika-svarūpa,* "whose essential nature is wholly auspicious" (*GBh* 18.73, p. 171); *antaryāmi-svarūpa,* "the essential nature of the Inner Controller" (*VedS,* para. 6); *vilakṣaṇa-svarūpa,* "whose essential nature is distinct from everything else" (*VedS,* para. 6); *vānmanasāparicchedya-svarūpa,* "whose essential nature cannot be grasped by speech or thought" (*GBh* 6.14, p. 99); *tad-antaryāmi-paramātma-svarūpa,* "the essential nature of the supreme Self who is the Inner Controller of that finite self" (*VedS,* para. 4); and *bhagavat-svarūpa,* "the essential nature of Bhagavan" (*VedS,* para. 78). Even more general are these statements in the *Vedārthasaṃgraha:*

"The Divine attendants and Divine abode are included within the essential nature of Brahman like such auspicious qualities as knowledge, strength, and sovereignty" (para. 132). "Just as knowledge etc. are the essential nature of the Supreme Brahman because they are mentioned as His essential nature in the Scriptures, so also the Form [rūpa] is that which is the essential nature of Brahman by the Scriptures" (para. 135).

6. "[Those who are not my devotees] do not know what are my titles, deeds, essential nature, and inherent nature, etc.," *nāma-karma-svarūpa-svabhāva-ādikam* (*GBh* 10.2, p. 87); ". . . obtaining a vision of Me as I am in My essential nature, inherent nature, qualities, and glorious realms," *svarūpa-svabhāva-guṇa-vibhūti* (*GBh* 18.55, p. 166); "[Never reveal this wisdom] to one who finds fault with My essential nature, My sovereign dominion, or My attributes," *matsvarūpe madaiśvarye madguṇeṣu* (*GBh* 18.67, p. 170).

7. *VedS,* para. 4.

8. *VedS,* paras, 136, 140.

9. *VSāra* 1.1.2, p. 16; 2.3.45, pp. 218-19. *GBh* 13.2, p. 117.

10. Personal conversation with Professor Anantha Rangachar.

11. *VedS,* para. 4, nn. 20, 21, pp. 184-85; *svarūpa,* "proper form" (where form is the principle of individuality, cf. *nāmarūpa*), free from adventitious adjuncts but (for R) possessed of essential properties; *svabhāva,* "this essential form in the process of being and becoming with and through its essential qualities."

12. This combination of terms seems also to have baffled Vedānta Deśika, for in his comment on these words of Rāmānuja in the *Tātparyacandrikā,* Deśika is forced to give two alternative explanations of Rāmānuja's usage, and the preferred explanation is contrary to his interpretation of the same terms elsewhere. Thus he first explains that the term *svabhāva* connotes association with the defining attributes of God, which are to be reflected upon in all meditations, but he adds that some say that it is svarūpa which stands for such qualities and that svabhāva signifies saulabhya.

13. *Viṣṇu Purāṇa* 6.5.79, quoted in *ŚBh* 1.1.1, p. 66; Thibaut, p. 87; Rangacharya, p. 111; Lacombe, p. 85; Otto, p. 89.

14. *ŚBh* 3.3.12-13, p. 323; Thibaut, p. 638.

15. This is emphasized in Rāmānuja's comments on the last six sūtras in order to prevent misunderstanding of the doctrine of the soul's "equality" with God. *ŚBh* 4.4.17-22, pp. 394-96; Thibaut, pp. 766-71.

16. *GBh* 6.30, pp. 57-58.

17. *VedS,* intro., p. 36.

18. Govindacharya, *Life,* pp. 135-36; cf. Ramakrishnananda, *Life of Ramanuja,* pp. 187-88.

19. Rāmānuja's followers made some further efforts to safeguard the importance of these other qualities by deriving them from the five essential attributes, especially from jñāna.

CHAPTER 7

1. *VedS,* para. 6.
2. *VedS,* paras. 10-39.

3. *VSāra* 1.1.1, pp. 6-10.
4. *ŚBh* 1.1.2, p. 105; Thibaut, p. 156.
5. *ŚBh* 1.1.2, p. 106; Thibaut, pp. 159-60; Rangacharya, pp. 232-33.
6. *ŚBh* 2.3.20, 23, 33.
7. Śrīnivāsadāsa, *Yatīndramatadīpikā*, p. 103.
8. *ŚBh* 3.4.21, pp. 311-12; Thibaut, p. 616.
9. *ŚBh* 1.1.13; p. 127; Thibaut, pp. 212-13; Rangacharya, p. 315.
10. *ŚBh* 3.3.33, p. 333; Thibaut, p. 653.
11. *ŚBh* 1.1.21, p. 138; Thibaut, p. 239; Rangacharya, p. 359.
12. *VedS*, para. 83.
13. *ŚBh* 1.1.21, p. 138; Thibaut, pp. 239-40; Rangacharya, p. 360.
14. *ŚBh* 1.2.8, p. 151; Thibaut, p. 265.
15. The last sentence is a free translation which seemed to me necessary in order to convey Rāmānuja's point in using this analogy. A more literal translation of the final clause would run: "so likewise there is no connection of the Supreme Self with any evil [doṣa] because there is absence of any cause of evil, by virtue of His being of a nature [radically] opposed to evil." *ŚBh* 3.2.20, p. 311; Thibaut, pp. 614-15.
16. It should be added that many Śaivite groups in South India are as concerned as Śrī Vaiṣṇavas are in becoming and remaining pure or sāttvic. Moreover, those Śaivite groups which do emphasize the use of abhorrent materials or practices think that thereby they are magnifying the Deity by demonstrating His transcendence of the finite realm of good and evil.
17. *ŚBh* 3.2.11, p. 307; Thibaut, pp. 239-40.
18. *ŚBh* 3.2.12, p. 308; Thibaut, pp. 609-10.
19. *ŚBh* 1.1.3, p. 111; Thibaut, p. 173; Rangacharya, pp. 251-52.
20. *ŚBh* 1.1.1; Thibaut, p. 78.
21. *VedS*, para. 2.
22. *VedS*, paras. 7-9.
23. *VedS*, para. 59. This rather free paraphrase is necessitated by Rāmānuja's use of the term *paramārtha*, "absolutely real." The more literal translations make it appear that Rāmānuja is criticizing the view that the finite realm of suffering souls in material bodies is real. In fact, of course, Rāmānuja defended this view against the Advaita. It is the notion that God's own essential nature is involved in the realm of saṃsāra which he is so sharply criticizing with this rather bitter humor. It is almost as if he were saying, "I should rather accept the Advaitin doctrine that this world is unreal than ever admit that God is involved in and affected by its imperfection."
24. *ŚBh* 1.1.1; Thibaut, pp. 131-35. *ŚBh* 2.3.18; Thibaut, pp. 543-44. *VDīpa*, Int. Skt., p. 5; Eng., p. 12. *VSāra* 1.1.2, pp. 21-22.
25. Govindacharya, *Life*, p. 32. Srinivasa Aiyengar refers to Yādava Prakāśa's interpretation only as "a very blasphemous and obscene rendering" but gives Śankara's interpretation in a footnote (*Life*, p. 48, n. 16).
26. The other disputes over scriptural interpretation with Yādava are also interesting in that they bring out other fundamental points of Rāmānuja's doctrine: first, that Brahman is not identical with His defining attributes but is the knowing subject who can possess them all; and second, that the

cosmos is neither identical with God nor an illusion but His real, though utterly dependent, creation (Govindacharya, *Life*, pp. 30-31, 43).

27. *ŚBh* 2.3.29; Thibaut, p. 550.

28. *ŚBh* 1.1.1, p. 63; Thibaut, p. 84; Rangacharya, pp. 106-7; Lacombe, p. 82; Otto, p. 79.

29. *VedS*, para. 142.

CHAPTER 8

1. *ŚBh* 1.1.21, p. 139; Thibaut, p. 240; Rangacharya, pp. 361-62.

2. *ŚBh* 3.2.15, p. 309; Thibaut, pp. 611-12.

3. Cf. also *ŚBh* 1.1.12; Thibaut, p. 206; and *VedS*, para. 136, where the emphasis is on texts proving also that He has a transcendent bodily form suitably adorned and is served by angelic attendants in His transcendent abode.

4. *ŚBh* 1.1.1, Thibaut, pp. 142-43; Rangacharya, pp. 204-6. *VedS*, paras. 69-74.

5. *ŚBh* 1.1.13, p. 132; Thibaut, p. 226; Rangacharya, pp. 336-37.

6. Van Buitenen, *VedS*, intro., p. 36.

7. *ŚBh* 2.3.14-15; Thibaut, pp. 537-38. Anantha Rangachar has suggested to me that this relative lack of interest might be otherwise explained. First, there might not have been any controversy in Rāmānuja's time about the details of the creative process; we have already noticed that Rāmānuja tends to concentrate his comments on controversial subjects. However, it is by no means certain that there was no such controversy; the variety in details, and even in major features, between the many accounts of creation in the Purāṇas and Āgamas would seem to indicate that these matters were engaging the minds of many of Rāmānuja's contemporaries. Secondly, Anantha Rangachar thinks that the context of discussion in commenting on the *Vedānta Sūtras* did not require futher elaboration of the process of creation. This may well be true with respect to certain concepts in the *Śrībhāṣya*, but we find this same indifference to cosmogonic details throughout Rāmānuja's writings. It seems preferable, therefore, to seek an explanation for this lack of interest in the basic structure of Rāmānuja's theology.

8. *ŚBh* 2.4.17; Thibaut, pp. 578-80.

9. *ŚBh* 2.1.32, p. 245; Thibaut, pp. 476-77.

10. *ŚBh* 2.1.33, p. 246; Thibaut, p. 477.

11. *VSāra* 2.1.33, pp. 160-61.

12. *ŚBh* 2.1.33, p. 246; Thibaut, pp. 477-78.

13. *VedS*, para. 42.

14. *VedS*, para. 42.

15. *VedS*, para. 107.

16. *GBh* 3.10, p. 26.

17. Kumarappa, *Hindu Conception of the Deity*, p. 263.

18. *GBh* 3.10.

19. Van Buitenen suggests that the concept of the Divine līlā "is best understood by its opposite *karman-*. It contains a free action (an action not resulting from a preceding action in an endless retrogressive succession) performed

to no purpose at all: no purpose that of necessity would result in new phalas for the agent to enjoy or to suffer" (n. 83 to his *VedS*, para. 14, p. 192). I would agree with van Buitenen's interpretation of Rāmānuja's conception of God's creative action, but I have not been able to discover any indication by Rāmānuja which would definitely show that he regards the non-karmic character of the Divine action as līla. It seems to me that it is the term *svecchayā* (according to His own will) that is the proper opposite of action determined by karma. God's creative action is both svecchayā and līlayā (see *VedS*, para. 107).

20. *VedS*, para. 82. I have expanded the literal meaning of the last sentence to give what seems to be its intent. The same idea is repeated in a slightly different wording in the following paragraph.

CHAPTER 9

1. *VedS*, paras. 17b-18a; last sentence following M. R. Rajagopala Ayyangar, *Vedartha Sangraha*, p. 51.

2. *VedS*, para. 20. I have translated *jīvāntaryāmirūpeṇa* as an instrumental indicating a cause, along with Rajagopala Ayyangar ("by being"), whereas van Buitenen translates "under the aspect of . . . " Raghavachar follows a different reading (rūpam) and translates simply: "Brahman, the inner ruler." Van Buitenen has noted three variant readings, *rūpe sarvaśarī*, *rūpi saśarī*, and *rūpam saśarīra.* He states that he prefers *rūpeṇa* on textual grounds. Rāmānuja often uses the instrumental to express cause, especially when he does not wish to emphasize the causal link too much, or when there is a causal clause modifying another compound in the ablative which also expresses cause. See *VedS*, p. 196; p. 82, n. 10; Raghavachar, pp. 17-18; and Rajagopala Ayyangar, p. 541.

3. Kumarappa, *Hindu Conception of the Deity*, pp. 232, 236. P. N. Srinivasachari calls the *śarīrātma-bhāva* the most essential truth of Viśiṣṭādvaita, but in his exposition of *Rāmānuja's Idea of the Finite Self*, he emphasizes prakāra (mode) as the fundamental category. See his *The Philosophy of Viśiṣṭādvaita*, pp. 95, 296-97, referring to his *RIFS*. Lacombe also follows the standpoint of *RIFS*, to which he refers, when he states: "It is the word 'mode' (prakara) which brings together all the aspects under which the creature can be envisaged in relation to its origin" (*La doctrine*, p. viii).

4. Both constructions are found in the same passage in *ŚBh* 1.1.1, p. 114; Thibaut, p. 135; Rangacharya, p. 195.

5. *ŚBh* 1.1.1, pp. 114-15; Thibaut, pp. 136-37; Rangacharya, p. 197.

6. *ŚBh* 1.1.1, p. 116; Thibaut, p. 138.

7. *ŚBh* 1.1.13, p. 133; Thibaut, p. 228; Rangacharya, pp. 340-41.

8. This is stated in many places. See n. 6 above, and also *ŚBh* 1.1.12; Thibaut, p. 271.

9. *ŚBh* 2.1.9, pp. 223-24; Thibaut, p. 424. The same definition is given even more briefly in *ŚBh* 1.2.2, p. 149; Thibaut, p. 262.

10. *VedS*, para. 76.

11. *GBh* 10.20, p. 92; 13.22, p. 123; 13.28, p. 125.

12. *GBh* 7.12, p. 65; 9.4, p. 78.

13. *ŚBh* 1.1.1, pp. 108-20; Thibaut, pp. 140-42. This passage and the adjacent paragraphs have been incorporated bodily in *GBh* 13.2.

14. *ŚBh* 2.1.23, pp. 241-42; Thibaut, pp. 469-70. This last sentence has been stated a number of times earlier; cf. the end of *ŚBh* 2.1.15; Thibaut, p. 459.

15. *ŚBh* 1.4.37, p. 215; Thibaut, pp. 405-6.

16. *ŚBh* 4.1.3, p. 368; Thibaut, p. 718.

17. *ŚBh* 1.1.13, p. 133; Thibaut, pp. 228-29; Rangacharya, p. 340.

18. *ŚBh* 1.4.22, p. 211; Thibaut, p. 396.

19. Van Buitenen, *VedS,* intro., p. 17.

20. *ŚBh* 2.1.14, pp. 225-26; Thibaut, pp. 427-28.

21. Ibid., p. 226; Thibaut, p. 429.

22. *ŚBh* 1.2.1, p. 149; Thibaut, pp. 260-61.

23. *ŚBh* 1.4.27, p. 214; Thibaut, p. 402.

24. *ŚBh* 1.1.13, p. 134; Thibaut, p. 230; Rangacharya, p. 343. The *Vedānta Sūtras* themselves were from ancient times known as *Śārīrakaśāstra,* and śāstra in this passage may refer to the name of the work being commented upon as well as to the doctrine it contains. Sukhtankar argues that the widespread use of the title of the word well before Śankara "certainly shows that Śārīraka (one possessing a body) was considered to be the principal denotation of Brahman" (*Teachings of the Vedānta,* pp. 8-9). Since Advaitins themselves have sometimes called Śankara's commentary on the *Vedānta Sūtras* the *Śārīrakabhāṣya* (incorporated into the names of the subcommentaries by Ānandatīrtha and Appaya Dīkṣita; see MW, p. 1066 ad "śārīraka"), they have evidently found an acceptable interpretation of the term, but Rāmānuja's explanation is certainly the natural one. It is to be noted that he does not make any further use of this title in his argument, whether because there were alternative interpretations or because he prefers to draw his support, not from the title, but from the text of the *Sūtras* and their content: the texts of Scripture.

CHAPTER 10

1. MW, pp. 138-39.

2. MW, p. 158, gives the primary meaning of *āśraya* as "that to which any thing is annexed or with which anything is closely connected or on which anything depends or rests."

3. *VedS,* para. 11.

4. This is a frequent phrase used by Rāmānuja to express the complete dependence of creatures on God; see, e.g., *GBh* 7.19, p. 67.

5. *ŚBh* 2.1.9; Thibaut, p. 424.

6. MW, pp. 551-52.

7. *ŚBh* 1.2.19-21, pp. 157-58; Thibaut, pp. 287-92.

8. *ŚBh* 1.3.8; Thibaut, pp. 307-8.

9. *ŚBh* 1.3.29, p. 184; Thibaut, pp. 333-34.

10. *ŚBh* 2.2.3, pp. 249-50; Thibaut, pp. 486-89.

11. *ŚBh* 2.3.40-41, p. 282; Thibaut, pp. 556-58.

12. *VedS,* paras. 89-90.

13. *VedS,* para. 77.

14. MW, p. 978; Bharadwaj, *Philosophy of Rāmānuja,* p. 220; F. Otto Schrader, *Introduction to the Pāñcarātra and the Ahirbudhnya Saṃhitā,* p. 50. Franklin Edgerton notes both Śankara's and Rāmānuja's comments on the word as it appears in the tenth chapter of the *Bhagavadgītā* and says that both the meaning of "lordship" or "power" (aiśvaryam) given by Rāmānuja and that of "varied manifestation" (vistāram) given by Śankara and Ānandagiri are contained in the word. "I have tried to suggest both by the term 'supernal manifestation'" (Edgerton, *The Bhagavad Gītā,* chap. 10, n. 3 [ad vs. 7]).
15. *GBh* 10.7.15-16, 18-19, 21, 31, 37, 39-41, pp. 89-96.
16. *GBh* 15.6, p. 136.
17. *GBh* 15, intro., pp. 133-34.
18. *GBh* 16, intro., and 16.1, p. 140.
19. *VedS,* para. 6.
20. *ŚBh* 1.1.1; Thibaut, p. 188.
21. *VedS,* para. 98.
22. *VedS,* para. 112.
23. *VedS,* para. 42.
24. *ŚarG,* paras. 5 and 17, pp. 174-75.
25. *VG,* para. 1, p. 178.
26. *VedS,* para. 81.
27. *ŚBh* 4.4.19, p. 395; Thibaut, p. 768.
28. *ŚBh* 1.3.7, pp. 170-71; Thibaut, pp. 305-6.

CHAPTER 11

1. MW, pp. 1088-89; van Buitenen, *Rāmānuja on the Bhagavadgītā,* p. 46, n. 10; *VedS,* p. 274, n. 636, referring to the *Karma Mīmāṃsā Sūtras* 3.1.2: *śeṣaḥ parārthatvāt,* "one constituent is accessory when it is subservient to another."
2. *VedS,* para. 121, p. 274, n. 636.
3. Bharadwaj, *Philosophy,* p. 110.
4. Ibid.
5. *VedS,* paras. 121-22.
6. *VedS,* para. 122, p. 275, n. 637.
7. *ŚBh* 1.1.1; Lacombe, para. 230; Skt., p. 129; Fr., pp. 155-56; nn. 974-75, 240-42. *VedS,* intro., p. 40, nn. 636-38.
8. M. R. Rajagopala Ayyangar, *Srimad Rahasyatrayasara,* p. 30.
9. Personal conversation with Professor Anantha Rangachar.
10. Aśeṣa-cid-acid-vastu-śeṣine . . . Viṣṇave namaḥ (*VedS,* para. 1).
11. *VedS,* para. 18; cf. especially Rajagopala Ayyangar's translation, *Vedartha Sangraha,* p. 51.
12. *VedS,* paras. 76, 80, 83, 90, 97, 106.
13. *VedS,* para. 78. Van Buitenen suggests that *rasa* is here taken in the double meaning of "essence" and "ecstasy" (*VedS,* para. 78, p. 238, n. 349.)
14. Van Buitenen, *Rāmānuja on the Bhagavadgītā,* intro., p. 46, n. 10.
15. *VedS,* paras. 142-44.
16. *GBh* 18.59, Skt., p. 167.
17. *GBh* 7.6, 7a, p. 64.
18. *GBh* 11.2, p. 97.

19. *GBh* 3.30, pp. 30-31.
20. *GBh* 9.27-28, pp. 84-85.
21. *GBh* 3.32; 7.16; 7.19; 9.27; 18.54; 18.73.
22. *GBh* 7.19, p. 67.
23. In the *Gadyatraya* and the *Nityagrantha,* the concept of the soul's metaphysical subordination or subservience (śeṣatā) to God is linked even more explicitly to the concept of service to God (kainkarya), service conceived not as a means to the end of winning the Lord's favor but as itself the end: the privilege of eternally serving God at His sacred feet. This is put several times in the *Śaraṇāgatigadya* as follows: "I desire to attain the eternal service [nitya-kainkarya, or May I become the eternal servant] of the Lord, which is of such a nature [rūpa] that one's sole delight [ekarati] is to be subservient [śeṣatā] in all situations" (paras. 2, 16, 17, 20). In the *Śrīrangagadya* there twice occurs a formulation of the same doctrine using different terms: "reflecting [or realizing] that the inherent nature of the self is to be one whose sole delight is eternal service [nitya-dāsya] eternally under God's control [nitya-niyāmya]" (paras. 1, 2).

In a number of these passages, it is said that this state of being God's eternal servant is produced (kārita) by a fervent love of God, which is itself engendered by the direct experience of God, achieved in supreme devotion. In the *Vaikuṇṭhagadya,* particularly, the term *paricarya* is frequently used as a synonym for kainkarya and dāsya. This term denotes especially the personal service rendered to a king or to a deity. It is first applied to the supernatural attendants of the Lord, such as Garuḍa, and then to the devotee. This means that the service to which the devotee aspires as his goal is the same kind which God's eternal attendants, who are always with Him in His supreme abode, are able to render Him. The metaphysical basis for such service is the soul's essential subservience as useful instrument or property at the disposal of the Lord (bhagavat-śeṣatā); that the finite self is actually allowed to share in such service to and attendance on the Supreme Lord is by virtue of God's grace (prasāda), and this state is actualized by the attainment of a state of fervent love for God, dependent on a mystical vision of Him, an experience which God grants only to those who are exclusively devoted to Him (*VG,* paras. 2, 5, 6).

In one sentence of the prayer of surrender in the *Śaraṇāgatigadya,* the soul's essential state of servitude (dāsya) is linked with the act of throwing oneself on God's mercy (śaraṇāgati): "As I utter the words, 'I have surrendered to Thee; I am Thy servant [dāsa]'; do Thou help me, who am Thy servant [dāsabhūtam] to transcend material nature [prakṛti] . . . which conceals Thy essential nature from me and which causes me to have false notions of my nature" (para. 12).

The terms *dāsya* and *dāsatā* in the Gadyas seem to signify both the eternal metaphysical relation (servitude, the meaning of śeṣatā) and the desired personal relation (service, the meaning of kainkarya). In this one passage there seems to be also, as in *GBh* 9.27, a connection of both servitude and service with the indispensable act (and attitude) of surrendering oneself to God (śaraṇāgati or prapatti). Neither in the *Gītābhāṣya* nor in the *Śaraṇāgati-*

gadya is this act and the faith which accompanies it a substitute for devotion to God, but it is the indispensable condition for God's action in destroying one's sins and engendering loving devotion to Him.

The few doctrinal passages in the *Nityagrantha* stress the doctrine which Rāmānuja develops in the *Gītābhāṣya* and which, as we have seen in the last two passages quoted, involves the idea that God is the Śeṣī, the principal person or owner. This is the doctrine that it is God who performs all the action in the worship of Him and possesses the subject, the object, and the means of worship. In the *Nityagrantha* this is linked with the idea of kainkarya developed in the Gadyas. The author states at the very beginning that he is describing the worship of a supremely exclusive devotee (paramaikāntī) whose delight is in the service of the Lord (bhagavat-kainkarya-ratiḥ). The worshiper is to reflect at the outset that "the Lord Himself . . . commences to cause Himself to be pleased by means of me, who am His śeṣa." Later on he states that the devotee "must begin the worship [pūjā] which is of the nature [rūpa] of complete or perfect [paripūrṇa] service [kainkarya]." Later the opening doctrinal reflection is twice repeated with some variation (pp. 181-82 in Annangarācārya's *Śrī-Bhagavad-Rāmānuja-Granthamālā*).

24. A. Govindacharya, *Śrī Bhagavad-Gītā.*

25. Rudolf Otto, *Die Gnadenreligion Indiens und das Christentum,* p. 27. The English version of this book is entitled *India's Religion of Grace and Christianity Compared and Contrasted.*

CHAPTER 12

1. *GBh* 15, intro., pp. 133-34.

2. *GBh* 15.17-19, pp. 138-39.

3. *VedS,* para. 42. *ŚBh* 1.1.1, pp. 66-67; Thibaut, p. 87; Rangacharya, pp. 111-12; Lacombe, p. 85.

4. *ŚBh* 1.1.1, p. 2.

5. *ŚBh* 1.1.1, pp. 66-67; Thibaut, p. 87. *VedS*, para. 42.

6. Commentaries on *ŚarG,* para. 5, by Periya Āccān Pillai and Vedānta Deśika.

7. *ŚBh* 1.1.1, pp. 69-71; Thibaut, pp. 89-90.

8. *ŚBh* 1.1.21, p. 139; Thibaut, p. 240; Rangacharya, p. 361.

9. The three passages referred to here are all from the *Taittirīya Āraṇyaka:* 10. 1-3, 3.13.2, and 10.11.1, the last being the Nārāyaṇa Anuvāka, also contained in the *Mahā Nārāyaṇa Upaniṣad* 9.8.3.

10. *VedS,* para. 103.

11. *VedS,* para. 102.

12. *VedS,* paras. 104, 108.

13. *VedS,* para. 94.

14. *VedS,* paras. 113-14.

15. *VedS,* para. 115. The "three bhāvanās" are interpreted quite differently by two of the translators, while Raghavachar leaves the word untranslated. Van Buitenen refers to *Viṣṇu Purāṇa* 6.7.47 ff. and defines the term as "creative potency manifesting itself in three successive ontological orders," those of the (subordinate) creator, the creation, and the mediators of creation (van Buitenen, *VedS,* p. 265, n. 585). Rajagopala Ayyangar, on the other hand, translates

"three kinds of mental effort." The first is the effort to perform works which will bring a reward of pleasurable objects; the second is the effort to perform the adoration of the Supreme; and the third is the effort required to perform both kinds of worship (Rajagopala Ayyangar, *VedS*, p. 166, n. 1).

CHAPTER 13

1. Bharadwaj, *Philosophy*, pp. 233-34.
2. *VedS*, para. 127.
3. *VedS*, para. 136.
4. *VedS*, paras. 128-31.
5. *VedS*, para. 132.
6. *VedS*, para. 135.
7. Quoting verbatim van Buitenen's translation, *VedS*, para. 34.
8. *VedS*, para. 135, p. 290, n. 748.
9. *GBh*, intro., p. 1.
10. *ŚBh* 1.1.21, pp. 138-39; Thibaut, pp. 240-42; Rangacharya, pp. 260-63.
11. Bharadwaj, *Philosophy*, pp. 134-38. *ŚBh* 2.2.42; Thibaut, p. 525.
12. *ŚBh* 1.2.2, p. 149; Thibaut, p. 262.
13. *ŚBh* 2.2.41, pp. 266-67; Thibaut, p. 525.
14. *VedS*, para. 34.
15. *GBh* 4.6, p. 36.

CHAPTER 14

1. *ŚBh* 3.2.40, p. 317; Thibaut, pp. 627-28.
2. *ŚBh* 2.2.3, p. 250; Thibaut, pp. 488-89.
3. *ŚBh* 2.2.41, pp. 266-67; Thibaut, p. 525.
4. Schrader, *Introduction*, pp. 29-42.
5. *ŚBh* 2.2.41.
6. Personal conversation with Professor K. C. Varadachari in Tirupati.
7. Paraśara Bhaṭṭar, *Sri Vishnu Sahasranama Bashya*, trans. L. Venkatarathnam Naidu, pp. 77-78.
8. *GBh* 4.11, p. 39.
9. *Yatīndramatadīpikā*, pp. 116-38.
10. *VedS*, para. 143.
11. *GBh* 4.4-8, pp. 35-37.
12. *GBh* 4.9, p. 37.
13. *GBh* 7.24-25, pp. 68-69.
14. *GBh* 9.11-13, p. 80.
15. *GBh* 11.18.
16. *GBh* 11.51.
17. *ŚBh* 1.1.21.
18. *ŚBh* 1.3.1, p. 166; Thibaut, p. 297.
19. *ŚBh* 1.1.21.
20. *VedS*, para. 107.
21. *VedS*, paras. 107, 112.
22. *VedS*, para. 113.
23. *ŚBh* 1.3.8, 1.3.13, 1.3.14, 1.3.20, 1.3.24.
24. *ŚBh* 1.4.1, p. 194; Thibaut, p. 356.

CHAPTER 15

1. *GBh* 7.24-25, pp. 68-69.
2. Raghavachar, *Introduction to the Vedarthasangraha*, p. 165.
3. *Vān-manasayoḥ abhūmi-bhūmiyor natajana-dṛśām* in the mangalaśloka at the beginning of the *Vedāntadīpa*. Cf. the phrasing in verse 21 of Yāmuna's *Stotraratna: vān-manas-atibhūmaye . . . vān-manas-aikabhūmaye*, "beyond the range [atibhūmi] of speech or thought . . . [yet] the sole object [aikabhūmi] of speech and thought."
4. *ŚBh* 2.2.3, p. 250; Thibaut, pp. 488-89.
5. *GBh* 6.47, p. 61.
6. *GBh* 7.17, p. 66.
7. *GBh* 9.22, p. 83.
8. *GBh* 7.19, p. 67.
9. *GBh* 7.27, p. 69; cf. *Gītārthasaṃgraha*, v. 29.
10. *GBh* 6.47, p. 61.
11. *GBh* 7.1, pp. 62-63.
12. *GBh* 8.15, p. 74.
13. *GBh* 9.14, p. 81.
14. *GBh* 9.4-5, p. 78.
15. *GBh* 8.14, pp. 73-74.
16. *GBh* 7.18, p. 67.
17. *GBh* 9.29, p. 85.
18. *GBh* 9.2, pp. 77-78.
19. *GBh* 7.18, p. 67.
20. *GBh* 9.26, p. 84.
21. This is Vedānta Deśika's definition in the *Gadyabhāṣyam*. Those of Sudarśana Sūri and Periya Āccān Piḷḷai are very similar. The reference is to the verse of the *Gītā* we have noted (7.18) in which the Lord calls His devotees "generous."
22. Parāśara Bhaṭṭar, "Śrīguṇaratnakośa," v. 58.
23. Sudarśana Sūri, *Gadyatrayavyākhyā*, commenting on the *Śaraṇāgatigadya*, para. 5.
24. Parāśara Bhaṭṭar's comment on name 83 in his commentary on the "Thousand Names of Viṣṇu," *Śrīviṣṇusahasranāmabhāṣyam*, Skt., p. 69; L. Venkatarathnam Naidu's Eng. trans. p. 70.
25. Sudarśana Sūri ad *ŚarG*, para. 5.
26. Parāśara Bhaṭṭar ends his comment on name 626 by stating that the following qualities concern "the highest extent of gracious condescension, which is most secret." The first of these is *vijitātmā*, interpreted as "Though linked with that supreme prosperity desired even by Lakṣmī, His mind is conquered by those who do reverence to Him." The next Divine name Bhaṭṭar reads as *vidheyātmā* and interprets to mean, "His nature is such that He is at the beck and call of His devotees." Name 632 is *anīśaḥ*; Bhaṭṭar says that the Lord is called "one who is not the Lord" because "He does not exercise His overlordship over persons solely devoted to Him; He is under their control with regard to such matters as His bath and decoration, and the conduct of the worshipping congregation [goṣṭhi]" (*Śrīviṣṇusahasranāmabhāṣyam*, Skt., pp. 157-58; Naidu, pp. 153-54].

27. Bhaṭṭar's comment on name 472, ibid., Skt., p. 132; Naidu, p. 130.
28. Sudarśana Sūri ad *ŚarG*, para. 5.
29. Periya Āccān Piḷḷai, *Gadyavyākhānam*, commenting on the *Śaraṇāgatigadya*, para. 5.
30. Vedānta Deśika ad *ŚarG*, para. 5.
31. Sudarśana Sūri ad *ŚarG*, para. 5.

CHAPTER 16

1. Rāmānuja's long comment on the first sūtra was translated by Rudolf Otto into German in 1917 and by Olivier Lacombe into French in 1938. The comparison with Sankara was understandably the main point in Thibaut's introduction to his translation of both Bhāṣyas in the Sacred Books of the East series. (The introduction comes at the beginning of vol. 34 [pp. ix-cxxviii], before he begins his translation of Śankara's Bhāṣya).

V. A. Sukhtankar wrote *The Teachings of the Vedānta according to Rāmānuja* as a thesis for the University of Vienna (1908). This is a brief work that confines itself to Rāmānuja's own constructive philosophical position, almost entirely on the basis of the *Śrībhāṣya* and the *Vedārthasaṃgraha.* In 1899 M. Rangacharya and M. B. Varadaraja Aiyangar published the first volume of their translation of the *Śrībhāṣya,* thus contributing to the emphasis on Rāmānuja's metaphysics, even though they indicated in their introduction (pp. v-vi) that the *Śrībhāṣya* was in the tradition of the Bhāgavatas, who stressed worship (bhakti) above wisdom (jñāna).

2. See the works of A. Govindacharya listed in the bibliography.
3. Cf. the following statement by Satyavrata Singh, in *Vedānta Deśika, His Life, Works, and Philosophy*, p. 145: "What ultimately happened was that after the Master's retirement, some of them leaned towards philosophy while others were snatched away by religion."
4. Kumarappa, *Hindu Conception of the Deity*, pp. xiii-xix.
5. Ibid., pp. 148-49, 162-63.
6. Otto, *Siddhānta des Rāmānuja*, p. 2.
7. Otto, *Gnadrenreligion Indiens*, pp. 117-18.
8. Van Buitenen, *VedS*, intro., p. 48.
9. Bharadwaj, *Philosophy*, p. ix; and p. 11, quoting A. A. Macdonell, *India's Past* (Oxford, 1927), p. 149.
10. Bharadwaj, *Philosophy*, p. 21.
11. Raghavachar, *Introduction to the Vedarthasangraha*, p. 5.
12. Ibid., pp. 5-10.
13. Kumarappa, *Hindu Conception of the Deity*, p. 186.
14. Ibid., pp. 187-88.
15. Ibid., p. 191. Kumarappa concludes his chapter on "The Nature of the Deity" with the following footnote. "It is obvious from the foregoing that Rāmānuja obtains most of his doctrines regarding the nature of the Deity from his own religious sect. That part of his teaching, however, which may be said primarily to reveal Upaniṣadic influence is that which describes thought and bliss as constituting the essential nature of Brahman, although, as our account of the Upaniṣads shows, the conception of Brahman as an all-

perfect Being characterised by grace is not altogether absent even in the Upaniṣads" (p. 193, n. 1).

16. *ŚBh* 2.1.2; pp. 218-19; Thibaut, pp. 408-11. Van Buitenen, *VedS*, intro., p. 33.

17. *VedS*, para. 133, p. 288.

18. *VedS*, para. 139, p. 294.

19. *Veds*, para. 94, pp. 251-53, quoting *Matsya Purāṇa* 290.

20. *Veds*, intro., pp. 35-36.

21. *VedS*, intro., p. 36, n. 100.

22. Ādidevānanda, in his introduction to the *Yatīndramatadīpikā* of Śrīnivāsadāsa, pp. v, xxix.

23. *Yatīndramatadīpikā*, p. 1.

24. Ibid., pp. 122-40.

25. The "Stotraratna," the "Catuśślokī" (four verses in praise of Śrī), and the *Gītārthasaṃgraha* (see the bibliography).

26. Kāñcīpūrṇa is the Sanskrit name of the disciple of Yāmuna who is called Tirukacci Nambi in the Tamil biographies. His hymn is called the "Devarājāṣṭakam" and is printed on p. 8 in the collection of Śrī Vaiṣṇava Sanskrit hymns (*Stotramālā*) edited by P. B. Annangarācārya.

27. Kūraṭṭāḻvān's (Kūreśa's) extant works are hymns included in the *Stotramālā* (pp. 14-41) and the text in verse and commentary in prose called the *Yamakaratnākaram* (see bibliography and chap. 17).

28. Parāśara Bhaṭṭar's four hymns are included in the *Stotramālā*, pp. 41-62. His major work is his commentary on the "Thousand Names of Viṣṇu" *Śrīviṣṇusahasranāmabhāṣyam*) otherwise known as the *Bhagavadguṇadarpaṇa* (see bibliography and chap. 17).

29. See Satyavrata Singh, *Vedānta Deśika.*

30. This conversational form is unfortunately lost in van Buitenen's condensed translation of Rāmānuja's *Gītābhāṣya,* in which the first and second person pronouns are changed to third person pronouns.

31. Commenting on certain scriptural texts, Parāśara Bhaṭṭar says, "Don't consider these quotations as empty praise [arthavāda], for they are not exaggerations [ativāda]." Further on he states, "Nāmasankīrtana is not an instance of the Mīmāṃsā category called *pūrṇāhuti-nyāya* [according to which the praise uttered at the end of a Vedic sacrifice is regarded as an exaggeration in the interests of emphasizing the importance of that sacrifice] because the pūrṇāhuti-nyāya is applicable only to such exaggeration as is present when the praise is a subordinate sentence in the ritual and contains flattery appropriate to a petition. On the contrary, even in the case of words of praise, unless there are objections based on some authority, it is rash to deprive the words of their proper meaning, for these are scriptural words possessing their own authority." (*Śrīviṣṇusahasranāmabhāṣyam,* intro. [after *sadeti*], pp. 22-33; Venkatarathnam Naidu, p. 23; Viraraghavacharya, pp. 32-33).

Compare also verse 3 of Kūraṭṭāḻvān's "Hymn to Śrī" ("Śrīstava"). "Poets think of *stotra* as ascribing to the person who is to be praised the good qualities of someone else, but that meaning of *stotra* does not apply when I praise Thee. Who can properly describe Thy treasury of excellent qualities, for they are beyond Vācaspati [the 'Lord of Speech'] ?" (*Stotramālā*, p. 40).

32. In his hymn in praise of the Goddess Śrī (Lakṣmī), Parāśara Bhaṭṭar has the following verse, "I am the only person qualified to praise Thee. 'Stotra' means: expanding the qualities of the person. That qualification rests with me because hearing my harsh words, such qualities of Thine as forgiveness [kṣānti], generosity [audārya], and mercy [dayā] will be revealed" ("Śrīguṇaratnakośa," v. 6, *Stotramālā*, p. 56).

33. The commentaries of Periya Āccān Piḷḷai (the "Twenty-four Thousand") and of Vaḍakku Tiruvīdi Piḷḷai (the "Thirty-Six Thousand," often called the *Īḍu*) refer in a few places to different interpretations of the same stanza by Āḷavandār (Yāmuna) and Uḍayavar (Rāmānuja). Among these are the following: 1.2.1 (only in the "Thirty-six Thousand"); 1.4.3 (in the "Twenty-four Thousand"; the "Thirty-six Thousand" attributes Yāmuna's interpretation to his disciple Tirumālai Āṇḍān); 2.9.8 (in both); and 3.3.6 (in both).

34. "Six Thousand" [*Ārāyirappaḍi Guruparamparāprabhāvam*], pp. 180-82; Srinivasa Aiyengar, *Life*, pp. 126-28; Govindacharya, *Life*, pp. 102-4.

CHAPTER 17

1. Pandit Agnihothram Rāmānuja Thatachariar of Kumbakonam has advanced the following arguments against the authenticity of the three Gadyas and the *Nityagrantha* (during conversations with Robert Lester and myself in Madras, 25-28 Sept. 1961).

> 1. The emphasis on śaraṇāgati (prapatti) is unlike the genuine Rāmānuja. It is true that in the *Śaraṇāgatigadya* this is still an anga (branch, subordinate part) of the path of bhakti. The author is thus following Rāmānuja's interpretation of the caramaśloka (*Gītā* 18.66). He is not expounding prapatti as a separate upāya (means to mokṣa) but is asking for cleansing from all his sins so that he might undertake and be successful in parabhakti, parajñāna and paramabhakti. In the *Śrīrangagadya*, however, śaraṇāgati is described as an independent means of attaining mokṣa.
>
> 2. The *Śaraṇāgatigadya* mentions a mantra (the "Dvayam") whose simple utterance is sufficient to remove all obstacles to the achievement of bhakti. No such doctrine is found in Rāmānuja's genuine works.
>
> 3. The *Śaraṇāgatigadya* has an act of surrender to the goddess Śrī before the surrender to the Lord. This Pāñcarātric doctrine is not found in the genuine works of Rāmānuja.
>
> 4. The *Śaraṇāgatigadya* and the *Nityagrantha* mention two other consorts besides Śrī, namely Bhūdevī and Nīlā, whereas Rāmānuja holds Śrī to be the only consort of the Lord.
>
> 5. All of these works make much of the concept of nityakainkarya, eternal service to the Lord (kainkarya is literally the state of readiness to serve: asking, "*kiṃ-karomi*?"—what shall I do?). This servant-master relationship implied in kainkarya is contrary to Rāmānuja's idea that the soul is equal with God in Vaikuṇṭha; that is, after release the soul enjoys equally with God the attributes of God (bhogasāmya).
>
> 6. In the *Śaraṇāgatigadya* the Lord tells the author he should live the rest of his life in Śrīrangam, and in the *Śrīrangagadya* the Lord is once addressed as "Śrī Ranganātha," which means that the image of the temple in Śrīrangam

is identified with the Brahman of the Upaniṣads. This is quite contrary to Rāmānuja's thought, for he never mentioned a particular image, and though he worshiped images he did not accept the Pāñcarātric theory adopted by later Śrīvaiṣṇavas that the image is a veritable incarnation of the Supreme Lord. All of these works are thus centrally concerned with the worship of the image, about which Rāmānuja says nothing. Moreover, the *Nityagrantha* gives only a secondary place to yoga or meditation according to the Upaniṣads and follows entirely Pāñcarātric and not Vedic rites.

7. The author of the *Vaikuṇṭhagadya* has indulged in poetic fancy in describing the transcendent realm (Vaikuṇṭha) in a way unsupported by Śruti, Smṛti, or even the Pāñcarātras. This is most irresponsible, for Vaikuṇṭha is not an imaginary place to be described by poets as they please, and it is quite unlike Rāmānuja, who tried to support his every statement with pramāṇa (scriptural authority), to write such a description. Moreover, Rāmānuja said nothing about Vaikuṇṭha in commenting on the last sūtra of the Brahma Sūtras, where we would expect him to say anything he thought important about it, since this is the point at which Śankara had described Vaikuṇṭha.

8. We must decide what Rāmānuja's ideas are primarily on the basis of the *Śrībhāṣya.* Second in importance is the *Vedārthasaṃgraha,* which refutes rival systems. The *Gītābhāṣya* is only third in importance, because Rāmānuja considered the *Gītā* to be only Smṛti (that is, not Śruti like the Vedas and Upaniṣads). The utterances of God in the form of an avatāra are not to be considered 100 percent perfect; they have to be rejected when they do not conform to the Vedas. The introduction to the *Gītābhāṣya* is careless in its use of terms, an indication that it also was not written by Rāmānuja himself.

9. These works were probably written two or three generations after Rāmānuja by those who accepted the idea of prapatti as an independent means to salvation. They may come after the three commentaries on the Āḻvārs that consider them to be "bhaktas" and before the commentary (the "Twenty-four Thousand") that describes them as "prapannas."

Lester generally accepted Pandit Agnihothram's arguments and incorporated them in his Ph.D. dissertation submitted to Yale University in 1962, entitled "The Nature and Function of Patañjalian-Type Yoga as the Means to Release (Mokṣopāya) according to Rāmānuja." The dissertation itself has not been published, but Lester has expressed his views on this subject in two articles. One of these, entitled "Rāmānuja and Śrī-Vaiṣṇavism," was read at the annual meeting of the American Association of Asian Studies in the spring of 1965. The main arguments of the paper are summarized later in this chapter. The other article, entitled, "Rāmānuja and Śrī-Vaiṣṇavism: The Concept of Prapatti or Śaraṇāgati," is published in *History of Religions,* 5:266-82. In the published article Lester argues that "while Rāmānuja prominently employs the concepts of *prapatti* and *śaraṇāgati,* he, in fact, supports neither the Tengalai nor the Vaḍagalai view" (p. 267). In order to establish this thesis he seeks to demonstrate that Rāmānuja did not author either the *Śaraṇāgatigadya* or the *Śrīrangagadya* (p. 267). For other reasons not presented in this paper, he holds that the *Vaikuṇṭhagadya* is also not authentic (p. 268, n. 6). Much of the paper is spent in showing the "basic discrepancy" between the conception of śaraṇāgati in Rāmānuja's admittedly genuine works and the conception in the *Śaraṇāgatigadya.* Lester notes more briefly several other discrepancies: "The *gadya's* concept of Śrī, as mediatrix between the devotee and Nārāyaṇa, its description of the means to release aside from *śaraṇāgati* as *parabhaktiparajñānaparamabhakti* and its concept of *nityakainkarya* as the highest good" (p. 279). He maintains that the service of the soul associated with śeṣatva in the *Vedārthasaṃgraha,* where it is called *sevā,* not kainkarya, has the form of bhakti and "applies only to the state of *saṃsāra,* not to the state of release" (p. 281, referring to van Buitenen's text, pp. 171-73). He concludes that "the author or authors . . . of the *gadyas* knew Rāmānuja's writings and that the theology of the *gadyas* represents a stage somewhere between Rāmānuja and Vedānta Deśika, close enough to the former that the writings could be attributed to him" (p. 282).

2. *VedS,* para. 143.

3. Partially following Franklin Edgerton's romanized text and translation of *The Bhagavad Gīta,* 1:176-77.

4. *GBh* 18.66, pp. 169-70.

5. *Gītārthasangraha-Gītāsāra,* vv. 61-62.

6. Meghanādāri Sūri in the *Mumukṣūpāyasaṃgraha.* The other divergent views of Meghanādāri Sūri spring from his conviction that there is one consistent teaching about prapatti in all of Rāmānuja's works. Prapatti, like parabhakti, may only be practiced by members of the three higher castes, because it is one of the Brahmavidyās, disciplines of meditation based on the Upaniṣads, which may only be studied by those castes. (This is an interesting view, because it shows that prapatti could be accepted by one who rejected what has often been considered the chief reason for its popularity and extensive development, its availability as a means of salvation to the great majority of people in South India who are outside the three higher castes.) Contrary to the later accepted view, prapatti is to be observed not only once but repeatedly. The term *sakṛt* of the Gadyas is understood not as "once" but as "at once" or immediately. Prapatti is defined as that mental consciousness which is entirely of the nature of a prayer for protection, bereft of all kinds of misconceptions and preceded by supreme faith, along with the knowledge of the Supreme as both the Upāya (means) and the Upeya (goal). The fruit of this spiritual discipline is not attained if there is a break in the continuity of the "supreme faith"; thus prapatti must be repeated.

7. *GBh* 18.65, p. 169.

8. *Gadyatrayam,* with the commentaries of Sudarśana Sūri, Periya Āccān Piḷḷai, and Vedānta Deśika.

9. Ibid.

10. Sudarśana Sūri in his *Gadyatrayavyākhyā*; Bhashyam's trans., pp. 37-91; Anantarangācārya's Skt. text, pp. 23-24.

11. Vedānta Deśika, *Gadyabhāṣyam* ad *ŚarG.*

12. *Stotraratna,* v. 3.

13. Vedānta Deśika, *Gadyabhāṣyam*; see *VG,* para. 1, p. 19, n.

14. *VedS,* para. 78, n. 349.

15. *Jitantā Stotra,* v. 15—*sarva-sthāsu . . . kinkaro 'smi.;* cf. v. 14—*kinkaro 'smi-iti. VedS,* para. 77, quotes v. 7.

16. *Stotraratna,* v. 46.

17. V. 17 of the *Jitantā Stotra* contains the words *tvam-prapannasya,* and v. 60 of the *Stotraratna* reads (in part): tvadīyas-tvadbhṛtyas-tava parijanas-tvadgatir-ahaṃ prapannaścaivam (I am Thine, Thy servant and Thy attendant; Thou art my goal, and I am one who has surrendered myself [to Thee])."

18. The extant works of the three converts are: Yādava Prakāśa (renamed Govinda Jīyar), *Yatidharma-samuccaya*; Yajñamūrti (renamed Aruḷāḷa Perumāḷ Emberumānār), *Jñānasāram* and *Prameyasāram*; Periya Kōil Nambi (renamed Tiruvarangattu Amudanār), *Irāmānuja Nūtrandādi.* The works of Kūrattālvān, Parāśara Bhaṭṭar, and Tirukkuruhai Pirān Piḷḷān are discussed below. Three disciples wrote devotional manuals like Rāmānuja's *Nityagrantha*: Parāśara Bhaṭṭar, *Kriyādīpam* (followed by the Tengalais in their domestic worship); Govinda (Embār), *Haryārādhanakrama* (40 stanzas); and Vangipurattu Nambi, *Nityagrantha* (526 stanzas). Two disciples of Rāmānuja's disciples also wrote important works: Nañjīyar's commentary on the *Tiruvāymoḻi,* called the "Nine Thousand"; and Viṣṇu Citta's commentary on the *Viṣṇu Purāṇa.*

19. *Jñānasāram,* v. 9.

20. Ibid., v. 23.

21. Ibid., v. 28.

22. Ibid., v. 24.

23. Ibid., v. 25.

24. Ibid., especially vv. 29-30, 32-37; and *Prameyasāram,* vv. 1, 2, 10.

25. Kōil Kaṇḍādai Nāyan, in his fourteenth-century Tamil work *Periya Tirumuḍi Aḍavu* [Aḍaivu], lists the *Gadyatrayavyākhyānam* as one of Kūraṭṭālvān's works (p. 60 in my Telugu script edition, which lacks a title page). Another lost commentary on the *Gadyatraya* is that of Viṣṇu Citta; this is referred to by Vedānta Deśika in his commentary (p. 24) on the *Śaraṇāgatigadya* because of a small textual variant in the text of "Viṣṇu Citta, etc." It is also quoted by Deśika in commenting on the second verse of Yāmuna's "Catuśślokī." These references are referred to in the editor's introduction to the three extant commentaries on the *Gadyatraya,* where he also notes Manavāḷamāmuni's reference to commentaries on the Gadyas by Nañjīyar and Piḷḷai Lokācārya (S. Krishnasvāmī Ayyangār, ed., *Gadyavyākhyānangaḷ: Commentaries on Rāmānuja's "Gadyatraya" by Sudarśana Sūri, Periya Āccān Piḷḷai, and Vedānta Deśika,* printed in Devanagari and Tamil script [Trichy: published by the editor, n.d.], pp. 1-2).

26. "Considering that souls bound in saṃsāra are always sinful, Thou forgivest them if they have merely the thought of approaching Thee" ("Śrīvaikuṇṭhastava," v. 61). "I am a fit receptacle for Thy mercy [dayā], for I have done no good deeds, have no perfect education, and am without devotion [bhakti]" (ibid., v. 88). "Knowingly or unknowingly I have committed a number of sins. There is thus no other way [for me]. Forgive me by Thy grace" (ibid., v. 89). "I don't have [that minimum of] faith for singing Thy name, praising Thee, or doing obeisance to Thee, [let alone] for meditating [on Thee]; nor do I even have devotion or desire for Thee" (ibid., v. 96). "If one has taken refuge with Him, whatever one's caste or character, the Beautiful One [Sundara] embraces Him because He is affectionate [vatsala]" ("Sundarabāhustava," v. 30). "Even the word 'refuge' [śaraṇam] would not appear without Thy grace

[prasāda]" ("Varadarājastava," v. 88). "I who am no devotee [abhaktaḥ] want to attain Thee solely by the word 'prapatti' [humble approach or surrender], which is difficult to obtain" (ibid., v. 92). "Those who worship Thee with devotion [bhakti] or otherwise by their good qualities, good deeds, and knowledge were made to be like this solely by Thy mercy [dayā]. That mercy is my strength" (ibid., v. 94). "I am not able to overcome my sins, so consider me Thy śeṣa [servant], as one who has no other refuge, being very inferior, and forgive me" ("Sundarabāhustava," v. 121).

27. "O Varada, I am without devotion, good qualities, or good deeds. I have not made a serious effort [to attain Thee], nor have I removed my evil deeds. If [nonetheless] I attain Thy feet, then such auspicious qualities of Thine as kṣamā [forgiveness or forbearance] and dayā [mercy] will become evident" ("Varadarājastava," v. 95). "If Thou savest only Those who are qualified to attain Thee and dost not save me, who have done no good works and have no other way [to attain salvation], that is not sufficient greatness for Thee" ("Śrīvaikuṇṭhastava," v. 99).

28. "It is not proper for Thee who art the Lord (Īśvara) to ignore even the sinner if he is one who may be deemed to have taken refuge with Thee. Thou possessest knowledge (jñāna], power [śakti], and compassion [kāruṇya]. Therefore my sin is not sufficient to obstruct the display of Thy attributes" ("Atimānuṣastava," v. 61). "My life should be full of yearning for Thee. Alas, though my desire for worldly objects is great, for Thy feet I have not even a particle of desire. If I am to be saved, Thou must bear me Thyself!" ("Varadarājastava," v. 87).

29. "Śrīvaikuṇṭhastava," v. 62.

30. "When those who have supreme devotion [parabhakti] toward the feet of the Beautiful One have attained release [mokṣa], they attain the status of eternal servants [nitya-kinkara] in the supreme abode [paramapada]" ("Sundarabāhustava," v. 83). "O how great is the gracious condescension [śītatva] and the affection toward His dependents [āśrita-vātsalya] of the Beautiful-Armed One who decorated the universe with His avatāras, in which He observed the duties [dharmas] of creatures in the world!" (ibid., v. 84). "Thou took the form of avatāras to make it easy for Thy devotees to approach in the place they requested" (ibid., v. 86). "To show Thy majesty [vaibhava] to Thy devotee, because of Thy affection Thou became visible to all, taking up residence in Thy own abode, Śrīranga" (ibid., v. 119). "It is established by the Vedas that Thou art under no one else's control, but we consider that Thou art under the control of others, dependent upon those who surrender to Thee. Thou art blamed in the world because, though Thou knowest everything, Thou dost not notice the faults [doṣa] of Thy devotee" ("Varadarājastava," v. 20). "O Varada, there is nothing for Thee to obtain that Thou dost not already possess. The creation, maintenance, and destruction of the universe is the result of Thy mere thought. Even so, Thou becomest incarnate [avatāra] in the families of inferior beings, such as the Vedic deities and men, in order to embrace [āśleṣṭum] Thy devotees and to crush those who cause [them] unhappiness" (ibid., v. 64). "O Creator of boons [Varaprada], Thou hast eagerly incarnated Thyself in the world because of Thy affection [vātsalya] for Thy

worshipers. Thou becamest accessible [sulabhaḥ] to them. Once when Thou wert tied [by Thy mother to the stone] Thou went weeping. What does this mean?" (ibid., v. 70). "May I always be in Thy presence serving Thee, yearning to be entirely Thy servant, without any other objective. My service should be in all places, at all times, and in all stages of life" (ibid., v. 98).

31. "Śrīvaikuṇṭhastava," v. 90.

32. The following verses from Parāśara Bhaṭṭar's hymns illustrate some of these favorite Śrī Vaiṣṇava themes. "Toward this Nārāyaṇa may my natural service [sahaja-kainkarya] take place at all times, in all places, and during all the stages of life" ("Aṣṭaślokī," v. 3). "Leaving all dharmas that I have prescribed to attain Me, in order to attain Me simply be eager and believe that only I am the refuge. I shall free you who firmly resolve this from the obstructions to attaining Me" (ibid., v. 7, paraphrasing *Gītā* 18.66, the caramaśloka). "Without any cause [akasmāt] Thou hast become an avatāra at Śrīrangam to protect the universe" ("Śrīrangarājastava" 2.52). "The incarnations Thou hast assumed are countless, like Thy qualities. In the shrines of the world Thou art worshiped, and Thou bearest everything. Thy entire existence is under the control of the priests [arcaka-parādhīna]. Thy condition is a touching one for those with tender hearts" (ibid. 2.74). "O Lord of Śrīrangam, who is there able to see my faults completely? Thou art pouring out Thy qualities into me, but I am not a [fit] receptacle for them" (ibid. 2.94). "Forgiveness [kṣamā] is granted to the offender only when he repents, but I am proud [dṛpta]. How [can forgiveness be granted] to such an offender? O Lord of Śrīrangam, Thou wilt nevertheless forgive me, for Thy forgiveness is endless" (ibid. 2.96). "Even with [Thy enemies] Kakāśura and Śiṣupāla, Thy forgiveness did not have sufficient scope, for they understood some of Thy attributes. In my case, O Varada, Thy forgiveness has free play, spreading everywhere, for I do not know even a particle of one of Thy attributes" (ibid. 2.97). "I must leave Thee, who hath said that Thou wouldst give fearlessness [abhaya] to those who only once surrender to Thee [sakṛt-prapannāya] [for even that I cannot do]. I am full of ego because I do not have the knowledge that leads to faith" (ibid. 2.101). "O Ruler of Śrīrangam, I have declared myself Thy burden. With the help of the righteous teachers [dhārmikās] I have uttered the word 'refuge' [śaraṇam]. Therefore carefully consider my case and accept me as Thy burden" (ibid. 2.102). "The quality of lordship is the fulfilling of the wishes of the supplicants. O Lord of Śrīrangam, please lift this creature, who is very low, by Thy own qualities" (ibid. 2.104).

33. "Śrīrangarājastava" 2.105.

34. *Śrīviṣṇusahasranāmabhāṣyam,* intro.; Skt., pp. 13-14, 17; Venkatarathnam Naidu, pp. 13, 18; Bhashyam, pp. 20, 25.

35. One striking verse of Bhaṭṭar's father, Kūraṭṭāḻvān, part of his short hymn in praise of the Goddess Śrī, expresses this theme, "I am very small; I have evil thoughts; I have no affection [for Thee]; and I have done Thee no service. Yet I am tasting [literally, licking] Thy fame, O Goddess. I am not afraid or ashamed, for I am ignorant. The river Ganges is not polluted by the dog that is lapping up [licking] the water, nor is the dog ashamed or fearful. The dog's thirst must be quenched" ("Śrīstava," v. 5).

Parāśara Bhaṭṭar seems even more concerned than his father with the wonder of the contact of the all-perfect Lord with such imperfect creatures, as the following stanzas from his hymns illustrate. "A purification is performed if there is even a false report of some inferior creature coming into Thy shrine, though not even coming near to Thee. Inferior to that creature am I, who am so close to Thee. O Lord of Ranga, what sort of purification wilt Thou then perform?" ("Śrīranganāthastotra," v. 7). "As the baby elephant plasters dirt on its head after it has bathed, so He who shines forth through both the Sanskrit and Tamil Scriptures dirties Himself with the words of my praise" ("Śrīrangarāja-stava" 1.16). "I love Thee, who are fit to be loved by Śrī. I am like a dog that touches the offerings for the homa sacrifice or like a dog buffeted by waves, the waves of the embryo, birth, old age, death, worldly afflictions and [the bondage of] deeds" (ibid. 2.99).

36. *Śrīviṣṇusahasranāmabhāṣyam,* intro., commenting on *naraḥ*; Skt., p. 19; Venkatarathnam Naidu, p. 20; Bhashyam, p. 28.

37. Ibid., Skt., p. 22; Venkatarathnam Naidu, p. 22; Bhashyam, p. 31.

38. Ibid., Skt., p. 23; Venkatarathnam Naidu, pp. 23-24; Bhashyam, pp. 33-34.

39. Tirukkuruhai Pirān Piḷḷan, Sanskritized Tamil commentary on the *Tiruvāymoḻi,* known as the *Ārāyirappaḍi* or "Six Thousand"; the expressions *āśritasulabha, -sulabhatatva,* or *-sulabhatā* occur, for example, in 1.3.1, 1.3.2, 3.4.6., 3.4.9.

40. Ibid., 1.3.9, 3.1.9, 3.4.6, 3.5, intro.

41. Ibid., *āśrita parādhīna* in 2.7.11 and *āśritaparatantra* in 2.7.12. Cf. Rāmānuja's phrase *āśritavātsalyavivaśaḥ,* which occurs at the end of his introduction to the *Gītābhāṣya* (see chap. 5).

42. Cf. the first line of v. 20 in Kūraṭṭāḻvān's "Varadarājastava": "It is established by the Vedas that Thou art under no one else's control, but we consider that Thou art under the control of others [parādhīnam], dependent [paratantra] upon those who surrender [praṇata] to Thee." There are several references to the boy Krishna allowing His mother to tie Him to the millstone: "Atimānuṣastava," v. 41; "Varadarājastava," v. 70; and "Sundarabāhustava," v. 109. This last reads: "When Thou took a mortal form, Thou made Thyself to be tied to the stone and Thou wert weeping; Thou art easily accessible to Thy dependents." Parāśara Bhaṭṭar expresses similar sentiment with respect to the Lord's dependence, in His image form, on His worshiper: "The avatāras Thou hast assumed are countless, like Thy qualities. In the shrines of the world Thou art worshiped, and Thou bearest everything. Thy entire existence is under the control of the priests [arcaka-parādhīna]. Thy condition is a touching one for those with tender hearts" ("Śrīrangarājastava" 2.74).

43. "Six Thousand" commentary, 1.3.8; 3.2.6.

44. Ibid., 3.2.8.

45. Ibid., 6.10.8.

46. Ibid., 3.3.6.

47. Ibid., 1.1.1.

48. Ibid., 2.3.5.

49. Ibid., 8.1.6. The term *nirhetuka* also occurs in Piḷḷān's comment on 1.6.3, 2.6.8, and 6.10.3.

50. Lester, "Rāmānuja and Śrī-Vaiṣṇavism," esp. pp. 4-8.

51. There are two Sanskrit verse biographies purporting to be by contemporary

disciples of Rāmānuja. One is the *Yatirājavaibhavam*, attributed to Andhra Pūrṇa (Vaḍugu Nambi in Tamil), one of Rāmānuja's first converts during his exile in the Hoysala kingdom (modern Mysore State). A translation is published in *The Indian Antiquary* 38 (May 1909): 129 ff. A. Govindacharya sent in a brief "Note" published in a subsequent issue (40 [May 1911]: 152), in which he challenges the authenticity of this verse biography. The work is not mentioned in medieval times and appears to be a rather late attempt to support the Vaḍagalai version of the events of Rāmānuja's life and his choice of successor.

The other verse biography is the *Divya Sūri Carita*, a much longer poem, most of which is concerned with the lives of the Āḻvārs. It is attributed to Garuḍa Vāhana Paṇḍita, a disciple of Rāmānuja's at Śrīrangam. Some verses from it are quoted in the "Six Thousand" *Guruparamparāprabhāvam*. However, B. V. Ramanujam of Annamalai University has challenged its genuineness in an article published in the *Journal of Indian History*. He claims that it was a Sanskrit verse adaptation based on the Tamil "Six Thousand" (some verses from it were inserted in the "Six Thousand" later on, he suggests). Ramanujam's arguments are weighty, and they have not been satisfactorily refuted by the indefatigable defender of Tengalai orthodoxy, P. B. Annangarācārya of Kāñcī (in a Tamil pamphlet embodying his views, written by T. V. Parathasarati under the title *Divyasūricarita Kāla Nirdaranam*). The question does not seem to me to have yet been adequately settled. Even if the *Divya Sūri Carita* is not by a contemporary disciple of Rāmānuja's, it may well contain other early traditions besides those included in the "Six Thousand." Ramanujam suggests that this poetic history is intended as an epic poem (kāvya), not meant to be taken as the work of Rāmānuja's disciple, and that it may well have been written by a descendant of Garuḍa Vāhana Paṇḍita, since the name is really a family title.

52. Certain views of recent and contemporary Śrī Vaiṣṇava scholars on this question should be noted. M. R. Rajagopala Ayyangar of Chromepet (Madras) thinks that the difficulties can best be reconciled if we recognize that Rāmānuja considered prapatti to be a particular form of bhakti, rather than an alternative means to salvation. According to Principal N. S. Anantha Rangachar of Bangalore, that variant view had been voiced a generation ago by H. Srinivasa Iyengar, a renowned pandit of Bangalore, who propounded the view that for Rāmānuja prapatti was only an anga (branch) of bhakti, not an independent means to salvation. Anantha Rangachar himself believes that Rāmānuja and his predecessors did practice prapatti as an independent means to attain salvation, but they did not discuss the modes, techniques, or constituent parts of prapatti. Later writers expressed a number of different opinions, before definite conclusions were reached by Vedānta Deśika and Piḷḷai Lokācārya. One of the views that Deśika opposes is that Rāmānuja regarded prapatti only as an anga of bhakti. M. Yamunacharya, on the other hand, follows the Tengalai tradition's insistence that prapatti is the only means to attain God. However, strictly speaking, prapatti is not a means to salvation but the acknowledgment that God Himself must accomplish men's salvation. Yamunacharya is therefore willing to recognize that for Rāmānuja prapatti was more a spirit pervading the religious life, including karma, jñāna, and bhakti, than the particular cultic act that it tended to become in the later schools.

53. Compare Parāśara Bhaṭṭar's interpretations of the following divine names in his *Śrīviṣṇusahasranāmabhāṣyam.* "The 'Great Lord of all the worlds' means: He is endowed with all riches in order to satisfy all those who sing His praise." "'The Cause of all beings and their existence' means: He is the cause of the existence of all beings, other than non-being. He shows grace [anugraha] to all because of His quality of not abandoning anyone" (commenting on names in stanzas 6 and 7 of the introduction). "'The All [Sarvaḥ]' means: He pervades everything; He looks upon everything as His own body and protects it" (name 25). "'The Constant One [sthāṇuḥ]' means: He who possesses firm grace [anugraha]. The touch of God does not rest with simply removing the defect from the soul, like ordinary purificatory rituals, nor with simply fulfilling the wish of the worshiper, like other divine beings [devatās] who preside over various rites. . . . Not even great obstacles impede His touch, nor is it removed or insulted. Even when He has extinguished all inconspicuous things and fulfilled all the wishes of His devotees, He does not stop for even a moment's rest [but continues to seek ways to increase their welfare]" (name 28). "'The Lord [Īśvaraḥ]'means: He is Īśvaraḥ because his aiśvarya [wealth] of usefulness is greater during His incarnations than in His supreme estate" (name 36). "He is called 'The Lord of all [Sarveśvaraḥ]' because He quickly accepts those who have taken refuge with Him [śaraṇāgatas], whether they are capable or incapable of attaining Him, in order to remove the delay and confusion" (name 97). "'The Unshaken One [Acyutaḥ]' means: He never leaves those who have surrendered to Him" (name 101). "The flow of grace [anugraha] toward His dependents cannot be measured. That is why He is called, 'Whose soul is immeasurable [Ameyātmā]'" (name 103). "'The adorner [Bhūṣaṇaḥ]': He who is the Lord of Śrī adorns Himself with the quality of gracious condescension, because of which He considers all to be equal. It is no discredit for a rich person to become a guest in a family without any means of support, to share with them their food and their livelihood. Quite the contrary, it redounds to his credit" (name 635). "'Wealth [Bhūtiḥ]': He is wealth because for those who do not have any means, internal or external, He is complete wealth. He is their wealth like a son or an esteemed friend" (name 636). "'He who is worshiped [Arcitaḥ]': Arca means incarnated as an image [arcāvatāra]. This incarnation is not far off, like His supreme state [paratva], nor is it like the celestial or human avatāras, which occurred at particular times and places, for He is always present in all the holy places and houses in a perceivable state [pratyakṣatva]" (name 640). "He is called 'the Entirely Pure Self [viśuddhātmā]' because He has given up His entire wealth to all His dependents" (name 642).

54. I have tried to respond to a number of the points raised by Pandit Agnihothram Rāmānuja Thatachariar (n. 1, above), and I deal with the question of the role of Śrī in chap. 18. Some points remain that require additional comment.

I find puzzling the reference to the utterance of the Dvaya mantra being sufficient to remove all obstacles to the achievement of bhakti. It is possible that Rāmānuja took the verbalization of the act of surrender in a secret and auspicious formula as a symbol for a surrender to God, not just as a particular act, but as a lifelong attitude that was the very basis of his religious life.

The occurrence of the names of a particular Divine image (Śrī Ranganātha) in a stotra-like work seems quite understandable, on the basis of the practice of both the Āl̲vārs and, more important in this respect, Yāmuna. The remarkable thing is really that a person who for so many years lived in Śrīrangam and worshiped in the temple should only once use the name of the presiding deity there. Rajagopala Ayyangar thinks that there is one parallel to this in the earlier works of Rāmānuja, that the "Śrīnivāsa" in the mangalaśloka of the *Śrībhāṣya* is a veiled reference to the Divine image, Venkaṭeśvara, in the temple at Tirupati. Whether or not there is such a parallel, the use of the name does not seem to me to imply an explicit acceptance of the Pāñcarātric theory of arcāvatāra about which, as Pandit Agnihothram rightly points out, Rāmānuja is completely silent. Pandit Agnihothram does admit, however, that Rāmānuja regularly worshiped images of the Deity. Now the passage in which the name Śrī Ranganātha appears is precisely such an act of worship. The idea that in such worship Rāmānuja could have accepted the image as a "mere symbol" runs contrary to everything we know about his religious environment.

It is difficult for an outsider to judge the appropriateness of the description of the transcendent realm in the *Vaikuṇṭhagadya,* but it does not seem to me to be so different from many Purāṇic passages as to justify the charge of "sheer poetic invention." It is quite possible that it draws much more freely on non-Vedic texts, without citing them, than do Rāmānuja's doctrinal works, but this is not a doctrinal work defining tattva (ontological categories) but a devotional writing which is meant to be helpful in daily meditation.

The final point that Pandit Agnihothram makes is actually basic to all the rest. He contends that in trying to decide whether the *Gadyatraya* and the *Nityagrantha* are genuine, we must compare them in the first place with *Śrībhāṣya,* recognizing that as Rāmānuja's most important work and the one which must be taken as defining his views on all subjects. He holds that the *Vedārthasaṃgraha* is of secondary importance and that the *Gītābhāṣya* is definitely even less important, since it is commenting on the *Bhagavadgītā,* which Rāmānuja recognized as Smṛti, a lower level of Scripture than the Śruti texts on which he is commenting in the *Śrībhāṣya.*

It is true that much of Rāmānuja's fame rests on the *Śrībhāṣya* and that it is there that he has most fully dealt with many metaphysical topics, but this does not mean that we must necessarily refer to the *Śrībhāṣya* to get Rāmānuja's definitive view on any topic. Pandit Agnihothram may prefer the *Śrībhāṣya* because of his particular theological views and his predilection for the Vedas, but the setting of the *Śrībhāṣya* above Rāmānuja's other works is as unwarranted on the principles of modern historical scholarship as it is abhorrent to the sentiments of the Śrī Vaiṣṇava community. As historians we must study each work seriously, keeping in mind its particular purpose and scope, and we have no basis for establishing any hierarchy in value or for assuming complete uniformity in views throughout an author's writings. Moreover, it is quite illegitimate to extend the principle of preeminence of Śruti above Smṛti to different works of Rāmānuja, for he has tried to base his comments in all his works on both Śruti and Smṛti.

55. Rajagopala Ayyangar, *Gadya-Traya,* intro., pp. 2-3; Bhashyam, *Śaraṇāgati Gadya,* p. iv.

56. Cf. van Buitenen, *Rāmānuja on the Bhagavadgītā*, intro., pp. 9-12, and *VedS*, intro., p. 32.

57. Van Buitenen, *VedS*, intro., pp. 32-33.

58. I have discussed one significant example of Rāmānuja's oral comments on the *Tiruvāymoḻi* at the end of chap. 18.

59. *ŚarG*, para. 5.

CHAPTER 18

1. MW, p. 803.
2. *VedS*, para. 127.
3. *GBh*, intro., p. 1.
4. *ŚarG*, paras. 1.5.
5. *VedS*, paras. 97, 127, 135.
6. *VedS*, para. 133.
7. *ŚarG*, para. 1, commentary by Sudarśana Sūri (*Gadyatrayavyākhyā*).
8. *ŚarG*, paras. 1, 5.
9. *NGr*, p. 182.
10. *ŚarG*, paras. 1, 7.
11. *VG*, para. 4, following Rajagopala Ayyangar's translation except for spelling.
12. *VG*, para. 4.
13. *NGr*, p. 184.
14. MW, p. 2098.
15. Kūraṭṭāḻvān's brief hymn in praise of Śrī ("Śrīstava") is distinguished from Rāmānuja's writing by its vivid imagery, but the understanding of the Goddess appears to be identical to that held by Rāmānuja: Śrī is united with Her Lord in all His activities. She, too, is supremely gracious, but this grace is as much connected with creation as redemption, and there is no suggestion that forgiveness is Her special function or that She must recommend sinners to the Lord. The first verse is an indicative statement: "The Lord [Bhagavān] pervades the entire universe, creating, maintaining, and destroying it, creating heaven, hell, and final liberation [mokṣa]. After He has been captivated [parādhīna] by the charming glance of Śrī so that He forms a common will [aikarasya] with Her, He ordains the entire universe. This is nothing but His sport." The poet ascribes to Śrī control over the wealth, beauty, and intelligence of all creatures. She is given a significant role in creation itself. "During the period of dissolution [pralaya], this universe lacked Thy grace and thereby lost its status. The same flower has now unfolded because of Thy soft glance. We take refuge with Śrī, who is the Queen of the God of gods" (v. 10). In the last verse, the poet takes "refuge" with Śrī, but this is because of the lordly power of Śrī rather than specifically because of Her forgiving nature. "May Lakṣmī, the Queen of Śrī Rangarāja, look also at me, for by Her momentary glance they [the created deities] become great lords" (v. 11).

Parāśara Bhaṭṭar wrote a much longer hymn to Śrī, called the "Śrīguṇaratnakośa." Most of the verses develop the same themes expressed in his father's shorter hymn. The following statements are of interest. "I bow down to Śrī, by whose glance the seven worlds are protected [pālita]" (v. 2). "The movement of Śrī's eyebrow is the authority for God's ranking all things, both material and animate" (v. 4). "Everything from the control over a small village to the lordship over the universe is the result of a few sparks of Thy glance" (v. 15). "Thy beloved created the universe for the sake of Thy play" (v. 19). "The inherent independence of the Lord comes only through Thy embrace. O Mother, . . . the Scriptures do not speak separately about Thee, for Thou art inside God" (v. 28). "O Śrī, by nature Thou art God's own property" (v. 31). In verse 32, Bhaṭṭar lists qualities shared by Śrī and Bhagavān, one of which is *praṇata-varaṇa-prema* (receiving and loving those who prostrate). In verse 34, he notes certain specifically masculine qualities of the Lord and the "appropriate feminine qualities" of Śrī "such as soft-heartedness [mradiman], being subordinate to one's husband [pati-pārārthya], compassion [karuṇa], and forgiveness or patience [kṣamā]." In verse 52, Bhaṭṭar approaches the later doctrine of Śrī. "Thy beloved sometimes becomes agitated by the shortcomings of the people of this world and acts like a father to correct them for their own good [hita]. [Then] Thou dost become like a mother to make Him forget their defects, saying 'What is this? In this world who is without defect?'" The final verse of the hymn is as follows: "May we live in this Śrīrangam for hundreds of years, being the dust of Thy feet, enjoying with our friends the wealth of the taste of Thy service without obstruction or sorrow and with joy. Thou art my father and mother and my dharma. Without any cause [akasmāt] please take mercy on us" (v. 61).

Tirukkuruhai Pirān Piḷḷān is the only one of Rāmānuja's disciples, to my knowledge, to use the term *puruṣakāra* (mediator or mediatrix), which later became standard in the understanding of Śrī by both Vaḍagalai and Tengalai Śrī Vaiṣṇavas. In addition to his comment on *Tiruvāymoḻi* 6.10.10 cited in the text, he has made some other comments with the same purport. In 1.4.7 the commentator paraphrases the anguished devotee to say, "If the Lord refuses even this message that I am wasting away, report it to Him in the presence of the Goddess Śrī [Piraṭṭi]."

16. K. C. Varadachari, *Idea of God,* pp. 111-12.
17. Ibid., p. 120.
18. Ibid.
19. Ibid., pp. 123, 124.
20. Ibid., p. 127.
21. Schrader, *Introduction,* p. 30.
22. Ibid., p. 31.
23. Ibid., p. 21.
24. Ibid., pp. 17-18.
25. Vaḍakku Tiruvīdi Piḷḷai, *Mupattārāyirappaḍi* [Thirty-six Thousand] or *Īḍu*, Commentary on Nammāḻvār's *Tiruvāymoḻi* 1.3, intro.
26. Govindacharya, *Divine Wisdom,* pp. 17-18.
27. Yāmuna's *Gītārthasaṃgraha,* v. 13. This work appears as an appendix in both van Buitenen's and Sampatkumaran's translations of Rāmānuja's *Gītābhāṣya.* The page references are: van Buitenen, p. 180; Sampatkumaran, p. 539. See also Bhashyam's translation *Gītārthasangraha-Gītāsāra* (with Vedānta Deśika's commentary), pp. 30-33. There is also a translation with extended

explanations by V. K. Ramanujachari: *Gītārtha Sangraha* by Yāmunārya; the translation of v. 13 is given on p. 66.

28. *Bhagavadgītā* 9.11-13.

29. *GBh* 9.11-13, p. 80.

CHAPTER 19

1. In 1887, Pieter Daniel Chantepie de la Saussaye, then Professor of the History of Religions at the University of Amsterdam, published the first volume of the first edition of his *Lehrbuch der Religionsgeschichte.* In 1891 this was published in an English translation by Beatrice S. Colyer-Fergusson, daughter of Friedrich Max Müller, with her father's encouragement and assistance. Only this first volume appeared in English, bearing the title, *Manual of the Science of Religion.* In his foreword the author states the intention of the second section of the first volume, called "Phänomenologischer Theil." "The phenomenological section might well be [*dürfte sein*] the first more comprehensive attempt so to order the principal groups of religious phenomena [*Erscheinungen*], without giving them a unified explanation from a single point of view [*ohne sie doctrinär einheitlich zu erklären*], that the most important aspects and points of view come forth of their own accord [*von selbst hervortreten*] out of the material." Chantepie de la Saussaye goes on to his subject as follows: "The science of religion has as its task the study of religion, of its essence [*Wesen*] and of its manifestations [*Erscheinungen*]. It divides itself naturally into philosophy of religion and history of religion. These two parts are most closely connected: philosophy would be vain and empty if while defining the Idea of religion it should lose sight of the factual material before us. Just as little can history dispense with philosophy: not only arranging and assessing [*Ordnung und Beurtheilung*] religious phenomena, but even determining that a particular phenomenon is of a religious nature, depends on some conception, even if only preliminary, of the essence of religion. . . . The collecting and grouping of various religious manifestations [*Erscheinungen*] forms the transition from history of religion to philosophy of religion" (pp. 7-8). Chantepie de la Saussaye omitted the phenomenological section from the expanded second and third editions of his *Lehrbuch* because he felt that it deserved a larger treatment in a separate work, but he never himself produced this larger phenomenology of religion. In a fourth edition (1925) published after Chantepie's death, Edvard Lehmann reintroduced this section under the title, "Erscheinungs und Ideenwelt der Religionen."

2. Three other polarities in Rāmānuja's conception of God have been suggested by a number of his modern interpreters: (1) transcendence and immanence, (2) unity and plurality, and (3) the Absolute Brahman and the God of religion.

The first of these polarities is expressed briefly by van Buitenen. "God is immanent inasmuch as He is the inner ruler of prakṛti and ātman but transcendent as He is entirely self-sufficient and does in no way depend on them. They are nothing but the spillings of the plenitude of His being which is eternally expanding and retracting, eternally creating and dissolving" (*GBh*, intro., p. 2). He contrasts Rāmānuja's conception with Śankara's: "Whereas for Śankara brahman is the *Other,* and he goes ever farther the way of excluding from its concept all that is related to the world, to the point of denying the reality of this world in the final analysis, Rāmānuja worships a God that is verily *Supreme* and includes in His concept all that is of the world, to the point of affirming this world just because it is related to God. Devout Vaiṣṇava if ever there was one, his vision can be understood. Viṣṇu, the god of incarnations *par excellence,* who in every age takes personally a hand in the direction of the world's affairs, god of preservation and maintenance, who pervades the Universe, the Viśvarūpa and omnipresent one, will lead his devotee to a very different conception of Absolute and World from that to which Śiva would inspire, the god of annihilation, who represents yogic renunciation and systematic abnegation" (*VedS,* intro., pp. 65-66).

S. S. Raghavachar lists what he considers nine elements of marvel in the nature of Brahman, as conceived by Rāmānuja, most of which hinge on the combination of transcendence and immanence. The first is Brahman's "uniqueness, transcendence, and utter magnificence." "His self-sufficiency and fullness of inward perfection is not reduced or altered by His exercise of cosmic control. . . . [It is] not a case of reciprocal dependence. . . . The infinite is related to the finite in a unique way. . . . God is one and undivided in His supreme reality of infinite perfection. But He becomes many. He maintains abiding unity of existence in and through infinite plurality of self-manifestation. . . . To such a vision of God comprehending the cosmic and the supercosmic . . . the pluralities of cosmic manifestation do not have their pluralizing effect. All is one supreme beauty and power, loveliness and grandeur, the one spirit of boundless light and joy" (*Introduction to the Vedarthasangraha,* pp. 100-2). Perhaps even more than the polarity of transcendence and immanence, it is the combination of unity and plurality both in God and in His Universe that impresses Raghavachar as a great marvel. We have seen that he refers to paratva and saulabhya in describing the Divine beauty, but in discussing the Divine "marvels" he does not mention the marvel that the Supreme Lord should descend into the world of imperfection and condescend to have fellowship with imperfect creatures.

K. C. Varadachari does note the importance of the Divine incarnations, but for him they are evidence of God's real transcendence. "God in the philosophy of Śri Rāmānuja is not merely transcendent and immanent to the universe but is also the redemptive Creator. . . . The theism of Rāmānuja claims to implement the truth of the Deity as immanent, as pervading everywhere and at all times, and transcendent as Governor and Enjoyer. His 'otherness' in respect of the created is finely and superbly represented by His unique descents into His creatures and Creation for purposes of greatest value and worth to mankind" (*Idea of God,* p. 143).

A major concern of A. Govindacharya's writings is to emphasize the Divine saulabhya. Rāmānuja's "message to man was the inalienability of the relation between God and the soul, in its several aspects of love. The main feature of his reform consisted in the declaration of God, not as cold, but as very loving" (*Divine Wisdom,* p. xiii).

P. N. Srinivasachari has clearly recognized the polarity of paratva and saulabhya in Rāmānuja's own thought. "The Lord of redemptive love sets aside His cosmic glory and *Īśvaratva* and delights to dwell in the hearts of all beings in spite of the filthiness of the body. . . . Eternally self-realized in His transcendental abode, He pours Himself into the cosmos and by His pervading identity imparts to it all the unique richness, colour and life. In His infinite love, He spurns His *Īśvaratva* and assumes human forms with a view to recover and redeem the prodigals and to revel in the ecstacy of communion with them. . . . The chief postulate of religion is the immediate knowability of God. There is a certain paradox in religious belief arising out of the contrary ideas of contrast and unity. The infinite majesty and goodness of God instill a feeling of human littleness and divine unapproachableness. At the same time religion has a living faith in eternal affinity and communion with Him. The sense of alienation that oppresses the finite self is finally subdued by the irresistibility of divine love and grace" (*Philosophy of Viśiṣṭādvaita,* pp. 54, 59, 67). Srinivasachari has rightly sensed the paradox, but his deriving it from "the contrary ideas of contrast and unity" does not quite fit Rāmānuja's thought. It is not the paradox of simultaneous likeness and unlikeness between the essence of God and the essence of the finite self but the twin facts of distance and nearness in their existential relations that occupy Rāmānuja. Moreover, Rāmānuja believes that God does not entirely divest Himself either of His cosmic glory or of His essential lordship when He descends to dwell *with* men (as an avatāra) or *in* them (as the antaryāmī).

3. See chap. 5, above.

4. Saint Thomas's own teaching may well have been more nuanced, more "Augustinian," and less rationalistic than that of his late scholastic and post-Tridentine interpreters. Certainly there have been a variety of positions in Christian theological thinking through the centuries on the nature of faith, reason, and intuition and on their mutual relations. Saint Thomas's synthesis of Aristotelian, Neoplatonic, and biblical traditions was at first regarded with grave suspicion by church authorities and never in the medieval period became the Roman Catholic theology par excellence. It was perhaps not until the nineteenth century that "Thomism" gained such preeminence in the Roman Catholic church, but it certainly had great influence on the thought of Western Europe from Saint Thomas's time onward, not least in the reactions it produced and in its indirect influence on the rationalist philosophies of the eighteenth-century Englightenment. Thomism formed an important link between interreligious philosophical discussions among Jews, Muslims, and Christians in the early Middle Ages and post-Enlightenment philosophies of religion.

5. There is another Roman Catholic view of general revelation that is historicist rather than rationalist: religions are considered to retain fragments of the original monotheism of Adam, confirmed through God's general covenant with Noah. It is the value of human religion passed down through all the generations since Noah that is here affirmed, rather than a general capacity of human reason to know God apart from revelation. This more positive Roman Catholic view of human religion generally also had its effect on missionary practice: the willingness to make accommodations to pre-Christian

practices and to regard such previous religion as in some sense a "preparation" for the Catholic church. Such a notion of preparation was and is easier for Roman Catholics to accept than for many Protestants. On the one hand, Catholics see a greater gulf between the Church and the People of Israel than do many Protestants (especially Calvinists); on the other hand, Catholics see a greater affinity between the religion of Israel and other pre-Christian religions than do Lutherans and Calvinists. Such a notion of "preparation" was of great importance for practical missionary policy, but it was of less concern for systematic theological assessment, since it was linked to the doctrine of *logoi spermatikoi,* the scattered seeds of the Divine reason, which were more readily discoverable in Greek philosophical systems than in pagan cults. This was true for patristic and medieval Christian theologians. It is only very recently that non-Christian cults have been positively evaluated by some contemporary Roman Catholic theologians. (See the following note.)

6. Recent Roman Catholic thinking on "theology of religions" has brought together two lines of previous thought: on the one hand, natural theology, man's capacity to know God apart from the revelation in Christ, and on the other hand, natural religion, the positive value of all human religion as a means for communion with God, whether or not this religion is seen in any historical continuity with the religion of Adam or Noah. A third line is the Augustinian emphasis on grace, sometimes reinforced by Protestant emphasis on the Christological determination of grace. The "Declaration on the Relationship of the Church to Non-Christian Religions" of the Second Vatican Council (Walter M. Abbott, S.J., ed., *The Documents of Vatican II* [New York: America Press, 1966], pp. 660-68) is significant in its general direction and certainly in what it does not say, e.g., other religions are not described as "superstitious." The specific formulations of different Catholic theologians vary considerably. Perhaps most influential are the views of Karl Rahner, worked out succinctly in his article, "Das Christentum und die nichtchristlichen Religionen," *Schriften zur Theologie* 5 (1962): 136-58. H. R. Schlette has elaborated his views in *Die Religionen als Thema der Theologie: Uberlegungen zu einer "Theologie der Religion"* (Freiburg: Herder, 1963). Roman Catholic missionaries in various countries have developed their theological views with reference to specific religious and cultural contexts. Some of the recent thinking of Jesuits in India is indicated in *Religious Hinduism* (Allahabad, 1964), by R. De Smet and J. Neuner, et al. The various works of Raymond Panikkar should also be noted, especially *The Unknown Christ of Hinduism* (London: Darton, Longman and Todd,

7. A striking example is F. R. Tennant, *Philosophical Theology,* 2 vols. (Cambridge: University Press, 1930).

8. In his discussion of the important third sūtra, *śāstra-yonitvāt* (Because Scripture is the source), Rāmānuja affirms that Brahman cannot be known by perception or inference, but only through Scripture. He therefore attempts to refute two arguments proving the existence of God. The first argues from Rāmānuja's own soul-body analogy: as we may infer the existence of an in-

dwelling soul from the presence of a living body, so we may infer the existence of a Supreme Soul animating and supporting the material world. Rāmānuja replies that even if the analogy is granted, it does not prove what is desired about the Supreme Soul, for the finite soul does not create its body or entirely support it. The analogy fails, however, because the material world lacks the breathing character of living organisms. The second argument is that the world is an effect that requires a number of causes: the agent, the material, the instrument for fashioning the material, the purpose in making it, and the person to be saved by the thing produced. Rāmānuja replies that it would first be necessary to prove that a number of finite souls could not produce the world, especially souls that had acquired remarkable powers through the efficacy of their sacrifices. Moreover, Rāmānuja doubts whether a world consisting of mountains and oceans has the character of a product or effected thing. There are also logical problems in determining whether the presumed Creator creates with a body or without it. (*SBh* 1.1.3, pp. 107-11; Thibaut, pp. 161-73. Cf. Kumarappa, *Hindu Conception of the Deity*, pp. 152-59.)

9. Walter G. Neevel, Jr., is discussing this question in his Ph.D. dissertation for Harvard University on the Philosophy of Yāmuna, now in preparation.

10. See n. 2 above. Rāmānuja explicitly attempts a refutation of the Vaiśeṣika position of Kaṇāda (similar to that of Nyāya) in the so-called *ārambhana-adhikaraṇa*, the group of sūtras (2.1.15-20) dealing with the origination of the cosmos. Rāmānuja here upholds the view that the effect (the pot) is non-different from the cause (the clay). The implication is clear that the material cause is primary and that Brahman in His causal state, with the world in subtle form as His body during the state of dissolution (pralaya) is that primary material or substantial cause of the universe in its present manifest state. (*SBh* 2.1.15-20, pp. 226-40; Thibaut, pp. 430-67.)

11. Neo-Reformation theology has reacted strongly against two of the intellectual currents that informed liberal Protestant thought: Schleiermacher's derivation of Protestant Christian theology from the particular Christian form of human religious experience, and Hegel's treatment of Christian religion as the rationally still-unclarified form of the culmination of human intellectual development and Divine self-disclosure. It is significant that Karl Barth places his critique of religion in the prolegomena of his dogmatics. He wants to reject religion or piety as the proper starting point for Protestant Christian theology. The section is entitled "Gottes Offenbarung als Aufhebung der Religion," which the English translators have rendered as "The Revelation of God as the Abolition of Religion" (*Die kirchliche Dogmatik*, vol. 1, pt. 2, pp. 304-96; *Church Dogmatics*, vol. 1, pt. 2, pp. 280-361).

12. Barth, *Church Dogmatics*, vol. 1, pt. 2, *The Doctrine of the Word of God*, p. 327.

13. This interpretation is advanced in a Ph.D. dissertation submitted to Yale University in 1963 by Allan W. Loy, entitled "The Theological Interpretation of the Relation of Christianity to Other Religions, with Particular Reference to Karl Barth." Loy seeks to demonstrate that *Aufhebung* has the same multiple meanings it has for Hegel and therefore would prefer *elevation* to the word *abolition* used by Barth's translators. "Barth does not mean by 'the abolition of religion' the dissolution of the religious capacity. Not only

does his view of the possibility of true religion rule out this interpretation, but [scattered] indications that he regards religion as something essentially human; the religious capacity is necessary to the human creature" (p. 85). When Barth does use *Aufhebung* in the sense of "abolition," he is referring, Loy maintains, not to the actual world of human religions, but to the formal category of human self-determination diametrically opposed to the grace of God in Jesus Christ (pp. 89, 97-98). "If Barth had broken through to the concrete and if he had taken fully into account the empirical reality of the religions, is it not possible that he may have found that religion and the religions also form a 'sphere of God's commanding' and that not only the political and the cultural life of man, but also his religious life is subject to that commanding in other terms besides 'crisis' and 'contradiction'?" Loy answers his own question affirmatively and spends much of his dissertation working out some of the implications of this unrealized possibility in Barth's theology.

14. "In His revelation God is present in the world of human religion." The connection between revelation and religion must "again be seen as identical with that event between God and man in which God is God, i.e., the Lord and Master of man, who Himself judges and alone justifies and sanctifies, and man is the man of God, i.e. man as he is adopted and received by God in His severity and goodness. It is because we remember and apply the Christological doctrine of *assumptio carnis* that we speak of revelation as the *Aufhebung* of religion." "A theological evaluation of religion and religions must be characterized primarily by the great cautiousness and charity of its assessments and judgments. It will observe and understand and take man in all seriousness as the subject of religion. But it will not be man apart from God, in a human *per se.* It will be man for whom (whether he knows it or not) Jesus Christ was born, died and rose again. It will be man who (whether he has already heard it or not) is intended in the Word of God. It will be man who (whether he is aware of it or not) has in Christ his Lord. It will always understand religion as a vital utterance and activity of this man" (ibid., p. 297).

The Dutch Calvinists Korff, Bavinck, and Kraemer have paid more explicit attention to the ambivalent nature and value of the human religious consciousness. F. W. A. Korff, *Het Christelijk Geloof en de Niet-Christelijke Godsdiensten* [Christian Faith and Non-Christian Religions]. J. H. Bavinck, *Religieus Besef en Christelijk Geloof* [Religious Consciousness and Christian Faith]. Hendrik Kraemer, *Religion and the Christian Faith.*

15. Richard Garbe, *India and Christendom.*

16. Barth, *Church Dogmatics,* vol. 1, pt. 2, p. 340.

17. Ibid., pp. 341-42.

18. Otto, *Gnadenreligion Indiens.*

19. Barth, *Church Dogmatics,* vol. 1, pt. 2, p. 344.

20. Bishop A. J. Appasamy has written much on this general subject. Of particular interest here is his little book on H. A. Krishna Piḷḷai, a non-Brahman Christian convert in the nineteenth century from Tengalai Śrī Vaiṣṇavism. The work is entitled, *Tamil Christian Poet: The Life and Writings of H. A. Krishna Pillai.* A more thorough study of Krishna Piḷḷai and his Tengalai Śrī

Vaiṣṇava background is given in D. Dennis Hudson, "The Life and Times of H. A. Krishna Pillai (1827-1900): A Study in the Encounter of Tamil Sri Vaishnava Hinduism and Evangelical Protestant Christianity in Nineteenth Century Tirunelveli District" (Ph.D. dissertation, Claremont Graduate School, 1970).

21. Cf. P. Y. Luke and John B. Carman, *Village Christians and Hindu Culture: Study of a Rural Church in Andhra Pradesh, South India.*

Bibliography

Texts and Translations of Rāmānuja's Writings, and Introductions to Specific Works and His Thought as a Whole

Anantarangācārya, N. S., ed. *Śaraṇāgatigadyam* of Rāmānuja with Sudarśana Sūri's *Vyākhyā.* Sanskrit. Bangalore: N. S. Anantarangācārya, 1879 Śaka.

Annangarācārya, P. B., ed. *Śrī-Bhagavad-Rāmānuja-Granthamālā.* Complete works in Sanskrit. Kāñcīpuram: Granthamālā Office, 1956.

Bharadwaj, Krishna Datta. *The Philosophy of Rāmānuja.* New Delhi: Sir Shankar Lall Charitable Trust Society, 1958.

Bhashyam, K. *Śaraṇāgati Gadya* of Rāmānuja. Text and translation with translation of Sudarśana Sūri's commentary. Madras: Ubhaya Vedanta Granthamala, 1959.

——. *Vedanta Deepa* of Rāmānuja [*Vedāntadīpa*]. Sanskrit text and English translation. Tamil translation by Uttamur Viraraghavacharya. 2 vols. Madras: Ubhaya Vedanta Granthamala, 1957-59.

Buitenen, J. A. B. van. *Rāmānuja on the Bhagavadgītā.* Condensed translation of *Gītābhāṣya.* The Hague: Ned. Boek en Steendrukkerij, 1953.

——. *Rāmānuja's Vedārthasaṃgraha.* Critical text and translation with notes. Poona: Deccan College Postgraduate and Research Institute, 1956.

Govindacharya, Alkondavilli. *The Life of Rāmānujāchārya.* Madras: S. Murthy, 1906.

——. *Śrī Bhagavad-Gītā, with Rāmānuja's Commentary in English.* Madras, 1898.

Hohenberger, A. *Rāmānuja: Ein Philosoph indischer Gottesmystik.* Bonn: Selbstverlag des Orientalischen Seminars der Universität Bonn, 1960.

——. *Rāmānuja's Vedāntadīpa: seine Kurzauslegung der Brahmasūtren des Bādarāyaṇa.* German translation. Bonn: Selbstverlag des Orientalischen Seminars der Universität Bonn, 1964.

Karmarkar, R. D., ed. and trans. *Śrībhāṣya of Rāmānuja.* University of Poona Sanskrit and Prakrit Series, vol. 1 (in three parts). Poona: University of Poona, 1962.

Kumarappa, Bharatan. *The Hindu Conception of the Deity, as Culminating in Rāmānuja.* London: Luzac, 1934.

Lacombe, Olivier. *L'Absolu selon le Védânta: Les notions de Brahman et d'Atman dans les systèmes de Cankara et Râmânoudja.* Paris: Librairie Orientaliste Paul Geuthner, 1937.

——. *La doctrine morale et métaphysique de Rāmānuja.* Text and French translation, with notes, on *Śrībhāṣya* 1.1.1. Paris: Adrien-Maisonneuve, 1938.

Lazarus, F. K. *Rāmānuja and Bowne: A Study in Comparative Philosophy.* Bombay: Chetana, 1962.

Manalapuzhavila, Antony. *Nature and Origin of the World according to Rāmānuja.* Alwaye (India): St. Joseph's Pontifical Seminary, 1966.

Narasimha Ayyangar, M. B. *Vedāntasāra of Rāmānuja.* Madras: Adyar Library, 1953.

Norton, James. "The Mahāsiddhānta of Rāmānuja's *Śrībhāṣya.*" Unpublished article.

Otto, Rudolf. *Siddhānta des Rāmānuja.* German translation of *Śrībhāṣya* 1.1.1. Jena: Eugen Diederichs, 1917.

Periya Āccān Piḷḷai. *Gadyavyākhyānam.* Tamil commentary. In *Gadyatrayam* with the commentaries of Sudarśana Sūri, Periya Āccān Piḷḷai, and Vedānta Deśika. Sanskrit and Tamil text in Telugu script. Kāñcīpuram: Śrīvaiṣṇavagrantha Mudrāpaka Sabhai, 1916.

Raghavachar, S. S. *Introduction to the Vedarthasangraha.* Mangalore: Mangalore Trading Assn., 1957.

——. *Vedārthasaṃgraha* of Rāmānuja. Text and translation. Mysore: Sri Ramakrishna Ashrama, 1956.

Rajagopala Ayyangar, M. R. *The Gadya-Traya of Rāmānuja.* Text and translation. Madras: published by the author, n.d.

——. *Vedartha Sangraha* of Rāmānuja. Translation with introduction. Chromepet (Madras): published by the author, 1956.

Ramakrishnananda. *Life of Ramanuja.* Madras: Sri Ramakrishna Math, 1959.

Rangacharya, M., and Varadaraja Aiyangar, M. B. *The Vedānta-Sūtras with the Śrī-Bhāshya of Rāmānuja.* Madras: Education Publishing Co., vol. 1, 2d ed., 1961, vols. 2 and 3, 1964, 1965.

Rangacharyulu, M. *Life and Teachings of Ramanuja, or the Spirit of Visishtadwaita.* Revised and edited by T. S. Parthasarathy. N.p.: Sri Bhashyakaraswami Avatara Mantapa Kainkarya Sabha, 1951.

Sampatkumaran, M. R. *The Gitabhashya of Ramanuja.* Madras: Professor M. Rangacharya Memorial Trust [1969].

Sen Gupta, Anima. *A Critical Study of the Philosophy of Rāmānuja.* Banaras: Chowkhamba Sanskrit Series Office (vol. 55), 1967.

Srinivasa Aiyengar, C. R. *The Life and Teachings of Sri Ramanujacharya.* Madras: R. Venkateshwar & Co., n.d.

Subramanian, T. N. "A Note on the Date of Rāmānuja." *South Indian Temple Inscriptions,* vol. 3, pt. 2. Madras Government Oriental Series, no. 157, pp. 145-60.

Sudarśana Sūri. *Gadyatrayavyākhyā.* Sanskrit commentary. In *Gadyatrayam* with the commentaries of Sudarśana Sūri, Periya Āccān Piḷḷai, and Vedānta Deśika. Sanskrit and Tamil text in Telugu script. Kāñcīpuram: Śrīvaiṣṇavagrantha Mudrāpaka Sabhai, 1916. English translation by K. Bhashyam under the title, *Sri Bhagavad-Ramanuja's Saranaagati Gadya,* in Ubhaya Vedanta Granthamala Series. Madras: Liberty Press, n.d.

——. *Śrutaprakāśikā.* Sanskrit commentary on Rāmānuja's *Śrībhāṣya.* 2 vols. New Delhi: Government of India, 1967.

——. *Tātparyadīpikā.* Commentary in Sanskrit on Rāmānuja's *Vedārthasaṃgraha.* Vṛndāvana, 1978 Śaka (equivalent to A.D. 1900).

Sukhtankar, Vasudev Anant. *The Teachings of the Vedānta according to Rāmānuja.* Vienna: Adolf Holzhausen, 1908.

Thibaut, George. *The Vedānta-Sūtras with the Commentary by Rāmānuja.*

Translation. Sacred Books of the East, vol. 48. Oxford: Clarendon Press, 1904.
Varadachari, K. C. *Sri Ramanuja's Theory of Knowledge.* Tirupati: Tirumalai-Tirupati Devasthanams Press, 1956.
Vedānta Deśika. *Gadyabhāṣyam.* Sanskrit commentary. In *Gadyatrayam* with the commentaries of Sudarśana Sūri, Periya Āccān Piḷḷai, and Vedānta Deśika. Sanskrit and Tamil text in Telugu script. Kāñcīpuram: Śrīvaiṣṇavagrantha Mudrāpaka Sabhai, 1916.
Viraraghavacharya, Uttamur. *Bhāṣyārtha Darpaṇa.* Modern Sanskrit commentary on Rāmānuja's *Śrībhāṣya.* Madras: published by the author, vol. 1, 1963, vol. 2, 1964.
Yamunacharya, M. *Rāmānuja's Teachings in His Own Words.* Bhavan's Book University, vol. 111. Bombay: Bharatiya Vidya Bhavan, 1963.

OTHER WORKS

Annangarācārya, P. B., ed. *Stotramālā.* Kāñcīpuram: Granthamālā Office, 1958. (N.B. Unless otherwise specified, references to Śrī Vaiṣṇava hymns in the bibliography and notes are to this collection of stotras.)
Anonymous. *Jitantā Stotra.* Ancient Śrī Vaiṣṇava hymn, with Periya Āccān Piḷḷai's commentary. Kāñcīpuram: Śrīvaiṣṇavagrantha Mudrāpaka Sabhai, 1919.
Appasamy, A. J. *Tamil Christian Poet: The Life and Writings of H. A. Krishna Pillai.* World Christian Books, no. 56, 3d series. London: Lutterworth Press, 1966.
Aruḷāḷa Perumāḷ Emberumānār. *Jñānasāram and Prameyasāram.* With Manavāḷamāmuni's commentary. Kāñcīpuram: Śrī Vaiṣṇava Grantha Mudrāpaka Sabha, 1916.
Barth, Karl. *Church Dogmatics.* Vol. 1, pt. 2. Translated by G. T. Thomson and Harold Knight as *The Doctrine of the Word of God.* Edited by G. W. Bromiley and T. F. Torrance. Edinburgh: T. & T. Clark [1956].
Bavinck, J. H. *Religieus Besef en Christelijk Geloof.* Kampen: J. H. Kok, 1949.
Belvalkar, S. K. *Vedānta Philosophy.* Pt. 1, lectures 1-6. Poona: Bilvakunja Publishing House, 1929.
Carpenter, J. Estlin. *Theism in Medieval India.* Hibbert Lectures, 2d series, 1919. London: Williams & Norgate, 1921.
Chantepie de la Saussaye, Pieter Daniel. *Lehrbuch der Religionsgeschichte.* 2 vols. Freiburg, 1887-89. The English translation by Beatrice S. Colyer-Fergusson was entitled *Manual of the Science of Religion.* London and New York: Longmans Green & Co., 1891.
Chethimattam, John B. *Consciousness and Reality: An Indian Approach to Metaphysics.* Bangalore: Dharmaram College, 1967.
Das Gupta, Shashi Bhusan. *Aspects of Indian Religious Thought.* Calcutta: A. Mukherjee, 1957.
Dasgupta, Surendranath. *A History of Indian Philosophy.* Vol. 3. Cambridge: University Press, 1961.
Devanandan, Paul David. *The Concept of Māyā.* London: Lutterworth Press, 1950.
Edgerton, Franklin. *The Bhagavad Gītā: Translated and Interpreted.* 2 vols.

Harvard Oriental Series, vols. 38-39. Cambridge: Harvard University Press, 1946.

Garbe, Richard. *India and Christendom.* Translated by Lydia G. Robinson. LaSalle, Ill.: Open Court, 1959.

Garuḍavāhana Paṇḍita. *Śrī Divya Sūri Carita.* Kāñcī: P. B. Annangarācārya, 1953.

Ghate, V. S. *The Vedānta, a Study of the Brahma-Sūtras with the Bhāṣyas of Śaṃkara, Rāmānuja, Nimbārka, Madhva, and Vallabha.* Government Oriental Series, Class C, no. 1. Poona: Bhandarkar Oriental Research Institute, 1960.

Gonda, Jan. *Die Religionen Indiens.* Vols. 1 and 2. Die Religionen der Menschheit, vols. 11 and 12. Stuttgart: W. Kohlhammer Verlag [1960, 1963].

——. *Inleiding tot het Indisch Denken.* Antwerp: Standard Boekhandel, 1948.

Gopinatha Rao, T. A. *Sir Subrahmanya Ayyar Lectures on the History of Śrī Vaiṣṇavas.* Madras: University of Madras, Government Press, 1923.

Govinda [Embār]. *Hari Ārādhana Krama.* 40 stanzas. In a collection of Śrī Vaiṣṇava manuals of worship (title page missing), pp. 49-51.

Govindacharya, Alkondavilli. *A Metaphysique of Mysticism (Vedically Viewed).* Mysore: published by the author, 1923.

——. "A Note on *Yatirāja-Vaibhavam.*" *The Indian Antiquary* 40 (May 1911): 152 (article dated 5 July 1910).

——. "The Astadasa-Bhedas." Reprint from the *Journal of the Royal Asiatic Society* (October 1910), pp. 1103-12.

——. *The Divine Wisdom of the Dravida Saints.* Madras: C. N. Press, 1902.

Hari Rao, V. N., ed. and trans. *Kōil Oḻugu: The Chronicle of the Srirangam Temple with Historical Notes.* Madras: Rochouse & Sons, [1961].

Harrison, Max Hunter. *Hindu Monism and Pluralism.* London: Humphrey Milford, Oxford University Press, 1932.

Hidding, K. A. H. *Mens en Godsdienst, Levende Godsdiensten Phaenomenologisch Belicht.* Delft: W. Gaade, 1954.

Hiriyanna, M. *Outlines of Indian Philosophy.* London: George Allen & Unwin, [1932].

Ingalls, Daniel H. H. "Sankara's Arguments against the Buddhists." *Philosophy East and West* 3 (January 1954): 291-306.

Jagadeesan, N. "History of Śrī Vaishnavism in the Tamil Country (Post Rāmānuja)." Ph.D. thesis in history, University of Madras, January 1967.

Kāñcīpūrṇa [Tirukacci Nambi]. "Devarājāṣṭakam," In *Stotramālā*, edited by P. B. Annangarācārya, p. 8.

Kōil Kaṇḍādai Nāyan. *Periya Tirumuḍi Aḍavu* [Aḍaivu]. (Title page missing.)

Korff, F. W. A. *Het Christelijk Geloof en de Niet-Christelijke Godsdiensten.* Amsterdam: Holland Uitgeversmaatschappij, 1946.

Kraemer, Hendrik. Introduction to *The Meaning of Religion,* by W. Brede Kristensen. The Hague: Martinus Nijhoff, 1960.

——. *Religion and the Christian Faith.* London: Lutterworth Press, [1956].

Krishnasvami Aiyangar, S. "The Yatirājavaibhavam of Āndhrapūrṇa (Life of Rāmānuja)." *The Indian Antiquary* 38 (May 1909): 129 ff.

Kristensen, W. Brede. *Inleiding tot de Godsdienstgeschiedenis.* Translated from the Norwegian by J. Kristensen-Heldring. Arnhem: Van Lochum Slaterus, 1955.

——. *The Meaning of Religion: Lectures in the Phenomenology of Religion.* Translated by John B. Carman. The Hague: Martinus Nijhoff, 1960.

Kulandran, Sabapathy. *Grace: A Comparative Study of the Doctrine in Christianity and Hinduism.* London: Lutterworth Press, [1964].

Kūraṭṭāḻvān [Kūreśa]. *Pañcastava* [Five Hymns]. Included in the *Stotramālā:* "Śrīvaikuṇṭhastava," pp. 14-21; "Atimānuṣastava," pp. 21-26; "Sundarabāhustava," pp. 26-34; "Varadarājastava," pp. 34-40; and "Śrīstava," pp. 40-41.

——. *Yamakaratnākaram with Commentary.* Madras: Śrīvaiṣṇavagrantha Mudrāpaka Sabhai, n.d.

Leeuw, G. van der. *Inleiding tot de Phaenomenologie van den Godsdienst.* Haarlem: De Erven F. Bohn, 1948.

——. *Inleiding tot de Theologie.* Amsterdam: H. J. Paris, 1948.

——. *Religion in Essence and Manifestation: A Study in Phenomenology.* Translated by J. E. Turner. London: George Allen & Unwin, 1938.

Lester, Robert. "The Nature and Function of Patañjalian-Type Yoga as the Means to Release (Mokṣopāya) according to Rāmānuja." Ph.D. dissertation, Yale University, 1962.

——. "Rāmānuja and Śrī-Vaiṣṇavism." Paper read at American Association of Asian Studies, 1965.

——. "Rāmānuja and Śrī-Vaiṣṇavism: The Concept of Prapatti or Śaraṇāgati." *History of Religions* (University of Chicago) 5 (Winter 1966): 266-82.

Loy, Allan W. "The Theological Interpretation of the Relation of Christianity to Other Religions, with Particular Reference to Karl Barth." Ph.D. dissertation, Yale University, 1963.

Luke, P. Y., and Carman, John B. *Village Christians and Hindu Culture: Study of a Rural Church in Andhra Pradesh, South India.* World Studies of Churches in Mission. London: Lutterworth Press, [1968].

Macnicol, Nicol. *Indian Theism from the Vedic to the Muḥammadan Period.* Religious Quest of India Series, 1915. Reprint. Delhi: Munshiram Manoharlal, 1968.

Meghanādāri Sūri, Ātreya. *Mumukṣūpāyasaṃgraha.* Bangalore: Eriṣ Mudrākṣaraśālāyām, 1910.

Monier-Williams, Monier. *A Sanskrit-English Dictionary.* Oxford: Clarendon Press, 1899.

Nañjīyar. *Onbadināyirappaḍi* [Nine Thousand]. Commentary on Nammāḻvār's *Tiruvāymoḻi.* S. Krishnamācārya's edition in Tamil script. Madras: Noble Press, 1925-30.

Nilakanta Sastri, K. A. *A History of South India from Prehistoric Times to the Fall of Vijayanagar.* 3d ed. Madras: Oxford University Press, 1966.

Otto, Rudolf. *Die Gnadenreligion Indiens und das Christentum.* Munich: C. H. Beck'sche Verlagbuchhandlung, 1930. English version entitled *India's Religion of Grace and Christianity Compared and Contrasted.* London: S. C. M. Press, 1930.

Parāśara Bhaṭṭar. *Bhagavadguṇadarpaṇākhyam Śrīviṣṇusahasranāmabhāṣyam.* Sanskrit text. Kāñcīpuram: P. B. Annangarācārya, 1964.

——. *Commentary on the Śrī Viṣṇu Sahasranāmam.* With Śankara's commentary. Translated by K. E. Parthasarathy. Madras: Ganesh & Co., n.d.

——. *Kriyādīpam.* 72 stanzas. In a collection of Śrī Vaiṣṇava manuals of worship (title page missing), pp. 52-57.

——. Four hymns included in the *Stotramālā:* "Śrīrangarājastava," pp. 41-55; "Śrīguṇaratnakośa," pp. 56-60; "Aṣṭaślokī," pp. 60-61; and "Śrīranganāthastotra," p. 61.

——. *Sri Vishnu Sahasranama Bashya.* Translated by L. Venkatarathnam Naidu. Tirupati: Tirumala Tirupati Devasthanams, 1965.

——. *Sri Vishnusahasranama with Nirukti Slokas.* Text and English translation of the introduction to Parāśara Bhaṭṭar's Bhashya, by K. Bhashyam. Edited by Uttamur Viraraghavacharya. Madras: Visishtadvaita Pracharini Sabha, 1960.

Periya Āccān Piḷḷai. *Irupattinālāyirappaḍi* [Twenty-four Thousand]. Commentary on Nammāḻvār's *Tiruvāymoḻi.* S. Krishnamācārya's edition in Tamil script. Madras: Noble Press, 1925-30.

Pinbaḻahiya Perumāḷ Jīyar. *Ārāyirappaḍi Guruparamparāprabhāvam.* Tamil in Tamil script. Trichi: S. Krishnasvāmī Ayyangār, 1968. An edition in Telugu script has been published in Kāñcīpuram by the Śrīvaiṣṇavagrantha Mudrāpaka Sabhai, n.d.

Rajagopala Ayyangar, M. R. *Srimad Rahasyatrayasara* of Vedānta Deśika. Translation with introduction. Kumbakonam: Agnihothram Ramanuja Thathachariar, 1956.

——. *The Stotra-Ratna* of Yāmuna. Text and translation. Madras: published by the author, n.d.

Ramanujam, B. V. "Divya Sūri Charitam." *Journal of Indian History* 13: 181-99.

Rangachari, K. *The Sri Vaishnava Brahmans.* Bulletin of the Madras Government Museum. Madras: printed by the Superintendent Government Press, 1931.

Śankarācārya, *Commentary on the Śrī Viṣṇu Sahasranāmam* together with the commentary of Parāśara Bhaṭṭar. Translated by K. E. Parthasarathy. Madras: Ganesh & Co., n.d.

Satyavrata Singh. *Vedānta Deśika, His Life, Works, and Philosophy.* Banaras: Chowkhamba Sanskrit Series Office, 1958.

Schrader, F. Otto. *Introduction to the Pāñcarātra and the Ahirbudhnya Saṃhitā.* Madras: Adyar Library, 1916.

Srinivasachari, P. N. *The Philosophy of Viśiṣṭādvaita.* Madras: Adyar Library, 1943.

Śrīnivāsadāsa. *Yatīndramatadīpikā.* Sanskrit text with English translation and notes by Swāmī Ādidevānanda. Madras: Sri Ramakrishna Math, 1949.

Subrahmanian, N. "The Brahmin in the Tamil Country (in Ancient and Medieval Times)." Unpublished article.

Thibaut, George. *The Vedānta-Sūtras with the Commentary by Śankarācārya.* Sacred Books of the East, vols. 34 and 38. London: Oxford University Press, 1904.

Tirukkuruhai Pirān Piḷḷān. *Ārāyirappaḍi* [Six Thousand]. Commentary on Nammāḻvār's *Tiruvāymoḻi.* S. Krishnamācārya's edition of the collection of commentaries called *Bhagavadviṣayam* in Tamil script. Madras: Noble Press, 1925-30.

Tiruvarangattu Amudanār. *Irāmānuja Nūtranḍādi.* Madras: Śrīvaiṣṇavagrantha Mudrāpaka Sabhai, 1904.

Tiruvenkaṭācāryar, Citrakūṭam Kaṇḍādai [ed.]. *Vārttāmālai* [Tamil Utterances of "Śrī Vaiṣṇavas beginning with Nāthamuni," printed in Telugu script with the title spelled *Vārtāmalai*]. Tiruvellikkeṇi: Śrī Sarasvati Bhandāra Mudrākṣaraśālai, 1887.

Vaḍakku Tiruvīdi Piḷḷai. *Muppattārāyirappaḍi* [Thirty-six Thousand], known as *Īḍu.* Commentary on Nammāḻvār's *Tiruvāymoḻi.* S. Krishnamācārya's edition in Tamil script. Madras: Noble Press, 1925-30.

Vangipurattu Nambi. *Nityagrantha* or *Kārikāḥ.* 526 stanzas. In a collection of Śrī Vaiṣṇava manuals of worship (title page missing), pp. 14-48.

Varadachari, K. C. *Āḻvārs of South India.* Bhavan's Book University, vol. 143. Bombay: Bharatiya Vidya Bhavan, 1966.

——. *Idea of God.* Tirupati: Sri Venkatesvara Oriental Institute, 1950.

Vedānta Deśika. *Yatiraja Saptati.* English translation by D. Ramaswami Ayyangar. Tirupati: Tirumala Tirupati Devasthanams, 1965.

Yāmuna. *Gītārtha Sangraha.* With English translation and explanatory notes by V. K. Ramanujachari. Kumbakonam: published by the translator, 1931.

——. *Gītārthasangraha.* With Vedānta Deśika's *Gītāsāra.* English translation by K. Bhashyam, together with a Tamil translation by Uttamur Viraraghavacharya. Madras: Ubhaya Vedanta Granthamala, 1960.

——. *Stotraratna.* Sanskrit text with English translation by Svāmī Ādidevānanda. Madras: Sri Ramakrishna Math, 1950.

——. Two hymns included in the *Stotramālā:* "Catuśślokī," p. 4; "Stotraratna," pp. 4-7.

Zimmer, Heinrich. *Philosophies of India.* New York: Meridian Books, 1956.

Index

Accessibility (*Saulabhya*), 77-81 passim; reason for this translation of *Saulabhya*, 11-13; balanced emphasis with the Divine supremacy in the *Gītābhāṣya*, 61; separate from God's essential nature, 98; in the Divine form, 173-75; two aspects of Divine, 187-90; emphasis on, by Rāmānuja's disciples, 223-230, 232; Rāmānuja's distinctive balance between Divine supremacy and, 235; transcendence-immanence or supremacy-accessibility, 244-48; comparison of Rāmānuja's doctrine of, 256; four aspects of the polarity of supremacy and, 257-58

Advaita (Non-duality). *See* Śankara

Agnihothram Ramanuja Thatachariar, 213-14, 218, 230, 235, 298-301, 306-07

Aiśvarya (Lordship), 162-63. *See also* Six qualities of the Lord

Amalatva (Purity), 90, 93, 103-11, 114

Anantatva (Infinite nature), 66, 93, 101-03. *See also* Five defining qualities

Antaryāmī (Inner Controller), 124, 135-40, 180-81, 186. See also *Hārda*

Anubhava-grantha, 248

Arca. *See* Image incarnation

Arcaka. *See* Temple priest

Asceticism. See *Sannyāsī*

Atomicity (*Aṇutva*), 102-03

Attributes (*Guṇas, dharmas*). *See* Qualities

Audārya. *See* Generosity

Auspicious qualities (*Kalyāṇaguṇas*): ascribed to the Lord in dedicatory verse of *Vedārthasaṃgraha*, 66; listed in first half of introduction to *Gītābhāṣya*, 77-80; often identified with the six qualities of the Lord (*ṣaḍguṇas*), 92; frequently differentiated from Brahman's essential nature, 95; linked with radical opposition to everything defiling as God's dual characteristics (*ubhayalingatva*), 106; declared by the Scriptures to belong to Brahman, 172; identified with God's nature (*svabhāva*), 255. *See also* Qualities

Authenticity of authorship: general question of determining, 18-20; relative reliability of Śri Vaiṣṇava authorship, 20-21; lack of concern with, in most modern studies, 21-22; of the *Vedāntadīpa* and the *Vedāntasāra*, 57-60; of the *Gadyatraya* and *Nityagrantha*, 62-64, 212-14, 217-23, 229-36, 298-300, 306-07

Avatāra (Incarnation), 179-86 passim, 187-90; emphasized in introduction to the *Gītābhāṣya*, 80; Viṣṇu understood as, 120, 166; completing the number of creatures in a particular category, 120; God possessing a bodily form in, 167; God's periodic descents as active intervention in the world, 176; God's retaining supremacy in, 250-51; comparability with Christian doctrine of, 256; two levels of, in the Lord's descents, 257-58. *See also* Incarnation (Christian)

Avidyā (Ignorance), 56, 59, 73. See also *Karma*

Ācāryas (Śrī Vaiṣṇava teachers), 13-14, 21, 24-26, 37, 46-47, 231

Ādhāra (Support), 68, 124, 128, 134-35, 190-91. *See also* Body-Soul relationship

Ādheya (Supported), 134. *See also* Body-Soul relationship

Āḻvārs (Poet-saints), 21, 24, 25, 47, 209-11, 218, 235, 248-51. See also *Divya Prabandham*

Ānanda (Bliss), 90, 93, 99, 103, 112, 152. *See also* Five defining qualities

Āśraya: as support, 134; as refuge, 135, 185-86, 187, 188

Bala (Strength), 162-63. *See also* Six qualities of the Lord

Beauty of the Divine Form, 170-75, 188-89. *See also* Auspicious qualities

Being (*Sat*), 51, 100-01, 116, 124-25, 151, 164

Bhagavadgītābhāṣya, 19, 49, 60-62, 154-56

Bhagavān (Lord), 159, 161-64 passim. *See also* Six qualities of the Lord

Bhakti (Devotion), 63, 86, 112, 152, 214-37, 296-300, 305*n*52

Bhaktiyoga (The path of disciplined devotion), 61, 78, 80; devotion described as love and knowledge, 112; devotion expressed in prose, 208-11; relation to *prapatti*, 214-37 passim

Bhedābheda (Difference and non-difference), 28, 59; criticized by Rāmānuja as vitiating God's perfection, 108-11
Bhūmī or Bhūdevī (Goddess Earth), 236, 238, 242, 298
Biographical sources, 24-48 passim, 213-14; usefulness for understanding Rāmānuja's life and teachings, 16-17; contrast between traditional biographies of Śankara and Rāmānuja, 20-21; relative reliability of Śrī Vaiṣṇava sources, 20-21; traditional sources on Rāmānuja's dispute with Kūraṭṭāḻvān, 95-97
Bliss. See *Ānanda*
Bodhāyana, 43
Body (*Śarīra*): Brahman's possessing a bodily form, 72, 167-75; the Lord's beauty of bodily form, 79; entities considered parts of Brahman as His body, 90; purity of God's bodily form, 105, 111; body defined as *śeṣa*, 147-51; the Lord's body in His incarnations, 183
Body-Soul relationship (*Śarīra-śarīri-bhāva*): definition, 124-29; God's perfection in this relation to the imperfect world, 129-33; God's independence of His cosmic body, 191; key to understanding Scripture, 247. *See also* Body; Embodied Self
Brahmā, 164-66. See also *Trimūrti*
Brahman, 10, 17, 158-59, 162, 164
Buddhists, 263, 269

Caramaśloka (*Bhagavadgītā* 18.66), 215-17. See also *Prapatti*
Caste, 25, 28, 32. *See also* Vaḍama Brahmins
"*Catuśślokī*" ("Four Verses" to Śrī), 242-43
Causality (*Kāraṇatva*): Brahman the material and efficient cause of the universe, 51, 54, 59, 114-17; the Supreme Self, the sole cause of all changes in the state of finite beings, 99-101; causation understood as transformation in the state of the universe, 134; doctrine that the effect is a transformation of the cause (*satkāryavāda*), 134; *Nārāyraṇa* identified as the Supreme Cause, 164, 166; Rāmānuja's emphasis on God's being the cause of everything, 261
Christianity: on a Hindu theology, 1-3; utilization in studying Rāmānuja's conception of God, 7; distinction between theological and phenomenological stances, 10-11; great marvel for Christian faith, 12; God's creatorship not part of His essential nature in, 97; love within the Godhead in theology of, 97; "Creation," the concept nearest to *vibhūti*, 146; Rāmānuja as theologian in usage of, 202-03; first question to theologians of, 258-64; second question to theologians of, 264-71
Coḻa Kings, 27, 44-45
Communion with God, 61, 72, 85, 86, 197, 198, 255
Compassion (*Dayā, Kāruṇya, Kṛpā*), 93, 97, 179, 184, 189-90, 197-98, 223
Consciousness. See *Jñāna*
Consorts of the Lord, 238-44. *See also* Bhūmī, Mediatrix of Grace, Nīlā, Śakti, Śrī
Controller. See *Niyantā*
Coordinate predication (*Sāmānādhikaraṇya*), 124-25
Creation-Emanation (*Sṛṣṭi*), 164-66, 180. See also *Vyūhas*
Creatorship, 114-23; Christian view of, 97; Christian views of the knowledge of God the Creator, 260-61. *See also* Causality

Dāsa (Servant, slave), 214, 222
Dasgupta, S. N., 14
Dāsyabhakti (Devotion of a servant), 94, 214, 221
Dayā. See Compassion
Dedicatory verses (*Mangalaślokas*), 63, 65-67
Descent. See *Avatāra*
Devotion. See *Bhaktiyoga*
Dharma, 183-84, 187, 215-16. See also *Avatāra*
Divine Abode (*Divyasthāna, Paramapadam*), 167-75
Divya Prabandham, 21, 26, 230-31, 235
Duties. See *Dharma; Karma*

Einfühlen (Empathy), 5. *See also* Methodology; Phenomenology of religion
Emberumānār, Aruḷāḷa Perumāḷ. *See* Yajñamūrti
Embodied Self (*Śarīrī*), 17, 51, 124-33, 135. *See also* Body-Soul relationship
Empathy, 5. *See also* Methodology;

Worship: in the temple, 37-38; purification of temple worship, 43; *Nityagrantha* as a manual for daily worship at home or in the monastery, 63, 65; in the *Gītābhāṣya*, 154-56; God rewards when offered pleasing worship (*ārādhita*), 178; stages in the Āḻvārs' devotional experience reflected in the Gadyas, 218; primacy of *dāsyabhakti* not excluding erotic symbolism and emotional fervor, 221; defense of chanting names of God (*nāmasaṃkīrtana*) by Parāśara Bhaṭṭar, 225. *See also* Service

Yādava Prakāśa, 28-29, 33, 110-11

Yajñamūrti (Aruḷāḷa Perumāl Emberumānār), 41-42, 223-24

Yāmuna (Āḻavandār), 8, 32-37 passim, 189, 225; occasional contrasts with Rāmānuja's views in the oral tradition, 17; summary of life and writings, 25-26; dates, 27; relation to Rāmānuja, 29-30; Rāmānuja instructed by five of his disciples, 38-41; his arguments against *māyavāda* used by Rāmānuja, 41-42; his *Gītārthasaṃgraha* closely followed by Rāmānuja, 60-61, 216-17; praised by Rāmānuja in the *Vedārthasaṃgraha*, 109; in contrast to Rāmānuja, sometimes composed in verse, 208; Rāmānuja diverges from Yāmuna's poetic interpretation of a verse of Nammāḻvār, 210-11; Agnihothram emphasizes difference between Yāmuna's position and Rāmānuja's, 213; praised in *Vaikuṇṭhagadya*, 219; Lester doubts Yāmuna considered himself a Śrī Vaiṣṇava *ācārya*, 231; connection of his *Siddhitraya* to the *Vedārthasaṃgraha*, 233-34; Gadyas show a conscious dependence on his hymns, 235; conception of Śrī in his *Catuśślokī* similar to Rāmānuja's view, 242-43, 246; his comments on some verses of the *Tiruvāymoḻi* reported in the "Thirty-six Thousand," 248; followed by Rāmānuja, 250-51; more influenced by the Nyāya school than Rāmānuja, 262